HEALTHY CLASSROOM MANAGEMENT
Motivation, Communication, and Discipline

Raymond M. Nakamura

California Polytechnic State University

Illustrations by Taimay North

 **Wadsworth**
Thomson Learning™

Australia • Canada • Mexico • Singapore • Spain • United Kindom • United States

Education Editor: Dianne Lindsay
Assistant Editor: Tangelique Williams
Editorial Assistant: Keynia Johnson
Marketing Manager: Becky Tollerson
Project Editor: Trudy Brown
Print Buyer: April Reynolds
Permissions Editor: Bob Kauser
Production Service: Progressive Publishing
   Alternatives
Photo Researcher: Progressive Publishing
   Alternatives

Copy Editor: Progressive Publishing
   Alternatives
Illustrator: Taimay North
Cover Designer: Laurie Anderson
Cover Image: William Hart, Photo-
   Edit; David Young-Wolff, PhotoEdit
Cover Printer: Webcom, Ltd.
Compositor: Progressive Publishing
   Alternatives
Printer: Webcom, Ltd.

Printed in Canada

1   2   3   4   5   6   7   03 02 01 00 99

For permission to use material from this text, contact
us by **Web:** http://www.thomsonrights.com
Fax: 1-800-730-2215 **Phone:** 1-800-730-2214

For more information, contact
Wadsworth/Thomson Learning
10 Davis Drive
Belmont, CA 94002-3098
USA
http://www.wadsworth.com

International Headquarters
Thomson Learning
International Division
290 Harbor Drive, 2nd Floor
Stamford, CT 06902-7477
USA

**UK/Europe/Middle East/
South Africa**
Thomson Learning
Berkshire House
168-173 High Holborn
London WC1V 7AA
United Kingdom

Asia
Thomson Learning
60 Albert Street, #15-01
Albert Complex
Singapore 189969

Canada
Nelson Thomson Learning
1120 Birchmount Road
Toronto, Ontario M1K 5G4
Canada

Library of Congress Cataloging-in-Publication Data
Nakamura, Raymond M.
   Healthy classroom management: motivation, communication, and discipline/by
Raymond M. Nakamura; illustrations by Taimay North.
     p. cm.
   Includes bibliographical references and index.
   ISBN 0-534-56727-4
   1. Classroom management—United States. 2. Teacher-student relationships—United
States. 3. Activity programs in education—United States. I. Title.

LB3013.N25 1999
371.102'4 21—dc21

                                                                                99-046273

Photo Credits
Pg. 3, © Michael Krasowitz/FPG International; pg. 31, © Ron Chapple/FPG International; pg. 53, ©
Jim Cummins/FPG International; pg. 83, © Arthur Tilley/FPG International; pg. 108, www.corbis.com;
pg. 132, www.corbis.com; pg. 163, www.corbis.com; pg. 189, © Arthur Tilley/FPG International; pg.
213, © Arthur Tilley/FPG International; Pg. 238, www.corbis.com.

To the Hoose family: Jim, Helen, John, Linda, Connie, Mike, and Cheryl. Thank you for accepting me as part of your wonderful family.

And to Mike and Toni Heinze. Thank you for your friendship and especially, for loving my children. Mike, your spirit will always be a part of me.

Contents

CHAPTER 8　COMMUNICATION: RESOLUTION AND THE CLASS MEETING　189

Part IV:　Discipline in the Healthy Classroom　211

CHAPTER 9　DISCIPLINE: DISCIPLINE STYLES AND THE GOALS OF BEHAVIOR　213

Preface

Healthy Classroom Management: Motivation, Communication, and Discipline is designed to help you with strategies and skills for building within each student the strength and ability to live a happy, healthy, and productive life in the classroom. This book is about understanding, meeting, and supporting the student's emotional and social needs and teaching students about responsibility, self-discipline, social interaction, and self-reliance in the classroom.

This book is about meeting the challenges of modern-day teaching so that you can learn to connect with your students in ways that will motivate them and help them to personally grow in school. Its intention is to provide you with an understandable and usable way of approaching your wonderful, yet awesome task of teaching and managing young people.

Healthy Classroom Management is divided into the following chapters:

Part I: The Foundation of the Healthy Classroom consists of three chapters and focuses on the foundation of student wellness, the teacher's role as a leader both in and out of the classroom, and the theoretical foundation for the classroom management strategies presented in this book.

Part II: Motivating Students in the Healthy Classroom consists of three chapters and focuses on the needs established by self-esteem research, resiliency research, hardiness research, and humanistic psychological theory. The chapters also include healthy strategies to help you motivate your students. These simple strategies are based on a foundation of mutual dignity and respect. The formula is simple: Give the students what they need, and the students will give you what you need. By meeting their basic psychosocial needs within an environment of intellectual and emotional freedom, you will help students to develop positive perceptions of themselves and motivate them to become the capable people they were meant to be. As a result, teachers will be setting the foundation to help students develop self-reliance, discipline, and responsibility.

Part III: Communication in the Healthy Classroom consists of two chapters and focuses on helping teachers develop positive interpersonal relations through healthy communication. Success will depend not only on how well you communicate your thoughts and feelings, but also on how well you listen. Communication skills are just as basic as driving a car—a person needs to know how to start and stop it. In between starting and stopping, one needs to know when to accelerate, when to put on the brakes, and how to keep the vehicle on course. Chapter 8 pulls together all the concepts of the book in a process called the Classroom Meeting. This meeting is designed to help teachers and students make plans and decisions, to provide encouragement, and solve problems. Classroom meetings improve communication, cooperation, and responsibility and, most important, reflect how fortunate the students are to have each other.

Part IV: Discipline in the Healthy Classroom consists of two chapters and focuses on helping you develop healthy discipline techniques that will help empower students to become self-reliant, self-disciplined, and responsible in their behavior. Part IV addresses discipline styles, why students misbehave, communicating appropriate behavior, and managing the classroom environment to reduce potential problems. Knowing the primary goal of most behaviors is the foundation for understanding most problems and knowing what kind of strategies to use in helping your students grow. Healthy classroom discipline empowers students and is based on treating them with dignity and respect rather than punishment and humiliation.

A unique feature of the book is the "learn by doing" activities that are distributed throughout the book. The three types of activities are listed below:

1. **Self-Assessments** consist of self-tests that are designed to help illustrate the principles supported in the book. These activities are designed to help you evaluate your own attitudes and behaviors while expanding your understanding of teaching issues in general.

2. **The Teacher's Corner** are observation and interview activities that require students to visit schools and observe what is taking place in the classrooms. The results of the observations and interviews generate powerful discussions.

3. **Discussion Activities** are experiential activities that reinforce some of the major points within the chapter. The activities are found at the end of each chapter. The activities are facilitated by the instructor or the students in the class. The activities are easy to prepare and facilitate and they provide an excellent opportunity for students to practice leadership roles. A guide for facilitating these experiential activities is provided in Appendix E.

Throughout this book, strategies are offered to help students grow both in and out of the classroom. Carefully evaluate the suggestions in these pages, and try to determine what will work for you—after all, you know your students better than anyone else. Do only those things that feel right to you; otherwise, your students will see right through the strategies. Teaching and the art of developing positive relationships with your students are not easy. There is no one magical technique for all teachers; however, whatever methods you choose, they must have a foundation based on mutual honesty, dignity, and respect.

In the end, *Healthy Classroom Management: Motivation, Communication, and Discipline* will help you enhance your leadership and management skills, examine your teaching philosophy, and most important, connect you with your students in healthy ways.

Acknowledgments

ealthy Classroom Management: Motivation, Communication, and Discipline was written and published with the help and assistance of numerous people. I am extremely grateful to be working with the outstanding team at Wadsworth. I wish to acknowledge two senior editors that I had the pleasure to work with: Joan Gill, who had the vision and confidence in the importance of this book, and Dianne Lindsay, whose commitments, high standards of professionalism, and personal attention made it all possible. I am also thankful to their two editorial assistants, Valarie Morrison and Tangelique Williams, for their assistance in this project.

I also wish to acknowledge the contributions of the following reviewers whose honest and thoughtful opinions and suggestions are incorporated in every chapter: Esther Barkat, West Virginia State College; Cindy Carlson, University of Texas, Austin; Janet Castaños, U. S. International University; Bruno J. D'Alonzo, New Mexico State University; Bill Danley, Southern Oregon University; Rosa Castro Feinberg, Florida International University; Anne Richardson Gayles-Felton, Florida A & M University; Belinda Laumbach, New Mexico Highlands University; Bruce M. Mitchell, Eastern Washington University; Sureshrani Paintal, Chicago State University; Cynthia Darché Park, San Diego State University; Ernest Ramirez, Villanova University; Al Stramiello, Mercer University; Angela Valenzuela, Rice University; and Verlic Ward, Walla Walla College.

A note of special thanks must be given to Taimay North for her creative and thoughtful illustrations. Your artistic talents added so much to this book. Thank you.

Two Notes to the Reader

A NOTE ON GENDER

For ease of reading, the author alternates between "he" and "she" in the text. This is not meant to stereotype or be exclusionary of either gender.

A NOTE ON TERMINOLOGY

It is important that we are sensitive to the names we use for ethnic groups. As the multicultural and intercultural terminology is debated, no single one term is deemed acceptable or "politically correct" because it implies that all other terms are disrespectful.

There is much variability in the terminology used in the area of intracultural and intercultural education. The media, professional disciplines, and geographical locations use a variety of terms that influence what people use. In addition, there still continues to be great discrepancies from within and outside of each individual culture. For example, many African-Americans still refer to themselves as blacks, and individuals from various Native-American tribes refer to themselves as "Indian."

Yet, clarification of terminology is important. It is also important that the reader not get stuck on a word or phrase. The terms used in this book are chosen because they are widespread, widely known, and comfortable to the author. The author asks the reader to look beyond the differences in terminology and to view this book in the content of its larger picture. Levels of acceptability with any particular terminology have changed and will change over time; however, feelings of utmost respect for the cultures and the people discussed herein are a primary motive for writing this book.

■

The Foundation of the Healthy Classroom

This part consists of three chapters and focuses on the foundation of student wellness, the teacher's role as a leader both in and out of the classroom, and the theoretical foundation for the classroom management strategies presented in this book.

1

■

The Healthy Classroom

Imagine going to school and encountering an exciting, inspiring, and intoxicating atmosphere. Students are brimming over with enthusiasm, commitment, and pride. They are eager to work hard, listen to the teacher's words, and are willing to share ideas. Some of the students are mentoring others; others are sharing and cooperating as they discuss the daily lesson.

They laugh easily and playfully kid with the teacher and among themselves. They enjoy being there. They like and respect the teacher.

As the class progresses, the students meet among themselves, sometimes going to the teacher with creative ideas and special requests. They approach each lesson and assignment with purpose and intensity. Each student continuously works on different ways to improve his or her skill levels.

When a student speaks, others listen. When a student takes leadership of a lesson, others are quick to respond and help because they know that on another occasion they may be the leader and need support. Each student has trust in the teacher because the teacher listens and is flexible enough to accommodate each of them whenever possible. As the teacher listens to the students' words, the teacher hears voices that are supportive, sincere, and personal. No one fears or hides from the teacher, nor is there any secretive mumbling behind the teacher's back. There is an atmosphere of support, trust, and respect with no antagonism because a philosophy of teamwork and partnership makes up the class structure.

The most penetrating aspect of the healthy classroom is that each person—whether it is the teacher, the student, the teacher's aid, or anyone associated with the class—is treated with dignity and respect. When the class shows that it truly cares about each individual student, each student will reciprocate this faith with loyalty and hard work. Students in a healthy classroom have a common vision, surrounded by shared goals, shared respect, and shared values.

Healthy Classroom Management is about building healthy classrooms and promoting student wellness. The foundation of the healthy classroom is built on the interpersonal relationships you, as a teacher, have with your students and the relationship that students have with each other. Healthy relationships require positive motivation, communication, and discipline. A healthy classroom will help students become the significant and capable people they were meant to be.

The concept of the healthy classroom may seem like a distant dream. For many teachers, it is. Many teachers sell themselves short, performing well below their full potential. Instead of striving for optimal performance, they accept stress and mediocrity as the norm. As a result, they lead stressful lives and build unhealthy classrooms. The concept of the healthy classroom is relevant to all teachers and schools. *Healthy Classroom Management* provides strategies to help you develop student wellness and healthy classrooms that are based on mutual dignity, respect, and trust.

STUDENT WELLNESS AND
THE HEALTHY CLASSROOM

The World Health Organization (1947) has the most widely recognized definition of health. It defined health as "a state of complete physical, mental, and social well-being and not merely the absence of disease and infirmity." An examination of this definition reveals that health is multifaceted and includes many components beyond just freedom from physical disease and pain. Historically, the definition evolved from a limited perspective that focused on hygiene, sanitation, and the absence of disease. Today, the definition of health encompasses physical, mental, and social dimensions. Health extends beyond the structure and function of the body to include feelings, values, and reasoning—it also includes the nature of interpersonal relationships. In recent years, the concept of holistic health has extended the definition to include intellectual and spiritual dimensions. The holistically healthy person functions as a total person. Some experts say that holistically healthy people have reached a "high level of wellness" (Payne & Hahn, 1995).

Wellness is a term that has gained popularity in the 1990s. High-level wellness suggests an optimistic way of looking at a person's health. Wellness is a process for the continuous self renewal that is needed for an exciting, creative, fulfilling life. Wellness is judged from the standpoint of reaching or achieving human potential. Student wellness is another way of looking at the fully functioning or self-actualized person. Self-actualization as theorized by Abraham Maslow (1987) refers to the desire for self-fulfillment—for becoming what one has the potential to become. Maslow viewed health as an equivalent to self-actualization.

Brylinsky and Hoadley (1991) summarized the concept of wellness:

Wellness reflects a feeling, a conscious perception, or the awareness by the whole person that his / her components and processes are not only under control, but are also working harmoniously as a unit. Wellness also reflects a person's attitude and his / her unique response to living.

Student wellness and the healthy classroom are complementary in concept. The healthy classroom is more than an absence of unruly and undisciplined students. It involves vitality, vigor, and general physical and mental well-being. The healthy classroom is an evolving process in which students are given the opportunity to develop and enhance all aspects of their physical, social, spiritual, emotional, intellectual, and environmental well-being. The healthy classroom is viewed as a continuous process in which students are given the opportunity to take some control of their own lives within the classroom by deliberately choosing behaviors that lead to a richer, more balanced, and satisfying state of being. The healthy classroom cannot be achieved without emotionally healthy students.

Dimensions of Student Wellness

It is important to recognize that each of the dimensions of student wellness is as important as the others, and that each dimension affects and is affected by every other. The following definitions and lists are adapted from the Wellness Project at California Polytechnic State University in San Luis Obispo, California.

Social Wellness Knowing yourself and feeling good about yourself are fundamental components of social wellness. Social wellness means enjoying your own company and interacting comfortably with people from a variety of backgrounds. Two basic components of social wellness are communication and interaction with others. The school setting contributes to helping children and youth make friends and developing the social dimensions of their lives.

A socially healthy classroom is a positive environment in which teachers help students to (1) have satisfying interpersonal relationships, (2) have positive interpersonal interactions with others, and (3) adapt to various social situations and daily behaviors.

Spiritual Wellness Spiritual wellness is a dynamic process through which an individual seeks to integrate beliefs and actions. Incorporated into this process is a growing appreciation of aesthetics, nature, the environment, and people of all cultures. A sense of purpose, direction, and awareness contributes to spiritual health resulting in hope, joy, courage, and gratitude. Spiritual wellness does not necessarily involve a belief in a supreme being or a specified way of living prescribed by a particular religion.

The spiritually healthy classroom means there is a feeling of unity among students within the classroom—a feeling of connection with others and with the school—and a guiding sense of meaning or value within the classroom. It means students care about and respect all students within the class.

Emotional Wellness Learning to cope with the stresses of life and the classroom is essential in maintaining emotional wellness. Keeping a positive attitude, being sensitive to one's emotional needs, and holding expectations in line with reality all contribute to good emotional health. Emotions influence the way we interact with people, how we perceive our world, and the way we reason. Emotional reactions such as feelings of self-esteem, self-confidence, trust, love, and many other emotional reactions are all part of one's emotional wellness.

The emotionally healthy classroom refers to the feeling component: students feel comfortable expressing emotions appropriately. Students who are emotionally healthy are not free of negative emotions like anxiety, frustration, and anger, but in an emotionally healthy classroom these emotions are not expressed in outbursts that affect the students' relationships with others or lead to inappropriate behavior.

Intellectual Wellness The continuous development of one's knowledge and skills defines intellectual wellness. It is the strong desire to learn from challenges and experiences. By incorporating new ideas into everyday life, the individual follows a pattern of ongoing intellectual growth. Intellectual wellness enables the individual to fully pursue learning about all aspects of life. It creates a broad and open outlook toward all types of learning in all kinds of environments.

The intellectually healthy classroom refers to a classroom where teachers give all students the opportunity to process and act on information, clarify their values and beliefs, and exercise their decision-making capacity. Teachers need to set high expectations for students and to provide the appropriate lessons to help achieve them.

Physical Wellness   A vital component of our daily lives is physical wellness. Physical wellness is not merely the absence of disease or illness, but is a balanced lifestyle focusing on learning about oneself to enjoy good health. Feeling safe and secure is part of physical wellness and means that students feel they are in control of their own selves within the classroom environment—they have mastery over their own being. Being physically well increases resistance to illness and enables one to cope better with stress. Maintaining alertness allows for full participation in learning as well as other situations.

The physically healthy classroom refers to students feeling physically safe and secure within the classroom and knowing that the school is committed to their physical safety. The physically healthy classroom means that students are not "bullied" by others and they know all safety precautions have been taken to protect them. Without a feeling of physical safety and security, students will find it difficult to move beyond strong fear and anxiety and will not be willing to enthusiastically explore new challenges. The physically healthy classroom happens when all precautions have been taken to ensure the students' physical safety and emotional well-being.

The physically safe classroom refers to classrooms that are protected and have no safety hazards or unsafe equipment. Safe classrooms have teachers who are committed to the students' safety and the students are comfortable within the environment. In addition, a safe classroom provides an environment that is conducive to learning. It provides an atmosphere that reflects the needs of minority students and women. The environment reflects the rich variety of cultural influences and traditions of today's social environment. Factors that threaten the healthy classroom include aggressive temperaments and behaviors, exposure to unethical teacher and student actions, and a culturally insensitive setting.

Psychosocial Wellness   Psychosocial wellness encompasses the intellectual, emotional, social, and spiritual dimensions of health. Psychosocially healthy people have managed to develop these dimensions to optimal levels. They have the ability to respond appropriately to life's challenges, disappointments, joys, and frustrations by summoning up inner resources. Their resiliency is strong and they are actively involved in the process of living rather than being trapped in despondency caused by the negative events in their lives (Donatelle & Davis, 1997).

The following is a personal examination or checkup list for each of the psychosocial dimensions of wellness.

Dimensions of student wellness.

A Personal Examination of Social Wellness

Being socially healthy means being socially active. As you reflect on your social wellness, here are some questions you may wish to ask yourself:

- How do I behave around someone with a disability?
- Have I had lunch with a friend lately?
- Who is the last person to whom I wrote a letter?
- What are the qualities I look for in a friend?
- When was the last time I engaged in a meaningful conversation?
- When was the last time I showed appreciation for someone?
- Do I share ideas, work, play, and possessions?
- Do I share conversations with persons of different cultures, ethnic backgrounds, or religions?
- Do I know my limits?
- Do I really listen to what others are saying?
- Am I able to laugh at myself and not take myself too seriously?
- Am I comfortable in expressing my opinions with peers, coworkers, administrators, and family members?
- Do I set aside time for myself?
- Do I include people of different lifestyles, ages, and cultural backgrounds within my social circle?

A Personal Examination of Spiritual Wellness

Being spiritually healthy means being spiritually active. As you reflect on your spiritual wellness, here are some questions you may wish to ask yourself:

- Have I spent time with someone less fortunate than myself?
- Have I attended a religious service of my choice?
- Have I explored the works of various philosophers, composers, and artists?
- Am I aware of the prejudices I hold, and am I striving to overcome them?
- Do I have a sense of forgiveness toward others and toward myself?
- Have I made an effort to put my convictions into actions?
- Do I feel my life has meaning and purpose?
- Am I comfortable defining and expressing my spiritual values?
- What are the sources of my inner strength? A religious background?
- Is there still a sense of wonder in my life about the world around me?
- Am I satisfied with the direction my life is going?

A Personal Examination of Emotional Wellness

Being emotionally healthy allows identity to develop and feelings to be expressed. As you reflect on your emotional wellness, here are some questions you may wish to ask yourself:

- Am I comfortable with my sexuality?
- Do I complete projects before the deadline?
- Can I identify how to relieve my tensions?
- Can I share my true feelings with friends?
- Am I comfortable with my intimate relationships?
- Do I find experiences that give me positive strokes?
- Would I consider joining an assertiveness group?
- Do I usually get a good night's sleep?
- Am I able to accept and learn from my mistakes?
- Do I express my anger in a healthy way?
- Do I consider how positive and negative stresses affect my personal growth?
- Is my direction in life clearly identified?
- Am I excited by each day?
- Do I feel pressure to conform?
- Am I working to reduce my fears?
- When I find something is not working do I try new behavior patterns?
- Do I take on more projects than I can handle?
- Do I have difficulty saying "no"?

A Personal Examination of Intellectual Wellness

Being intellectually healthy means being intellectually active. As you reflect on your intellectual wellness, here are some questions you may wish to ask yourself:

- Do I discover new pursuits and challenges?
- Have I joined interest groups?
- Am I becoming well-versed in an area of my choice and interest?
- Do I enjoy exploring the world of art, music, and the classics?
- Do I have confidence in managing my time and planning ahead?
- Do I believe I am achieving my potential?
- Am I able to consider different viewpoints in decision making?
- Am I able to listen to others before making critical judgments?
- Do I exercise my voting privilege and support candidates of my choice?
- Is goal-setting something I do regularly?
- Do I use a sense of humor to put problems into perspective?
- Am I stimulated by new ideas?
- Do I change chores into challenges?
- Do I plan and adhere to a monthly budget?
- Do I seek daily information on current trends and events?

Psychosocial health is the result of a complex interaction between a person's history and conscious and unconscious thoughts about and interpretations of the past (Donatelle & Davis, 1997). The major focus of this book is on encouraging the psychosocial dimensions of health in the classroom. When the psychosocial dimensions of health are achieved within the student, he or she is more likely to be motivated to achieve, cooperate, and take on new challenges.

Mutual Respect and Trust

Creating the healthy classroom is a process. It is not something that automatically occurs. The foundation of the healthy classroom is based on the development of two important ingredients: mutual respect and trust. Without respect and trust it is difficult to encourage the psychosocial dimensions of wellness. Respect and trust lie at the core of healthy interpersonal relationships. The development of these two components requires patience. They cannot be acquired overnight, but must be proven over time. Students will listen to your words and then observe how you act on those words. If your actions do not back up your words, respect and trust will not develop.

Respect Respect is enormously important in teaching because it means that the teachers and students are highly regarded, honored, or esteemed. Although respect is usually ceremoniously acknowledged in conversation and at special gatherings, it is often largely ignored in the daily workings of the classroom. The lip service that is given to respect comes in many forms, such as:

- Developing rules or a code of ethics for all students while making special exceptions for some students.

The foundation of a healthy classroom is based on the development of two important ingredients: mutual respect and trust.

- Asking for opinions of students and never acting on them.
- Touting opportunities for women while not promoting women's teams or students on the same basis as men's.
- Touting opportunities for ethnic minority students while not promoting them on the same basis as the majority students.
- Voicing a loud commitment to sportsmanship and fair play in school sports while pressuring students to commit illegal or questionable acts on the athletic field.
- Voicing a commitment to academics while pressuring teachers to keep student athletes eligible by changing grades.

Both students and teachers suffer when the human element in school is disrespected and devalued. When relationships are dishonest, class policies are unfair, and communications are secretive or degrading, students will develop low morale and the teacher will have difficulty working with students. Absenteeism, tardiness, early departures, passivity, indifference, and belligerence are some of the other symptoms of disrespect. These are also the symptoms of an unhealthy classroom. Building respect is created by understanding its components and acting on them.

Trust Trust is a firm belief or confidence in the honesty, integrity, reliability, and fairness of the teacher and/or student. It is something that requires time to mature and can be lost in a few seconds of thoughtlessness. Once lost, it is difficult to recover, and in some cases it may be lost forever. Distrust will break down morale, loyalty, and performance and leads to cynicism, retaliation, destructive rumors, and other forms of anger.

Trust is a two-way street; it involves both the ability to trust others and the quality of being trustworthy ourselves. If trust does not flow in both directions it will eventually break down. Trust is composed of the following qualities:

- Honesty or the believability of your words. Inconsistencies will destroy trust. Once students stop listening, you will never be taken seriously.

- Your commitments are backed by your actions. If students cannot depend on you to fulfill your commitments, they will become indifferent to your words.
- Concern for the students' emotional and physical welfare. As a teacher, you do not abuse feelings. Each student is important. You protect the students from humiliation or unnecessary criticism, allowing them to perform with comfort and security.

Control and Wellness: Empowerment

Motivating students to behave in healthy ways is a difficult task. You can inspire motivation, but the real motivation must come from within the student. Thus, it is not easy for you to motivate your students. Knowing about healthy classroom behavior is one thing; achieving it is quite another.

Many studies have shown that having a sense of control over one's own life is beneficial to one's health. The phase *locus of control* means one's sense of where the control over one's life lies. An *internal locus of control* means the student feels he or she has control of his or her own behavior in the classroom, while an *external locus of control* means the student believes his or her life is under the control of other people or powers.

The benefits of an internal locus of control fall into at least two categories. First, having the feeling of being in control of your own life is immensely rewarding in and of itself. Second, and especially important, is the fact that there can be little motivation to make positive behavior choices if you believe that your life is controlled by people or forces outside of yourself and beyond your control.

Within the last few years, educators and counselors have used the term *empowerment* to describe the process in which individuals or groups of people gain increasing measures of control over their behavior. Empowered students are taught to rely on their internal locus of control. Empowered students do not blame others for their negative situations, but focus on producing constructive

Empowerment is used by educators and counselors to describe the process in which individuals gain increasing measures of control over their behavior. Empowered students rely on their internal locus of control.

Self-Assessment: Are You a Nurturing Person?

This assessment is for individuals who are considering going into the teaching profession. How you respond to people in your daily life will be a barometer of how you will respond to your future students. *Treat the results as a guide only. There is a margin of uncertainty in all surveys of this kind.*

Instructions: Mark one answer for each question. Four points are awarded for a "yes" answer, two points are awarded for a "maybe" or neutral answer, and no points are awarded for a "no" answer.

DO YOU:	YES	MAYBE	NO
1. Like being with young people?	—	—	—
2. Listen to others without making judgments of their words or actions?	—	—	—
3. Maintain your composure during stressful interactions with other people?	—	—	—
4. Accept success graciously without being arrogant or obnoxious?	—	—	—
5. Display faith and confidence in the abilities and judgments of others?	—	—	—
6. Treat all people fairly and equally regardless of their color or ethnic background?	—	—	—
7. Control your temper under pressure situations?	—	—	—
8. Accept all people for who they are rather than what you want them to be?	—	—	—
9. Act as a positive role model for others?	—	—	—
10. Accept criticism from others?	—	—	—
11. Admit to others when you are wrong?	—	—	—
12. Accept responsibility for your errors graciously without blaming others or making excuses for your errors?	—	—	—
13. Eliminate your swearing or use of other inappropriate language?	—	—	—
14. Go the "extra" mile for others when they are in need of help?	—	—	—
15. Have reasonable classroom rules that students feel are fair?	—	—	—
16. Talk honestly with people?	—	—	—
17. Treat people with respect even though some may dislike you?	—	—	—
18. When angry, clearly express your inner feelings in a respectful manner?	—	—	—
19. When necessary, become involved in the personal problems of others?	—	—	—
20. Let others be in charge of activities even though you know you can do them better?	—	—	—
21. Allow yourself the time to take more classes or seminars in subjects such as adolescent psychology or multicultural education?	—	—	—
22. Help others set realistic goals for themselves?			
23. Stop using put-downs and criticizing words when motivating or disciplining others?	—	—	—
24. Accept compliments or encouraging words without making excuses or explanations?	—	—	—
25. Search for, identify, and acknowledge the strengths of others regardless of gender, disability, color, or ethnic background?	—	—	—

SCORING

Points

100	Is impossible for most ordinary, truthful people
75–99	Yes, you will probably be a nurturing teacher
50–74	Yes, you can learn to be a nurturing teacher
49 or less	Are you sure that you are in the right profession?

change through dialogue and collaboration. Only when students realize that they can make a difference will they become empowered. The healthy classroom provides an environment of empowerment.

Making the Commitment to the Healthy Classroom

One of the goals of this book is to help you develop the motivation to create student wellness and a healthy classroom. Making the commitment to student wellness and the healthy classroom involves making changes in your own behavior that enhances the health and well-being of your students and improves the quality of life in the classroom. You must make changes in your own behavior before changes can be made in a student's behavior.

Creating student wellness and the healthy classroom is about developing the psychosocial dimensions of wellness by raising the level of self-esteem and resiliency in students and motivating and managing them from the inside out. Just as skilled architects design buildings to be inspiring, to stand strong, and to resist the elements over the years, effective teachers build in students the strength and skills to live healthy, happy, and productive lives both in and out of the classroom. Like architects, effective teachers know that to build strong and independent structures and to build a foundation for healthy self-esteem and resiliency one must work from the inside out. Self-esteem and resiliency are discussed further in Chapter 3.

The inner framework that you help build within your students evolves through the quality of your relationship with them. Students look to significant adults in their lives, as well as their peers and classmates, for a reflection of who they are and how they are. Students will observe your responses and reactions; they hear your words and sense your body language. They also sense your feelings and notice whether they are taken seriously and listened to and whether they are respected and enjoyed. The conclusions that students draw from these reflections often become their truth or the inner framework that tells them who they are and what they might expect in school.

Creating student wellness and the healthy classroom is not an easy one-step recipe. Creating lasting behavior changes in your students requires careful thought, individual analysis, and considerable effort. As you will soon discover, changing your own beliefs, attitudes, values, actions, and behaviors that have been developing from your infancy is difficult; changing the beliefs, attitudes, values, and behaviors of others is even more challenging.

THE TEACHER'S CHALLENGE:
FOUR CRITICAL ISSUES

The pursuit of excellence for all students should be the keynote of American educational thought as we move into the twenty-first century. Education is emerging as a vision of, and an art in, human development and human self-realization, but the pursuit of excellence is hardly possible without knowledgeable, creative, and nurturing teachers. In the age of unprecedented societal changes and challenges, unprecedented societal evolution and revolution, the teacher will not be able to inspire and guide all students without being a person of indisputable professional competence, displaying the highest standards of scholarship and moral integrity. Mere information is no longer enough; both a penetrative insight into, and a broad outlook on, our changing society and its children are needed. The teacher who is out-of-touch with what is happening in our diverse society and with its children is poorly qualified to teach any subject or any grade.

Significant changes continue to take place in education as we move into the twenty-first century. Just as the nations of the world are moving from dependence to independence and from independence to interdependence, our children are making parallel journeys in life and school. The child in life is dependent; the adolescent strives for unlimited independence; the full-fledged adult discerns that the fundamental law of human existence is interdependence. Hence, interdependence is synonymous with moral autonomy—liberty within the order, inner and outer peace, and maturity in human relationships (Paplauskas-Ramunas, 1968). One of the greatest challenges that you face is helping children navigate through this sometimes turbulent journey.

Before exploring the ways you can create healthy classrooms, four separate but integrated forces that are affecting the direction of educational practices will be explored: (1) equality, (2) diversity, (3) the increasing power of the student, and (4) the goals of our children. These forces are redefining the nature of teaching and the interpersonal relationships that occur between you and your students and consequently affect the development of student and classroom wellness. The theme and relevance of these four issues are integrated into the remaining chapters throughout the book. Those teachers who ignore or underestimate their impact will find it almost impossible to build student wellness and the healthy classroom.

Equality

Advancement in our social system has moved toward a society that demands that all people, regardless of race, gender, disability, or ethnic background, have the right to be treated as equals. As a result, schools are also experiencing these positive changes and teacher-student relationships have gone through significant transition and change. The traditional methods of influencing students come from an autocratic past in which students were to conform to the demands of the authoritative teacher. The democratic evolution, however, has promoted a process of equalization where most students resist disrespectful demands from those who try to assert authority over them.

Some teachers are disturbed at the thought that their students are their equals. It is true that teachers have more knowledge, experience, and skills than the students have, but these things do not confer automatic superiority. Equality means that any student, despite his individual differences and abilities, has an equal claim to dignity and respect. Neither teacher nor student is inferior. No individual ability or trait such as sex, age, color, wisdom, money, status, or position guarantees superiority, the right to dominate, or the right to be disrespectful to others.

The central guidepost in education should be that all children regardless of sex, social class, ethnic, racial, or cultural characteristics should have an equal opportunity to learn in school.

Equality in this context means that all students are equal to teachers in terms of human worth and dignity. You and your students both have specific roles and responsibilities within the classroom. Each of you has your own functions, knowledge, experiences, and ambitions, but all of you are equal in terms of human dignity and respect.

As the autocratic process weakens and you can no longer forcibly impose your will, students gain greater freedom in determining their own motivation and direction. In a democracy, every student is entitled to respect and to self-determination within the limits prescribed by the social structure of the school and society. Self-determination is fundamental in a democracy. Students, however, do not always act in socially acceptable ways or approach their academic responsibilities in constructive ways. A student's positive or negative behavior is often related to his or her self-concept, perception of himself or herself and others, and the methods of finding a place for himself or herself in the classroom and society.

The real challenge for you lies in your ability to create the healthy classroom by building positive self-esteem and resiliency within your students and creating an atmosphere that is encouraging to them. The foundation of the healthy classroom is the interpersonal relationship that you have with your students and the relationship that students have with other students. Building healthy interpersonal relationships based on mutual dignity, understanding, trust, and respect is the foundation of teaching.

Diversity

Diversity in this discussion is divided into ethnic/racial diversity and exceptional children.

Ethnic/Racial Diversity Historically, America has been viewed as a place where people of any color or ethnic background could come and pursue their economic and social dreams. However, it has only been over the last few decades that America is facing the reality of that ideal. In the past few decades, Trimble (1995) stated "America has truly grown into a beautiful complex mosaic of every conceivable skin color from existing populations and descendants of what sometimes appears to be a countless number of countries. To add to the complexity of the mosaic, even the make-up within each diverse group is complex and diverse in its language, norms, mores, and ethnic and cultural traditions." Each race has different ethnic groups, and different ethnic groups have different cultures.

This transition is moving at a greater pace in the major metropolitan areas where the U.S. Bureau of Census projects that the ethnic and racial minorities will be well over 65 percent by the turn of the century. The National Multicultural Institute (1997) reported that: (1) over the next 20 years the U.S. population will grow by 42 million. Hispanics will account for 47 percent of the growth, blacks 22 percent, Asians 18 percent, and whites 13 percent; (2) Miami is two-thirds Hispanic and San Francisco is one-third Asian-American; and (3) by the year 2000, English will be the second language in California. Ethnic minority students now make up the majority of the student population in 25 of the nation's largest school districts. The majority of the public school students in California, the nation's most populous state, are ethnic minorities.

As a result of this process, evolutionary changes are taking place in our nation's classrooms; the societal impact and repercussions will have far-reaching effects upon the development of contemporary education. The increasing racial and ethnic diversity within our nation's classrooms has become one of the most significant challenges our teachers of today and tomorrow face. Working with and understanding our diverse society should be one of the most important concerns in modern education. The central guidepost in education should be that all children regardless of sex, social class, ethnic, racial, or cultural characteristics should have an equal opportunity to learn in school. Inherent in this ideal is the concept that racism, sexism, and discrimination will be continually fought against.

This transition is, unfortunately, compounded by the fact that many ethnic minority students are not achieving academic success in mainstream American schools. As a consequence, fewer ethnic minority students will enter college and this will ultimately have an impact on the numbers of ethnic minorities entering the professional workforce.

The National Association of Independent Schools projected that a shortfall of 2 million teachers will occur by the start of the twenty-first century (AACTE, 1989). It is estimated that California alone will be short 200,000 teachers in the same time period. The Research About Teacher Education (RATE) 111 study (AACTE, 1989) of elementary school teacher education students reported:

1. The number of female candidates was 76 percent

2. Ninety-one percent were white

3. Thirty-three percent were married

4. Less than 7 percent were people of color or of international descent

5. Nearly half spoke no language other than English

6. Less than 25 percent came to college from over 100 miles away, with over 75 percent reporting wanting to return to their suburban or rural hometowns to teach

7. Among the 8 percent who came from major urban settings to attend college, 33 percent would consider returning to those cities to teach

While the percentage of ethnic minority students in the nation's schools is increasing rapidly, the percentage of ethnic minority teachers is decreasing sharply. In 1980, ethnic minority teachers made up 12.5 percent of the nation's teachers. If current trends continue, ethnic minority teachers will make up about 5 percent of the nation's teachers by the turn of the century (Hope-Franklin). In 1997 in California, our most diverse state, minority students made up 60 percent of the 5.5 million students (K–12), but only 21 percent of the teachers were minorities (Guthrie, 1997). In comparison, 54 percent of the students were minorities and only 18 percent of the teachers were minorities in 1990. The Minority Teacher Development Program (Chole), established in 1990, initiated efforts to meet this need by recruiting African-American, Latino, and Asian-American teachers.

We are at the dawn of a global era where education may be the very starting point, central point, and ending point of all human endeavors, undertakings, and achievements. Never before has the race between education and social catastrophe been so clear. As the people of various nations and cultures move closer together, education will play a major role in convincing humankind that all people are born equal and that we all share a common goodness that is stronger than any agreement, treaty, or league. Appendix G contains a listing of multicultural magazines and journals that would be helpful for the teacher to review in order to gain a better understanding of the diverse cultures represented in his or her classroom.

Although poverty is not exclusively linked to ethnic/racial minority groups, there is a strong correlation between the two. It is almost impossible to talk about the health and educational experiences of minority groups without talking about their economic circumstances. Many poor minorities are undereducated, unemployed, or work at minimum wage jobs, and are geographically concentrated in large cities and ghetto areas. Substantial evidence suggests that poverty, underemployment, and living in a single-parent home pose significant risks of the development of health problems, particularly in behavioral health areas (Reed et al., 1993).

Poverty significantly affects health and wellness, and, in particular, affects the education of young people. For example, disproportionately large numbers of students from lower socioeconomic levels drop out of school and while in school are assigned to low-ability groups beginning very early in their school experiences. These students are seen by teachers as less able academically, are

Diversity in the United States

The four dominant multicultural populations (Native-Americans, Hispanic-Americans, Asian and Pacific Islander Americans, and African-Americans) are increasing in size at a rate greater than the dominant population. The American Council on Education (1988) reported that by the year 2000, one-third of all school age children and 42 percent of all public school students will be of ethnic minority backgrounds.

It is important to bear in mind that the labels "Native-Americans/American Indians," "Hispanic/Latino," "Asian-Americans and Pacific Islanders," and "African-American/Blacks" are designations of convenience, and while the subgroups to which they are applied show some commonalities, they are culturally, demographically, and linguistically diverse. Because each subgroup differs along so many dimensions, the practice of aggregating data in epidemiological studies of social problems, practices, and prevalence under the above summative labels masks the important differences in at-risk status. National aggregated data for the subgroups listed under these convenient labels is therefore of very limited utility for program planning in regions dominated by a specific cultural subgroup.

Native-Americans/American Indians
The two groups consisting of Native-Americans are American Indians and Native Alaskans as Native-Americans. Each group, in turn, consists of many subgroups. The 1992 Census registered 2,134,000 Native-Americans in the United States. Native Alaskans consist of Aleuts, Eskimos, and Indians. The Bureau of Indian Affairs recognizes approximately 315 American Indian tribes or bands.

Hispanic-Americans/Latinos
The Hispanic population is the second largest minority population next to African-Americans in the United States. The three major groups that exist in this category are: Mexican-Americans (Chicanos), Puerto Ricans, and Cubans. The 1992 Census registered 24,238,000 Hispanic-Americans in the United States. The majority of Hispanics live in the five Southwestern states of Arizona, California, Colorado, New Mexico, and Texas.

Asian-Americans and Pacific Islanders
The six major groups of Asian-Americans are Chinese, Filipino, Japanese, Asian Indian, Korean, and Vietnamese; there are numerous smaller subgroups as well. The 1992 Census listed a total of 8,401,000 Asian-Americans in the United States.

African-Americans/Blacks
African-Americans make up the largest population of minorities. The 1992 Census listed a total of 31,635,000 African-Americans in the United States. African-Americans come from several specific cultural experiences that differ in language, values, and beliefs. They come from Africa, the Caribbean, and from the Americas, including urban and rural areas. African-Americans are disproportionately concentrated in central cities or Southern states. In 1990, 81 percent of blacks living in the United States were living in metropolitan areas.

assigned to a low-ability track, and perhaps are condemned to that level for the rest of their academic lives (Peterson et al., 1984). Oakes (1990) has critically looked at the concept of tracking and sees it as a way of keeping certain groups of people in their place. She believes that the procedure used to identify, label, regroup, and instruct children tends to lead to a control of knowledge that made it hard for them to ever catch up with the children placed in a higher track.

How can we prevent the development of negative and harmful expectations for students? Gollnick and Chinn (1998) summarized this question in the following way:

Table 1.1 Persons and Families below Poverty Level

Selected Characteristics by Race, Age, and Family	1994	1995
All persons	%	%
All races	14.5	13.8
White American	11.7	11.2
African-American	30.6	29.3
Hispanic-American	30.7	30.3
Asian/Pacific Islander	14.6	14.6
Families		
All races	11.6	10.8
White American	9.1	8.5
African-American	27.3	26.4
Hispanic-American	27.8	27.0
Asian/Pacific Islander	13.1	12.4
Families with female householder, no husband present		
All races	34.6	32.4
White American	29.0	26.6
African-American	46.1	45.1
Hispanic-American	52.0	49.4

SOURCE: Adapted from U.S. Bureau of Census: Poverty in the United States, 1996, www.census.gov/main/www/subjects.html

Teachers, counselors, and administrators must be aware that they can consciously fall into such behavior because they have learned that poverty is the fault of the individual. As a result, students are blamed for circumstances beyond their control. Instead, educators should see as a challenge the opportunity to provide these students with the knowledge and skills to overcome poverty (p. 67).

Women and children represent 80 percent of the poor people in the United States—the majority of which are people of color. Table 1.1 provides a picture of poverty for the years 1994 and 1995. The United States 1994 federal poverty level for one person was $7,500; $9,000 for a couple; and $14,500 for a family of four. The 1995 poverty threshold for a family of four was $15,569.

Minorities with the worst health status and poorest access to health care live in communities that have inadequate housing, poor nutrition, poor sanitation, and high rates of physical, emotional, and sexual abuse. People living in poverty experience poorer health, which is reflected in a higher incidence of chronic diseases, a higher mortality rate, and poorer survival rates (National Center for Health Statistics). In addition, students from poverty have a much higher dropout rate from school.

There is little question that something must be done in the schools to help counter the inequitable environments from which an increasing number of our students come from. As an educator, you must become aware of the communities of poverty and fear. You must read widely in the area of social class, particularly focusing on the problems of the poor. Clearly, there is a need for the voices of the powerless and oppressed to be recognized and heard (Shapiro et al., 1995).

Exceptional Children   Nearly 25 million Americans from every ethnic and socioeconomic group fall into one or more of the categories of exceptionality. Exceptional people include students with disabilities and giftedness. Heward (1996) defined exceptional children as children that:

> differ from the norm (either below or above) to such an extent that an individualized program of special education is required to meet these children's needs. The term exceptional children includes children who experience difficulties in learning and children whose performance is so superior that special education is necessary to help them fulfill their potential. Thus, exceptional children is an inclusive term that refers to children with learning and/or behavioral problems, children with physical disabilities or sensory impairments, and children who are intellectually gifted or have a special talent (p. 8).

As a teacher, you should first and foremost maintain the exceptional student's self-esteem by considering the student first in your words and thoughts. A person's disability, for example, should be described accurately, if it needs to be included in the message, but it is more important to emphasize his or her abilities than his or her disabilities. "Ray, who has a visual impairment, uses a cane for mobility" is more appropriate than "Because he is blind, Ray needs a cane." The use of the term *person with a disability* is preferable to the term *disabled person* to promote the person's self-esteem and recognition as a person first (Pierson, 1999).

Unfortunately, not all exceptional children are fully accepted into the mainstream culture and are often labeled in negative ways. Many labels placed on exceptional people, especially those with learning disabilities and mild mental retardation, are demeaning and stigmatizing. The opposite, however, occurs with individuals with visual impairments who usually have public empathy and are given significant public support. Efforts by various organizations and individuals are underway to help society view individuals with disabilities primarily as persons and to view the disabilities as only secondary to who they are. Every exceptional child who is mainstreamed into the regular classroom wants to be valued, accepted, and considered "normal" within that environment. Wolfensberger (1983) states "the most explicit and highest goal of normalization must be the creation, support, and defense of valued social roles for people who are at risk of social devaluation" (p. 234). Gollnick and Chin (1998) state:

> The arguments against integrating children with severe disabilities have often been centered on the presumed inability of nondisabled children to accept their peers with disabilities. In reality, some of the reservations may be more a reflection of educators who themselves are unable or unwilling to accept the dignity and worth of individuals with severe disabilities (p. 179).

Laws Designed to Help Students with Disabilities

The Education for All Handicapped Children Act (EHA) (Public Law 94-142) passed in 1975 provides the following:

1. A free and appropriate education for all children with disabilities.
2. Safeguards to protect the rights of children with disabilities and their parents.
3. Education of children with disabilities with nondisabled children to the maximum extent possible in the least restrictive environment.
4. Testing to determine or to assess whether or not the child does need special education; or evaluation to determine what the needs are and what the placement should be.
5. An Individualized Education Plan (IEP), which is a written document to be individualized to the needs of a single child, rather than to a class or group of children. The special education plan is to be specifically designed to meet the child's needs.
6. The parents are to be given an equal voice in the educational program given to their children. This equal voice is assured in the development of the child's IEP.

Individuals with Disabilities Education Act (IDEA) (Public Law 101-476) was passed in 1990 and amended and renamed PL 94-142. The amendment extended the definition of special education to include instruction in all settings, including the workplace and training centers, and extended the definition of exceptional children to include students with autism and traumatic brain injury.

The Americans with Disabilities Act (ADA) (Public Law 101-336) was enacted in 1990 with the purpose of extending to people with disabilities civil rights similar to those now available on the basis of race, color, sex, national origin, and religion through the Civil Rights Act of 1964. It prohibits discrimination on the basis of disability in the private sector and in state and local governments, public accommodations and services, including transportation provided by public and private entities. It also includes provisions for telecommunications relay services.

Title II of the ADA provides comprehensive civil rights protections for "qualified individuals with disabilities." An "individual with a disability" is a person who (1) has a *physical or mental impairment* that substantially limits a *"major life activity,"* or (2) has a record of such an impairment, or (3) is regarded as having such an impairment. Examples of physical or mental impairments include, but are not limited to, such contagious and noncontagious diseases and conditions as orthopedic, visual, speech, and hearing impairments, cerebral palsy, epilepsy, muscular dystrophy, multiple sclerosis, cancer, heart disease, diabetes, mental retardation, emotional illness, specific learning disabilities, HIV disease (whether symptomatic or asymptomatic), tuberculosis, drug addiction, and alcoholism. Homosexuality and bisexuality are not physical or mental impairments under the ADA.

"Major life activities" include functions such as caring for oneself, performing manual tasks, walking, seeing, hearing, speaking, breathing, learning, and working. Individuals currently engaged in illegal drug use are not protected by the ADA.

Schools must provide *reasonable accommodations* for students with disabilities. Reasonable accommodation is a modification or an adjustment to the school environment that will enable the student with a disability to perform essential school functions. Reasonable accommodation also includes adjustments to assure that a student with a disability has rights and privileges in school equal to those of nondisabled students. Examples of reasonable accommodation include making existing facilities used by students readily accessible to and usable by an individual with a disability; modifying school schedules; acquiring or modifying equipment; providing qualified readers or interpreters; or appropriately modifying examinations or programs. Most modifications within a classroom setting are readily achievable in most cases. School districts have many resources and consultants that work with disabled student services and a teacher should work with them in conjunction with the student and his or her parent(s) to achieve "reasonable accommodations."

The Education for All Handicapped Children Act (EHA; PL 94-142), the Individuals with Disabilities Education Act (IDEA; PL 101-176), Section 504 of the Vocational Rehabilitation Act Amendments of 1973 (PL 93-112), and the Americans with Disabilities Act (ADA; PL 101-336) guarantee all exceptional children the right to free and appropriate education and freedom from discrimination resulting from their disability. Gollnick and Chinn (1998) state:

> Despite these mandates, equality still eludes millions of individuals with disabilities in this country. Insensitivity, apathy, and prejudice contribute to the problems of those with disabilities. The laws can force services for individuals with disabilities, but only time and effort can change public attitudes (p. 81).

Laws make it virtually impossible for any educator or student not to encounter exceptional students in their teaching and everyday experiences. It is, therefore, imperative that all teachers be trained to be sensitive to the needs of exceptional students. A summary of different disabilities is discussed in Appendix F.

The Power of the Student

Regardless of the budget, the number of teachers, the kinds of equipment, or the incorporation of innovative technology, the success of any classroom or school will ultimately be determined by the participating students. Students are more than just names that appear on the enrollment sheets because every student ultimately becomes the center of every strategy, goal, or vision. The reality is that how students think, work, and feel dictates the direction and success of the classroom and school. Success is generated through the spirit and minds of all students—through their competence, capacity, and commitment. Advantages will go to the teachers who understand this and know how to guide, motivate, and manage their students. It should be obvious that mismanaging students will create costly liabilities for the classroom and the school.

Young people, regardless of their gender, ethnic background, or color, are full of energy, imagination, enterprise, and when given encouragement, they develop motivation and hope. Teachers as significant adults and role models must be careful not to diminish any student's beliefs and dreams of finding himself or herself and his or her place in school and society. Just by being a student, he or she will challenge you to respond to some of his or her unspoken questions: What kind of person am I? Do you really care about me? Can I make a positive difference in this classroom? How can you as my teacher help me? How do I fit in with the rest of the class? Are you willing to accept me? Will you treat me with dignity and respect? Will you help prepare me for what lies ahead? These questions, of course, are not answered in your words, but by your actions and behaviors that support those words.

These are important questions because they go to the core of every student. The answers to these questions tell them who they are and what they are worth. Students have within themselves vast resources for understanding and for altering their self-concepts and self-directed behavior. To take each student seriously is to help his or her progress into becoming the capable person he or she was meant to be. If you are to enhance the individual growth and development of your students you must ask yourself such questions as: How do I create an atmosphere and curriculum that values diversity and encourages cooperation among children from all backgrounds? Am I acting on any prejudicial assumptions about people that are contradicting the human values that I am trying to teach? Am I supporting any certain preconceived characteristics that give some students a better chance to learn over other students? Most important, how can I reach out to all of my students and raise their levels of self-esteem? Motivating students to become the capable people they were meant to be is one of many challenges all teachers face.

Common Goals

The goals of students and teachers are complementary. Students are in the process of growing and developing and trying to determine who they are and what role they will play in life. Many young people will use school as a means to that end. Payne and Hahn (1995), in their book *Understanding Your Health,* listed four of the most important developmental tasks that are critical for young people to accomplish. These are: (1) forming an initial self-identity, (2) establishing a sense of relative independence, (3) assuming increasing levels of responsibility, and (4) developing the social skills needed for social interaction. If these skills sound familiar, they are. These are some of the same positive goals that teachers have for their students: responsibility, self-reliance, self-discipline, and social interaction. These are also the same goals of the healthy classroom.

Students, of course, may not be able to verbalize these tasks or even be aware that they are in the process of fulfilling their developmental tasks, but the students' behavior and actions clearly reflect them. You must understand these tasks, recognize your own role in this process, and, whenever possible, provide the skills and strategies to help your students achieve these tasks.

Forming an Initial Self-Identity Many young people use school as a means of attaining some self-identity. For most of childhood and adolescence, adults see children as someone's son or daughter. Very few people recognize children as unique people. Young people usually wish to present their uniqueness and competencies. Young people are constructing perceptions of themselves both internally and externally and are formulating behavioral patterns that will project this identity to others. One's identity will be based on the judgments, both good and bad, that one makes in the classroom as well as in life. Using good judgment requires openness to new information, the ability to see other alternatives, and the courage to make decisions. Most important, it requires the willingness to evaluate the choices. How people adjust to their frustrations and stresses in school will influence who that person is. Young students who lack these skills will find themselves in a continual series of crises because they cannot apply effective solutions to their problems.

Each student is a unique individual functioning within the total classroom structure. That uniqueness contributes to the total personality of the classroom.

One of the teacher's goals should be to encourage students to develop social skills for social interaction.

Each student must be given the freedom to search for his or her own identity within the guidelines of acceptable classroom participation. Students cannot be placed into a teacher's preconceived mold. Participation in school is just one small piece of a larger puzzle that can help young people answer the question "Who am I?"

Establishing a Sense of Relative Independence In childhood, the primary responsibility for socialization lies within the family. However, as youngsters begin to move through adolescence, they want some degree of separation from that dependent relationship. They seek out their peers and move to outside activities that begin to disengage them from the family. Within this process, individuals must develop self-discipline, which requires self-evaluation, self-understanding, and recognition of one's own feelings, goals, and the willingness to accept responsibility for one's own actions. School is just one of many activities that can be a safe, secure path toward independence. Young people will need to draw on physical, emotional, social, intellectual, and spiritual strengths that they have attained from both family and teachers to undertake the school experiences that will bring independence.

Assuming Increasing Levels of Responsibility All young people are expected to assume increasing levels of responsibility. This is a significant part of adulthood. In school the opportunity to assume responsibility can come from a variety of sources. Responsibility is involved in establishing new friendships, helping others to achieve, cooperation in classroom work, being on time, fulfilling school assignments and schedules, and a variety of other tasks. The ability to assume responsibility requires recognizing limits and identifying what needs to be done. Weakness in this area will cause students to blame others or the system and to see themselves as victims.

Developing the Social Skills for Social Interaction The fourth developmental task is that of developing appropriate and dependable social skills. Participation in the school classroom requires the ability to function and communicate with different kinds of people. Students will probably need to refine a variety of social skills, including communication, which requires a person to express oneself clearly and to be able to listen to others. These interpersonal skills are necessary for making friends, joining groups, developing intimacy, and managing conflict. Weakness in this area shows up as dishonesty, inability to share feelings, and difficulty in giving and receiving love or help.

TEACHERS CAN MAKE A DIFFERENCE

You have a unique opportunity to make significant contributions for change. You can create within your small classroom a unique environment in which you can reach your students, raise their level of self-esteem, win their cooperation, and instill in them the ideal values of society. The classroom that promotes wellness gives all students a miniature world in which they can try out their skills and explore themselves. How they respond and what they learn will later contribute to their adult performance. Being sensitive to the needs of each student is one of the greatest vehicles to helping each one of them reach his or her human potential.

Students deserve the best, and over time, what goes around, comes around. If students are respected and accepted, they will learn to respect and accept; if students are abused and rejected, they will learn to abuse and reject. Young students will imitate. They reflect how you think, how you communicate, what you value, how you solve problems, what you do with feelings, how you care, and how you are in the world. Whether you know it or not, you are teaching and modeling self-esteem—or a lack of it—to all of your students all of the time.

SUMMARY OF MAJOR POINTS
IN CHAPTER 1

1. The healthy classroom is designed to create student wellness through positive relationships based on mutual dignity, respect, and trust.

2. Today, health and wellness are viewed as multifaceted concepts that encompass physical, emotional, spiritual, social, and intellectual dimensions.

3. Maslow equated self-actualization with health.

Class Discussion	CHAPTER 1

Note: Review Appendix E before facilitating this activity.

Equality Does Not Mean Sameness
Time: 3–5 minutes (discussion not included)
Objective: Participants learn that equality does not mean sameness.
Materials: A one dollar bill, one dollar in coins (3 quarters, 2 dimes, and 1 nickel), 100 pennies, a silver dollar (if available), 10 dimes, 20 nickels, and 4 quarters.

Procedure:

1. Select one volunteer for each of the different dollar amounts.
2. Have the volunteers sit at a desk or table and place a different one dollar amount in front of each volunteer.
3. Ask the volunteers if any of them has an amount that is more than another.
4. Ask the volunteers which dollar would be of more value if the person wanted to enclose a dollar inside a birthday card and mail it to a child.
5. Ask the volunteers which dollar would be of more value if the person wanted to get a 65 cent beverage from a coin-operated vending machine.
6. Ask the volunteers which dollar would be of more value if the person wanted to play the quarter slot machines in Las Vegas.
7. Ask the volunteers which dollar would be of more value if you took a child to a carnival where he could try to pitch pennies onto a plate to win prizes.
8. Ask the volunteers which dollar would be of more value if you needed to make a telephone call from a public phone booth.
9. Ask the volunteers which dollar would be of more value if you needed to park your car at a metered spot.
10. Ask the volunteers which dollar would be of more value if you wanted to give your child a "special" dollar (the silver dollar if you have one).
11. Comment that the dollars are "equal" in one sense, but that each still retains its own unique properties and strengths.

Suggested Discussion Questions:

1. In what ways are the two amounts of money "equal?" or "not equal?"
2. If you establish an equalitarian relationship with your students, will you lose your uniqueness? Why?
3. How can you apply this demonstration to your teaching philosophy?

4. Self-actualization refers to self-fulfillment, namely, the tendency for a person to become actualized in what he or she is capable of becoming.

5. Psychosocial health encompasses the intellectual, emotional, social, and spiritual dimensions of wellness.

6. The healthy classroom is based on mutual trust and respect.

7. Empowerment is a process in which individuals or groups of people gain increasing measures of control over their behavior.

8. Empowered students are taught to rely on their internal locus of control.

9. Effective teachers know that to build strong and independent structures and to build a foundation for healthy self-esteem and resiliency one must work from the inside out.

10. The inner framework that teachers help build within their students evolves through the quality of the relationship between them.

Class Discussion	CHAPTER 1

Note: Review Appendix E before facilitating this activity.

Behavioral Characteristics of A Good Teacher
Time: 20–25 minutes (discussion not included)
Objective: To help participants understand that good teaching requires a teacher to be respectful, trusting, and accepting.

Materials:

2 large sheets of butcher paper for each group
Different colored felt tip pens (a blackboard and chalk can be used if butcher paper and pens cannot be obtained)
Masking tape for each group
Pair of scissors for each group
A list of Teaching Behaviors for each group (see list below)

Procedure:

1. Divide the class into groups of 4–6 participants.
2. Distribute large sheets of butcher paper and felt tip pens to each group.
3. Using one sheet of butcher paper, each group is to brainstorm a list of adjectives they believe best describes the positive behavioral characteristics or traits that they think are required for good teaching.
4. After each group brainstorms the list, they are to prioritize the list by choosing what they believe are the four most important traits.
5. On the other sheet of butcher paper, each group is to draw a teacher's shield (see the following example) and divide it into four parts. Tell the groups to be creative in their art.

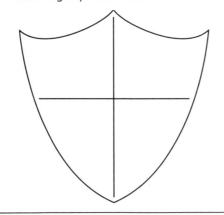

6. After the four traits are chosen, write one trait in each of the four sections on the teacher's shield.
7. The teacher's shield should be taped on a wall in the room.
8. Next, the group is to study the "List of Teacher's Behaviors" (see following list) and select which ones they believe will contribute to the traits that they listed on the teacher's shield. Each group is to cut them from the sheet and tape them on the butcher paper next to the shield. Place the others in a pile.
9. The groups join together for the discussion.

Suggested Discussion Questions:

1. Why did you choose to list those four specific characteristics as qualities you desire in a good teacher?
2. Can you recall any personal experiences that are related to the characteristics you listed?
3. Were you surprised by any similarities or differences of opinions with the people in your group?
4. Were you surprised by any similarities or differences of opinions between the different groups within the classroom.
5. Comparing the list of statements and words that you taped next to your teacher's shield to the list that you placed in a pile, do you see any type of consistent pattern in your selections? If so, what is the pattern?
6. Which of the statements and words would contribute to developing positive behaviors in the students?
7. Which of the statements and words would contribute to creating rebellious students?
8. What other words or statements can you add that will contribute to developing positive behaviors in the students?
9. What other words or statements can you add that will contribute to creating rebellious students?
10. What have you learned from this lesson and how can you apply it to your teaching career in the future?

List of Teacher's Behaviors

Works with teachers to solve problems   Insists on own way
Uses power to create a win/win situation   Accepting
Utilizes joint problem solving   Looks for reasons behind students behaviors
Controlling   Always has the answers
Empowering   Allows mistakes
Punishes   Listens without judgment
Shares feelings with students   Solves and fixes problems for students
Respects different ideas

---

11. One of the greatest challenges that teachers face is helping children navigate their journey from dependence to independence and from independence to interdependence and finally from interdependence to living life in all its fullness.

12. Four important social forces that are influencing education include the concepts of equality, diversity, the power of the student, and developmental student goals.

13. The four dominant multicultural populations in the United States are African- Americans, Asian and Pacific Islander Americans, Native-Americans, and Hispanic-Americans.

14. Many laws have been passed that guarantee all exceptional children the right to free and appropriate education and freedom from discrimination resulting from their disability.

15. Teachers do have a unique opportunity to make significant contributions for change in educational practices.

Teacher's Corner: Observing and Interviewing to Assess the School's Multicultural Program

Directions for Observation

This exercise is a combination of observation and interview. You will have to interview a teacher or administrator to answer some of the questions in the following survey.

Observe a multicultural student for about one hour. Check the appropriate box for each of the questions in this survey.

YES	NO	OBSERVATION
—	—	Does the school have a statistical record of the different multicultural groups?
—	—	Are the different multicultural groups recognized in the school curriculum?
—	—	Are different multicultural groups recognized in the books and other educational materials?
—	—	Do the majority of students recognize and value the various cultures?
—	—	Does the school have a culturally diverse faculty?
—	—	Are multicultural students disciplined more than the mainstream students?
—	—	Are more multicultural students suspended than the mainstream students?
—	—	Does the library have a variety of materials on culturally diverse groups?
—	—	Are multicultural students represented in school organizations such as clubs, teams, cheerleading, etc.?
—	—	Are outside speakers from different cultures invited to speak at school assemblies or similar functions?
—	—	Are different cultural holidays recognized?
—	—	Are parents of multicultural students represented in administrative decisions?
—	—	Does the school have a general school policy that recognizes the needs of the different cultural groups?
—	—	Does the faculty meet periodically to discuss multicultural issues?
—	—	Does the school have a strong rationale for multicultural education?

Directions for Interview

After the observation of the class, use the following questions to guide an interview with the student. Feel free to ask your own questions.

1. Do you think you are treated fairly in school? Why?
2. What do you like about school?
3. What don't you like about school?
4. Why kinds of problems do you have at school?
5. How do you take care of those problems?
6. What are some similarities between your own culture and the mainstream culture?
7. What are some differences between your own culture and mainstream culture?

Analysis

As a result of your observations and interview, what important lessons can you apply to your present or future teaching strategies?

2

■

The Healthy Classroom
Teacher

Little happens in a relationship until the individuals learn to trust each other.

DAVID JOHNSON

Who you are and what you do in the classroom has a tremendous influence upon the students that you teach. The words that you speak and how you say them, your body language, your facial expressions—from pursing your lips or drawing your brows together to smiling—all have an impact on the atmosphere that you create for each student and the class as a whole. This is referred to as your teaching or leadership style.

You are a leader of young students and you must plan, organize, direct, and coordinate the efforts of your students; set goals; maintain the class; handle conflict; and much more. Leadership goes beyond just teaching academic skills. Good teachers incorporate leadership techniques into their teaching. You are more than an instructor—you are a leader. The following list presents some differences between instructors and leaders (Goode-Vick, 1985):

1. An instructor's job is to teach a skill, a technique, an activity, or a subject, while a leader's aim is to improve character and citizenship.

2. An instructor is primarily activity- or subject-centered on how well the student is performing, while a leader is person-centered and concerned about attitudes, ideals, values, goals, and the future.

3. Instructors watch what is happening with test scores, while a leader is concerned with what is happening to the students.

4. An instructor stresses and uses position, rank, and authority to get compliance, while a leader uses influence to motivate students.

TEACHING STYLES

It is important that you know your style of teaching or leadership. Each and every day you communicate messages that tell each student how you feel, not only about the students, but also about yourself. It may be scary for you to see who you really are, but it is also reassuring to know who you are not. The good news is no matter what inadequacies you might possess, once you become aware of the kind of teacher you are you can take steps to become even better. By its very nature, teaching is a series of learn-by-doing experiences. This means that you can change your leadership style.

The Autocratic or Controlling Teacher

Many teachers mishandle their power and misperceive their role as a leader. Few teachers are taught the art of leadership. Consequently, they tend to model the way they were taught. Unfortunately, many teachers imitate ultra-strict behaviors and refuse to give the students any freedom or responsibility in the mistaken belief that control is what gets things done and handing it over to anyone else will hinder success. Controlling teachers usually work extremely hard and are admired for their intensity; after all, they plan, direct, control, and coordinate. In fact, controlling or directive teachers will usually find themselves physically and emotionally involved in every activity of the job because they believe that without them, the job will not be done right. These teachers are afraid that if they lose control, they will lose everything.

The autocratic teacher controls and directs and makes most of the decisions. They give the student the message that "I am the boss and you will do as I say." Autocratic teachers believe that they not only have the knowledge and experience, but also power to make students do what they say. They expect students to listen and comply rather than listen to hear their words or feelings. Everyone has had experiences with individuals like this, experiences that often provoked both anger and frustration. In the long run, healthy individuals cannot sustain positive relationships with individuals who treat them as inferior and incapable.

Autocratic teachers mistakenly believe that when they constantly direct and correct, they are helping their students to flourish and grow. They believe that their words are the only truth and solution to any problem. Students respond to these messages in some of the following ways:

The teacher never listens to me.

The teacher treats me like a two-year-old.

He just pushes me around.

Why can't she be nice once in a while?

Why is she always picking on me?

Is he ever pushy!

Why doesn't she just shut up?

I hate him.

I'm never going to tell her anything again.

I'm just going to ignore him.

Im going to quit.

I'm going to get even.

My feelings don't really matter.

The teacher doesn't even know who I am.

If a teacher hears similar statements from his or her students, they are probably telling the teacher something that goes beyond their spoken words. Their underlying message is that the teacher is controlling and/or demanding. The students are telling the teacher that they feel discounted and that what they think really does not matter. A teacher who chooses to motivate students through fear instead of respect will have a class that never reaches its full potential.

How Students Respond to the Autocratic Teacher A demanding, controlling teacher elicits many behavioral symptoms from the students. If students are displaying any of the following behaviors, the teacher should ask himself or herself what might be happening to cause the feelings that they represent:

Talking back

Anger

Stubbornness

Uncooperativeness

Lying

Disrespectful attitude

Defensive attitude

Keeping a distance from you (both physically and emotionally)

Controlling and directive teachers justify their approach with the belief that they are providing the students with the structure and discipline that are necessary to succeed in life. Most psychologists would suggest that structure and discipline are most effectively developed in an atmosphere of love, acceptance, and warmth. Many autocratic leaders are successful in sports and business, but they are often unsuccessful in human relationships. Many people in positions of authority say they would rather be respected than liked. Wouldn't it be better if they could have both?

Just think about how many schools achieve mediocre success with students who are treated disrespectfully. Imagine what might happen if those schools had students who were fully engaged, energized, appreciated, and empowered.

The Permissive Teacher

Permissive teachers are often ineffectual teachers who create frustration, disorder, and confusion in the classroom. Two types of permissive teachers include the inadequately trained teacher and the teacher who is just too lazy to meet teaching obligations or is unavailable or preoccupied with other issues. The message of the uncaring, permissive teacher to his or her students is "I cannot give you what you need. I am overwhelmed," or "You are not terribly important to me." The permissive teacher who is aloof, cold, impersonal, or uninterested in his or her students usually finds it very difficult to motivate students to put out any extra effort.

The permissive teacher who is afraid and lacks confidence is often afraid of not being liked by his or her students and has a difficult time saying "no." They feel relatively helpless, and their teaching responsibilities are overwhelming to them. They feel inadequate, and teaching enhances their inadequacy. They are very immature and do not know how to assume responsibility. Permissive teachers make few decisions, give little direction, and usually provide limited teaching. The students of permissive teachers respond in these ways:

I don't respect her.

I can't count on her.

I feel sorry for him.

Boy, is he a joke!

She's just our babysitter.

He's just putting in his time.

I'm not important.

She is never around for me.

He doesn't even bother to try and pronounce my name correctly.

He only cares about the other students. He doesn't care about me.

How Students Respond to the Permissive Teacher If students are displaying any of the following behaviors the teacher should ask himself or herself what might be happening to cause the feelings that they represent:

Lack of respect

Manipulative tactics

Frequent angry outbursts

Withdrawal

Anxiety

Frustration

The Healthy Teacher

Healthy teachers are democratic teachers who empower their students. To empower is to give ability to or to make effective or powerful. Healthy teachers empower their students by giving them opportunities to express their individuality and, at the same time, validate or affirm them by:

- providing a safe and confirming atmosphere
- giving them the feeling that they are accepted and cared for regardless of the situation
- listening to them and taking them seriously
- being honest and open
- believing that they are capable of solving their own problems
- providing choices and allowing them to learn from the consequences of their choices

The healthy teacher provides power and control by giving the students only as much power and control as they can handle responsibly. The message that empowering teachers convey is "I like you. You are a good person. I trust you." Students respond to messages from the healthy teacher in some of the following ways:

He likes having me around.

She trusts me.

She gives me responsibility.

He takes me seriously.

She listened to me.

He was willing to change his mind.

He takes an interest in me.

She thanked me.

She thinks that I contribute.

How Students Respond to the Healthy Teacher As a result of the consistent words and actions of the healthy teacher, students respond in some of the following ways:

Confidence

Resourcefulness

Helpfulness

Enthusiasm

Happiness

Cooperativeness

Responsibility

Empathy

Healthy teachers who empower want the best for their students. Of course, they want them to reach their academic potentials, but they also want them to be good, successful, happy, and capable people in the process. Have confidence in your students. They are able and willing to cooperate when treated with dignity and respect, and they can learn problem-solving skills that encourage self-control. Some ways of empowering students include:

- allowing the student to develop the capacity to set their own goals and the desire to reach them
- accepting each student as a unique individual
- giving them responsibility
- accepting their opinions
- making each student feel capable of succeeding
- being a good listener
- establishing reasonable limits for behavior
- allowing students to share in the decision-making process
- providing a safe environment
- organizing and planning lessons
- taking time with each student
- establishing fair discipline policies

Empowerment means letting the students flourish and grow, giving them more responsibility, accepting their ideas, and providing an atmosphere that promotes self-confidence. It is what leads to healthy classrooms.

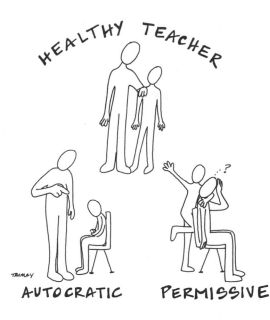

HEALTHY TEACHER

AUTOCRATIC   PERMISSIVE

Time-out: What Kind of Teacher Are You?

This exercise lists certain phrases that we all say some of the time. The situations and the words you use may be slightly different from what is listed below, but the message is still the same. Check off only those phrases that you think you say often.

If you are not currently teaching you can still check off items on the list. If you find that you are using a lot of the phrases in your everyday life, you will probably be using them when you become a teacher. You may also want to think about a former or current teacher and check off the phrases that apply to him or her.

If you are a teacher, if your students are cooperative and if you are willing to hear the answers, have your students rate you with this list. Compare their list with yours. You may be surprised.

1. I told you to do it now.
2. I don't know. That's not my area of expertise.
3. I'm really proud of you.
4. Because I said so.
5. What do you think I should do?
6. I like the way you did that.
7. I can't believe you did that again.
8. Do whatever you want.
9. Thanks for helping me out.
10. Get over here, now!
11. It doesn't matter that it's wrong, go on to the next problem.
12. You've put a lot of work into getting better.

13. I make the rules around here.
14. I can't deal with this anymore.
15. You have really stayed in great shape.
16. Stop it this minute!
17. Don't bother me right now.
18. You must be disappointed. You worked so hard on that project.
19. Why don't you do it this way.
20. I'm busy. Just go and sit down and work on anything you need to.
21. That's a great idea. Let's do it.

Scoring and Analysis

Questions 1, 4, 7, 10, 13, 16, 19 are all statements of the autocratic or controlling teacher.
Questions 2, 5, 8, 11, 14, 17, 20 are all statements of the permissive teacher.
Questions 3, 6, 9, 12, 15, 18, 21 are all statements of the healthy teacher.

Count your check marks for each of the three categories. If you checked more than four statements in any category, you have some tendencies to fall into that style of teaching. It is important that you understand the effects of the messages you are sending to your students. How are they feeling when they hear your words?

Congratulations if you scored high in the healthy teacher category. You are doing a good job in helping your students reach their potentials.

EXPANDING TEACHER LEADERSHIP
ROLES BEYOND THE CLASSROOM

Most teachers, if they have a choice to be anywhere, would prefer to be in their classroom and doing what they were trained to do—teaching children. Most would prefer to leave the policy making to the policy makers, the administrating to the administrators, and parenting to the parents (Teachers Leading the Way, 1998). Teachers often comment how much more fun teaching would be if they did not have to attend all the meetings, work with uncooperative parents, and do all the "extras" that administration is asking them to now do. Most teachers, however, realize that the traditional perception of teachers working solely in the classroom helping children learn is a thing of the past. The role of teachers and their responsibilities has been going through significant changes in recent years.

In recent years, schools, families, and communities have gone through significant changes and the need to improve our schools has required teachers to take on new roles and responsibilities that go beyond their traditional classroom leadership role. Although teachers are still expected to focus most of their energies and attention on classroom responsibilities, they have been required to rechannel some of that energy into other roles; in particular, leadership roles outside of the classroom.

The concept of teacher leadership has extended beyond the classroom and teachers today are being asked to do many things that past traditional teachers were not required to do. Some examples include:

- Communicating more with parents and families on how they can help their children reach higher academic standards
- Communicating what every student needs to know and be able to do, both personally and in the development of curriculum and programs
- Integrating technology into instruction
- Developing partnerships with community and businesses
- Helping to improve assessments and use the results to improve teaching and learning
- Collaborating with other teachers
- Participating in teams and school-level decision making
- Having "master teachers" mentor new teachers

Today's teachers are expected to participate in the development of policies, help administrators make decisions, and help parents find ways to support their children's education. Teacher contributions are critical to making education reform efforts succeed. When teachers participate in improving education, the changes are more likely to work because they understand the support they need to do their jobs well.

Redefining Teacher Leadership Roles

In 1996 the Department of Education hosted the National Teacher Forum to discuss such questions as "Why is teacher leadership needed?" "What forms can teacher leadership take?" and "What steps can teachers take to become effective leaders?" One hundred and twenty exemplary public and private school teachers attended this forum to answer these questions (Teachers Leading the Way, 1998). They concluded that in order for education to continue to improve, teachers must be involved in the process. They recommended that schools find ways to allow teachers to expand their leadership roles outside of their traditional roles. New leadership roles for teachers can include:

- Participating in professional teacher organizations
- Working with administrative management teams to plan improvements within their school
- Being part of curriculum teams to develop academic standards and revise curriculum and assessments to reflect new standards
- Participating in professional development programs that include the sharing of ideas with colleagues aimed at helping teachers improve skills needed to help students reach high standards
- Providing input in personnel decisions
- Improving facilities and technology
- Working with parents
- Defining what students need to know and be able to do (developing standards and assessments for curriculum areas)
- Creating partnerships with the community
- Creating partnerships with businesses and organizations
- Creating partnerships with colleges and universities to prepare future teachers
- Mentoring new teachers
- Becoming politically involved at the local, state, or national level
- Promoting the efforts of teachers through public relations programs

The list of leadership roles for teachers will continue to grow as teachers become more comfortable as education leaders outside of the classroom.

The School as a Community

Two important pieces of legislation were passed in the mid-1990s that recognized the need for building school, community, and family partnerships. Goals 2000: Educate America Act included the following goal: "Every school will promote partnerships that will increase parental involvement and participation in promoting the social, emotional, and academic growth of children." It encourages parent involvement in education and provides for the creation of family information and resource centers. It also encourages local community-based reforms to meet the needs of every student at risk. Title I of Goals 2000 specifies and mandates programs and practices of partnership in order for schools to qualify for or maintain funding. The other important piece of legislation was the Improving America's School Act (IASA), which also included goals to increase parent involvement through parent training, school-parent compacts to improve student achievement, and requiring school districts and parents to develop written parental involvement policies.

Because of the recognition for the need for such partnerships, government legislation has given schools and community organizations the responsibility to work together to help schools meet the many and varied needs of today's students and parents. Schools have been given the responsibility to become service organizations where educational, psychological, and social needs of students and their families are to be addressed in a well-planned, holistic manner. We all recognize that school personnel alone cannot help children cope with or begin to solve the problems of drug abuse, teenage pregnancy, violence, gangs, poverty, theft, vandalism, suicide, and sexually transmitted diseases. By working cooperatively, community agencies can relieve schools of the burden of changing high-risk behaviors and have direct access to the students through referral or immediate contact on the school campus. This three-way partnership can help parents and the school, and ultimately help the child who is at risk.

What Is a Family?

As we move into the twenty-first century, the concept of family has changed considerably. The traditional view of the ideal American family embraces the image of a lifelong monogamous marriage and the nuclear family pattern of husband and wife living together with their children in the same home. Research has shown that American families have undergone dramatic changes in the last 30 years. There has been a shift from traditional, nuclear families to families consisting of single people, single older people, unmarried couples, and extended families (Sweet & Bumpass, 1987). Divorce, remarriages, working parents, single-parent families (especially many headed by women), grandparent parents, foster parents, gay parents, and various configurations of the blended family have changed the traditional image of the nuclear family. The diversity of values, characteristics, and lifestyles that arise from such elements as geographic origin, level of acculturation, socioeconomic status, education, religious background, and age level reveal such traditional categorization to be inaccurate and ultimately unproductive (Boyd-Franklin, 1989).

According to McLaughlin (1993) only 7 percent of all American school-age children live in a home with two parents who are married to each other, only one of whom works outside the home. Almost 75 percent of mothers whose children are in school do work outside the home and close to 25 percent of all children under 18 live with only one parent. This translates to 9.3 million single parents in America.

Parent Involvement in Education

In communities where parents are involved in their children's education, students generally achieve more than children whose parents do not become involved in school activities (Useem, 1990). Henderson (1997) stated: "The evidence is now beyond dispute. When schools work together with families to support learning, children tend to succeed not just in school, but throughout life." Henderson's research reported that when family is involved, students show:

- higher grades and test scores
- better attendance and homework completion
- more positive attitudes and behavior
- fewer placements in special education
- higher graduation rates
- greater enrollment in post-secondary education
- more effective transition to work
- increased civic responsibility and citizenship

Because parent involvement is important to the success of children, it is imperative that schools finds ways for parents to become and stay involved in their childrens' education. However, what is meant by parental involvement is not always clear, nor is it clear as to what type of involvement makes the most difference.

Steinberg et al. (1996) studied 12,000 high school students over a 3-year period and determined that the type of parent involvement that has the most impact on high school students is not the type that parents practice most often—such as checking homework and encouraging their children to try harder. Steinberg and colleagues reported that these types of behaviors do not harm a child's performance in school, but by themselves, they surprisingly have little positive effect on student performance—especially once a child has reached high school. They determined that the key to making a difference is involvement in programs that physically bring the parents into the school, such as attending school programs, extracurricular activities, teacher conferences, and "back to school" nights. Steinberg and his colleagues determined that when parents take the time to attend a school function it sends a strong message about how important school is to the parents and, by extension, how important it should be to their child.

Stevenson and Baker (1987) determined that when parents attend parent-teacher conferences, participate in the Parent Teacher Associations (PTAs), and help in their child's selection of courses, they positively influence their child's achievement. Hidalago et al. (1995) summarized nine studies that showed that family practices concerning a child's education are more important for helping

Four Types of Parents

+ Supportive of child (for example, often encourages)

+ Active participant (for example, attends and helps at school functions)

+ Supportive of child (for example, cares for well-being)

− Inactive participant (for example, rarely comes to school activities)

− Not supportive of child (for example, ignores child and doesn't encourage)

+ Active participant (for example, attends event only to be seen)

− Not supportive of child (for example, is abusive or homeless)

− Inactive participant (for example, no communication with school)

1. Parents in the +, + box are most likely to attend workshops and conferences, help in the classroom, and do whatever they can to get involved in their child's education. This portion of the grid is not always possible for every parent (e.g., working parents or discomfort in this type of role) and should not be the ultimate goal of parent involvement.

2. Parents in the +, − box simply are not "joiners," even though they have an emotional investment in their child's education.

3. Parents in the −, + box are parents who are visible at school functions, but do not provide an emotionally supportive environment for their child's education at home.

4. Parents in the −, − box are unsupportive and do not participate and, obviously, the most difficult to reach.

students succeed in school and in general than are family structure, economic status, or characteristics such as race, parent education, family size, and age of child. Hidalago et al. (1995) summarized six studies that showed that schools must take leadership in developing and implementing practices that enable more parents to become and remain involved in their children's education. They also concluded that when schools develop their programs of partnership, families appreciate the assistance, more families become involved, and more students improve their achievements, attitudes, and behaviors.

What Is Parent Involvement?

Vandegrift and Greene (1992) believe that a popular notion among parents and teachers is that parents are "involved" when they actively participate in school-sponsored activities (e.g., PTA, parent conferences, parent training workshops, committee meetings, etc.) or help their children in ways visible to their children and others (reading in the classroom, helping the teacher grade papers, or assisting with homework). This idea, according to Vandegrift and Greene, has two key elements. First, parents are supportive because they are sympathetic, reassuring, and understanding and this shows a high level of commitment to their children and their education. Second, parents are active because they are doing something that is observable. This combination of level of commitment and active participation is what many people believe constitutes an "involved parent." In rethinking parent involvement, Vandegrift and

Greene created a grid that separated the notions of support and participation along a continuum.

McLaughlin (1993) reported that more than one-half of American parents (53 percent) belong to a parent's group through the school. Thirty-five percent are in the PTA, 22 percent in a Parent-Teacher Organization, and 12 percent in a Booster Club. She also reported that more African-American parents (62 percent) sign up than Caucasians (52 percent) or Latinos (48 percent). Adults in the highest income bracket are also twice as likely to belong to a parent group as those in the lowest-income bracket (74 percent vs. 38 percent).

Barriers to Parent Involvement

Teachers recognize that when parents are involved in their children's education, positive things will happen. Getting parents involved, however, requires good planning and removal of any barriers that prevent participation. Bey and Turner (1996) reported the following four barriers to parent involvement:

1. Physical and economic barriers relate to the frustrations parents have in making arrangements to attend school functions, such as needing a babysitter, transportation to school, and getting time off from work. For example, low-income parents are often limited in their ability to buy materials and make financial commitments for activities such as field trips or bake sales.

2. Social barriers are limitations due to family problems. Some parents have their own personal and social issues, such as drug dependency, alcoholism, mental illness, and homelessness that prevent them from becoming involved. Many families who live in poverty face greater challenges in their everyday life (shelter, clothing, and food) and their focus is on survival, not school. It may be unrealistic to start improving parent(s) involvement, especially among populations at risk.

3. Emotional barriers occur when parents are afraid to speak out, not wanting to cause problems for their children or feel uneasy talking with school personnel whose knowledge about the educational process exceeds their own. Many parents are simply not "joiners" or perceive many school events as socially uncomfortable.

4. Communication barriers refer to the methods used to keep parents informed and the welcome they receive when attending school functions. If parents do not speak English, then written and verbal communications should be in their native language. Many non-English speaking parents look up to the teacher as authority. This makes it difficult to express their candid opinions or genuine concerns.

Since garnering parent support for their children and for their education is a prerequisite for improving parent involvement, the best way to elicit support is by improving communication and meeting parents where they are. A closer examination of these barriers reveals that they are related to "needs." In order to overcome these barriers we must address the parent's needs. Parent's basic needs

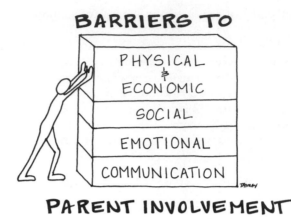

are no different than the children's. Every parent needs to feel: (1) accepted and that they belong, (2) significant, (3) capable, and (4) physically and emotionally secure. The secret is to know who your parents are, what their needs are, and to have in your school's repertoire as many options for involvement as possible. The following list presents a few suggestions for increasing parent involvement:

- Do not intially require high levels of commitment or participation.
- Match a task or a strategy of involvement with a parent's own need and ability.
- Set up meeting times that are responsive to working schedules and personal responsibilities.
- Learn to listen and act upon what you have heard.
- Provide transportation to certain events for low-income families.
- Offer a broad range of activities to encourage support and participation, including non-threatening low-commitment opportunities, such as attending or helping at events that occur in the evening or on weekends, such as athletic events, suppers, intramural events, neighborhood clean-up days, fund raisers, and class trips.
- Use telephone calls, personal notes, and information sheets to keep parents up-to-date on the learning goals, objectives, and activities covered in class.
- Personalize home-school communication.
- Make expectations reasonable. Tell parents what your expectations are of them, and ask for the same back from them.
- Set goals together. Goals should include the child, the family, and the school.
- Set up parent advocates who are willing to work directly with other parents, especially those parents of an at-risk or special-needs child.

The Importance of Healthy Communication
between Teacher and Parent

It is essential that you establish healthy, two-way communication between the school and the parent(s). Most parents are willing to become involved in their children's education if you let them know what you are trying to accomplish and how they can help. By becoming partners through healthy communication, you can work together to create better programs and opportunities for students. Occasionally, parents may feel uneasy talking to school personnel whose knowledge about the educational process exceeds their own. You, therefore, need to outreach to parents and not wait for them to become involved. Actively seek information and learn to be a good listener. Following are several ways you can establish and maintain two-way communication with parents:

1. Send home written information such as newsletters, announcements, congratulatory notes, letters, and reports about school assignments and goals so that parents know what is going on in the classroom, at school, and in the community. Find any excuse to report success to the parent or guardian of a student whose previous school performance has been unsatisfactory. A brief encouraging note may make a significant difference in the way a student's family feels about the school. Also, encourage parents to send notes to you if they have any questions or concerns.

2. Talk to parents by telephone. Let them know when they can reach you at school by phone. Use the telephone as an adjunct to the written information that you send home. Call periodically and let them know when things are going well and not just for the purpose of telling the parent(s) that the child is experiencing learning or behavioral problems at school. Be a good listener and encourage parents to ask questions or make comments.

3. Prepare for Parent Back-to-School Night as you would for an important lesson. Make the classroom as attractive, interesting, and entertaining as possible. This is an opportunity to let the parents experience what their children are experiencing. This is also an opportunity for you to tell the parents what you and their children are learning and doing. Place the names of the students on their chairs whenever possible or place each student's work folder on top of a desk. Share your plans and ask for input or advice from the parents. If you need help, invite the parents to participate. If you need parent supervision on a field trip, tell them. If you need special construction work on a class project, tell them. If you need special parent help in the classroom, let them know. If you give parents opportunities to help, you might just get them.

4. Prepare for parent-teacher conferences. These meetings serve as a basis for parents' involvement in the educational development and experiences of their children. How you handle these conferences has a strong influence on how the parent(s) will perceive you and the school. Establish a purpose and a set agenda. These meetings must be conducted in an atmosphere of dignity and respect and be free of blame and embarrassment. Use healthy

communication that is friendly, nonthreatening, fair, and presented in a businesslike manner with parents and teachers having an equal stake in the conference's success. Together, both parent(s) and teacher can establish a possible plan of action to promote the child's academic and personal achievement and provide suggestions that parents and teachers can use to help reinforce the child's successes and overcome any weaknesses. Always end the parent-teacher conference on a positive note.

It should be noted that many teachers are now moving away from the parent-teacher conferences and having parent-teacher-student conferences because they believe it is disrespectful to talk about students and make decisions about them when they are not present and involved. The same principles that are used in the parent-teacher conference are used when the student is involved. The communication must be friendly, nonthreatening, fair, and presented in a businesslike manner with parent, teacher, and student having an equal stake in the conference's success. The purpose of parent-teacher-student conferences is to encourage and empower the child, the parents, and the teacher as a team with the same goals.

Linking School and Family Partnerships and Multicultural Education

It is almost impossible for minority families in America to maintain a traditional family structure. This is true, in particular, with children. As children become more acculturated to mainstream society through school and peers, conflict often arises between them and their family when traditional customs, behaviors, and values differ from the dominant culture. Vega (1995) cited numerous studies that indicated that acculturation and the associated changes in household structures are linked with family dysfunction, low family pride, and higher levels of personal disorganization, especially adolescent pregnancy, deviant behavior, and drug use.

Conflicts in interpersonal relationships often occur for minority children because many traditional behaviors and values are unconsciously modeled and learned and become a natural part of their emotions and may conflict with the dominant culture. Ethnic minority families, and, in particular, children must also make psychological sense out of the dominant culture's sometimes disparaging view of them, deflect negative messages about themselves, and negotiate racial barriers under all kinds of conditions (Greene, 1992). Many culturally diverse children must face particular challenges in the course of their development that are not encountered by their white counterparts.

Family structure has a tremendous influence on the physical and mental health of its members. There are many myths about certain minority families that have painted a negative portrait of their functioning and the emotional and physical health problems that they encounter. It is important that educators, counselors, health practitioners, and policy makers understand the family structure (both its strengths and weaknesses) of minority families. This understanding can serve as a foundation for preventive and therapeutic work.

PARTNERSHIP PROGRAMS

- combat prejudice
- increase sensitivity to cultural behaviors & customs

It is important for partnership programs to reach out to culturally diverse parents and students and to include multicultural issues in the curriculum.

Hildalgo et al. (1995) believe that well-designed programs of partnership must mobilize all families to help their children to develop pride in their history and culture, bolster self-esteem, and contribute to a sense of community. When parents of different cultural groups work together at school and in the community, they send powerful messages to children about the importance of family in education and about cooperation among adults. Students' self-acceptance and self-confidence as learners within the school are affected by how the school accepts, respects, and appreciates them and their families and culture. It is essential that topics and approaches of multicultural education be added to the school curriculum and to partnership programs.

Most parents value and support education because they see education as a means to a better life for their children. However, many minority parents resist becoming involved with school for a number of reasons. Some feel alienated because they believe the school does not support their cultural values. Others feel intimidated because they believe they do not have the necessary educational background to be involved with their children's education or believe that education should be left to the schools.

As stated earlier, it is important for partnership programs to reach out to culturally diverse parents and students and to include multicultural issues in the curriculum to help combat prejudice and increase sensitivity to cultural behaviors and customs. Children need to be proud of their family and culture, not ashamed.

Connecting the School and Parents of Exceptional Children

It is equally important that you meet with the parents of any exceptional child to discuss any questions or concerns that either party may have. You should request information on the child's needs and any literature on the child's disability if this seems appropriate. For example, you may have fears or worries about what to do if the student becomes ill, has a seizure, or hurts himself or herself while in school. Working with parents can provide reassurance about these fears and also let you know how to handle these situations if they should occur.

You may also feel that you need some help in successfully meeting special needs of students in the classroom. By joining with the parents, you can explore ways to meet classroom and personal needs of the student. Developing a communication process (telephone, conferences, notes, etc.) between you and the parent(s) is an important way to share and solve concerns before they become insurmountable problems.

Connecting the Family and the School to Community Services

For many children, their health and social and economic well-being is being threatened in communities where poverty, drug abuse, juvenile crime, teenage pregnancy, gangs, AIDS, and violence have become the norm. When children attend school abused, hungry, and/or neglected, wellness and success is almost unattainable. Community partnerships refer to the involvement of any institutions or agencies that share in the development or success of the children. This includes programs that coordinate and provide access to community support services for children and their families. School personnel must work with community organizations to assist in providing services to the school, parents, and children that deal with the complex problems that extend beyond the academic environment. Many community social agencies have services and support for families because they have a shared interest in the positive development of its children.

Because each school and community is unique, no one single partnership program is perfect for all situations. Each school must evaluate its students, parents, and community services to determine what is best for their individual situation. Some schools have developed full-service programs that are one-stop centers, where educational, health, and social requirements of students and their families are addressed in a single location within the school campus. In many communities these one-stop schools have become the neighborhood hub, where children and their families want to be. These full-service, one-stop schools provide the following services:

- Family services which provide social services, including immigration, employment, and housing consultation. Social workers and mental health counselors are also on hand to serve students and family.

- Primary health and dental clinic are on the premises.

- After school programs for children, such as educational enrichment, mentoring, sports, computer labs, music, and art programs.

- Evening programs that offer classes for parents such as English, computer literacy, aerobics, job training, and parenting classes.

- Staying open weekends and summers to offer many opportunities for cultural and family participation.

FAMILY   SCHOOL

COMMUNITY

This three-way partnership enables schools and community organizations to meet the many and varied needs of today's students and parents.

Other schools have developed partnerships with public mental health, social services, health, probation, police, housing, and drug and alcohol services, as well as nonprofit health and service agencies. The schools link the parents and students to these organizations through referrals.

The proverb "It takes a village to raise a child" has received much attention in recent years. Very few would argue against the idealism behind this proverb; however, in the real world, this ideal is difficult to achieve because few of us live in cohesive communities. Within most communities there is little coordination between the schools, the family, and the community social agencies. Given these circumstances the schools must take the first step by adapting to create community within the school and classroom. We must do so not only for the children, but for their families and the community because our links with one another have eroded over the years.

By developing school, family, and community partnerships we increase the possibility of success for all our children. By working together, school, family, and community partnerships can improve school programs and climate, provide family services and support, increase parents' skills and leadership, connect families with others in the school and in the community, and help teachers with their work (Epstein, 1995). However, the guiding force behind creating such partnerships is, of course, to help all children succeed in school and later in life.

SUMMARY OF MAJOR POINTS
IN CHAPTER 2

1. Healthy classroom teachers encourage an atmosphere of support, trust, and respect. They have an underlying philosophy of teamwork and partnership.

2. There are three basic teaching styles:

   - The autocratic teacher controls and directs and makes all the decisions.
   - The permissive teacher makes few decisions and provides little teaching.
   - The democratic or healthy teacher gives the students the opportunities to express their individuality and at the same time validates them by:
     - providing a safe and confirming environment
     - accepting and caring for them regardless of the moment
     - listening to them and taking them seriously
     - being honest and open

3. Teachers must instruct, but they must also be leaders.

4. Healthy leadership is a process that is based on respect and trust.

5. Healthy teachers encourage the two basic principles of participation and psychological ownership.

6. Today's teachers are expected to participate in the development of policies, help administrators make decisions, and help parents find ways to support their children's education.

7. Schools must find ways to allow teachers to expand their leadership roles outside of their traditional roles.

8. Two important pieces of legislation (Goals 2000: Educate America Act and Improving America's School Act) included goals to increase parental involvement in promoting the social, emotional, and academic growth of children.

9. There has been a shift from traditional nuclear families to families consisting of single people, single older people, unmarried parents, single-parent families (especially many headed by women), grandparent parents, foster parents, gay parents, and various configurations of the blended family.

10. When family is involved with school, students show:

    - higher grades and test scores
    - better attendance and homework completion
    - more positive attitudes and behavior
    - fewer placements in special education
    - higher graduation rates
    - greater enrollment in post–secondary education

Class Discussion   **CHAPTER 2**

Note: Review Appendix E before facilitating this activity.

Prioritizing Your Teaching Values
Time: 5–10 minutes (discussion not included)
Objective: To help the participants recognize how their values will affect their teaching philosophy and behavior.
Materials: A copy of "Prioritizing Your Teaching Values" for each participant.

Procedure:

1. Distribute "Prioritizing Your Teaching Values" and have participants fill it out.

2. Have participants form triads to discuss their rankings.
3. Have all participants gather together.

Suggested Discussion Questions:

1. What did you learn about yourself?
2. What did you learn about others?
3. What about the activity surprised you?
4. How can this activity be of value to you as a future teacher?

Prioritizing Your Teaching Values

A value is:

1. Something that is desirable or worthy of esteem for its own sake
2. A thing or quality having intrinsic worth
3. Something you include in your life even when you have to give up something else.

As a teacher, what values would you model and hopefully instill in your students? Prioritize the following list, as well as any other values which you would care to include. Number from the most important to the least important beginning with the number 1 as the most important.

_____ Unconditional acceptance of others

_____ Trustworthiness

_____ Fairness

_____ Thoughtful of others

_____ Hard work

_____ Courage

_____ Cooperation

_____ Honesty

_____ Good sense of humor

_____ Doing what is right

_____ Self-respect

_____ Independence

_____ Responsible

_____ Self-discipline

_____ Something not mentioned on list

_____

- more effective transition to work
- increased civic responsibility and citizenship

11. Parent involvement includes being supportive of their children's education and actively participating in school functions.

12. Barriers to parent involvement include physical and economic, social, emotional, and communication barriers.

Teacher's Corner: Supporting Teacher Leadership

This assessment is designed to help you determine whether school administration is supportive of teachers taking on new leadership responsibilities. Ask a school administrator or teacher the following questions.

Does School Administration:

1. Compensate teachers with monetary adjustments or reduced teaching schedules for taking on certain leadership roles that extend beyond the classroom or school?

   - If yes, how are teachers rewarded at your school for taking on extra leadership responsibilities?
   - If no, what are the policies or reasons that prevent compensation or release time?

2. Encourage teachers to take on leadership roles outside their normal classroom responsibilities? For example, leadership roles in professional organizations; becoming politically involved at the local, state, or national level; or participating on committees or personnel actions.

   - If yes, what types of new leadership roles have teachers at your school become involved with?

3. Create opportunities for new leadership roles, but still allow teachers to remain in the classroom? For example, creating "master teachers" who assume extra responsibilities such as working with less experienced teachers, incorporating innovative technology into teaching, or allowing teachers to become liaisons for community, business, or parent functions.

   - If yes, what are the opportunities that are provided teachers?
   - If yes, how many of your teachers have taken on new leadership roles?

4. Provide opportunities for teachers to continue learning? For example, encouraging teachers to attend conferences, take university classes to enhance learning in their professional area, create in-service days, encourage teachers to apply for fellowships, or take leadership classes.

   - If yes, how does school administration fund teachers to pursue some of these activities, such as professional conferences or classes?
   - If yes, what kind of continuing education are your teachers involved in?

5. Provide teachers with information about outside grant funding possibilities?

   - If yes, what types of grant proposals are encouraged within your school district?
   - If yes, are teachers given release time for grant support writing?
   - If yes, what types of grant funding have your teachers received?

Conclusion: Although there is no assessment score for this evaluation, it should be obvious that teachers need support from other teachers and school administration as well as from outside the profession. Greater support will encourage the development of more leaders. The more leadership opportunities that teachers are given will, ultimately, lead to greater commitment to our children.

13. Healthy communication with parents is essential in getting them actively involved in their children's education.

14. A well-designed partnership must mobilize all families to help their children to develop pride in their history and culture, bolster self-esteem, and contribute to a sense of community.

15. Community partnerships refer to the involvement of any institutions or agencies that share in the development or success of the children.

16. By developing school, family, and community partnerships we increase the possibility of success for all our children.

3

■

The Foundation of Healthy Classroom Motivation

What we see depends mainly on what we look for.

JOHN LUBBOCK

HEALTHY CLASSROOM MOTIVATION

ealthy Classroom Management is about human relationships, behavior, understanding, and meaning. The concepts within this book will help you unlock the positive human potentials within your students and, consequently, help them become the capable people they were meant to be. By meeting the needs of your students in the psychosocial dimensions of wellness, you can begin developing the healthy classroom.

How do you create the behavior changes that promote the psychosocial dimensions of wellness of any given individual? The answer to this question has been debated for years and probably will continue to be debated far into the future. The reason, of course, is the difficulty in accumulating empirical data in this area. Countless theories have been developed that attempt to explain human behavior, yet no single theoretical model has been universally accepted. Models are constantly modified in response to new situations. While complete agreement on how to create changes in the psychosocial dimensions of wellness may be impossible to reach, some progress toward identifying the major determinants of psychosocial health has been made through the collection of data from surveys, interviews, and observations over many years.

Healthy Classroom Management has its foundation rooted in self-esteem research, resiliency research, medical research on "psychological hardiness," and humanistic psychology. The conclusions drawn from each of these areas all focus on the principle of understanding and meeting basic human needs. The model for *Healthy Classroom Management* can be used as a guide for promoting positive behaviors as well as assessing negative behaviors. A discussion of each of these four areas follows.

Self-Esteem

In the mid–1980s, the California legislature formed a task force to address the major social concerns that confronted the young people of California. The California Task Force (1990) determined that self-esteem is the likeliest candidate for a *social vaccine,* something that empowers us to live responsibly and inoculates us against the lures of crime, violence, substance abuse, teen pregnancy, abuse, chronic welfare dependency, and educational failure. The task force determined that the lack of self-esteem is central to most personal and social ills that plague our nation. Students who lack healthy self-esteem lack the resiliency to cope with and rebound from adversity or challenging life events in a positive or constructive manner. The concept of self-esteem and resiliency are key themes to psychosocial wellness.

Some of the key findings of the task force report are:

- Because children spend so much of their time in school, the school environment plays a major role in the development of self-esteem. Schools that feature self-esteem as a clearly stated component of their goals, policies, and practices are more successful academically.

■   Young people who are self-esteeming are less likely to become pregnant as teenagers.

■   People who esteem themselves are less likely to engage in destructive and self-destructive behavior, including child abuse, alcohol abuse, abuse of other drugs (legal and illegal), violence, crime, and so on.

Regardless of age, race, creed, sex, or sexual orientation, an affirming environment in the home, school, workplace, and community is crucial for nurturing self-esteem. This is a personal and public responsibility that we need to recognize, accept, and undertake. The choice to esteem one's self is also a decision for which each of us, ultimately, is personally responsible, no matter what our backgrounds may have been.

The task force challenged every school district to adopt the promotion of self-esteem and personal and social responsibility as a clearly stated goal, integrated into its total curriculum, policies, and operations. School boards should establish policies and procedures that value staff members and students and serve to foster mutual respect, esteem, and cooperation.

Definition of Self-Esteem   Defining self-esteem is difficult and different researchers, educators, and mental health professionals have offered a variety of definitions. Many of these definitions or conceptualizations have overlapped and focused on what individuals think and feel about themselves and about their abilities to meet certain challenges and accomplish certain tasks. Some of the confusion about what self-esteem really is occurs because "definitions that place too much of the spotlight on how we think and feel about ourselves can prompt some people to confuse self-esteem with self-centeredness and conceit." The California Task Force adopted this as its official definition:

> Appreciating my own worth and importance and having the character to be accountable for myself and to act responsibly toward others.

This definition defined self-esteem not only in terms of "appreciating my own worth and importance," which is consistent with most definitions of self-esteem, but expanded the meaning by adding "having the character to be accountable for myself and to act responsibly toward others." This latter part includes the view that self-esteem cannot be separated from the way we behave toward others. Consequently, self-esteem is not limited to one's self, but must include our relationships with others.

The Importance of Having Healthy Self-Esteem   If students feel good about themselves and have confidence that they can achieve success, they are well on their way to becoming capable in school. A person's self-esteem is all part of a person's personality. Personality is extremely complex and consists of many variables or traits. Our self-esteem is developed from the sum total of the many variables that make-up our personality. Each one of us possesses some personality traits and lacks others and it is the combination of these traits that helps define who we are and how we think about ourselves at any particular moment. Because we all have the ability to improve or acquire personality variables, we are all subject to change. Thus, our personality and self-esteem are not static but constantly changing as we learn to adjust to life events.

Dreikurs (1964) supported the theory that if given the opportunity and appropriate encouragement, individuals will grow in positive ways. Individuals are basically made up of the sum total of their experiences and, consequently, positive experiences will have an impact on the development of healthy self-esteem. Research reported in the California Task Force to Promote Self-Esteem and Personal and Social Responsibility (1990) supports the theory that a positive sense of self-worth is critical to learning and growing. Students who feel accepted and believe that they are competent and worthwhile develop positive attitudes about what they can accomplish and are equipped to handle frustration and problems both in and out of school. In addition, students who have healthy self-esteem are more willing to take on new challenges. Their positive beliefs also help them to become more compassionate, responsible human beings.

Youngs (1991) states that "self-esteem is central to what we make of our lives—the loyalty we have to developing ourselves and to caring about others, and it is at the heart of what we will achieve in the course of our lifetime. Perhaps nothing affects health and energy, peace of mind, the goals we set and achieve, our inner happiness, the quality of our relationships, our competence, performance, and productivity, quite as much as the health of our self-esteem."

Self-efficacy and *self-respect* are the dual pillars of healthy self-esteem. If either is absent, self-esteem is impaired (Brandon, 1969). How people view themselves and how much self-worth they possess will affect their health, relationships, competence, goals that are set and achieved, performance, and happiness. This self-image or inner picture will influence how people will treat themselves and others.

Self-efficacy means confidence in your ability to think and in the process by which you judge, choose, and decide. It is knowing and understanding your interests and needs. It incorporates self-trust and self-reliance (Brandon, 1969). It is your perception of your ability to take on and successfully complete tasks. This belief stems from your past experiences. For example, practicing diligently on the piano has helped you successfully play a difficult musical piece; therefore, you believe that more diligent practice will do the same for you on future musical pieces.

Self-respect means assurance of your values. It is an affirmative attitude toward the right to live and be happy, toward freedom to assert your thoughts, wants, needs, and joys. The experience of self-respect allows for mutual regard of others and makes possible a non-neurotic sense of fellowship with them (Youngs, 1991).

SELF-ESTEEM

Self-efficacy and self-respect
are the dual pillars of healthy
self-esteem.

Students with healthy self-esteem are not egotistical. They have an inner happiness based on feelings of self-worth and respect. They are happy with themselves and happy with who they are. They do not waste their time or energy trying to impress others and do not try to be like others. They know they are valued, and they value themselves.

Everyone has a self-image that is based on one's self-esteem. Every person perceives himself or herself in some positive or negative way—pretty, ugly, overweight, skinny, athletic, clumsy, or different. Everyone has adjectives that describe themselves. A person's self image is a result of the kinds of reinforcements he or she receives from parents, peers, relatives, friends, teachers, and other community members.

Having students with healthy self-esteem is essential to the healthy classroom. As an empowering teacher, you must help your students to believe in themselves by nurturing the inner picture that develops in each one of them.

Resiliency

An important trait associated with healthy self-esteem is resiliency—"the capacity to spring back, rebound, successfully adapt in the face of adversity, and develop social, academic, and vocational competence despite exposure to severe stress or simply to the stress that is inherent in today's world" (Henderson & Milstein, 1996, p. 7). Bernard (1992, p. 24) proposed a similar definition and referred to resiliency as "that quality in children who, though exposed to

---

Characteristics of Persons with High Self-Esteem

An individual with high self-esteem:

- Seeks opportunities to engage in challenging and stimulating experiences.
- Accepts responsibility for his or her actions without blaming others or making excuses.
- Acknowledges his or her strengths and achievements.
- Loves self and others.
- Works well with others.

- Enjoys the company of others.
- Balances time spent alone and with others.
- Asserts self without harming or manipulating others.

SOURCE: "Adjustment and Growth in a Changing World," by V. Napoll, J. Kilbride, and D. Tebbs, 1996, Minneapolis: West Publishing Co. In *Concepts for Healthy Living* by S. Alters and W. Schiff, 1998, Pacific Grove, CA: Brooks/Cole Publishing Company, p. 31.

---

significant stress and adversity in their lives, do not succumb to the school failure, substance abuse, mental health, and juvenile delinquency problems they are at greater risk of experiencing." Fostering resiliency occurs by integrating certain attitudes and behaviors with students into the interactions you have with them. These attitudes and behaviors are the same building blocks used to help build healthy self-esteem within your students.

Bernard's (1991) research identified the following four consistent factors that help describe the resilient child:

- *Social Competence.* This includes prosocial behaviors such as flexibility, empathy and caring, communication skills, and a sense of humor. Masten (1994) felt that resilient children have a sense of humor, in that way they can generate comic relief and find alternative ways of looking at things. They can also laugh at themselves and ridiculous situations. Resilient children—from early childhood on—also tend to establish more positive relationships with others, gaining protection from peers and assistance from adults.

- *Problem-Solving Skills.* These skills include the ability to think abstractly, reflectively, and flexibly and to attempt alternative solutions for both cognitive and social problems. Rutter (1984) reported that resilient children have the ability to think abstractly, reflectively, and flexibly, and to attempt alternate solutions for both cognitive and social problems.

- *Autonomy.* This refers to a strong sense of independence, a sense of power, self-discipline, self-efficacy, self-identity, impulse control, or someone with an "internal locus of control." The resilient person has the ability to act independently and exert some control over his or her environment.

- *Sense of Purpose/Future.* This includes such factors as healthy expectancies, goal-directedness, success orientation, educational aspirations, belief in a bright future, and a sense of coherence.

Resilient Adult Characteristics Henderson and Milstein (1996) attributed the following characteristics to a resilient adult. The criteria of a resilient adult is

Resiliency is an important trait associated with healthy self-esteem.

very similar to the criteria of a self-actualized person and the psychosocial dimensions of wellness.

1. Have positive relationships
2. Are adept at problem solving
3. Are motivated for self-improvement
4. Have attained educational goals
5. Are involved in activism and social change
6. Have a sense of faith
7. Construe some meaning and usefulness from stress, trauma, and tragedy they have experienced

Psychological Hardiness

Kobasa (1979) tried to sort out exactly what personality traits help some people resist health-eroding stress. Her research separated three attitudes that seemed to separate corporate executives labeled "hardy" from executives more likely to fall ill under stress. She labeled these three attitudes the "three C's" of hardiness— commitment, control, and challenge. The hardy executives stayed *committed* and involved in whatever they were doing and in the experiences presented by life. This commitment, in turn, offered them a sense of purpose that gave meaning to their lives and environment. They eagerly undertook their work and obligations and were unlikely to give up under pressure.

These executives also saw themselves as being in charge or *control* of their lives. They had an internal locus of control, believing they are in control of the rewards and punishments in their lives. They had a feeling of mastery over their circumstances; they were less likely to feel helpless in the face of change and more likely to perceive options in the face of stress.

Finally, these executives sought *challenges*. They saw change as a challenge rather than a threat. Hardy people are more resistant to stress because they choose to face it.

People who believe they are in control of events, who are committed to their work and other life goals, and who are invigorated and challenged by change are less likely to be detoured from wellness.

In recent years, researchers have added a fourth "C" to psychological hardiness. Researchers have long suspected that close, supporting relationships encourage health—that to the three C's of hardiness should be added a fourth—*connectedness*. Berkman and Syme (1979) concluded that isolated, lonely people were dying at twice the rate of their more socially connected peers. Marmot and Syme (1976) found that members of Japanese families who retained the spirit of group interconnectedness or *amae* after immigrating to the United States retained superior patterns of health over those who did not. The Japanese concept of *amae* expresses a belief that the well-being of the individual depends on the cooperation of others and the goodwill of the group. Williams et al. (1992) reported that heart disease patients were three times as likely to die within 5 years of diagnosis if they had no spouse or good friend in whom to confide.

The growing evidence that health is directly related to social support and connectedness to others has led to the establishment of therapy groups from people with everything from drug dependency to cancer. The primary benefit of groups may be that they allow people to share feelings and emotions, reducing social isolation and increasing the sense of connectedness that research has so clearly tied to health.

Finally, some have suggested that the "s" in the "4 C's" of hardiness should be defined as *spirit*. In many people, the accumulation of dissatisfactions and distress has left them with a sense of emptiness—a lack of purpose, meaning, and coherence in life—causing their pain. For them, the crisis is spiritual and its resolution central to establishing that wholeness that is the source of true health (Poole, 1993).

Spirit is difficult to define and impossible to measure, yet its existence has been unquestioned and has been a part of every society throughout history. For many people, that difficult-to-describe element that gives zest to life is the spiritual dimension. Spiritual health is that belief in some unifying force that gives purpose or meaning to life or to a sense of belonging to a scheme of existence greater than the merely personal. For some people, this unifying force is nature; for others it is a feeling of connection to other people coupled with a recognition of the eternal nature of the human race; for still others, the unifying force is God or another spiritual symbol (Donatelle & Davis, 1997).

Because spirit cannot be measured makes it hard to "prove" its effect on health. Spiritual qualities, however, such as love, altruism, and caring have been linked to health. Even though the affect of one's spirit on health cannot be measured, the association between healing and spiritual behaviors has been demonstrated by the success of Alcoholics Anonymous and similar self-help groups and studies on the influence of prayer and religion. A review of 200 studies on religion and mental health concluded that, in general, churchgoers showed lower suicide rates, lower rates of drug use, lower divorce rates, greater marital happiness, and lower rates of depression (Gartner et al., 1991).

Psychological hardiness is a personality trait that helps some people resist health eroding stress.

Few would disagree that the willingness to assume responsibility for one's behavior while at the same time enlisting the influence of spirit can be a powerful force for psychosocial health.

Humanistic Psychology

Humanistic psychology includes the following similar but distinct approaches: humanism, perceptualism, and existentialism. Collectively, these three approaches seek to understand people in terms of how they perceive themselves and what influences them to behave the way they do. In other words, they center on humans as social beings who are influenced and guided by the personal meanings they attach to their experiences.

Humanistic psychology begins with the assumption that teaching is a relationship between people that involves human behavior, understanding, and experiences. Therefore, humanism centers on the affective domain that is the cultivation of emotions. Humanistic psychology theorizes that man and woman are basically good and the biological imperative for positive growth and development unfolds naturally in the presence of certain environmental attributes.

It is beyond the scope of this book to fully explore each of these approaches, but a brief description for each of these approaches follows. Further discussion of humanistic psychology is found in Appendix A.

Humanistic Psychology The humanistic approach is concerned with helping people actualize their potential and with bettering the state of humanity. Humanistic psychological theory is based on the idea that people are motivated not only to satisfy their biological needs, but also to cultivate, maintain, and enhance the self. Humanistic psychologists believe that behavior is motivated by a desire for personal growth and achievement and that it involves free choice and the ability to make conscious, rational decisions. Maslow, the "father" of humanistic psychology, developed the theory that people achieve emotional well-being by meeting a hierarchy of needs: physiological needs, security needs, love and belonging needs, self-esteem needs, and self-actualization needs. Most humanistic psychologists believe that we have the power not only to understand our behavior but also to actively change it and, thus, to mold our own personalities. In addition, when basic needs are met, then resiliency has a chance to grow.

Self-actualization refers to self-fulfillment, namely, the tendency for a person to become actualized in what he or she is capable of becoming. Before achieving higher levels of Maslow's hierarchy and eventually becoming self-actualized, people must first fulfill the lower level needs. Maslow (1987) viewed "health" as equivalent to self-actualization, the characteristic features of which he identified through the study of persons in public life whom he deemed to be self-actualized. Graham (1985) reported that Maslow's self-actualization features included:

- superior perception of reality
- increased acceptance of self, others, and nature
- increased spontaneity and greatly increased creativity
- increased autonomy and resistance to enculturation
- richness of emotional reaction
- increased identification with the human species
- changed interpersonal relationships
- a change in values and a more democratic value structure
- an ability for spiritual experiences

Rogers referred to the "fully functioning person" instead of the self-actualized person. According to Rogers (1961), a person en route to becoming "fully functioning" usually exhibits characteristics such as the following:

- He tends to move away from facades. That is, he moves away from a self that he is not and moves toward the self that he really is.
- She tends to move away from "oughts." In other words, she ceases to guide her conduct in terms of what she "ought" to be or "ought" to become.
- He tends to move away from pleasing others and begins to be more self-directing.
- She tends to move away from meeting others' expectations and moves toward meeting her own expectations.
- He tends to be more accepting of himself and able to view himself as a person in the process of "becoming." That is, he is not upset by the fact that

he does not always hold the same feelings toward a given experience or person, or that he is not always consistent. The striving for conclusions or end states seems to decrease.

- She tends to move toward being more open to her experiences in the sense of not having to blot out thoughts, feelings, perceptions, and memories that might be unpleasant.

- He tends to move in the direction of greater acceptance of others. That is, he is able to accept the experiences of others.

Perceptual Psychology Perceptual psychologists believe that the reality of an event lies in the perception of the event. Fundamental to this point of view is the belief that our behavior is influenced by the personal meanings we attach to our perceptions of those experiences (Hamachek, 1978). How we feel about the event determines our perceptions of the event and, consequently, we may be powerless to change the event but can change how we feel about the event.

Existential Psychology The existential approach shares with humanistic psychology an emphasis on individual uniqueness, a quest for meaning in life, freedom and responsibility, and a phenomenological (understanding the person's subjective world of experience) approach to understanding the person and a belief that the individual has positive attributes that will eventually be expressed unless they are distorted by the environment. Existentialism also stresses individual responsibility, but it stresses responsibility to others as well. Self-fulfillment is not enough.

MEETING HUMAN NEEDS: A PREREQUISITE TO THE HEALTHY CLASSROOM

Plants require good soil, an adequate water supply, and lots of sunshine to grow and to flourish. If one neglects their needs—soil, water, and sunshine—plants may wilt and die. Young students also need optimal growing conditions. They too have basic needs on both a physical and emotional level. Meeting these basic needs molds the inner framework that builds the foundation of healthy self-esteem, resiliency, and hardiness. These human needs must be met for appropriate psychological motivation and growth to occur both in and out of the classroom.

The Basic Psychological Needs

Although people come into this world dependent on others for their survival, everyone has the innate desire to grow and become independent. Young people need others, others need them, and the need to be self-sufficient is basic to all people. These needs are like the soil, water, and sunshine. Understanding basic human needs and nurturing the young student's growth and development are the foundation on which teaching should be built. The basic needs discussed in this chapter and throughout the book are consistent with building resiliency, self–esteem, and hardiness in students.

If you are going to motivate, empower, and manage your students you must know and respond to their basic needs. A parent, of course, should have little difficulty identifying the needs of his or her own child. However, a teacher in the classroom filled with many students may find it far more difficult to respond to the basic needs of each individual student. Each student is often seen as only one small part of a much larger whole. It is easy for a student's basic needs to be overlooked in a group. You must always remember that human needs do not exist in a social vacuum. Human emotional needs develop and find expression through relationships such as that between you and your students. The basic needs of feeling accepted, significant, capable, and safe are briefly discussed in the following paragraphs. These four needs are consistently discussed or referred to in the research on hardiness, self-esteem, resiliency, and humanistic psychology.

The Need to Be Accepted The need to be accepted and to belong is an important human need and is the foundation of the others. All human beings need to feel they are accepted and have a sense of belonging to some group, such as with family, peers, or other organizations. Without a sufficient amount of acceptance and belonging, people will perish just as surely as if you deprive them of food and water. Young students need to know that you care about them and are on their side. The concept of acceptance in this book is based on respect, affirmation, caring, empathy, fairness, sensitivity, and warmth. Acceptance is recognizing and appreciating the student's intrinsic worth. You do not have to feel that you must love every student, but you must accept each student unconditionally, not contingent on anything particular about the individual. The student does not have to accomplish anything to receive this acceptance. Each student has inherent value, and so acceptance is not something to be earned. Students who are accepted unconditionally will absorb the message that they are needed, worthwhile individuals even when they are progressing slowly or when they make mistakes.

Belonging means that people must feel connected with other people to feel secure. This sense of security enables them to reach out and identify with others in a positive way. Creating acceptance and belonging in the classroom is discussed in Chapter 4.

The Need to Feel Significant Students need to feel that they are significant or important, that their participation in the classroom has meaning and purpose, that they make a difference, that their existence matters, and that they are needed. Students need to feel that their contributions are appreciated and necessary. Students will give up or lose their motivation to compete or progress when they believe that they are not important to the classroom and its members. The need to feel significant is discussed in Chapter 4.

The Need to Feel Capable The need to feel capable or competent means that students need to feel that they can take on responsibility and that they are skilled and can do things well. Teachers and students who feel capable know that they can learn to do things. They recognize that there is often as much to learn from failure as from success. They are challenged by tasks even though they face difficult odds. They have inner strength and reasoning power that keeps life and school in proper perspective. The need to feel capable is discussed in Chapter 5.

The Need to Feel Safe and Secure Students need to feel that they are safe and in control of themselves while performing in the school environment, that they have mastery over their well being. Without a feeling of physical and emotional safety or security, a student will find it difficult to move beyond fear and anxiety. Strong fear and anxiety will hinder performance and promote possible injury. Intense fear or anxiety can affect thinking, remembering, behavior, and physical performance. How long a student will stay in school is directly related to how safe he or she perceives the school environment to be. The need to feel safe and secure is discussed in Chapter 6.

You cannot be expected to meet every basic need all of the time, but you must express awareness of and concern for these needs. Students cannot be neglected. All plants need sun, water, and good soil, but different plants need different amounts of each. Give a cactus too much water and it will weaken, withhold sunlight from a rose and it will wilt. The same principle applies to students. They all have basic needs, but each student is unique.

Students who believe that they are capable, significant, accepted, and safe develop a positive attitude about coping with the problems and frustrations that frequently occur in school as well as life. Students who believe that they are capable, significant, accepted, and safe will be more resilient and motivated to succeed. Positive beliefs reinforce the "I can do it" or "Just do it" attitude. On the other hand, students who believe that they are not capable, significant, accepted, or safe, seldom find fulfillment and meaning in their school participation. They will find it difficult to help their classmates do the same. Unhealthy students will make it difficult to build healthy classrooms.

Meet their needs and students will thrive. Ignore or abuse these needs and the classroom will be dysfunctional. Symptoms such as demanding undue attention, seeking revenge, quitting, rebelling, always seeking approval, fear, and self-doubt are signs of dysfunctional and unhealthy classrooms. Missing class, withdrawal, passive efforts, and jealousy among students are also common symptoms found in the unhealthy classroom.

You must believe that most problems can be resolved by working on and improving human relationships, because once you meet the students' needs, students will usually meet yours. Nurturing teachers will find ways to be sensitive to the basic needs of all students. Being aware of and attending to those needs is an investment that will bring immediate and future behavioral dividends.

Understanding basic human needs and nurturing the young student's growth and development are the foundation on which teaching should be built.

The Difference between Needs and Wants

It is important to recognize that wants and needs are separate matters. *Wants* can be frivolous and greedy and often are never satisfied. In many cases, if one want is met, there will be at least two more to replace it. *Needs* are the deep roots of one's existence. They are meaningful, worthy, and not as changeable as wants.

Students *want* fame; they *need* recognition. Students *want* prestige; they *need* respect. Students *want* freedom and permissiveness; they *need* discipline. Students *want* ease and comfort; they *need* achievement and work. Students *want* sympathy; they *need* empathy. Students *want* approval; they *need* acceptance.

A modified version of Conklin's (1979) rule is "to the extent that a teacher gives students what they need, they will give the teacher what he or she needs." This is the key to leading, motivating, guiding, and influencing students. Unfortunately, many teachers have this simple rule backwards.

Some teachers believe that a student should get praise and recognition after putting forth some extra effort. Some teachers will start having confidence in their students only when the students start performing adequately in the classroom. You, however, must recognize and encourage students to bring forth the extra effort. You must express confidence in students first, then they will try with greater effort.

That is the way the rule works. First, you give students what they need; then they will give you what you need. This requires patience and knowing what it is students need, how to give them what they need, and what it is you, the teacher needs, and what you are willing to give in order to get it.

It is important for teachers to focus on giving students what they need rather than giving them what they want.

This rule is not about manipulating and moving students around for one's own satisfaction and ego or about developing strategies for gaining power and dominance. It is not about finding emotional buttons to push to get one's own way. This rule is about giving and succeeding.

Applying Resiliency Principles in the Classroom

To develop resiliency in children takes a collaborative effort that includes their families, schools, and communities. Each of these environmental factors alone are important, but together they are synergistic. Bernard identified the following key factors that help build resiliency in children:

- *Having a caring and supportive relationship with at least one person.* The whole nature of the healthy classroom is based on this concept. You must accept, nurture, and create positive opportunities for your students. Noddings (1988, p. 32) said, "It is obvious that children will work harder and do things—even odd things like adding fractions—especially for people they love and trust." You must provide unconditional positive regard and encouragement. Optimally, every child should have several adults he or she can turn to for help. Teachers must work together with the family and community to provide a caring and supporting relationship.

- *Setting and communicating high expectations.* This step is consistent in self-esteem, resiliency, and academic success literature. It is imperative that teachers set both high and realistic expectations to be effective motivators. Setting low expectations only reinforces the students to adopt low expectations for themselves.

Teacher's Corner: Discovering the Potential of Each Student

This exercise is a treasure hunt designed to help you (1) discover the potentials in each of your students, and (2) make sense of what you uncover. Be honest.

If you are not a teacher-in-training, choose a student or friend and discover his or her potential.

1. Observe and talk with a student during the week, and write a description of him or her. Pretend that you are writing it to someone who has never met the student. Describe each student physically, emotionally, intellectually, socially, and athletically. How does the student act in school and in the class? Does the student get along with others? What is it about him or her that you have difficulty accepting? Is the student even-tempered? Does he or she have a lot of friends? Does the student interact socially with others? Does he or she have a sense of humor? How does the student dissipate nervous energy? What do you like best about the student? What does he or she do outside of school? What are his or her athletic talents? What does the student do that annoys you? Does the student study effectively? Is he or she performing up to his or her present capabilities? What keeps the student from improving? What is the student doing that is making him or her perform better? Is the student a responsible person? What are his or her limits? What are his or her bad habits?

Keep your description as detailed as possible. Keep adding to it during the week. You will find yourself thinking about the student and looking at him or her more carefully. You will discover qualities and behaviors that you never noticed before. Add to your description by checking with other people such as parents, other teachers, and friends. You will probably be surprised and delighted by the added insights.

2. Now analyze your description by constructing a list of the positive qualities that you want to nurture and the negative qualities that you want to change. This partial list is written about Marie, a senior in high school.

POSITIVE QUALITIES	NEGATIVE QUALITIES
Pleasant manners	Easily frustrated by other students
Great sense of humor	Too much of a perfectionist
Good grades	Loses temper too easily
Knows a lot about chemistry	Not very outgoing with others
Determined	Stubborn, bossy

Examine the Positives

Look for positive qualities that already exist. Reflect on those qualities and appreciate the student for having them. Continue to reinforce those behaviors with recognition, praise, or reward. The student will learn to value those qualities and see himself or herself as capable and special in these areas. If the list is long, choose a few qualities to begin with and gradually add others to your reinforcement strategy. In time, you will get used to finding the special qualities in each student.

Examine the Negatives

Both positive and negative behaviors are based on fulfillment of one or more of the basic emotional needs. When a student starts a fight with a classmate, shows off in an obnoxious way, complains about rules, or deliberately misses practice, he or she needs something. If you can determine what need is being expressed, you can help that student meet the need in a more appropriate manner.

For every item on the negative list, ask yourself these three questions:

1. What need does this behavior really reflect?
2. How can I help meet this need in a more positive way?
3. Can I find a positive quality in this behavior?

Reevaluating Some of the Negatives

Carefully reexamine the negative list and identify some of the items that are really your problem and not the student's. Are some of the things you listed a matter of your own personal preferences? No amount of nagging or reminding will change a shy, quiet student into a verbal, outgoing classroom leader. Forget about hairstyles and dress; you will only create tension or conflict and, in the long run, spoil the relationship.

- *Creating opportunities for students to participate.* This means that you must provide students with meaningful, valued activities and roles and give them opportunities to solve problems, set high but realistic goals, work with others, and make important decisions relevant to their own participation in the classroom.

Henderson and Milstein (1996) developed a resiliency wheel that listed three additional protective factors. They are:

- *Increase prosocial bonding.* This refers to involving students in prosocial activities such as sports, art, music, drama, volunteering in community organizations, and/or participating in school services. The more connections that students can make with adults and other young people in positive activities will help foster resiliency.

- *Set clear, consistent boundaries.* This involves the development of school and classroom rules, policies, procedures, and norms. Many of these rules should involve student input and be clearly communicated so there is no misunderstanding of the interpretation. Most important, the boundaries must be coupled with appropriate consequences and consistently enforced.

- *Teach "life skills."* These include cooperation, healthy conflict resolution, communication skills, problem solving, and decision making. When these skills are adequately taught and reinforced they provide young people with an arsenal to resist such adolescent perils as the use of alcohol, cigarettes, other drugs, sexual activity, and violence. Conflict resolution and communication skills are discussed in later chapters.

The Role of Perceptual Psychology in Psychosocial Wellness

How students feel about themselves has a direct effect on how they live all aspects of their lives, including school. Their feelings of self-worth form the core of their personalities and determine the use they make of their minds and bodies. Teachers who empower students must guide them to believe in themselves. Even though a student may not believe in himself or herself in other aspects of life, you can empower that student in the classroom. By doing so, the student will have added a positive piece to the foundation of his or her own self-image.

Everyone, whether they realize it or not, has a self-image. Everyone perceives themselves in some way—smart, fast, different, motivated, lazy, incompetent, shrewd, or misunderstood. Everyone has adjectives that describe themselves. It is the "I" behind the eyes. It is the "I" who thinks, hears, talks, and feels. It is the "I" that perceives and interprets all that comes at us.

De Boer (1984), for example, reported that high school women rated their science ability lower than males even though their actual performance was generally better. De Boer felt that this negative self-perception in science ability is an important issue and one of the reasons why women have reduced participation in science courses and careers. In addition, Allen (1986) reported that male students outnumber female students by 2 to 1 in computer programming courses. More female students perceive computer programming as too difficult, partly because computer courses are usually based within the mathematics department. In 1991, the American Association of University Women (AAUW) reported that teachers still continue to have lower expectations for girls than for boys, and stated:

> Whether one looks at preschool classrooms or university lecture halls or at female or male teachers, research spanning 20 years consistently reveals that males receive more teacher attention than do females. In preschool classrooms boys receive more instructional time, more hugs, and more teacher attention. The patterns persist through elementary school and high school. (p. 68)

Of all the judgments and beliefs that students have, perhaps none is more important than the ones they have about themselves. Their beliefs about themselves are telling factors in determining their success and happiness in school and in life. Their self-images are based partially on the kind of reinforcements they receive from their friends, peers, teachers, and classmates everyday. Every outward expression of your face and body, whether positive or negative, reflects the secret truths that you hold within your heart.

All students need to see themselves as significant and worthy. They need to believe that their existence in the classroom makes a difference and that what they do with their time, energy, and talent is meaningful to themselves and others. They need to know that they are worthy of your attention and that they are cared for, accepted, and belong. All students want to feel valued. If they don't feel valued, their effectiveness and commitment are diminished. You must continue to work on, maintain, and improve the self-images of all students because self-image is an important motive behind behaviors in, as well as out of, the classroom.

A person who is continually treated as inferior by people will eventually perceive that he or she is inferior. Once the perception of inferiority becomes established, it becomes the foundation by which that person acts. Such a person will act inferior in relation to others, and other people will reciprocate by treating the person as inferior.

The historical Rosenthal and Jacobson's (1968) study, "Pygmalion in the Classroom" reported that when children were "stereotyped" as being exceptionally bright and treated by the teachers in such a manner (e.g., positive facial expressions, tone of voice, supportive statements, behaviors of acceptance) they reciprocated by assuming that role. The following list includes some of their findings:

1. The general climate factor, which consisted of the overall warmth a teacher exhibited, was shown more to high expectancy students.
2. Students for whom high expectations were held received more praise for doing something right than students for whom low expectations were held.
3. High expectancy students were taught more than low expectancy students.

Teachers must continue to work on, maintain, and improve the self-images of all students because self-image is an important motive behind behaviors in, as well as out of the classroom.

4. Students for whom the teacher had higher expectations were called on more often and were given more chances to reply, as well as being asked more frequent and more difficult questions.

Rosenthal and Jacobson's original study was eventually faulted because of methodological weaknesses (Brophy & Good, 1974). But further research has continued to support the general principles of the study.

Some teachers, unfortunately, expect less of some multicultural students, and thus, these students produce less. The historic U.S. Commission on Civil Rights (1973) study of 429 classrooms determined that Mexican-American students were treated less favorably than the Anglo students. The term Anglo was used instead of Western European American in this study. The study concluded that:

1. Many teachers unconsciously assumed that Mexican-American students were more unruly and consequently needed more discipline. As a result of this unconscious assumption, Mexican-Americans were scolded more often than Anglos and consequently, the interactions between Mexican-American students were less favorable and resulted in less interaction with the teachers. Teachers spoke more frequently with Anglo students than Mexican-American students.

2. Many teachers unconsciously assumed that Mexican-American students were less bright, which resulted in the teachers asking more difficult questions of the Anglo students. As a result of this, Anglo students were praised more and challenged intellectually more than were Mexican-Americans.

3. The quality of verbal and nonverbal interactions favored Anglo students over Mexican-American students.

These teachers unconsciously assumed that Mexican-Americans were more violent, less intelligent, and had difficulty with the English language. As a result, they treated the students according to their expectations, and the self-fulfilling prophecy held true.

Later studies have continued to support some of the findings of the 1973 Civil Rights Study. Oakes (1987) concluded that patterns of lower achievement and underparticipation for minorities and poor children begin early in the educational process and the discrepancies grow larger the longer the students stay in school. Oakes found that in junior high school, minority and white students from low-income groups typically take fewer courses in mathematics and science. Gamoran and Berends (1987) reported that disproportionately large numbers of students from lower socioeconomic levels are assigned to low-ability groups beginning very early in their school careers and that teachers generally view high-track students positively and low-track students negatively. Peterson et al. (1984) reinforced earlier studies by reporting that children of lower socioeconomic status were seen as less capable academically by teachers and assigned more frequently to low-ability tracks.

The 1992 AAUW report presented evidence that there is a difference in the kinds of interactions associated with white and black children and their teachers. It reported that African-American females have fewer interactions with teachers than white females, but they actually attempt to initiate interaction more often than white females or males of either race. African-American students are perceived less favorably by their teachers and are seen as less able as other students (Rosser, 1989). Harris and Carlton (1990) also reported that African-American students have fewer verbal interactions with their teachers. Ortiz (1988) reported that instructional programs for Hispanic children tend to be remedial, as teachers do not believe that Hispanic children are capable of academically demanding work, and that teachers tend to avoid interaction and eye or physical contact with their Hispanic students. Olson (1988) reported that teachers made more derogatory and embarrassing remarks in front of the class about immigrant students because of the language difficulty. Conversely, Pollard (1989) reported that the academic performance of African-American students is enhanced when they perceive their teachers as being supportive and helpful.

Teachers must be aware of any prejudices they themselves hold against members of any group, in particular, minority groups. Otherwise, discriminatory practices will surface in the form of self-fulfilling prophecies that harm students and perpetuate societal inequities.

Similar to the self-fulfilling prophecy is the concept of "sustaining expectation effect." This condition exists when the teacher accurately assesses the student's ability but does not alter that expectation when a student improves or regresses over time. For example, a perceived "A" student continues to get A's even though some of the work is of lesser quality. The teacher graded the papers on her high expectation rather than the quality of the work.

This effect can also be applied to a student who is labeled by the teacher as a "C" student. The student has always turned in reasonable but not outstanding work. However, the student is inspired to work harder and the quality of work improves. The sustained expectation effect prevented the teacher from accurately perceiving the improvement and the student receives another "C." Cooper and Good (1983) reported that sustaining expectations are more common in classrooms than are self-fulfilling prophecies.

The Role of Existentialism in Psychosocial Wellness

The concept of freedom is an important part of existential psychology and an important part of any classroom. Freedom can be discussed from a variety of contexts, such as religion and government. The type of freedom applied to the classroom is "freedom of the mind."

Freedom of the mind is an "inner liberty"—a freedom of the inner person that exists aside from any outward choices or alternatives that may have come from external or environmental situations. Gensemer (1980) views freedom as subjective rather than objective, psychological rather than physiological, attitudinal rather than behavioral. Students must have the freedom to think, to feel, and to perceive because these are prerequisites to help them become the capable persons they are meant to be. Within this context, students must be allowed to express their feelings, intellectual thinking, and perceptions without fear of punishment, being told that they are wrong, or being judged. However, this freedom can only be symbolic in certain instances. What a student thinks and what the student does must be separated. Although we may not believe or accept the views of a racist, that racist has the right to own those views. However, the racist does not have the right to act out those feelings or express those feelings if they interfere with the freedom of others. In addition, you cannot allow students to express freedoms that are beyond the rules of the school or society. Freedom of the mind also implies the responsibility to outwardly respect the freedom of others.

You must be willing to allow freedom, which is more than the mere giving of permission to students to be more self-directive. It means a sacrifice of some presumed "controls" over students, which must be made if one believes in the basic concept of humanism and wishes to use it in teaching. For example, humanistic teachers must:

- Be willing to accept that all people are different and allow flexibility within the curriculum to allow some freedom in the information that is learned
- Recognize that student progress is not based entirely on standardized norms, but also on the student themselves
- Include the values and interests of the students and not just the imposed values of standardized tests

The preceding examples are within the philosophy of humanistic psychology because they promote individuality, freedom to think, and self-discovery—all of which promote the concept of the humanistic "self."

You can help contribute to the healthy classroom by providing a learning environment that helps meet the needs of the students. You can review programs as to whether they meet safety and security needs (e.g., fire drills, child abuse awareness, violence prevention programs, appropriate safety rules and regulations), and acceptance and belonging needs (e.g., class meetings, friendship groups, counseling and psychological services, genuine caring for children). For developing esteem (e.g., feelings of being significant and capable) and wellness needs (e.g., students are responsible, self-disciplined, and self-reliant) you must be creative in your approach to teaching by developing meaningful lessons that connect to the lives of your students. The more the needs are satisfied in the relationship between you and your students, the more they will be motivated to work and aspire to achieve.

The High School Dropout:
A Profile of Unfulfilled Needs

How dropouts are to be counted makes a big difference in what the public will come to understand as the level of seriousness of the problem. There are three commonly used types of dropout rates:

1. *Event dropout rates* measure the proportion of all students from grades K–12 who drop out in a single year without completing high school. The federal government generally uses this statistic. The problem with this measure is that when we count dropouts as a ratio of all students who leave school in a district, the number is relatively small since very few students drop out before grade nine. When statistics reflect the event rate for grades 9–12, the rate is around 5 percent. According to U.S. Secretary of Education Richard W. Riley, in 1995 the event dropout rate for grades 9–12 is holding at around 5 percent, which translates to some 500,000 young people (Thomas, 1997).

2. *Status dropout rates* measure the proportion of the population that has not completed high school and is not enrolled at one point in time, regardless of when they dropped out. The statistics for status rates are kept between the ages of 16–24. The status rate for this group is 11 percent. The status dropout rate represents approximately 3.4 million dropouts in October 1992 (Goal 2 High School Completion).

3. *Cohort dropout rates* measure what happens to a single group (or cohort) of students over a period of time. An example of this would be to follow a group of students from one high school class throughout their expected high school career and a bit beyond and noting when they drop out. The cohort rate between grades 8 and 10 was 6.8 percent in 1988 eighth-graders. The cohort rate between grades 10 and 12 for 1990 sophomores was 6.2 percent (Goal 2 High School Completion).

Who Drops Out? Dropout rates differ greatly by ethnicity. Dropout rates are higher for blacks, Hispanics, and Native-Americans than for whites. When blacks and whites from similar social backgrounds are compared, however, dropout rates for blacks are not higher, and in some cases may be lower, than those for whites. Rates for Native-Americans and Alaskan Natives are quite high, while those for Asian students are very low. According to the U.S. Department of Education Statistics (USDES), Hispanics continue to drop out at higher rates than any other groups (Thomas, 1997). Thomas also reported that according to the report, in 1996, 9 percent of Hispanics left school before completing a high school program, compared to 6.7 percent for blacks and 4.1 percent for whites. In 1996, according to the report, a lower percentage of Hispanics completed high school, 62 percent, compared to 91.5 percent for whites and 83 percent for blacks. McKay (1988) reported Mexican-American students not only have higher dropout rates, but they also tend to leave school earlier than do blacks or whites. It has been estimated that about 40 percent of Mexican-Americans drop out of high school before the Spring semester of their sophomore year. Seller (1989) reported that in the mid-1980s, the high school dropout rate of Latinas (women) was more than double that of whites and blacks and the high school dropout rate of teenage mothers suggests that needs of these young women were not being met in traditional schools.

The 1996 statistics on Native-Americans and Asian-Americans were not reported, but in 1993–1994, the dropout rates were 4.3 percent for Asian-Americans and 8.9 percent for Native-Americans (Goal 2 High School Completion).

Dropout rates are related to individual and family demographic and socio-economic characteristics. Dropout rates are higher for students from low socio-economic backgrounds, single-parent families, and non-English family backgrounds. Young adults living in families with incomes in the lowest 20 percent of all family incomes were five times as likely as their peers from families in the top 20 percent of the income distribution to drop out of high school according to the U.S. Department of Education's Statistics (Thomas, 1997). Research also shows that family background strongly influences the propensity to drop out of school and accounts for virtually all the racial differences in dropout rates (Rumberger, 1983). Students whose parents or siblings were dropouts are themselves more likely to drop out. The same is true for those who marry and have children before graduating from high school. The dropout rate is greater in cities than in suburbs and nonmetropolitan areas. Dropping out is most prevalent in the West and South. According to the USDES, high cumulative dropout rates in the South of 13 percent and 13.9 percent in the West are greater than the dropout rates of 8.3 percent in the Northeast and 7.7 percent in the Midwest.

The earlier the grade from which a student drops out of high school, the less likely it is that the student will later complete high school. As a group, Asian dropouts are most likely to return and complete high school, while Native-American and Hispanic dropouts are least likely to return and finish. Black and white dropouts do not differ in their completion rates in the first few years after dropping out of high school. Dropouts from high socioeconomic backgrounds or those with high grades are more likely to return then those from low socio-economic status families or with poor grades (Goal 2 High School Completion).

The Cost of Dropping Out   The economic cost of dropping out is clear. In 1992, the national unemployment rate for high school dropouts was twice the rate of those who graduated but did not attend college. The median annual earnings of high school dropouts working full-time ($12,809) is only two-thirds that of high school graduates. Over their lifetime, high school dropouts will earn only about 75 percent as much as high school graduates, and less than half of what college graduates are likely to make during their lifetime. In any given year, the likelihood of slipping into poverty is about three times

The Dropout: A Profile of Unfulfilled Needs

higher for high school dropouts than for those who have finished high school (Schwartz, 1995).

Unfulfilled Needs Although the research on school dropouts is still unclear and the dynamics of school completion are not well understood, the research does point out some important factors. As discussed earlier, certain factors such as race/ethnicity, socioeconomic factors, and family influences are correlated with dropping out. These factors are often beyond the control of the school and the teacher. However, according to Meyer's (1995) analysis of the literature, there are also a number of institutional and personal factors that can be attributed to students dropping out. Institutional and personal factors are influenced by both the teacher and school. They include:

- *Academic achievement.* Low standardized test scores and poor classroom achievement increase the chances of dropping out. Students who are given high expectations and treated as capable are more likely to achieve success.

- *Education aspirations.* Dropping out is a process that begins in elementary school and becomes more likely to occur as students accumulate negative experiences in the upper grades. Low educational aspirations are correlated with increased negative experiences in educational, emotional, and social experiences.

- *Self-concept or feelings of self-worth.* A student with poor self-concept is more likely to become a dropout. Poor self-concepts are often developed from an accumulation of negative experiences in school. When students feel the teacher doesn't care about them, have difficulty getting along with others, are placed in low-level academic tracks, or do not feel a part of the class, they often develop feelings of despair and drop out. Poor self-concept may also be related to substance abuse, which is also correlated with dropping out.

- *Poor school records.* For many students, the accumulation of academic, social, and emotional negative experiences increases the probability of low attendance, truancy, suspension, and expulsion.
- *Retention.* Retention in a grade for failure is also correlated with dropping out.
- *Alienation from school life.* A national study by Eckstrom et al. (1986) found that one of the main characteristics of dropouts is alienation from school life.

SUMMARY OF MAJOR POINTS
IN CHAPTER 3

1. *Healthy Classroom Management* has its foundation rooted in self-esteem research, resiliency research, hardiness research, and humanistic psychology.

2. The California Task Force determined that self-esteem is the likeliest candidate for a social vaccine, something that empowers us to live responsibly and inoculates us against the lures of crime, violence, substance abuse, teen pregnancy, abuse, chronic welfare dependency, and educational failure.

3. Self-esteem is defined as "appreciating my own worth and importance and having the character to be accountable for myself and to act responsibly toward others."

4. The dual pillars of healthy self-esteem are self-efficacy and self-respect.

5. Resiliency is "the capacity to spring back, rebound, successfully adapt in the face of adversity, and develop social, academic, and vocational competence despite exposure to severe stress or simply to the stress that is inherent in today's world."

6. Four traits of a resilient person include social competence, problem-solving skills, autonomy, and a sense of purpose/future.

7. The 4 C's of hardiness are commitment, control, challenge, connectedness, and spirit.

8. Humanistic psychology includes the following similar but distinct approaches: humanism, perceptualism, and existentialism.

9. All students regardless of gender, disabilities, race, or ethnicity share common basic human needs.

10. The basic psychological needs discussed in this chapter are consistent with building resiliency, self-esteem, and hardiness.

11. The basic needs discussed in this chapter are related to acceptance, significance, competence, and safety and security.

| Class Discussion | CHAPTER 3 |

Note: Review Appendix E before facilitating this activity.

Nurturing the Student

Time: 20 minutes (discussion not included)
Objective: To help participants recognize the basic needs of people.
Materials: A small variety of plants including some that look great, some wilted, some in bloom, a cactus, and perhaps a weed. A plant for each participant is ideal, but not absolutely necessary. (Pictures of different plants can be substituted, but is not quite as impressive as real plants.) Chalk board and chalk or a flip chart with marking pens.

Procedure/Suggested Discussion Questions:

1. Pass out a plant to each participant or one plant to a small group of participants.
2. Each participant or group is then requested to make some comments about their plant. Have the participants compare their plant with the others. Ask the participants if they were able to keep the plants which one would they choose and why? How many got their favorite plant? If you received a daisy but wanted a tulip, is there anything you can do to turn your daisy into a tulip?
3. Record responses to the following questions on the blackboard. Since you got the plant that you got, what do you need to do to help your plant develop into its full potential? (possible answers: water, light, good soil, sunshine, shade, tender loving care, quiet music) What happens when any of these needs are neglected?
4. Do all of these plants need the same amount of water, sunlight, etc.? Why?
5. Ask each group to identify something positive about their plant and then relate this to the importance of finding the strengths in each student.
6. What do students need to develop their full potential?

7. Do all students need the same amount of nurturing? Why?
8. What have you learned from this exercise to help your students?
9. Take a few minutes to think about something specific you would like to do differently as a result of your increased insight from this activity. Be specific about what you want to do, why you want to do it, and exactly when you will do it.
10. Allow time for anyone who would like to share their commitment.

Needs in the Teacher-Student Relationship

Time: 5–10 minutes (discussion not included)
Objective: To help participants recognize that relationships are based on trust, acceptance, respect, and dignity.
Materials: A copy of the "Needs in the Teacher-Student Relationship" check list for each participant.

Procedure:

1. Distribute the "Needs in the Teacher-Student Relationship" check list and allow participants a few minutes to complete.
2. Have participants form triads to discuss and share their thoughts and answers on the survey.
3. Gather all participants together.

Suggested Discussion Questions:

1. What did you learn about yourself?
2. What did you learn about others?
3. How do you feel when others treat you in respectful ways?
4. What were you feeling or thinking as you were filling out the survey?
5. How can you apply what you learned from this activity to your teaching philosophy?
6. How can you apply what you learned from this activity to your everyday life situations? (For example: between boy friend and girl friend, husband and wife, parent and child, etc.)

CHAPTER 3

Needs in the Teacher-Student Relationship

Please check any of the following statements that apply or applied to you in your experience as a student and prioritize them according to the needs you felt most strongly about.

I want(ed) my teacher to:

____ 1. Treat me in a warmer and friendlier manner.

____ 2. Allow me to make more decisions.

____ 3. Expect less accomplishment from me.

____ 4. Have more confidence in my abilities.

____ 5. Be less directive.

____ 6. Accept me as an important member of the class.

____ 7. Have more respect for my judgment.

____ 8. Be more interested in me rather than my academic abilities.

____ 9. Give me more praise for my accomplishments.

____10. Criticize me less.

____11. Be more confident that I could be trusted with responsibilities.

---

12. Wants and needs are separate matters. Needs are the deep roots of one's existence. They are meaningful, worthy, and not as changeable as wants.

13. The following key factors help build resiliency:

   ■ Having a caring and supportive relationship with at least one person

   ■ Setting and communicating high expectations

   ■ Creating opportunities for students to participate

   ■ Increasing prosocial bonding

   ■ Setting clear, consistent boundaries

   ■ Teaching "life skills"

14. How students feel about themselves has a direct effect on how they live all aspects of their lives, including school.

15. All students need to see themselves as significant and worthy.

16. It is possible to change someone's perception of himself or herself.

17. Students must be given the freedom to think, feel, and perceive because these are prerequisites to help them become the capable persons they were meant to be.

18. Freedom of the mind also implies the responsibility to outwardly respect the freedom of others.

19. About 5 percent of high school students drop out between grades 9–12.

20. Dropout rates differ by ethnicity. Dropout rates are higher for blacks, Hispanics, and Native-Americans than for whites.

21. Dropout rates are related to individual and family demographic and socio-economic characteristics.

22. Other factors related to dropping out include academic achievement, educational aspirations, and self-concept.

23. In any given year, the likelihood of slipping into poverty is about three times higher for high school dropouts than for those who have finished high school.

Teacher's Corner: Observing and Interviewing Teachers

Concern: Do teachers treat all students fairly by arranging the classroom environment to affirm, encourage, and recognize them? Are teachers unknowingly biased toward certain students?

Directions for Observation

Observe a teacher for about one hour. Check the appropriate box for each of the questions in this survey.

Yes	No	Observation
__	__	Are minority students (ethnic and racial, language deficient, exceptional, class, and gender) seated together?
__	__	Are certain students seated away from the teacher?
__	__	Does the classroom have materials placed on the wall that reflect diversity?
__	__	Are materials bright and cheerful?
__	__	Did students interact with each other during lesson?
__	__	Are the students grouped during lesson?
__	__	If yes to above question, are the groups arranged heterogeneously (gender, race, and academic ability)?
__	__	If yes to above question, do the groups change from one group to another?
__	__	If yes to above question, did the students change from one group to another in an orderly fashion?
__	__	Are rules, procedures, or other cues visibly posted for all students to see?
__	__	Did the teacher interact in a positive manner with all students?
__	__	Did the teacher modify his or her oral pace and syntax to facilitate learning for those students who have special needs?
__	__	Did the teacher make culturally biased or sexist statements?
__	__	Did the teacher reprimand certain students more than others?
__	__	Did students make more positive statements as opposed to negative statements to each other?
__	__	Did the teacher use an effective teaching strategy for the lesson?
__	__	Did the teacher use a variety of teaching strategies?
__	__	Did the curriculum materials presented during the lesson reflect cultural diversity?
__	__	Are there different cultural magazines available in the classroom? (For example: *Ebony, America's Magazine, Asian Week,* or *American Indian Art*)

Directions for Interview

After the observation of the class, use the following questions to guide an interview with the teacher. Feel free to ask your own questions.

1. Do you have a specific strategy for working with students who may be limited in the Standard English language? If so, what is it and how did you arrive at it?
2. What kind of strategies have you developed to help create a supportive and accepting climate for all students? What are they and how did you develop them?
3. Do you have access to resources and materials for creating a multicultural classroom? If so, where do find them?

Analysis

As a result of your observations and interview, what important lessons can you apply to your present or future teaching strategies?

PART II

Motivating Students in the Healthy Classroom

This part consists of three chapters and focuses on the needs established by self-esteem research, resiliency research, hardiness research, and humanistic psychological theory. The chapters also include healthy strategies to help you motivate your students. These simple strategies are based on a foundation of mutual dignity and respect. The formula is simple: Give the students what they need, and the students will give you what you need. By meeting their basic psychosocial needs within an environment of intellectual and emotional freedom, you will help students to develop positive perceptions of themselves and motivate them to become the capable people they were meant to be. As a result, teachers will be setting the foundation to help students develop self-reliance, discipline, and responsibility.

4

■

Motivation: Acceptance and Significance

At the heart of personality is the need to feel a sense of
being lovable without having to qualify for that acceptance.

MAURICE WAGNER

MOTIVATION AND ACCEPTANCE

Acceptance—the sense of belonging, of being connected to those you care for—is one of the most compelling motivations that any student regardless of gender, color, or ethnic background has. Nothing contributes to one's self-esteem, resiliency, and overall wellness more than being accepted by another. For many students, being accepted by their teacher, classmates, or peers is just as important as being loved by their parents. It is important that they feel accepted by those whom they consider to be important to them—you as the teacher and their classmates or peers. There is nothing more sad and frustrating than being surrounded by people yet feeling only loneliness on the inside.

All students need to feel that there is some meaning to their existence in the classroom. As discussed in the previous chapter, the research on school dropouts is still unclear and the dynamics of school completion are not well understood. The research does, however, indicate that being unaffiliated—not belonging—is one of the major causes of dropping out of school. A national study (Eckstrom et al., 1986) found that one of the main characteristics of dropouts is alienation from school life.

Many students, in particular minority students, do not feel that they are really accepted, but only tolerated, in their schools. The unacceptance is reinforced by the fact that some schools have not traditionally valued their ethnicity, history, heritage, or language. Even their cultural mannerisms in talking, behaving, moving, and living are sometimes perceived as unacceptable or inferior.

Just because a student becomes a member of the class does not necessarily mean he or she will feel a part of the class. Belonging means a variety of things to different students. It can mean new friendships, cooperation with others, peer acceptance, feeling valued by the teacher and/or classmates, and excelling in academics.

Many teachers are initially surprised to find out just how important they are to their students. When students are asked to list the most meaningful people in their lives, teachers rank just behind parents (Brookover & Erickson, 1969). Being in this position, you have a significant impact on both the physical and emotional growth and development of your students.

Messages of Acceptance

You can build a sense of acceptance and belonging by actions as well as words. You should show an interest in all of your students, from the brightest student to the least talented member of the classroom. By having a student in the classroom you have made a commitment to him or her—regardless of his or her background. It is not always possible to "connect" during class. What is most important to students is that you are interested in them as individuals and not just because of their classroom ability or cultural background. Take some time outside of class to interact and find out what is going on in their lives. "How's it

Nothing contributes to one's self-esteem, resiliency, and overall wellness more than being accepted by another.

going?" and "Can I be of any help?" are simple openers that will make it clear to all students that they count in the life of their teacher.

According to Clarke (1978), the following messages of acceptance can be expressed verbally or by the teacher's actions:

- You have a right to be here.
- I'm glad you are who you are.
- It's okay for you to have needs.
- You don't have to do tricks to get attention and approval.
- You can stand up for the things you believe even if there is some risk involved.
- You can own the consequences of your actions; others don't have to rescue you.
- It's okay to make mistakes as long as you accept responsibility for making amends.
- You can express your own thoughts and feelings without fear of rejection.
- It's okay to disagree.
- You can trust your own judgment.

By accepting students for who they are and building on their strengths and successes rather than their weaknesses and failures, you can help students cope with their problems; develop self-confidence, responsibility, and self-reliance; and learn to accept themselves.

BELONGING

NEW FRIENDSHIPS

COOPERATION WITH OTHERS

PEER ACCEPTANCE

FEELING VALUED BY TEACHERS & CLASSMATES

EXCELLING IN ACADEMICS

Accepting Students for Who They Are

Students need to know that you accept and care about them, that you have their best interests at heart, that you want them as part of the classroom, and that you appreciate them for their contributions. Students need to feel that you are working with them to become all that they are capable of becoming both in and out of the classroom. Acceptance is unconditional—not contingent on anything particular about the individual who is accepted. It is inherent and not earned.

An ancient Chinese proverb says, *"A child's life is like a piece of paper on which every passerby leaves a mark."* You have an opportunity to leave a mark of caring and acceptance.

A Simple Gesture

The following excerpt is by Glenn Van Ekeren (1988). Although this story is related to sports, its implications apply to life in general.

> History was made in the baseball world in 1947. It was in that year that Jackie Robinson became the first black baseball player to play in the major leagues. The Brooklyn Dodgers' owner, Branch Rickey, told Robinson, "It'll be tough. You are going to take abuse, be ridiculed, and take more verbal punishment than you ever thought possible. But I'm willing to back you all the way if you have the determination to make it work."

In short order, Robinson experienced Rickey's prediction. He was abused verbally and physically as players intentionally ran him over. The crowd was fluent with their racial slurs and digging comments. Opponents ridiculed Robinson as well as the Dodger players.

Around mid-season, Robinson was having a particularly bad day. He had fumbled grounders, overthrown first base, and had an equally disastrous day at the plate. The crowd was celebrative in their boos. Then something special happened. In front of this critical crowd, Pee Wee Reese walked over from his shortstop position, put his arm around Jackie Robinson, and indicated his acceptance of the major league's first black baseball player.

Robinson later reflected, "That gesture saved my career. Pee Wee made me feel as if I belonged."

Consider the number of newcomers who happen into our lives every week. They too are awaiting for the displayed acceptance from the crowd. But more important, they need to feel as if they belong in our world and are considered an important contributor. We have a significant impact on the lives of others by simply letting them know we accept them.

Demonstrating That You Care
For and Accept Each Student

Most teachers probably care for and like most students they teach. However, because of personal shortcomings such as unconscious biases, stereotyping students, lack of cultural understanding, and faulty communication styles, some teachers do not make all students feel cared for or accepted.

The more caring and acceptance you can give to students, the more you will help your students to care. The more they have, the more they will be able to give away. The less they have, the less they can give away. Students who feel cared for and accepted will not need to use or abuse others to find their place in the classroom setting. If you can learn to give caring and acceptance away it will always come back with added interest. Conversely, if you give anger and hate away, they too will always find their way back to you.

Sometimes, teachers who really care about their students do not' know how to convey that caring and acceptance. Following are some strategies that communicate caring and acceptance.

Take All Students Seriously The things that happen in the lives of the students both in and out of school are of tremendous importance to them. You should value what they share. By listening and taking an interest in what they do you let them know that they are being taken seriously, that you care for them, and that they can always come to you.

Listen Carefully This is one of the most basic and important life skills. It tells the students that they are valuable and worthy of your time and attention. The U.S. Commission on Civil Rights (1973) reported that taking time to listen to a student share a personal experience may be sometimes difficult, but repeatedly refusing to listen to the same students tells them their lives and experiences are unimportant.

Tell Students That You Care for Them   If you really care about someone, you should say it directly. Don't drop hints or beat around the bush. Don't be coy or embarrassed. Say, "I'm glad you are a part of this classroom" or "I really enjoy being with you." These are significant statements to the students. These kinds of statements help students to feel connected to you and give them an idea of how you feel about them.

Touch Respectfully   Because touching can be a sensitive issue, many teachers have adopted self-imposed rules that forbid physical contact between themselves and their students, even though they know that appropriate touching can carry a message of care and respect. It is obvious that nobody wants any personal rights violated; however, touching can be done without having sexual or abusive connotations. For example, handshaking is an acceptable form of greeting among most Americans; however, some cultures view touching as a very personal matter and teachers must be aware of this fact. If you want to shake hands with a child but are not sure whether that child wants to be touched, simply ask respectfully if it is okay to shake hands.

The question that most teachers ask is "What is appropriate touching?" Part of the answer is based on why you are touching someone. If you are disciplining a student, your touch is going to be rejected; however, if you are encouraging or praising a student, an appropriate touch is usually welcomed. A safe zone of touch is from the shoulder to the hand. A "pat" on the shoulder, a handshake, and a "high" five are just some of the ways that a teacher can show caring and acceptance.

Smile   Sometimes a sincere smile is all that is needed to make a connection that says, "I care about you and support you."

Use Simple Hand Gestures   Acknowledging students with a "thumbs up, an okay sign, a hang-loose sign, or a simple wave to say hello or good-bye signal recognition, acceptance, and caring.

Provide Sincere Encounters   Every student needs occasional sincere encounters with you, the teacher. A sincere encounter is simply focused attention. It is a vital contact that is direct, special, and unique for each individual student. Students are highly sensitive to the degree of focused attention they receive. When it is lacking, they know. If you use this time to do mental note taking, students will know. Wandering thoughts such as "I need to remember to call in for my appointment" and "I've got to get ready for my next class" during sincere encounters will only put distance in the relationship. Students are sensitive to your inner presence. Without it, time together is wasted and sometimes harmful. Your lack of "inner presence" can be easily interpreted as a negative message

Use simple hand gestures to acknowledge students and signal recognition, acceptance, and caring.

because your behavior is indifferent and the student may feel that you are not interested in him or her.

However, learning to focus attention does not come automatically. Just as a coach might teach an athlete to focus on the moment for competition, you must recognize that sincere encounters require concentration and practice. Most teachers have spent so many years hurrying and concentrating on things to do, that it is hard to switch to focusing on the moment during a sincere encounter.

Just as a student is expected to focus during an academic test or an athlete during a competition, you need to let go of every peripheral thought and concentrate on the here-and-now. There must be no planning ahead or reminiscing. You must be totally with the student, even if only for a few moments. You need to let go of everything except the sincere encounter.

Obviously, the more encounters the better. Realistically, teachers are busy, and sincere encounters do take time. When classes are large, the thought of sincere encounters can be overwhelming. However, a teacher does not have to give exclusive attention all the time. It is when the teacher never has time that students will feel unfulfilled. If students occasionally feel your heartfelt presence, they will accept times when your attention is elsewhere.

You need to think about ways in which you can make students feel connected with you. Busy teachers need to find creative ways to let the students know that they count. A simple note sent in the mail can have a lifelong impact. You can plan to connect with your students by making it a priority to simply set aside a small amount of time on a regular basis and meet with one or two different students. Simply writing it into a daily or weekly schedule and not allowing other things to interfere with that scheduled time is a positive practice. This practice will be well worth the investment of your time. It does not take much. It is often the little things that win the biggest points. When students feel the quality of your presence, they will conclude that they matter. Most adults who look back on their school years will always remember the teacher who took the time to get to know them.

Be Sensitive to Terminology Terminology changes over time as ethnic and cultural groups continue to explore who they are through their history and their relationship to the dominant culture. In the 1990s the following terms gained general acceptance:

African-American: In the 1960s the term Negroes was replaced with blacks and Afro-Americans. In the 1990s the term African-American gained general acceptance. The Census report still uses the term black.

Asian-American: Most Americans of Asian ancestry do not want to be referred to as "Orientals." In California, Asian-American and Pacific Islanders are the terms that are currently preferred. However, as the cultures of the students are differentiated, most of them would prefer to be identified by the origin, such as Japanese-American, Chinese-American, or Thai-American.

Hispanic-American: This is the general accepted term. However, most Americans of Mexican ancestry prefer Chicano or Latino or Mexican-American to Hispanic-American.

Native-American: Native-American is the accepted term. There are two groups of Native-Americans: American Indians and Native Alaskans.

White-American: The term white or Caucasian has given way to the term Western European American in some literature, although the Census reports still use the term white. The term Anglo is also used.

To find out what terms are used and accepted within a community, you need to simply ask your students. The vocabulary has also changed for individuals with disabilities. Individuals are no longer referred to as "handicapped" but as "individuals with disabilities" or as "students with physical disabilities."

Develop Activities to Create Acceptance among Students Creating an atmosphere of acceptance between you and your students and students with other students helps promote positive attitudes between everyone involved. Acceptance promotes a positive class identity and pride among students, reduces prejudices and biases, and diminishes stereotyping. There are numerous books available that include student activities that can help promote positive human relationships.

Be Sensitive to the Pronunciation of Names Students take pride in their names and every teacher should learn to pronounce each name correctly. Continual mispronunciation or using "nicknames" to avoid pronouncing a name is disrespectful.

Prepare in Advance If you are aware that a new student will be in the class, you should prepare in advance to insure that the student is accepted. For example, if a student with a disability is mainstreamed into the class, you should learn about the disability. If possible, you should observe the student prior to receiving the student in the classroom. If necessary, the classroom should be prepared to accommodate any child with physical or sensory disabilities. Aisles should be wide enough to accommodate a wheelchair. Shelves should be lowered and obstacles removed. You should confer with a special education teacher about the necessary accommodations. Help all of the students to understand and accept children with disabilities in the classroom. Most important, whenever possible, meet the student prior to receiving him or her in the classroom. See Appendix F for a guide for working with disabled students.

Facilitate the acceptance of exceptional students You can facilitate the acceptance of a child with a disability by exhibiting an open and positive attitude. Students tend to imitate the attitudes of the teacher. If you are uncomfortable or negative toward a disabled student, the students will be also. If you are accepting and positive, the students will also be accepting and positive. An attitude of openness will help you recognize that students who have disabilities are useful members of society. Most students who are mainstreamed into the regular classroom have mild disabilities. This means that they are more like other students than they are different from them. Most of them will finish school, find jobs, and become part of the communities in which they live (Banks & Banks, 1993).

Incorporate Classroom Activities That Help Promote Acceptance among Your Students See Appendix B for practical classroom activities that help promote acceptance.

Personal Biases Affect Acceptance

Educators cannot begin to treat ethnic minorities, women, children of poverty, and the disabled fairly until they understand that these students are of equal human worth and value. This acceptance will only begin when teachers begin to examine the true qualities of these groups and begin to destroy the racial, sexist, and social myths and stereotypes that exist in society. There are a variety of reasons for prejudice, but most often it is the result of a conflict in cultural values as opposed to some articulated philosophy.

Some teachers, unfortunately, find it difficult to completely accept some students for who they are. Many teachers carry biases or prejudices into their profession. Their biases are their sets of beliefs, values, and assumptions that they hold because of past experiences and their philosophy of life. They will like some students better than others. Some students, because of their background, sex, appearance, abilities, size, nationality, behavior, or socioeconomic status will be more appealing than others to a given teacher.

In addition, a teacher may inwardly feel that students are not talented enough, outgoing enough, or smart enough. The student never completely measures up to what the teacher wants. While many teachers rarely display overt rejection, they may, unconsciously and unwittingly, express their lack of acceptance in more subtle ways, such as displaying disappointment, anger, irritation, passivity, or by becoming overly critical, protective, and demanding.

It is essential that teachers be fair in their treatment of all students. Teachers must focus on their own areas of personal bias. A teacher must ask himself or herself, "What preconceived notions do I have about young people in relation to their ethnicity, gender, or personal differences? Do I generalize about certain groups of people and create stereotypes? Do I undervalue comments made

Time-out: Are You Prejudiced?

Each of us, because of our personal experiences, carries biases and prejudices into our profession. Some of your values, beliefs, and assumptions are so ingrained that you are usually unaware of them. Consequently, you will generalize about certain groups of people and create stereotypes. If you trick yourself into believing that your subjective opinions are true facts, you lose a tremendous opportunity to see students as they really are. It is important that you examine yourself honestly and carefully to help you take stock of your inner feelings.

The purpose of this quiz is to help you determine your familiarity with and acceptance of people who are unlike yourself. *Treat the results as a guide. There is always a margin of uncertainty in questionnaires of this kind.*

Score Your Questions:

1. Never   2. Seldom   3. Sometimes   4. Often
5. Always

1. _____   Do you have negative feelings about children who are from poverty areas?
2. _____   Do you feel girls are not suited for classes like auto mechanics and woodshop?
3. _____   Do you feel uncomfortable where you are different, for example, where you are surrounded by others who are disabled or of a different color and/or speak a different language?
4. _____   Do you dislike males who have "feminine" traits or females who have "masculine" qualities?
5. _____   Do you tell ethnic jokes or jokes about disabled individuals?
6. _____   Do you discount opinions of students who are different from you (for example, someone who has brown skin, has a heavy accent, is disabled, or is of a particular nationality)?
7. _____   Do you believe girls are less mathematically inclined than boys?
8. _____   Do you dislike the African-American style of rapping in terms of voice volume, facial gestures, hand movements, and posturing?
9. _____   Do you ever try to learn or speak the language of some of your students from different cultures?
10. _____   Do you dislike the idea of interracial dating or marriage?
11. _____   Do you converse with close friends (not acquaintances) and speak negatively about some minority group or groups?
12. _____   Do you resent the special opportunities given to ethnic minorities?
13. _____   Do you avoid taking the time to study the different cultures that your students represent?
14. _____   Do you find assertive female students to be pushy or abrasive?
15. _____   Do you feel it is ever appropriate to imitate certain ethnic groups by overexaggerating certain stereotypical ethnic speech patterns or mannerisms?

Add your scores for all 15 statements. The total represents your score.

Score: What do your answers mean?

60–75 You probably have a number of cultural biases and tend to have a fear of or are intolerant of people of different cultures. You need to work on overcoming your prejudices by separating opinion or emotional reaction from the hard truth. Seek a professional who can help you in this process.

35–59 You appear to have some biases, but you are somewhat aware of your biases and try to treat people equally whenever possible. Keep plugging away. Continue to expand your knowledge and diversity.

Below 35 You have few ethnic or cultural biases and tend to judge most people individually, rather than by placing them into generalized groups. Congratulations!

by speakers whose English is accented differently than my own? Do I discourage ethnic minority students or young women from undertaking projects that require difficult qualitative and/or quantitative work?" These are just some of the questions that teachers need to sort through to separate facts from opinions.

All students need to be accepted for who they are without having to qualify or change for that acceptance. A teacher must look carefully at and accept each student as he or she is. At certain times, a teacher may not always have to accept what a student does; however, a teacher must learn to focus on the student's behavior rather than his or her personality. It is the behavior that is wrong and that can usually be corrected. Making mistakes or acting-out in inappropriate ways does not make the student a bad person and a teacher must be able to differentiate between the two. Attacking the person instead of the behavior will only create greater distance in the teacher-student relationship.

MOTIVATION AND SIGNIFICANCE

Students who feel purposeful have an inner knowledge that their participation has meaning and direction. Feeling a sense of purpose is one of the deepest human needs. Students with a sense of purpose have specific goals for what they want to do and be. Having purpose makes them feel like somebody. They become motivated, optimistic, and energized in the process.

Making Students Feel Significant

It is your responsibility to help each student discover personal meaning by helping him or her to determine his or her purpose and provide the support necessary to accomplish it. This means helping each student set and achieve worthwhile goals. When students are involved in decisions, they will feel accountable for what happens.

You act as a guide by helping all students determine the direction in which they should be heading. When they have a goal, students know where to focus their time and energy to increase the likelihood of success. Best of all, success in an area leads to success in another area—and that is the whole idea. Students who have no goal have nothing to aim for, and over time they will hit that nothing with great success. Goal setting leads to a sense of purpose and future. It is one of the important steps in helping children build resiliency. Positive outcomes of this process include goal directedness, healthy expectancies, success orientation, achievement motivation, educational aspirations, sense of participation, sense of coherence, and hopefulness.

Setting Goals

There are five easy steps to help students set goals:

1. *Determine whose goal it is.* If students do not really want something, chances are they won't make the commitment needed to achieve it. A smart teacher helps all students see each goal as their own. If a student "owns" the goal, he or she will be more motivated toward achieving it. When you are helping students set goals, take a few minutes to talk about what they are going to get out of accomplishing it—the benefits. The more reasons they think of for achieving the goal, the stronger their desire will be. A stronger desire will result in greater effort.

2. *Make sure the goal is attainable.* The student has to believe that the goal is achievable. It does not have to be easy, but the student should have a fair chance of meeting it. In contrast, if the goal is too easy, what's the challenge?

3. *Divide the goal into small, achievable steps.* Goals seem a lot easier to reach when they are broken down into manageable tasks. Long-term goals need to be broken down into a series of smaller short-term goals. Each small accomplishment should be recognized as the student moves toward the greater whole.

4. *Set realistic deadlines.* Setting deadlines forces the teacher and the student to plan and organize. A deadline also acts as a point of reference to determine success in achieving the short- and long-term goals. It forces an evaluation to determine where the student is at that point in time.

5. *Put the goal in writing.* Asking the student to put the goal in writing helps him or her to clarify it as well as organize and plan it. It helps to internalize the goal. The goal should also be posted where the student can see it. Crossing off each short-term goal as it is accomplished has wondrous effects.

Leaders Help Others to Reach Goals

The following story by Glenn Van Ekeren (1988) stresses the importance of setting goals.

> Paul "Bear" Bryant, the football coach who won 323 major college football games, more than any other coach in history, used a technique from which all leaders could benefit. At the beginning of each football season at Alabama, Bryant had every member of his squad write out his personal goals. Only after reading and studying those goals did Bryant design a game plan and objectives for his football team.
>
> Why did this work so well? This simple technique had a threefold message. Bryant was conveying to his team: (1) I care about you and what you want; (2) you should be thinking ahead; and (3) we are building a team in which each of you can pursue your personal goals and I'm going to include those goals in our total team plan in as many ways as possible.

The challenge for schools is to engage youth by providing them opportunities to participate in meaningful, valued activities.

Knowing this, Bryant's squad gave their coach all they could give, and in so doing they strove for their own personal goals as well as producing strong, winning records year after year.

Note: Other coaches may have surpassed Bryant's record since 1988, when this article was written.

Participation and Involvement

The need to feel needed is often more powerful than the need to live. People have even committed suicide when they felt that their lives had no meaning or significance. Wehlage (1989) has confirmed that teenagers who feel alienated from family, school, or the community are more likely to abuse drugs, get pregnant or father a child, fail in school, commit vandalism, develop depression, or commit suicide. Wehlage stated, "The challenge clearly for these social institutions—and especially for the schools—is to engage youth by providing them opportunities to participate in meaningful, valued activities and roles—those involving problem-solving, decision-making, planning, goal setting, and helping others."

Bernard (1991) states, "Once again, the operating dynamic reflects the fundamental human need to bond—to participate, to belong, to have some power or control over one's life. When schools ignore these basic human needs, they become ineffective and alienating places."

Sarason (1990) says it well: "When one has no stake in the way things are, when one's needs or opinions are provided no forum, when one sees oneself as the object of unilateral actions, it takes no particular wisdom to suggest that one would rather be elsewhere."

PSYCHOLOGICAL OWNERSHIP...

... or possession translates into pride and loyalty as one's participation becomes relevant and focused and consequently leads to commitment.

Every student is waiting for you to give him or her some responsibility, something that he or she can feel good about. When it happens, it is almost miraculous. Things begin to happen in ways that nobody, not even you or the student, could ever have guessed.

A simple test to determine the social climate of a school is to answer the following questions:

1. Which students traditionally receive most of the social rewards of the school? How many were female, male, exceptional, or ethnic minority students? Are certain students excluded?

2. Are male, female, disabled, or ethnic minority students actively involved in activities such as cheerleading, the debate team, the school play, or other similar activities?

3. How many ethnic minority or disabled students are in leadership positions?

4. Who is in charge of the multicultural student clubs or activities? Are they members of the majority group?

5. Are ethnic minority students or exceptional children chosen to represent the school in school social functions such as "open house" or escorting important guests?

6. Does the school's sports program equally support both men and women?

Empowerment Through Participation

Healthy classrooms cannot afford to house unruly students, insecure teachers, or a class structure that stifles involvement and innovation. To prevent this, you must encourage two basic principles: participation and psychological ownership.

Participation goes beyond performance. True participation means that students who are in the class have a right and responsibility to contribute. It means that students share responsibilities and work together with classmates and the teacher to accomplish mutual class goals. It means that all students have a right and responsibility to contribute to and share in the successes and failures of the class. Participation validates a student's existence in the class because what he or she does has meaning and has impact both on the class and on others.

Psychological ownership or possession arises when the student recognizes that his or her efforts do make a difference and that his or her contributions are an integral part of the total class process. Possession translates into pride and loyalty because one's participation becomes relevant and focused and consequently leads to commitment. Without emotional connections there is indifference because nothing really matters.

Providing Opportunities for Contribution

Every student as a classroom member must be given the opportunity to be meaningfully involved and valued. Kurth-Schai (1988) reported, "youth participation in socially useful tasks is associated with heightened self-esteem, enhanced moral development, increased political activism, and the ability to create and maintain complex social relationships." When students are needed as contributors, they will bond, grow in dignity and self-respect, and get involved.

Here is a partial list of activities in which students can become involved:

1. Organizing and planning lessons
2. Leading discussions
3. Making classroom activity plans
4. Managing classroom equipment/supplies
5. Caring for recreational equipment
6. Helping to teach less skilled classmates
7. Maintaining the classroom
8. Helping to select books
9. Maintaining a calendar of events
10. Writing articles for the school newspaper
11. Being the audio-visual manager
12. Being the public relations director for the classroom
13. Creating posters and announcements
14. Raising funds for special projects
15. Preparing classroom "social" functions
16. Being a computer consultant
17. Being the classroom statistician
18. Creating bulletin boards
19. Being a messenger for the teacher

Try to find a job for everyone in the class. If you cannot think of job options, have the class brainstorm different ideas to create a list of classroom jobs that need to be done on a regular basis. If there are not enough jobs for everyone, have the class create a system of job assignment and rotation. Remember involvement leads to accountability, accountability leads to ownership, and ownership will lead the students to involvement. Involvement is a cyclic process.

Setting Boundaries on Student Participation

How much should you let students really do? This is a tough question because each teacher, classroom, and situation is different. A discussion of these three factors follows.

1. *The teacher.* Each teacher has his or her own value system and many teachers feel compelled to assume the responsibility for all decision making. Each teacher must examine the importance that he or she places on organizational efficiency, personal growth of students, and classroom success. Teachers also differ greatly in the amount of trust they have in their student's abilities as well as their feelings of security when they allow students to make decisions.

2. *The students in the classroom.* Each classroom is different, being made up of people with different personalities, and different wants and abilities. Some want more responsibility; others need more independence. Some will have the necessary knowledge and experience to deal with a problem; others may not be interested in the problem.

3. *Situations.* Situations will vary in complexity. Such factors as the pressure of time, the nature of the problem, and group effectiveness will all play a role in how much input students might have in planning.

These three factors will influence your action in a decision-making situation. There is no one absolute answer. You should start slowly by allowing students to make decisions in nonthreatening situations. For example, little harm is done if a student makes mistakes while in charge of classroom maintenance. On more important issues such as helping other students with their lessons, you can work closely with students to help guide them through the process. Small steps are taken in the beginning, and as the students learn to walk on their own, you can gradually relinquish input to empower your students in the decision-making process. When students begin to take ownership of the situation, they are more motivated to participate.

The successful teacher is one who can accurately perceive when it is necessary for him or her to direct and make decisions but can provide the freedom of decision making to the students when it is called for. The hardest part of this process is letting go of your control and entrusting students with responsibilities. When you do, you will see that students are capable of doing more than you thought they could and all of you will feel better about yourselves in the process.

Teacher's Corner: "Why Aren't My Students Motivated in Class?"

Ms. Foster was frustrated by the attitude of many of her students. They did not seem motivated in class. Each evening she took much of her work home. She diligently planned each lesson. Activity by activity, drill by drill, and strategy by strategy, each had a specific purpose. Before each class, she lectured to her students and gave an overview of the lesson and its purpose. She carefully explained the reason behind each activity, drill, or strategy. She thought that if the students knew the purpose, they would be more responsive to her demands. She thought, "How could my students not respect and appreciate me for all the work I'm doing? No other teacher in the school does as much as I do." But she also thought, "Why aren't they responding? How can they be so unmotivated?"

During classes, she was often frustrated and pleaded with her students to get motivated. Phrases like, "Come on, you're being lazy" or "You're not working very hard" or "I give up!" were repeated continuously throughout her classes. Choice words reflecting anger and frustration were also beginning to surface. Yet, the energy level never really rose. Ms. Foster's tolerance was reaching its limits.

Multiple Choice

If you were Ms. Foster which of the following would you do?

A. Continue designing activities, drills, and strategies and explain their purposes, and hope that the students will become motivated once they truly understand and appreciate your efforts.
B. Show your anger and frustration by yelling more.
C. Use some form of punishment to motivate the students.
D. Allow the students to have input into the lessons.

Response D is correct. Student motivation during class can be enhanced if students have input into the lessons. Allowing input provides a number of advantages:

- It forces the students to think critically about the class's specific needs.
- With input, the students will take greater ownership of the class. The greater the ownership, the greater the motivation to participate. It assures the teacher that the students know the basics behind the lessons because they are implementing them in class.
- The students grow and mature. They become more responsible, self-reliant, and self-disciplined.
- Working together builds teamwork between the students and the teacher.

Response A does not work. Ms. Foster has always planned and explained the lessons and the students were not responding. Why continue this strategy if it is not working?

Response B may work for a short time, but in the long run, screaming and yelling will only distance the teacher from the students, and soon the yelling will increase as the students begin to ignore the teacher.

Response C may also work for a short time, but in the long run, like screaming and yelling, punishment will distance the teacher from the students.

Delegation of Responsibility

How much should you participate with the students once you delegate responsibility to them? This depends on whether your presence will inhibit or facilitate the planning process. There may be some instances when you should step back or leave to allow students to solve the problem by themselves. At other times, you can contribute beneficial ideas. However, if you are delegating responsibility, you need to clearly indicate that you are merely a contributing member of the group rather than the leader.

Student Decisions

What if you do not like the decision that the students have made? A teacher is always held responsible for whatever decision the group makes. Therefore, you must be ready to accept whatever risk is involved when you delegate decision-making power to your students. However, you cannot give your students more freedom than your superiors have given you. Therefore, limitations must be set. To reverse a decision will only create distrust and disrespect and will send the message that the students are incapable. If a wrong decision is made, it becomes a wonderful opportunity for learning.

Culturally Sensitive Lesson Plans Increase Significance

Motivating students to learn and participate in the classroom is your job because most students do not usually come inherently motivated. Students usually wait for some kind of invitation or signal from you that indicates to them that they are welcome, that they belong, that they are capable of success, and that they are an important member of the class. The kind of invitation or signals received will often contribute to the motivational energies of the students.

The things most culturally diverse students know as a result of their experiences outside of school (home, community, and culture), are very different from the things a white teacher might expect them to know. As a consequence, what is presented in class must be culturally meaningful to minority students. If information is presented without cultural considerations, minority students may feel that their significance in the classroom is at best peripheral, or at worst an unwelcome intrusion. Students are motivated when materials are relevant to them and their culture or gender. When educators incorporate teaching materials that include the perspectives and the experiences of culturally diverse populations, minority students respond with greater enthusiasm. Love (1985) stated that "knowledge must have a special relationship with the learner if it is to be learned." Learning about one's culture within the concepts basic to each discipline reinforces the student's importance or significance.

Sleeter and Grant (1991) examined textbooks used in grades 1 through 8 and found the following:

- Whites still consistently dominate textbooks, although their margin of dominance varies.

- Whites still receive the most attention and dominate the story line and lists of accomplishments in most textbooks.

- Women and people of color are shown in a much more limited range of roles than are white males.

- Textbooks contain very little about contemporary race relations or the issues that most concern people of color and women.

- Textbooks continue to convey an image of harmony among different groups and contentment with the status quo.

Even though Sleeter and Grant found the inclusion of more women and people of color in current textbooks, they still continued to highlight the status of white males and failed to develop the depth and importance of women and people of color.

On the other side of this issue is the fact that many children from the macro-cultural come to school with preconceived negative attitudes toward people who are different from them (Lasker, 1970). As a consequence, you must work to change these negative attitudes and develop strategies that encourage positive attitudes about economic, cultural, and racial differences.

The curriculums in some schools do not always reflect a diverse society. Gordon, Miller, and Rollack (1990) noted that African-Americans and other students of color are asked to learn and relate to material that:

1. has not been often reproduced in their community or culture

2. is not presented from their perspective

3. tends to ignore their existence and often demeans their personal characteristics

4. may distort or misinterpret data

5. makes unwarranted generalizations that differences are deficits

A lack of cultural sensitivity in the curriculum creates an atmosphere where majority students may come to believe that they are superior to the opposite gender and other racial and ethnic groups. It denies students the opportunity to study and benefit from the knowledge, perspectives, and experiences of other cultures and groups.

Present day textbook authors have fortunately recognized the serious cultural gaps that existed in past textbooks which contributed to the ignorance, stereotyping, and underestimation of many ethnic minority groups and women. Within the past few decades publishers have become sensitive to cultural issues and as a result, have evaluated their textbooks, other learning materials, and lessons for bias. However, as a precaution, teachers should continue to evaluate textbooks and other learning materials. If gaps appear, you must supplement learning activities with additional materials to redress bias. An excellent activity is to have the students evaluate books for bias (see "A Checklist for Evaluation of Books and Materials" at the end of this chapter).

Any curriculum that diminishes a student's experiences and culture creates a mirror that does not reflect his or her aspirations and hopes. If the curriculum undermines the student's capacity for full intellectual development and their lives are not matters for serious attention or concern, this will hamper their professional success. Also, if limited views of minority students are overtly or subtly communicated by teachers, other students will experience a reinforcement of their own negative views about minority students, especially because persons of knowledge and status confirm such views. This, of course, hampers a student's ability to relate to minority students as equals and work with them in collaborative situations.

Banks and Banks (1995) developed the following four-level approach (the four levels are inverted and should be read from the bottom–up) to multicultural curriculum reform:

Level 4: The Action Approach. Students make decisions on important personal, social, and civic problems and take actions to help solve them.

Level 3: The Transformation Approach. The structure of the curriculum is changed to enable students to view concepts, issues, events, and themes from the perspectives of diverse ethnic and cultural groups.

Level 2: The Additive Approach. Content, concepts, lessons, and units are added to the curriculum without changing its structure.

Level 1: The Contributions Approach. Heroes, heroines, holidays, foods, and discrete cultural elements are celebrated occasionally.

In summary, given the extent to which many racial/ethnic cultural histories have been omitted or obscured in the curriculum, it would seem important to develop material that is more sensitive to the many racial/ethnic cultures by providing readings, insights, contributions, and ideas related to the many groups. This would counter, to a degree, the earlier errors. This would also introduce all students to knowledge and perspectives to which, in all likelihood, they have not been exposed.

SUMMARY OF MAJOR POINTS
IN CHAPTER 4

1. One of the most compelling motivations that any student has is the need to be accepted.

2. A teacher's acceptance of a student should be unconditional, not contingent on anything particular about the individual who is accepted.

3. Teachers can show they care about their students by:

- Taking them seriously
- Listening carefully to the students
- Letting them know that you care about them
- Touching students respectfully and appropriately
- Smiling at them
- Using simple hand gestures of approval
- Providing sincere encounters with each student
- Becoming sensitive to cultural terminology
- Developing activities to create acceptance among students
- Being sensitive to the pronunciation of names

| Class Discussion | CHAPTER 4 |

Note: Review Appendix E before facilitating this activity.

Putting Labels on Students
Time: 20 minutes (discussion not included)
Objective: To help the participant understand the damage that labeling can have on the development of the students.

Materials:

1. Sticky labels, such as computer mailing labels or index cards with tape. One label or card for each participant.
2. Each label will have a positive or negative descriptive word(s) on it, such as: learning disabled, shy, gifted, clumsy, teacher, forgetful, star student, class bully, HIV positive, teacher's pet, visually impaired, physically handicapped, emotionally disturbed, developmentally delayed, speech delayed, aggressive, out-spoken, stuck-up, English language learner, attention deficit disorder (ADD), attention deficit hyperactive disorder (ADHD), cheerleader, computer "geek," pretty, top athlete, and class leader.

Procedure: A label is placed on the backs of each participant. The participant, of course, does not know what is written on the label.

Tell the group that they are gathered in the gym and waiting for the bus to arrive to take them on an all-day field trip. While they are waiting they are to mill around responding to people's labels. (10–15 minutes)

Suggested Discussion Questions:

1. What were you feeling when people where talking to you?
2. Were you able to guess your label? What were some of the clues?
3. Did you find yourself changing your behavior in any way as people talked with you?
4. Do you think there are any "good" labels? Why?
5. In you own personal life, do you think you have labeled certain people?
6. If so, what can you do differently?
7. Do you think you have been labeled? Is their anything you can do to make people see you differently? How?
8. If not, what can you do?
9. What have you learned from this activity that you can apply to your future teaching philosophy and behavior?

- Preparing in advance to receive a new student, in particular, a child with a disability.

4. Some teachers find it difficult to completely accept students for who they are. Their personal biases affect their acceptance of them. It is essential that you be fair in your treatment of different students and not let your biases or prejudices interfere.

5. Students will develop perceptions of themselves that are based on how they think others see them.

6. The three factors (the teacher, the students, and the situation) will determine how much responsibility the teacher can give to the students.

7. Teachers need to find ways in which all students can contribute within the classroom structure.

8. All students need to feel that their participation makes a difference and that their existence and contributions to the classroom really matter.

Class Discussion   **CHAPTER 4**

Note: Review Appendix E before facilitating this activity.

Recognizing Uniqueness
Time: 20 minutes (discussion not included)
Objective: Participants learn to appreciate similarities and differences.

Materials:

1. A piece of fruit such as a banana, orange, or apple for each participant.
2. A basket to hold the fruit.
3. Place chairs in a circle.

Procedure:

1. Give one piece of fruit to each participant.
2. Ask each participant to study his or her fruit carefully for 30 seconds.
3. Ask each participant to describe one characteristic of his or her fruit. Urge the participants to use all of their senses. Each person will take turns making his or her observation. Go around the circle twice.
4. After sharing their observations, place the basket in the middle of the circle and ask the participants to put their fruit in the basket. Mix the fruit up.
5. Tell the participants to now retrieve their fruit. Wait until all fruit is retrieved.

Suggested Discussion Questions:

1. What did you learn from this experience?
2. Can what you learned from this experience be applied to people?
3. Which is more basic and primary—similarities or differences?
4. Although there are marks or blemishes on the fruit, they helped you identify it. What does this fact teach you about people?
5. Process more by asking participants what they learned about the long range effects of recognizing similarities and differences in people.

---

9. Successful schools have clear and high expectations and a high level of participation.

10. The teachers must help each student set and achieve worthwhile goals.

11. The process of setting goals includes the following:

   - Determine whose goal it is
   - Make sure the goal is attainable
   - Divide the goal into small achievable steps
   - Set realistic deadlines
   - Put the goal in writing

12. The curriculums in many schools do not reflect a diverse society.

13. Teachers can help students understand various cultures by having students study the overlapping values and ideas and differences of the various cultures.

14. When teachers incorporate teaching materials that include perspectives and the experiences of culturally diverse populations, multicultural students respond with greater enthusiasm.

Teacher's Corner: Observing Teacher's Physical Closeness and Appropriate Touching Behavior of Students

Concern: Do teachers validate students by standing close to them or do they keep them at a safe distance? Physical closeness for this observation is when the teacher stands at least within an arm's distance. Do teachers appropriately touch students to be helpful to the student or to affirm, encourage, and recognize them? This observation is to also determine the number of times the teacher appropriately touches students in the classroom

Directions for Observation

Observe a teacher for about one hour. The observer makes a slash mark in the appropriate PC (physical closeness box) by the student's name each time the teacher stands within an arm's distance of a student while presenting a lesson. A recognition is recorded.

1. When the teacher stands in a stationary position and within an arm's distance of the student.
2. When the teacher is approached by a student and stands within an arm's distance.
3. For each contact. If the teacher remains near or with one student for a long period of time, only one recognition is recorded. Duration of time is not recorded.
4. Each time the teacher leaves the students and returns, another recognition is recorded.

No recognition is recorded if the teacher merely walks by the student.

The observer makes a slash mark in the appropriate T box (touch) by the student's name each time the teacher appropriately touches a student.

Appropriate touch: When the teacher touches the student from the shoulder to the hand or a gentle tap on the back in a manner that reflects encouragement, helpfulness, recognition, acceptance, and so forth. Examples include shaking hands; a high five; a gentle touch on the back, shoulder, or elbow.

Inappropriate touch: Touching the student on the head is considered inappropriate touch for various cultural reasons. Some students may also perceive touching of the head as patronizing or condescending. Hugs, in many situations, are very appropriate. Hugs, however, are not normally perceived as appropriate in the classroom.

Note: No recognition is recorded if the teacher touches the student inappropriately or for disciplinary behavior, punishment, power, or some type of rejection.

Summary

The observation data is tallied to determine how often the teacher stands close to the student and which students are appropriately touched. Discuss the results of the observations.

Observation Sheet

NAME OF OBSERVER _____   DATE _____

NAME OF TEACHER _____   TIME _____

OBSERVATION: PHYSICAL CLOSENESS (PC)   CLASS _____
                 TOUCHING (T)

ETHNIC CODE: AF = AFRICAN AMERICAN
                  AS = ASIAN AMERICAN
                  HA = HISPANIC AMERICAN
                  NA = NATIVE AMERICAN
                  WA = WHITE AMERICAN
                  DS = DISABLED STUDENT
                  CP = POVERTY STUDENT

NAME	ETHNIC	GENDER	RECOGNITION CODE			
			PC	PC	PC	PC
			T	T	T	T

Teacher's Corner: A Checklist for Evaluation of Books and Materials

Sending the Right Messages to Our Students

Concern: Students are exposed to many different types of reading materials from comic books to textbooks with a variety of general magazines, novels, and non-fiction books in between. In addition, children receive many messages through television and movies. Many of the messages that our children receive, unfortunately, are false, misleading, inappropriate, and/or conflict with the philosophy and goals of our educational programs. You must, therefore, be conscious of the messages that come through your words and actions. You must also evaluate the messages inherent in the materials you provide in the classroom. You must carefully evaluate and select books that reflect messages that are consistent with the philosophy and goals of our educational programs.

Directions: Use this checklist to evaluate books in the classroom or school library.

Look for Messages in School Books

Evaluate the Characters

Yes	No	
__	__	Do the characters accurately reflect the personalities and lives of real people?
__	__	Is there realism in the way the characters act and react?
__	__	Is the language appropriate to the story?
__	__	Are characters stereotyped? Be especially aware of how minorities and gender roles are portrayed.
__	__	Do the characters change in positive and/or negative ways?
__	__	Do the characters resolve their own problems?
__	__	Do the character's display strengths and weaknesses?
__	__	Is their lifestyle represented fairly and respectfully?
__	__	Do the characters reflect moral and/or social values?

Situation or Plot

__	__	Do the characters have power over their own lives?
__	__	Is the environment within the story realistic?
__	__	Is the situation within the story realistic?
__	__	Are the outcomes within the story realistic?

Illustrations or Pictures

__	__	Do the illustrations depict ethnic, age, cultural, economic, ability, and sexual differences respectfully? (Illustrations can be humorous; but they must fit the context of the story line and be consistent in portrayal.)
__	__	Is the style of illustration appropriate to the story?
__	__	Are the characters illustrated in realistic and not stereotypical manner?

Message(s)

__	__	Are the underlying messages of the story respectful and truthful?
__	__	Are there hidden messages which are demeaning in any way or which reinforce stereotypes?

5

■

Motivation:
Feeling Capable

Presume not that I am the thing I was.

SHAKESPEARE

MAKING STUDENTS FEEL CAPABLE

Children and adults develop perceptions of themselves based on how they think others see them. Students will find in the eyes and attitudes of educators who teach them mirrors in which they discover and perceive themselves. How students perceive themselves through you will be a major factor in how they comprehend themselves in the classroom.

The student's self-image becomes internalized as the student tests himself or herself in the school environment. The student adopts attitudes of worthiness or worthlessness as he or she ventures through school with an eye on the teacher's reactions. It is easier for students to develop positive attitudes about themselves if they are with teachers who see them as competent, responsible, and worthwhile.

Individuals see themselves as they think others see them. The words and attitudes that you choose and the way you use them significantly contribute to a student's destiny. Words and attitudes have the power to lift up or put down. If you fill students with visions of incompetence, failure, and worthlessness the student will probably perform poorly. When students hear you call them "average," "different," or "lazy," they may not only think of themselves as average, clumsy, or lazy but behave in that manner as well. You can assist in forming a positive view by focusing on the student's capabilities. If you encourage and affirm a student's capabilities, the student will respond with greater confidence and maturity.

Your language and attitudes can have both positive and negative effects. On one hand, words can create barriers that block trust, confidence, performance, and communication. The absence of achievement is most often due to a genuine belief that one could never achieve at a high level. As significant adults in the lives of children, some teachers reflect attitudes or use words that undermine the student's self-confidence. Attitudes and words can make students feel inadequate, incapable, and destroy the positive beliefs that the students may have in themselves. It is a language of disrespect for others. It can be nasty, condescending, and harmful.

The job of motivating students to have greater aspirations in life and school is essentially the task of working on their self-images. Any time you find students reflecting indifference, negativity, and pessimism about their own abilities you have much work to do.

However, the language and attitudes of teachers can also have the opposite effect. Words can consistently affirm and validate young people by instilling a belief in their capabilities and potential. Words can be respectful, caring, encouraging, and not charged with negative emotions. Words can be positive.

Your most fundamental task is to provide a learning environment that fosters the students' perceptions of themselves as capable, significant, and accepted. Everyone knows that having a positive self-image is important, yet concerned and caring teachers often interact with students in such a way as to promote a lowered self-image. Many destructive words keep repeating themselves simply because the teacher does not know of better ways to deal with problems.

Barriers Constructed by Teachers
That Obstruct A Student's Success

Teachers sometimes set up their students for failure. They may do it unintentionally, but they do it just the same. The following paragraphs list some barriers that obstruct a student's success.

Maintaining Standards That Are Too Low Instead of allowing students to develop and test their strengths and abilities in a variety of ways, a teacher may confront them with his or her own prejudices, preconceptions, and beliefs. The teacher, because he or she lacks faith in the students' abilities or has unknown biases, sets his or her own standards by which the students must perform. Unfortunately, some teachers treat multicultural students as though they are incapable of learning because they have the mistaken belief that the student's culture and background is inferior and, therefore, reflects on the student's capabilities. As a consequence of this attitude, the teacher has low expectations of achievement for these students.

Too often teachers train students at the level at which they think the students are rather than at the level at which they could or might be. If teachers treat students as the teachers think they are, the students may stay that way. If it is the teacher's job to help students grow and change, then he or she must allow them to grow and change.

Making assumptions prevents growth and development. By assuming, we say, "What you were before is all I allow you to be now." Once a student is placed into low-ability groups in elementary school he or she is likely to continue in these tracks in middle school and junior high; in senior high the student is typically placed in non-college preparatory tracks (Oakes, 1988). Students in low tracks and ability groups do not improve their self-esteem. On the contrary, they experience a loss of self-esteem and a worsening of their attitudes toward school (Grossman, 1995). Fortunately, teachers and schools are making a critical move away from the deleterious effects of tracking and ability grouping, which Oakes and others have persuasively documented (O'Neil, 1992).

It seems more logical for a teacher to encourage students to find out what is possible than to make assumptions that may keep the students from reaching their potential. A teacher should examine what is possible today and build higher levels of confidence in his or her student's abilities as growing and changing individuals.

Garcia (1982) concluded that teacher expectations are more influenced by negative information about pupil characteristics than positive data. As a result:

1. Teachers who do not have high academic expectations for Latino students ask them low-level memory, recall, and convergent questions; do not praise or encourage them as often as Anglo students; use lower standards of judging the quality of their work; do not call on them as frequently; and feed them academic pablum.

2. Counselors who do not believe girls or ethnic minority students can master math and science skills do not schedule them into these classes.

3. Special purpose instruction for ethnic minorities tends to be remediation and for Anglo students it tends to be enrichment.

4. Presumed high-achieving Anglo students who do not live up to their expectations are described as underachievers. These attitudes and expectations cause wide disparities in how educators interact with Anglo and minority students in the day-to-day operations of schools and, thereby, perpetuate educational inequalities among them.

5. Schools use culturally biased tests and procedures used to diagnose student needs and to evaluate their performance. For instance, tests may require skills in scenarios about situations that are not relevant to the cultural backgrounds and life experiences of ethnic minorities. Thus, multicultural students are placed at a disadvantage because they may know the skill or subject matter but be unfamiliar with the contextual scenario.

6. Many ethnic minority students are "tracked" into the lower level academic groups which perpetuates the stereotypical image of an incapable ethnic minority student and reinforces the feeling of superiority of the majority group. This process also leads to isolating students along cultural, racial, or economic lines and thereby perpetuating in-school segregation.

In addition to Garcia's study, Simpson and Erickson (1983) reported that white teachers gave white male students more verbal and nonverbal praise while using more nonverbal criticisms toward African-American males. Sadker and Sadker (1985) also reported that teachers would accept incorrect answers from African-American students with a verbal "okay." As a result of this behavior, African-American students were denied useful information about the quality of their performance. Natriello, McDill, and Pallas (1990) reported that teachers have lower academic expectations of poor children. Lowered expectations frequently reinforce themselves and children will often internalize what the teacher believes.

In relation to gender issues, Campbell (1984) concluded that teachers give males more feedback and check their work more often. When males answered questions incorrectly, they were encouraged to try harder. When females answered incorrectly, they were praised for trying. Bossert (1981) reported that teachers called upon males to perform tasks that involved manual skills while females were more likely to be requested to conduct housekeeping chores and secretarial tasks. Fennema and Peterson (1986) reported that in high level math achievement male students were given more feedback than female students. Female students were given no feedback more often than male students.

Schools that establish high expectations for all students and give them the support necessary to achieve them have incredibly high rates of academic success. Rutter (1984) concluded that successful schools shared certain characteristics: an academic emphasis with high standards, teachers' clear expectations

"Academic" Success

high expectations & support

Schools that establish high expectations for all kids and give them the support necessary to achieve them have incredibly high rates of academic success.

and regulations, and a high level of student participation. Weinstein (1991) reported that expectations of teachers for their students have a large effect on academic achievement. Equally important, Rutter found that the number of problem behaviors experienced by students decreased over time in the successful schools and increased in the schools that had low expectations of their students. Low expectations decreases motivation and increases alienation that may lead to dropping out and the interrelated problems of drug abuse, violence, teenage pregnancy, and so on.

Expectations influence how students think and how they will approach a particular task. Howard and Hammond (1985, p. 20) reported:

> When people who are confident of doing well at a task are confronted with unexpected failure, they tend to attribute the failure to inadequate effort. The likely response to another encounter with the same or a similar task is to work harder. People who come into a task expecting to fail, on the other hand, attribute their failure to lack of ability. Once you admit to yourself, in effect, that "I don't have what it takes," you are not likely to approach the task again with great vigor.

Students with negative expectancies will lack confidence and the belief that they have the abilities to succeed. Students with positive expectancies will blame their failures on a lack of effort rather than the lack of ability, something they can rectify. Low expectancies can lead to a self-fulfilling prophecy of failure.

All students have multiple self-images that are constantly shifting between highly positive and fearfully negative. On one day they may feel quite capable as a mathematician; on the next day they may feel like a failure. Students cannot be stuck into specific slots or reduced to computerized data. Besides being unique, students are ever-changing entities. Just when you think you have them figured out, they surprise you by being better than what you imagined or even the opposite of what you imagined. Young students are not fixed pieces of computer software; they are dynamic, ever-changing, unique, and capable.

Evaluating a Student's Social Behaviors Based on Cultural Biases In addition to academic expectations, teachers must have realistic expectations of the students' emotional and social behaviors. Teachers mistakenly expect, demand, and require students, to think, behave, understand, speak, see, and do things as they do. Teachers need to respect their students and recognize that they are still children in the process of becoming adults. Youngsters are still searching for their identity, discovering themselves and sorting out their feelings about who they are. It is a very important time in their lives. Young students are going to make mistakes, act out, do things that are considered foolish or immature, speak out, and be influenced by their peers and culture. Teachers must recognize that young students are only doing their "job." It is their job to individualize and become independent and capable. Teachers must recognize and respect this process and provide any necessary support. An adult's unrealistic expectations produce impotence, frustration, hostility, and aggression in young people.

As a result of cultural biases, many minority students face greater difficulties. For example, minority students for whom educators have low expectations are suspected of dishonesty and cheating when they defy these expectations by performing well. In addition, school administrators who expect greater discipline problems from ethnic minorities tend to treat their rule infractions with harsher punishment.

What teachers must realize is that the student is not bad; only the behavior or performance is bad. In addition, it is possible that the negative assumption of the behavior based on biases of the teacher is at fault. A student is not "dumb" if he or she fails an exam. The performance on the test was bad, but things can be done to improve the results of future tests. Focus on test improvements, not on the student. Students will sense the distinction. Young students are neither good nor bad; however, what a teacher thinks makes it so. Students will become aware of the teacher's faith in them. It will give them added encouragement to overcome difficulties, which will seem less formidable to them now that they have been minimized.

Not Recognizing the Different Learning Styles Because there are very few homogeneous classrooms, all teachers must be prepared to use a variety of instructional practices, be aware of the limitations of various teaching strategies, and most importantly, recognize the distinctive learning styles of students, in particular, different racial and cultural groups. If teachers are not sensitive to the cultural backgrounds of their ethnic minority students, they doom many of them to failure. Morris (1978) defined cultural sensitivity as the ability to identify patterns and behaviors of minorities in schools.

Many teachers, unfortunately, have the mistaken belief that students will learn in the same manner as they do. If a teacher has a tendency to learn from the written word, he or she has a tendency to write a lot and have his or her students do a lot of reading. If a student, however, has a strong preference for auditory learning he or she may be at a disadvantage. Students gather information in a variety of ways. Some learn more efficiently through a visual modality, while others may learn by auditory or kinesthetic experiences. Teachers must become familiar with learning style research. Examples of two such research perspectives include Kolb's Learning Style Inventory (Kolb, 1984) and Ramirez and Castaneda (1974) who created a Behavior Rating Scale designed to evaluate whether students are field-sensitive or field-independent learners. This scale, in particular, is a useful tool to evaluate students from different ethnic groups and gender stereotypes.

Not only do teachers have a particular preference for a learning style—they tend to teach in the manner that they have been taught to learn. In addition, the culture in which the teacher was raised will have a significant influence on learning style. Students who share the same cultural background as the teacher will have a distinct advantage over others who do not share the same background.

Many of the instructional procedures used by schools originate from an Anglo-Western European orientation that significantly differs from the cultural values and experiences of many bicultural students. Teachers need to understand their own and their minority students' cultural values, attitudes, experiences, and behaviors that have a direct effect on the instructional process.

Ethnic minority students may fail, not because of a lack of mastery of the subject, but because of their unfamiliarity with format and style. As a consequence of this process, ethnic minority students are at a disadvantage from the start. While many minority students are struggling to translate their mastery of the subject into a testing style they are unaccustomed to, the majority students are busy demonstrating their knowledge of the content. Unfortunately, if teachers do not recognize this process, they will conclude that the ethnic minority student's failure is due totally to their failure to master the subject matter. Consequently, in order to judge the capabilities of all students fairly, a wide variety of carefully chosen methods and evaluations should be used so that no one single group consistently has the advantage over another.

Teachers must begin to develop strategies that meet the educational mission in ways that do not (1) totally compromise or ignore the cultural backgrounds, values, and experiences of the ethnic minority students, or (2) compromise the expectations of high academic standards. Educators must begin to seriously examine how they go about teaching skills and making information more relevant and effective in the daily lives of their minority students.

The following section briefly discusses some of the different learning styles. There is a great deal of literature concerning this subject and a comprehensive review of the literature is beyond the scope of this section. The purpose of this section is to only introduce the subject as a "barrier" to student success. *It is also important to recognize that specific learning styles are not unique to any particular group. There will be variation within and among different multicultural groups.*

African-Americans Schools generally cherish verbal learning (e.g., lecture, teacher-student discussion, question-answer) and written demonstrations of achievement. These styles, however, run counter to the performance styles of some African-American students and other ethnic minority groups. Many African-American children are exposed to high-energy, fast-paced home environments, where there is simultaneous variable stimulation (e.g., televisions and music playing simultaneously and people talking and moving in and about the home freely). Hence, low-energy, monolithic environments (as seen in many traditional schools) are less stimulating (Franklin, 1992).

Boykin (1982) demonstrated that African-American children engage in "high energy level" activities both in and out of the classroom. These activities were called "psychological behavioral verve." Thus, the African-American cultural socialization process emphasizes aural, verbal, and participatory learning rather than written performance. For some African-American students, the spoken language is the primary mode of communication, whereas schools tend to stress written communication. As a result, African-Americans generally tend to be much more proficient in demonstrating their abilities when they can talk about them rather than write about them.

Many African-American students tend to function better in less formal environments in which students and teachers work closely together to achieve common goals. In particular, on problem-solving situations as opposed to memorization of facts. In other words, the group process or collaborative learning is a preferred style of instruction (Gay, 1975). However, most academic activities in our schools are based upon competition and individual achievement. Tests in school, for example, are almost always individual rather than group exercises. The whole trend in education in recent years has focused on different modes of individualized instruction, such as computerized instruction, programmed texts, independent study projects, and learning stations. Even at school academic honor assemblies, the students are honored for their individual achievements. Very seldom are students honored for group efforts.

Hale (1978) has suggested that African-American students do not perform as well in school when they are required to learn independently; in particular, when using educational hardware. They may have a need for interaction with the teacher and their classmates because they often are accustomed to learning being associated with interpersonal interaction in the family.

Native-Americans Many Native-Americans are accustomed to observational or imitative learning in their home cultures—it is a process of doing. Children in the majority of Native-American families participate in most family and community affairs. In fact, children are revered and welcome to such occasions. It is not uncommon then, for children to accompany their parents to community meetings, bingo nights, or even their place of employment. In sharp contrast, a mainstream white teenager would "rather die" than to have to bring a younger sibling to a teenage gathering, but this would be acceptable to Native-American teenagers who do not generally exclude younger children. As a result of this constant and close proximity, the child has the opportunity to observe, evaluate, and then practice a multitude of situations and skills with a minimum of verbal preparation or interchange.

This observational and imitative style of learning, of course, contrasts sharply with the learning styles most often fostered in most mainstream American schools. Even though this style of learning is universal to all people, according to Scribner and Cole (1981), "observation is a very limited technique in the overwhelmingly linguistic environment of the school."

Native-American children are also raised in an environment where parents and community allow them much freedom and movement to explore, imitate, and discover. This way of raising children is in direct contrast to what is expected in schools. For example, many Native-American children enter school expecting freedom of movement, but encounter restrictive movement; they expect visual-spatial kinesthetic learning, but encounter verbal learning; and they expect "learn by doing" experiences, but receive indirect and vicarious learning. Pepper (1976) reported that Native-Americans learn faster when the teaching style uses the concrete approach that moves to the abstract from practice to theory, but most schools follow the Western European American model that moves from theory to practice.

In addition, many Native-Americans do not traditionally converse by asking each other questions in their day-to-day speech. This may stem from their cultural value of not interfering or intruding with another person's affairs. As a result, Native-American students do not like being involved in strategies that involve questioning. However, question asking is one of the dominant verbal strategies employed in most schools. As a result of cultural differences, Native-American children may not ask questions in class.

Thus, many Native-Americans find it difficult to transform their knowledge from one performance style to another. As a result, the format of written tests or activities may be more of a problem for them rather than the content and substance of the learning task.

Incorporating collaborative/cooperative learning, group projects, lessons that incorporate manipulative devices, experiments, practical as opposed to theoretical lessons, experiential activities, and informal settings that allow movement is conducive to Native-American learning style.

Mexican-Americans The Hispanic culture requires good students to be passive learners—to sit quietly at their desks, pay attention, learn what they are taught, and speak only when they are called upon. This is in contrast to Anglo educational methods which require students to show initiative and leadership, to volunteer questions and answers, and to question the opinions of others (Grossman, 1984). The Anglo "inquisition" style is highly hostile to the Mexican-American attitude of tolerance (Burger, 1972).

Group interactions and relationships are an important cultural behavior that supports the value of community togetherness. Thus, many Mexican-Americans tend to be involved in collective and collaborative efforts than individualized efforts, therefore, Mexican-American students attempt to work together on tasks. Kagan, Zahn, and Gealy (1977) stated, "If Mexican-American children are more group- or family-oriented, they may be discriminated against by educational and psychotherapeutic practices predicated upon strong individualistic motivation. Understanding the social motive development of Mexican-Americans may provide a basis from more responsive public institutions." This preference, of course, is quite different from the competitive and individualistic classrooms in mainstream American schools.

Mexican-American students also tend to speak out less in formal classroom settings. Cortes (1978) stated that Mexican-American children are traditionally reared with the belief that to be well-educated, in the family sense, is to show courtesy to others, especially to show deference to elder members of the family, priests, and teachers. As a result, teachers must not be too quick to label this behavior as a result of poor language skills or disinterest and lack of attention.

Cortes (1978) suggests that the use of group motivation and rewards, the expansion of cooperative class activities, and the facilitation of a strong personal relationship with the teacher be incorporated to help meet the learning style needs of Mexican-American students.

In summary, if one is aware of the different learning styles and is willing to make adjustments in delivery of the lessons to accommodate these styles, all students will achieve more. This process does not mean that a teacher is to discard the things that he or she has been doing, but it means adding to and making adjustments to help all students stretch and grow in a variety of ways.

Teachers must also avoid falling into the trap of believing that ethnic minority or majority students are limited in the way they learn. For example, it is wrong to think that African-American students can only learn orally as opposed to visually, or Native-Americans can learn only visually and are incapable of learning verbally. By making this assumption another racial stereotype is created. What is being suggested is that teachers need to build on the students' strengths, but also to encourage students to engage in activities that are less preferable so that they can explore and gain strength in all areas.

Criticizing or "Dumping On" Students When They Are Already Down Criticism is closely related to the behavior of expecting. When a student fails to live up to the teacher's expectations or standards, he or she will often be criticized for that failure. Criticism contributes to lowered self-images. The more criticism students receive, the more likely they will be to avoid doing the things that engender that criticism. Such statements as "You will never be good at math" or "That's the second time you've failed to turn in your homework— I guess you'll never be responsible" are the tools that students use to sculpture a poor self-image. Teachers often believe that they are providing help to their students when they constantly correct and criticize them, assuming the student will grow from these negative remarks. There are other ways to help encourage and motivate students to a more effective performance. Criticism is the least effective and perhaps the most damaging of all the available techniques.

The language of criticism includes such statements as "Why don't you ever . . .?" "How many times do I have to tell you?" and "When will you ever grow up?" Teachers must realize that a young student's view of the world is different from an adult's view of the world. Teachers are faulting the student for not seeing what the teachers see. Criticizing responses are based on disrespect and will ultimately lead students to failure. Ridicule, put-downs, blaming, fault-finding, comparing, and labeling are also common. Messages that judge or criticize will make students feel inadequate and unworthy. These messages will begin to chip away at the student's confidence, potential, and abilities. Students will often respond to these messages with defensiveness, anger, and withdrawal because they need to protect their self-images.

The more teachers rely on external criticism, the greater the chance that the student will internalize these words. Before long, the student will create a self-image based on self-criticism. Nobody enjoys being criticized. Teachers should not build on weakness—only on strength. Unfortunately, some teachers spend too much of their time watching to see what their students are doing wrong and criticizing them for it instead of finding what is right and building on those strengths. As Dreikurs (1964) stated, "anyone who stops to think will realize that we really do follow our noses. If our nose points to mistakes, we arrive just there. If we center our children's attention upon what they do well, express our confidence in their ability, and give them encouragement, the mistakes and faults may die from a lack of feeding."

Teachers seem to live in a sort of fear that their students will learn bad habits and do things the wrong way. They watch their students constantly and try to prevent mistakes. They constantly correct and criticize. Such an approach shows a lack of faith in the students. It is discouraging and sometimes humiliating. With a constant emphasis on the negative, the student loses the energy to progress toward achievement.

When students are constantly corrected and criticized, they may get the feeling that they are always wrong and become very fearful of making mistakes. This fear may cause many students to lose their ability to function and may even cause them to give up in despair.

In addition to criticism, teachers often resort to verbally attacking their students with put-downs or name-calling. A put-down is a humiliating remark or degrading gesture directed at some aspect of one's behavior or action. How students deal with put-downs makes a statement about their self-concepts and self-esteems. The sad part is that if they accept the negative remark, their self-perception is going to suffer and affect their ability to succeed. In reality, disparaging remarks do not really reflect the students' inferiority or inadequacy; they reflect the low self-esteem and poor self-image of the teacher who makes the remark. Teachers who make disparaging remarks are reflecting their own unhappiness. They are trying to feel better by feeling superior to the student.

Recognition and encouragement are powerful tools. Encourage and recognize students for attempting a task, even if it was unsuccessful, and acknowledge them for taking the risks. Using recognition and encouragement creates an environment in which students know they are being supported for their efforts.

Talking Too Much and Not Allowing the Students to Discover Useful Explanations for Themselves Teachers who play the "know-it-all" role try to show their students that they have traveled life's roads for a long time and have accumulated most of the answers. Consequently, they lecture, advise, and make appeals to the students' reason. They try to show how superior they themselves are. Though lecturing is a legitimate function of the teacher-student relationship, students regard them as illegitimate at times. Teachers must try to become aware of when "logic and facts" begin to evoke defensiveness and resentment.

Lecturing is the most widely used teaching method, but it is also one of the least effective. It is an excellent example of one-way communication. The teacher is the only one who is active. The only indication a teacher receives of student understanding is nonverbal. The teacher cannot be sure that the students understand. It is also boring; it allows for no interaction. It does not allow the student to disagree or agree with expressed viewpoints, and, most importantly, it does not require the student to take any responsibility for learning.

Too often, teachers step in and explain things instead of helping students to discover the meaning of an event for themselves. Rowe (1986) reported that teachers seldom allow much time for a student to reply to a question. The average wait time is less than one second. After the second, the teacher will usually respond with the answer. When additional time is given (3 to 5 seconds) the quality of the reply, as well as the number of students who become involved, increases.

Some teachers even mistakenly believe that it is their job to explain everything before anything happens and more frequently after something happens. Teachers, in the role of the "know-it-all" or in the name of expediency, will step in all too quickly and explain to the students something that the students have not yet experienced. When a student makes a mistake in class, the teacher feels he or she must explain what happened. However, truly effective teachers work with students to help them develop useful explanations for themselves. If a student can figure it out by himself or herself, the teacher can be assured that he or she really understood what happened. Further growth can then occur. The student will become more independent and confident in his or her decision making when new situations arise.

Teachers often become frustrated because a student keeps on making the same mistake over and over. Each time the mistake is made, the teacher explains what happened, why it happened, and what can be done to fix it. By stepping in too quickly, teachers prevent students from thinking through the occurrence and learning from it.

Reflection on one's experience is a far more effective teacher than teachers could ever be. A teacher can help students to internalize the learning by helping them to reflect on the experiences that occurred. It is a process of understanding what happened, why it happened, and how one can learn from it. Instead of quickly explaining and lecturing, Glenn and Nelson (1989) suggest that one may ask thoughtful questions such as "What do you think happened?" "What do you think caused that to happen?" and "How could you do it differently the next time?"

This process conveys the message that the student is capable of developing good judgment, mastering situations, and gaining understanding. As a result of

Reflection on one's experience is a far more effective teacher than teachers could ever be.

this process, a mistake, if budgeted right, can be investment spending for the future. By explaining and lecturing all the time, teachers slow the development of the student's judgmental skills as well as his or her sense of feeling capable and competent. Of course, the teacher must provide an evaluation when it is clear that the student does not know what is correct or incorrect. If the behavior or performance is correct, the teacher should recognize and acknowledge the student for it and tell the student what he or she liked about it.

Excessive Directing For the sake of efficiency, expediency, and time, teachers find it easiest to direct, order, or command students to do things. When teachers step in too quickly and direct, they produce hostility and resistance and, most importantly, block communication. These messages tell a student that his or her feelings or needs are not important and he or she must comply with what the teacher wants (e.g., "I don't care if you have to go to the bathroom; wait until you're excused," or "Stop complaining. You are the biggest baby in the classroom," or "I know what's best for you, so do it now!"). Being directed makes people feel impotent and frustrated. Ordering or directing also implies that the other student's judgment or knowledge is inferior to the teacher's.

Unfortunately, some teachers add to their directing threats of punishment for refusal to comply (e.g., "Stop complaining or I'll give you something to really complain about."). These messages evoke fear and hostility and make the student feel fearful and submissive. Some students will respond to threats by doing something they have just been warned not to do, just to see whether the consequences promised by the teacher will materialize.

In general, the more directive teachers are, the more rebellious and resistant students become. In addition, when teachers are constantly directing, students will respond by doing nothing at all or less than what was expected. A very authoritative high school teacher once said that he directed his students to clean the classroom before leaving for the day. Most of the students tried to leave and did nothing to help. The teacher then proceeded to scream at the students and hovered over them as they were forced to clean the classroom. As a matter of defense, the coerced students reverted to passive-aggressive behavior by leaving a few items out to irritate the teacher.

If instead of being directed, students are invited or encouraged to assist or contribute, they are generally more willing to cooperate. After learning a different behavioral model, that same teacher discussed in the preceding paragraph was faced with a similar situation, but this time he said, "I would appreciate anything you could do to help me clean-up the classroom before we leave." Most of the students cooperated and picked up things, straightened the chairs, and cleaned the chalkboard. Some even asked if there was anything else they could do. By inviting their contribution, the teacher encouraged their participation and promoted extra effort.

Not Accepting the Diversity of Language or Dialect As the cultural mosaic in the United States continually evolves, it brings with it a rich diversity of languages and dialects. Within each community, different languages such as Spanish, Vietnamese, Chinese, French, Russian, German, and many others can be frequently heard. In addition, over 200 Native-American languages have continued to survive in America. Banks and Banks (1993) state "that diversity of language can enrich the lives of those who use such languages and the lives of those privileged to come into contact with it."

As a result of the diversity in the United States, schools are challenged with working with children who are limited in their ability to communicate in standard English. It has been estimated that over 80 languages are represented in the Los Angeles student population.

The complexity of the situation is further enhanced with the various indigenous dialects of English, such as pidgin, Creole, Gullah, and Black English that various populations living within the United States bring into the classroom. The dialects are briefly defined as follows:

- *Pidgin English* is a simplified form of English that evolves as new immigrants from different language backgrounds form new communities and begin to communicate with each other.

- *Creole* is the adoption of a pidgin as the accepted language of the community. Examples of Creole include such dialects as Louisiana French Creole and Hawaiian Creole (a combination of Hawaiian, Japanese, Chinese, Portuguese, English, and Ilocano).

- *Gullah* is an English and West African dialect spoken in North and South Carolina, Georgia, and the northern portion of Florida.

- *Black English or ebonics* is spoken by a large segment of the African-American population. Unlike Gullah and Creole, Black English has spread throughout the United States.

These different dialects are not accepted in most schools and are usually considered inferior to standard English, although each of these dialects has an internal linguistic infrastructure and a set of grammar rules just as any other language does. Schools have historically attempted to eliminate or discourage the use of the community dialect in the classroom. Many African-Americans, in particular, have suffered the negative consequences of this action because schools have singled out their nonstandard communication patterns as an important reason for academic failures. No research supports this premise. However, if teachers support this premise, they will not affirm these dialects because they believe these dialects will perpetuate failure.

Children who communicate in a different dialect may be Standard English deficient, but they are not language deficient. They are simply linguistically different, but they are not deficient. What contributes to failure is that teaching practices are usually not linguistically supportive and language becomes a source of inequity for students who are labeled as deficient. This is not an argument for or against use of different dialects within the school system nor the role of ESL (English as a Secondary Language) programs, because there is a great deal of debate on these issues. It is, however, important for teachers to work with students without demeaning the dialect. To deny the language is to deny the culture and to deny the culture is to deny the student.

Helping Students with Disabilities

Students with disabilities, like other students, must learn to trust themselves and their abilities to achieve success. They must trust their ability to make choices and to relate to others. A great deal of a student's success will depend on you. The degree of confidence a student with a disability shows in the classroom is related to the amount of confidence you and his or her classmates have in him or her. The barriers that were discussed earlier in the chapter apply to all students, including students with disabilities. The barriers discussed in the following paragraphs also apply to all students, but special reference is made to student with disabilities.

When students with disabilities are expected to do certain things, the implied message is, "The teacher would not expect something of me if I really could not do it. I must be capable of meeting the teacher's expectations." Your trust and confidence in your student will become the trust and confidence in himself or herself. If you pity your student, if you are afraid he or she cannot succeed, he or she will probably feel pitiful and afraid to try. A summary of suggestions (Pearlman & Scott, 1981) to help students with disabilities follows:

Do not be physically overprotective. Encourage your student to try whatever he or she feels capable of doing and whatever you feel he or she may be able to do. Almost every school has one or more success stories of students with disabilities who achieved beyond what was expected. To cite just a few examples of people who have been given the opportunity to try, there are football teams, ski clubs, gymnastic teams, and wrestling teams with members who only have one leg or arm. Students who are blind, or visually or hearing impaired, have participated on bowling, golf, and martial arts teams. Many have gone on to become champions. In addition, each year the Special Olympics is a success story for every child who participates.

Time-out: Stroking Yourself

Who is your biggest critic? You probably are. When you make a mistake or do something stupid, do you start an internal monologue of criticism? If you do, you need to turn the internal criticism into internal stroking. You already know that you can tear yourself down; you also have the ability to build yourself back up.

Internal stroking helps to develop a loving and positive attitude toward yourself. It means that you strive to see the best in yourself and to like yourself. If you do not like yourself, others probably will not like you either.

Part 1

Draw a line down the middle of a piece of paper. On the left side, write down all of the negative thoughts that you had about yourself today. Focus on statements such as:

"How could I be so stupid?"

"I look like a slob."

"How could I have forgotten? What a dummy!"

"Why did I say that? I can be so critical!"

Part 2

After recording your negative thoughts, take a deep breath and relax. Put your pencil away and close your eyes for a moment.

After a moment or two, slowly open your eyes, pick up your pencil and on the right side of the paper write positive replies to the criticisms you recorded on the left side. Create a dialogue between the two sides:

"How could I be so stupid?"

"I'm not stupid. I just made an honest mistake. I apologized and did what I had to do to correct it. No one is perfect. I can handle this, and I can forgive myself."

"I look like a slob."

"No I don't. I just got a little stressed today. I think I'll wear that new shirt tomorrow. People will take notice."

"How could I have forgotten? What a dummy!"

"I'm no dummy. Things were just too hectic this morning. Next time I'll plan ahead a little better and put what I need to bring in my briefcase the night before."

"Why did I say that? I can be so critical!"

"I mean well and don't intentionally try to hurt people's feelings. The next time I'm going to take a deep breath and focus on the positive things."

Overcoming your critic is not easy. Don't get discouraged. It takes time. After all, your critical voice has probably been with you for years. But the more loving strokes you give yourself, the greater chance you will have of overcoming your critics.

Do not be mentally overprotective. Do not solve problems, provide answers, or make any choices for your student if he or she is capable of doing so. Allow extra time if he or she needs it to deliberate. Do not speak for the student. Give him or her every chance to communicate with others even if he or she has difficulty being understood. Ask the student's opinion when appropriate. Provide mental challenges in which you believe he or she can experience success. Do not work down to his or her level, but encourage him or her to rise to the challenge.

Do not be emotionally overprotective. A student with disabilities must deal with many social situations to maintain self-respect and confidence. He or she must also be able to deal with his or her own feelings. If you feel sorry for the student, he or she will no doubt begin to feel sorry for himself or herself. Trust him or her not only to respond to others, but also to handle the emotions such encounters elicit. Words of encouragement, not pity, are needed. Also, do not interfere in your student's disagreements. Allow him or her to handle his or her own problems with others. Whether he or she is emotionally mature or immature for his or her age, the student will deal on the level where he or she is able to cope and others will learn to adapt and relate to him or her.

If the student is a victim of remarks, stares, and/or pity, make certain insofar as possible, that he or she understands that the problem belongs to those who exhibit such behavior and not to him or her. A simple explanation about the lack of education and understanding of others should alleviate some discomfort. If he or she is unable to deal directly with others' inappropriate responses to his or her disability, you may want to deal with it yourself. If, however, he or she is capable of dealing with it, do not deny the student the chance to develop greater self-respect. Allow the student to deal with it himself or herself.

STRUCTURE FOR SUCCESS
RATHER THAN FAILURE

The absence of achievement is most often due to a genuine belief that one could never achieve at a high level. Consequently, the job of motivating students to have greater aspirations in school is essentially the task of working on their self-perceptions. Any place where you find negativity, pessimism, or indifference you have an assignment for self-perception improvement to work on. Here are some ways to help students succeed:

1. Adjust the degree of challenge or difficulty of a skill according to the student's present ability.
2. Make certain that students are both physically and mentally prepared before moving on to new skills.
3. Structure the physical and emotional environment so that it is organized and supportive.
4. Give students plenty of time to practice before they move on to new skills.
5. Help students establish specific and achievable goals for improvement.
6. Schedule specific time blocks that allow the students to take their time or work at their own pace.
7. When students reach physical or mental blocks to improving, go the extra mile and provide the needed help.
8. Prepare students for unexpected situations that may catch them off guard by having them practice various situations that they may unexpectedly encounter.

9. Let students know that it is okay to fail and that failure can be a wonderful opportunity for learning.

10. Maintain daily or ritual routines.

In addition to the above recommendations, teachers can increase success by applying a variety of instructional techniques that can enhance the success of students.

Instruction Strategies That Promote Success, Not Failure

Following are a few suggested strategies that can help promote success in healthy classrooms. This list is not comprehensive.

1. *Grouping children on a heterogeneous basis as opposed to ability grouping and tracking.* The detrimental effects of tracking and the low quality of instruction associated with low-ability groups is well-documented. Heterogeneous grouping means having high, middle, and low ability students of different genders, races, and ethnic groups working together for a common purpose.

2. *"Assigning competence" to low-status students.* Teachers assign competence by observing students while they are working on a variety of tasks or assignments. The teacher searches for strengths or special abilities in each student such as art, athleticism, dexterity, computer operation, or others. The teacher then publicly focuses the remainder of the student's attention on those special abilities. This often motivates low-status or poverty students to want to participate more.

3. *Using a variety of assessments to evaluate student achievement.* Garcia (1982) reports that standardized testing tends to favor middle-class white students. As a result, Banks and Banks (1993) reported that academic achievement level scores for African-American, Hispanic-American, and Native-American students are lower than whites. Even though mathematics and reading scores on the SATs have improved significantly over the last 20 years, they are still lower than white student scores. According to Garcia, one of the contributing reasons for this discrepancy is that ethnic minority students are usually asked lower-level questions because teachers have lower expectations for certain minority students. Teachers, of course, should rely on a variety of methods for evaluating students. They should include written and oral tests, student group and individual projects, observations, and group and individual student reports. They should also test at a variety of levels—recall, comprehension, application, analysis, synthesis, and evaluation.

4. *Using a variety of proven instructional cooperative learning strategies.* Cooperative learning is a pedagogy that provides personal power and group support. Each student is responsible not only for his or her learning, but for other group members' learning as well. Implicit in this strategy is that cooperative learning is democratic, it requires students to take responsibility for themselves and others, and heterogeneity and diversity are valued.

SUMMARY OF MAJOR POINTS
IN CHAPTER 5

1. The teacher's words can consistently affirm and validate the students by instilling a belief in their capabilities and potential.

2. Barriers that condemn students to failure include:

   - Maintaining standards that are too low.
   - Evaluating the students' social behavior according to adult standards or evaluations based on expectations that have not yet been achieved.
   - Not recognizing the different learning styles of students.
   - Criticizing or "dumping on" students when they are already down.
   - Talking too much and not allowing the students to discover useful explanations for themselves.
   - Excessive directing.
   - Not accepting the diversity of language.

3. Teachers can help students with disabilities become capable by not being physically, mentally, and emotionally overprotective.

4. Teachers can structure students for success rather than failure.

5. Teachers can supply instructional strategies that promote success, not failure.

Class Discussion	CHAPTER 5

Note: Review Appendix E before facilitating this activity.

Relabeling: Turning Positives into Negatives
Time: 15–20 minutes (discussion not included)
Objective: To help participants recognize that the negative views that they hold about certain people can also be seen as positive traits if one is willing to look past their bias and see the behavior from another view.
Materials: A copy of the "Relabeling" exercise

Procedure:

1. Distribute "Relabeling" exercise and ask participants to read section A.
2. Ask participants to think about individuals that they believe have negative behaviors and/or traits and list them. (5 minutes)
3. After the list is completed ask the participants to determine if the listed behavior or trait is really their problem and not the other person's. For example, is the thing you listed a matter of your own personal taste?
4. Next, ask the participants to study the listed behaviors and ask them to reevaluate the list and label them in a more positive view. (5 minutes)
5. If the participants cannot relabel the behaviors, ask them to list them on the blackboard.
6. Have the rest of the participants make suggestions for the traits that are listed on the blackboard. (2–10 minutes)
7. Gather all participants together.

Suggested Discussion Questions:

1. What did you learn about yourself?
2. What were you thinking during the experience?
3. Did you have trouble relabeling? Why?
4. What will you start or stop doing after this experience?

Relabeling*

Section A

A PERSON WHO…	COULD BE CALLED…	OR COULD BE CALLED…
changes his or her mind a lot	wishy-washy	flexible
isn't orderly	sloppy, piggish	spontaneous
believes what others say	gullible	trusting
takes risks	impulsive	brave

Section B

List some negative behaviors or traits of individuals that you know, but do not list their names.

Negative Behaviors:

1. _____

2. _____

3. _____

4. _____

What are the negative labels that you have given each of these behaviors:

1. _____

2. _____

3. _____

4. _____

Relabel the behaviors with positive labels:

1. _____

2. _____

3. _____

4. _____

Class Discussion   CHAPTER 5

Note: Review Appendix E before facilitating this activity.

Goal Setting Exercise
Time: 15 minutes (discussion not included)
Objective: To help participants set goals for themselves.
Materials: A copy of the "Goal Setting Plan" for each participant.

Procedure:

1. Distribute a copy of the "Goal Setting Plan" to each participant.
2. Explain the difference between a long-term (general) goal and a short-term (measurable) goal and that the short-term goal is the basic action plan that is going to help achieve the long-term goal.
3. Explain: Research has indicated that specific small daily goals or specific action plans (I will do my math homework every evening) are more effective than general long-term goals (I will improve in math this year).

   More examples:

   - Long-range goal: I will get better at my backhand.

   - Short-range goal: I will practice my backhand drills for 30 minutes at every practice.
   - Long-range goal: I will lose some weight this year.
   - Short-range goal: I will complete a daily food diary each day for the next two weeks.
   - Long-range goal: I will not be tardy again.
   - Short-range goal: I will wake up 15 minutes earlier each morning for the next two weeks.
   - Long-range goal: I will improve my social skills.
   - Short-range goal: I will talk with my friends during our daily lunch periods.

4. Have the participants fill out parts A and B of the goal setting plan. (5 minutes)
5. After parts A and B are completed, explain that short-range goals must be reasonably flexible because potential barriers can keep the best plans from being accomplished. For example, how do you exercise when it rains or the gym is closed for repairs?

(Continued)

Class Discussion   (*Continued*)

6. Have participants fill out part C of their goal setting plan. (5 minutes)
7. Have participants get a witness signature.
8. Gather everyone together for group discussion.

Suggested Discussion Questions:

1. What did you learn from this experience?
2. Do you think a teacher should help each student set goals for the school year? Why?

3. Do you think a teacher should set goals and share them with his or her students? Why?
4. Do you think students should periodically give themselves rewards as they accomplish the short-term goals? Why?
5. If so, what kinds of rewards do you want to give yourself for achieving your short-term goals?

Name: _____

Date: _____

Date of beginning action plan(s) _____

Date long range goal will be accomplished _____

Witnessed by _____
                              (Signature)

Goal-Setting Plan

A. Long-Range Goal:

_____

_____

B. List one or two short-term goals (action plans) to help achieve the long-range goal:

1. _____

   _____

2. _____

   _____

C. Keep your goals reasonably flexible. Think about potential barriers that can affect your action plan.

Barriers   *Strategies for Overcoming Barriers*

_____   _____

_____   _____

_____   _____

Class Discussion	CHAPTER 5

Note: Review Appendix E before facilitating this activity.

Learning from Mistakes
Time: 20 minutes (discussion not included)
Objective: To help participants understand that mistakes provide opportunities for learning.
Comment: Teachers usually mean well when they try to motivate students to do better by making them feel bad about their mistakes. However, we fail to check out the results of our good intentions. When we see the fallacy of our misguided intentions, we are then open to see with a new perspective how empowering it is to see mistakes as wonderful opportunities to learn.

Materials: "Mistakes Interview Form" for each participant.

Procedure:

1. Participants pair up and interview each other using the "Mistakes Interview Form" (allow five minutes for each partner).
2. After interview, discuss the following questions with the total group.

Suggested Discussion Questions:

1. What insights did you gain from participating in this activity?
2. Are you willing to make some new decisions about mistakes?
3. What are they?

Mistakes Interview Form

1. Think of a time during your academic career when you made a mistake and your teacher was supportive and encouraging. (If you can't think of an academic experience, use any experience from your school experiences and think how supportive and encouraging your coach, advisor, counselor, etc., were.)

   - What mistake did you make?
   - What was the result of what you did?
   - What did your teacher do to support or encourage you?

2. Think of a time when you made a mistake and your teacher was not supportive or encouraging, but punitive or verbally abusive. (If you can't think of an academic experience, use any experience from your school experiences and think how supportive and encouraging your coach, advisor, counselor, etc., were.)

   - What mistake did you make?
   - What was the result of what you did?
   - What did your teacher do to punish or verbally abuse you?

3. How have you changed from these experiences?

Teacher's Corner: Do Teachers Ask Certain Students Lower-Level Questions in the Academic Process?

Concern: Do teachers ask certain students lower-level questions and other students higher-level ones? The levels are based on Benjamin Bloom's Taxonomy of Educational Objectives (1956)

Part 1. Types of Questions

Directions for Observation

Observe a teacher for about one hour.
A. The observer makes a slash mark by the LQ box (lower-level question) by the student's name each time the teacher asks a student a lower-level question in an academic lesson.

Lower Level   *Cognitive Process*

Level 1: Knowledge recalling factual information
Example: Can you name three different cultural groups that are classified as Asian-Americans?

Level 2: Comprehension using information
Example: What is the difference between Native-Americans and Native Alaskans?

Level 3: Application applying principles
Example: If Ray has 10 feet of lumber, how many 3-foot boards can he make?

B. The observer makes a slash mark by the HQ box (higher-level question) by the student's name each time the teacher asks a student a higher-level question in an academic lesson.

Level 4: Analysis: Explaining relationships or making inferences
Example: Why do you think people from other cultures want to move to the United States?

Level 5: Synthesis: Making predictions
Example: What do you think would happen if the affirmative action law is repealed?

Level 6: Evaluation: Making judgments or stating opinions
Example: What do you think about Proposition 187?

Part 2
Concern: Do teachers dignify student responses with analytical feedback?
A. The observer makes a slash mark in the BA box (brief affirmation) by the student's name each time the teacher responds to an answer with a brief affirmation. Examples of brief affirmations are "yes," "no," "that's right," "okay."

B. The observer makes a slash mark in the FA box (focused affirmation) by the student's name each time the teacher responds to an answer with a focused affirmation. Examples of focused affirmations are listed below:

1. Reflecting back the student's ideas.
2. Getting students to consider alternatives.
3. Seeking clarification.
4. Assisting, hinting, or prompting the student with the answer.
5. Holding the student accountable for the answer by letting the student know that you will ask him or her at a later time.
6. Dignifying an incorrect response by giving a question for which the response would have been correct. For example, "John Steinbeck would have been the correct answer if I asked you who wrote the *Grapes of Wrath*."

Summary
The observation data is tallied to determine which students are recognized and listened to and which are not. Discuss the results of the observations.

Observation Sheet

NAME OF OBSERVER _____   DATE _____

NAME OF TEACHER _____   TIME _____

OBSERVATION: LOWER LEVEL QUESTION (LL)   CLASS _____
              HIGHER LEVEL QUESTION (HL)
              BRIEF AFFIRMATION (BA)
              FOCUSED AFFIRMATION (FA)

ETHNIC CODE: AF = AFRICAN AMERICAN
              AS = ASIAN AMERICAN
              HA = HISPANIC AMERICAN
              NA = NATIVE AMERICAN
              WA = WHITE AMERICAN
              DS = DISABLED STUDENT
              PC = POVERTY STUDENT

NAME	ETHNIC	GENDER	RECOGNITION CODE					
			LL	HL	LL	HL	LL	HL
			BA	FA	BA	FA	BA	FA

6

■

Motivation:
Health and Safety

It is better to know the patient that has the
disease than the disease that has the patient.

WILLIAM OSLER

Children must be safe and healthy to be able to learn and they must learn how to be safe and healthy to assure their optimal health. Millions of infants and children, unfortunately, live in unsafe and threatening environments and suffer from poor health. These factors leave them vulnerable to physical and learning disabilities and long-term problems, such as illiteracy, failure in school, and incarceration as juveniles (Project TEACH, 1993). The health and learning ability of a child are inextricably connected.

Childhood is a critical time of development. This is no less true for the development of good health than it is for social, educational, emotional, and moral development. It may be easier to prevent the initiation of some behaviors, such as smoking and alcohol and drug use, than to intervene once such behaviors are established. Likewise, it may be easier to establish healthful habits, such as those related to hygiene and dietary and physical activity patterns, during childhood than later in life (U.S. Department of Health and Human Services, 1990). This chapter focuses on the following issues:

1. Health problems in the twenty-first century
2. Youth health problems
3. Minority health problems
4. School health and food services
5. Physical and emotional safety in the classroom

Education, safety, and health are interrelated. Children whose lives are touched by violence, hunger, substance abuse, early pregnancy, depression, or hopelessness are not healthy children. Children who are unhealthy are children whose learning is impaired. Not only can education contribute to improving health, but also, conversely, a child's health status is a major determinant in educational achievement. In order to improve academic achievement, schools and other institutions must devote more attention to the health and safety of students (Project TEACH, 1993).

The greatest threats to health are "social morbidities." National statistics reflect the increasing impact of health problems that are largely preventable. Many of these problems are strongly influenced by social environment and/or specific behaviors, many of which are established during youth and extend into adulthood (Project TEACH, 1993).

The health and learning ability of a
child are inextricably connected.

HEALTH CONCERNS OF THE
TWENTY-FIRST CENTURY

The health of our nation is of particular interest to the federal government
because its *Healthy People 2000: National Health Promotion and Disease Prevention
Objectives* was designed to significantly improve the nation's health in the
twenty-first century. The United States Public Health Service has set many
health-related goals for the United States. Some of its goals are to reduce mortality and morbidity rates from various diseases and infections; such as heart disease, cancer, and sexually transmitted infections; reduce legal and illegal drug
use; reduce homicides, accidents, obesity, and teenage pregnancies; and improve
the personal quality of life for every individual. In general, the purpose was to
help Americans live longer and better lives by receiving better health services
and practicing healthier lifestyles. In addition, *Healthy People 2000* specifically
points out the inequities in health, especially as they relate to minority groups
and the need to make health services equally available to all Americans.

A major strategy within the report is focused on the concept of prevention.
Individuals can prevent illness and promote health and wellness by taking personal responsibility for choosing and living more positive lifestyle behaviors.
Taking personal responsibility can help reduce the number of self-induced illnesses and problems. A second focus is on removing barriers that prevent access
to equal education, health care, employment, poverty, and an overall better
quality of life. See Appendix D for a brief review of the barriers that prevent
minority populations from receiving good health care.

To develop the needed programs to accomplish the goals of *Healthy People
2000* will not be an easy task because our behavior is not the only factor

involved in our health. One's genetics, access to health care, the environment in which we live, and one's economic status are important influences. Each of these factors, whether acting alone or together, can influence our health and wellness. These factors vary from individual to individual and from group to group. For example, an individual with a genetic predisposition to coronary artery disease is at higher risk of having a heart attack. If this person is not educated about heart disease and lacks adequate health care, he or she is more likely to suffer from more dangerous complications from coronary heart disease and have a lower quality of life.

Health Problems and Youth

The number one killer of children 14 years and under is injuries (15 deaths per 100,000 youths), which far outnumbers cancer (3.5 deaths per 100,000 youths). The remaining causes of death are (3) congenital anomalies, (4) homicide, (5) heart disease, (6) pneumonia/influenza, (7) suicide, (8) meningitis, (9) chronic lung disease, and (10) HIV infection (Kochanek, 1995).

The leading causes of death of young people 15 to 24 are, in rank order: injuries, homicide, suicide, cancer, heart disease, congenital anomalies, HIV, pneumonia/influenza, stroke, and chronic lung disease. Injuries, the leading cause of death, are significantly higher than all other causes of death. Forty-eight deaths per 100,000 youth will result from injuries, compared to 14 for homicide and 12.5 for suicide (Kochanek, 1995).

Mortality rate maps for young adult infectious diseases show highest rates in southern and central parts of the country; the high rate counties are rural and significantly poor, with large percentages of Hispanic and Native-Americans (Goldman, 1991).

The Center for Disease Control Youth Risk Behavior Surveillance System was an effort to determine the health risks of youth in this country through national, state, and local surveys conducted in 1990, 1991, and 1993. Some of the results of the survey are noted in the box on page 136.

While the percentages reported give an overall picture of risk behaviors of today's youth, it should be noted that there are significant differences between males and females, among people of different ethnic groups, and in different age groups. Kahn and Charles (1995) reported:

- Males were most likely to report injury-related behaviors and smokeless tobacco and illegal drug use
- Females were most likely to report suicide-related behaviors
- White students reported more tobacco use
- Black students reported carrying more weapons, being involved in more physical fighting, and sexual behaviors
- Hispanic students reported more alcohol use and cocaine and crack use
- Weapon carrying, lack of condom use, and physical fighting occurred more frequently in grades 9 and 10

Behaviors that Contribute to Unintentional Injuries

Behavior	Percent of Students	Behavior	Percent of Students
Rarely use seat belt	19.1	Suicide attempt	8.6
Ever ride motorcycle	26.7	**USE OF TOBACCO, ALCOHOL, AND OTHER DRUGS**	
Rarely use motorcycle helmet	40.0	Alcohol use	80.9
		Cigarette use	69.5
Ever ride bicycle	75.3	Marijuana use	32.8
Rarely use bicycle helmet	92.8	Smokeless tobacco use	11.5
Ever drink and drive	35.3	Cocaine use	4.9
		Steroid use	2.2
Behaviors that Contribute to Intentional Injuries		**SEXUAL BEHAVIORS**	
Carrying a weapon	22.1	Sexual intercourse	53
Carrying a gun	7.9	Lack of condom use	52.8
Physical fight	41.8		
Suicide ideation	24.1		

SOURCE: L. Kahn and W. Charles, 1995, "Youth Risk Surveillance—U.S., 1993," *Journal of School Health, 65(5),* p. 163.

- Alcohol, tobacco, and other drug use and sexual behavior was reported more frequently in grades 11 and 12

Over 90 percent of teachers reported having students in their classrooms with psychological or emotional problems and over 70 percent reported having children with unhealthy lifestyle habits, family violence or abuse, and poor nutrition. Fifty percent reported having kids coming to school with untreated illnesses.

Porter/Novelli PR Agency (1992) also reported that many elementary school children come to school sick, disturbed, and abused. Teachers reported students suffering from problems with vision and hearing, psychological/emotional problems, unhealthy lifestyles, family violence and abuse, poor nutrition, violent behavior, lack of regular care, untreated illnesses, and drug/alcohol abuse among their students.

THE TEACHER'S ROLE IN EDUCATING STUDENTS ABOUT HEALTH BEHAVIORS

You can provide instruction that will help young people make decisions that promote health and prevent disease. You can promote good health through reinforcement of positive health behaviors, positive role modeling, and participation in school-wide efforts to improve the health of students. You may teach health in three ways:

- Direct instruction, which involves the organization, coordination, and presentation of material to students in an organized health class.

- Integrated instruction, which involves the organization, coordination, and presentation of material to students in the course of study of subjects other than health. Ideally, both direct and integrated instruction occurs in biology, social science, and home economics classes, for example.

- Incidental Classroom Health Education, which is a personalized and spontaneous teaching approach in which health issues are discussed in response to students' questions or educators' initiatives. Random incidental instruction occurs at "teachable moments." Planned incidental instruction can occur during a community immunization program, a clinic visit, or school club meetings in which students become personally involved in a learning experience (Project TEACH, 1993).

Discussions of the high-risk health behaviors are discussed in Appendix C, which covers the following health topics:

- Sexually transmitted diseases
- Alcohol, tobacco, and other drugs
- Teenage pregnancy
- Teenage sexual intercourse
- Suicide

Health Status of Minority Americans

Native-Americans Native-Americans and Alaska Natives, as a whole, still lag behind the U.S. general population in terms of general health. Today's Indians are among the poorest, least educated, and most neglected minority groups in America. Unemployment rates are high. Fifty percent are unemployed and a considerable number are underemployed (Olson & Wilson, 1986). When compared to national averages, Native-Americans have the highest rate of alcoholism (438 percent greater), tuberculosis (400 percent greater), diabetes (155 percent greater), accidents (131 percent greater), homicide (57 percent greater), pneumonia and influenza (32 percent greater), syphilis (300 percent greater), and suicide (27 percent greater) (Olson & Wilson, 1986, U.S. Indian Health Service, 1993). Many feel that alcoholism is the number one health problem facing Native-Americans and contributes to many Indian deaths and illnesses (such as liver disease, suicide, accidents, homicide, diabetes, birth defects, and pneumonia).

Hispanic-Americans The Hispanic population includes a larger family size, younger median age, families clustered in large U.S. cities, and less favorable socioeconomic status than the majority population. Twenty-two percent of Hispanic Americans live below the poverty level versus 11 percent of non-Hispanic families. When compared to the majority population, Hispanic Americans have higher rates of AIDS and other sexually transmitted diseases, accidents, diabetes, homicide, and chronic liver disease, but have lower chronic disorders such as vascular diseases, neoplasms, and heart disease.

Asian Pacific Americans Despite limitations, epidemiological researchers and health care policymakers went so far as to conclude, on the basis of limited data, that the health status of Asian Pacific Americans as a group is remarkably good (U.S. Office of Disease Prevention and Health Promotion, 1987). In addition, "they are, in aggregate, healthier than all (other) racial/ethnic groups in the United States (U.S. Department of Health and Human Services, 1985). However, more recent health status data of different Asian Pacific Americans have uncovered particular problems with hepatitis B. In particular, Asian Pacific American subgroups suffer equally, and in some cases greater, with the same problems as the majority population, such as heart disease, cancer, HIV/AIDS, substance use and abuse, domestic violence, suicides, and mental health problems. Two infectious diseases that have seriously effected immigrants of Asian and Pacific subgroups are tuberculosis and hepatitis B. As more immigrants with these infections move to the United States serious health problems within the Asian communities may arise unless specific health programs that attack these issues are developed.

African-Americans African-Americans are disproportionately concentrated in central cities or southern states. In 1990, there were 30.8 million African-Americans in the United States with 81 percent living in metropolitan areas. The poverty rate was 28.2 percent, compared to the United States total of 10.4 percent. When compared to white Americans, they are usually poorer, less likely to graduate from high school or college or to hold professional or white-collar positions. Compared to white Americans, African-Americans have higher infant mortality rates, lower life expectancies, higher mortality rates at earlier ages, and higher rates of homicide, stroke, cirrhosis, diabetes, and AIDS.

McBarnette (1996) reported that 60,000 more African-Americans than white Americans die each year as a result of cancer, cardiovascular disease, chemical dependency, cirrhosis of the liver, diabetes, homicide, and accidents. African-American women are four times more likely to die in childbirth, and their children are three times more likely to die within the first year of life than white children (McCord & Freeman, 1990).

See Appendix D for discussions of the barriers to health care that minority Americans encounter.

Cultural Sensitivity

An effective school health program must also allow for cultural diversity. Special population groups, including racial and ethnic minority groups, often need targeted program efforts. It is important to realize that the community consists of individuals or groups who have different or multiple cultural identities. These variations in the way people identify with a particular culture reflect the influence of several factors, including responses to different experiences in the following:

- Their own historical, socioeconomic, and political experience
- Education
- Family and peer influence
- Primary language
- Religion
- Age at time of immigration
- Where they lived and length of time in the United States
- Citizenship status
- Whether or not the individual resides in an integrated community

Cultural Customs and Behaviors

Culture provides a set of implicit and explicit guidelines that an individual learns as a member of a particular group, and that tells him or her how to view the world and how to behave in it in relation to other people and to the environment. Culture provides a lens in which the individual perceives and understands the world he or she inhabits, and learns how to live within it.

Individuals become culturally conditioned and this conditioning becomes an integral part of how they interpret and judge the behavior of others. The cultural framework that evolves becomes the "truth" or "belief" by which the individual interprets the world. Therefore, each individual has his or her own cultural interpretation of the truth. Difficulty can arise when an individual encounters a different culture that disregards his or her cultural truth or when others grossly misinterpret his or her cultural truth.

The cultural truths or beliefs that may transcend into health truths are often different from the mainstream medical truths of the dominant Western-trained medical profession and society. Cultural factors can be causal, contributory, or protective in their relation to health and wellness and they are numerous. Different cultures have different beliefs about such things as family dynamics, gender roles, sexual behavior, diet, personal hygiene, body image alterations (e.g., body piercing, cosmetic surgery, tattooing, obesity, slimness), dress, use of drugs (e.g., tea, coffee, alcohol, hallucinogens, alcohol), leisure pursuits, and the use of nontraditional medical practitioners.

Illness is also a sociocultural construct. As a result, each culture provides a culturally relevant diagnosis or cause and a framework for appropriate intervention. Within this framework, different cultures provide explanations for why the illness occurred. These cultural beliefs are important in the treatment process of any illness and also in the prevention of illness. In addition, not all beliefs are clearly visible to those outside of the culture. For example, if religion is tightly woven into the culture's view of health, healing may be one of the primary responsibilities of religion. Thus, religious practices may be an integral part of that culture's health care system.

Examples of Cultural Factors That Affect Health

In certain cultures, for example, the male, by virtue of nothing other than his gender, is dominant and as a consequence, the woman loses control in her sexual relationship. If the man chooses to not use a condom, the woman then loses control of her fertility and her ability to prevent disease.

Many Hispanic, Asian, and African-American men come from cultures that reject the use of condoms and believe that extramarital sex with numerous partners enhances the male identity. As a result, the cultural consequence can be seen in an increase in unwanted pregnancies and HIV/AIDS, single mothers, cervical cancer, and major contributors to morbidity and mortality.

To argue for the use of condoms without understanding the cultural truth will have no effect. Without knowing the culture, it is impossible to know the people. Also, to disregard their cultural truths is to disregard them. This, in turn, effects how minorities believe they are perceived in mainstream society and, ultimately, effects their self-esteem and self-worth.

School Health and Food Services

Teachers play an extremely important role in the physical health of students. All teachers are an integral part of any comprehensive school health program. All schools should provide health services that include screening, intervention, and remediation of various health conditions. The school nurse most often coordinates school health services. Other professionals who make up the school health services team include the school physician, dentist, social worker, and speech pathologist (Anspaugh & Ezell, 1995). You can be of special assistance in working with the school health services team by contributing to the assessment of students. Health assessment of students is important for at least three reasons:

1. Assessment can help detect any disorder that may not be easily recognized but needs medical attention. Treatment may be more successful if a problem is detected early rather than discovery and treatment at a later stage when the condition may have caused more damage (e.g., speech, heart, visual, and emotional problems).

2. Identification of some signs that may not in themselves indicate illness, but if they persist may indicate abnormalities (e.g., perceptual, growth, or motor abnormalities).

3. Health assessments help determine the effectiveness of any treatments a child may be receiving or received (e.g., Did the infection clear up after treatment? or Did the child's ability to read improve with the new prescribed glasses?)

You can help in the assessment process by observing, keeping records on, and referring children.

Observations Observations consist of everything noticed through all of your senses. You are in a unique position to observe students in a closed environment

Teachers can be of special assistance in working with the school health services team by contributing to the assessment of students.

on a daily basis over a period of time. You can, for example, evaluate a child when you notice that the child holds a book too close to his or her eyes, does not respond when spoken to in an ordinary voice, or walks with a slight limp. While greeting each child at the door, you may notice if the child appears different or similar to the day before. To be specific, you can observe students' physical, cognitive, social, emotional, and language performance in comparison to age-cohort peers (Miller et al., 1996). Your observation is organized into signs and symptoms. Signs are characteristics that any person may see or observe, such as redness, vomiting, convulsions, or bleeding. Symptoms are what the child feels and describes to the teacher, such as feeling pain, nausea, or dizziness. Objective signs often accompany symptoms.

Young children are not always able to express themselves or describe how they feel. It is important for you to practice asking the right questions and recording accurate notes. For example, it is more valuable to say that Jose has a sore throat, a cough, and reddish colored cheeks than to say Jose looks ill. Accurate observations are more meaningful and avoid misinterpretation of what may be wrong with the child.

Keeping Records Keeping records contributes to the total health history of a student and supplies a pertinent up-to-date written account of past and present problems. Records provide information on past illnesses and operations, injuries, physical disabilities, immunizations, habits of living, and other pertinent health information. Keeping records also serves as a guide for further questions. You should also be familiar with the content of the student's health history that is kept in the nurse's office. The permanent records may often give the teacher clues to understanding the child's behavior.

Referring Referring children to appropriate health resources for help is another way in which you can help students. You are not expected to diagnose or treat suspected illness or conditions. You are, however, in a position to assist the child by making appropriate referrals, according to school policy, to other

---

Stay at Home Guidelines

Appearance/Behavior
Unusually tired, pale, difficult to awake, confused or irritable, lack of appetite. These problems are sufficient reason to exclude a student from school.

Diarrhea
Three or more watery stools in a 24-hour period, especially if student acts or looks ill.

Ear Infection
A student may attend school after receiving medical treatment (understand ear infections can cause permanent hearing loss and even more serious problems).

Eyes
Thick mucus or pus draining from the eye is pink eye. The student probably can attend school immediately after starting medical treatment ask about your school's policy).

Fever
A temperature of 101 or higher and confusion, diarrhea, earache, irritability, rash, sore throat, vomiting, cough, or headache.

Lice/Scabies
Students cannot return to childcare or school until their hair has been treated with lice shampoo and the dead eggs ("nits") have been combed or picked out.

Rash
Body rash, especially with fever or itching.

Sore Throat
Body rash, especially with fever or swollen glands in the neck.

Vomiting
Vomiting two or more times within the past 24 hours.

Common Cold
If the student has minor cold symptoms but does not have the symptoms described in this guideline, the student may not need to be kept home from school. A long-term (chronic) greenish nose discharge, and/or a chronic cough are symptoms that should be seen by a doctor.

SOURCE: Porter/Novelli PR Agency, September 1992, Health Care and a Child's Ability to Learn: A Survey of Elementary School Teachers, Chicago.

---

members of the school health team such as counselors, the school nurse, or physical educator or other professionals within the community.

When Is a Child Too Ill to Be in Your Class?

A student should not be sent to school with an illness that could be spread to other students, if the student would be miserable all day, or if the student's presence would distract the other children. Noted above are guidelines developed by Project TEACH (1993) for when a student should stay home from school. You might check to see if your school has its own set of stay-at-home guidelines.

School Food Services

Nearly two-thirds of all school children in the United States receive about a third of their daily nutrients from the school food service program (Miller et al., 1996). For most, this is provided as a part of the school lunch program. In some communities, other provisions, such as breakfasts and after-school snacks for children with working parents in economically disadvantaged communities, are made to feed children as part of the school program (Miller et al., 1996).

The Health Framework for California Public Schools (California Department of Education, 1994) states an effective nutrition services program is basic to successful learning in schools. Hungry children can neither learn nor achieve their potential in physical development, level of activity, or mental ability. Nutrition services can help to alleviate the physical signs and behaviors related to hunger and improve the resistance to some communicable diseases.

School lunch programs should also provide food choices that are consistent with common dietary recommendations such as increasing the consumption of whole grains, fruits, and vegetables and light consumption of fat, salt, sugar, and empty-calorie foods.

You play an important role in identifying and referring children who may not be getting adequate nutrition or displaying unusual eating behaviors. In addition, you have the opportunity of integrating nutrition into your curriculum.

PROMOTING PHYSICAL AND EMOTIONAL SAFETY

Feeling safe and secure means that students feel they are in control of their own selves within the classroom environment—they have mastery over their being. Without a feeling of physical and emotional safety and security, students will find it difficult to move beyond strong fear and anxiety in order to be willing to enthusiastically explore new challenges. Strong fear and anxiety limit students—sometimes in small ways, sometimes in ways so large they become imprisoned by them.

This need is not about the fear and anxiety that are related to the improvement of test performance, therefore, it is not about whether or not mild anxiety and fear may improve performance or whether or not too much will cause the student's performance to become awkward or deteriorate.

This need is about the fear and anxiety that are related to daily situations when the student's physical safety and emotional well-being are threatened. It is about feeling fear and anxiety and having no control over the situation. This chapter is about understanding the need for both physical safety and emotional security within the class environment.

Students must see the classroom arena as a place (1) where all precautions have been taken to ensure their physical safety, and (2) where their emotional well-being is not being violated. It is important for any teacher to make safety (both physical and emotional) the highest priority. Without a feeling of safety, students will become victims of fear and anxiety. Would most people stay on a job if they were afraid for their own physical or emotional safety? The answer would be "probably not."

How long students will stay in school is directly related to how safe and orderly they perceive the classroom and school environment to be. This perception of safety is also related to how well they will perform on a daily basis and how much they will respect and trust their teacher and classmates. Unfortunately, not all teachers and schools provide a safe environment for their students.

How long adults stay on a job is determined largely by whether or not they consider the environment to be safe and orderly. This perception is also related to their level of performance and productivity, how much trust they have in their fellow workers, and how much they support their boss. Employees who do not feel safe while at work suffer more depression and mood swings and have the highest absenteeism and quitting rates. Therefore, it would be prudent to apply the same results to the academic environment.

PHYSICAL SAFETY/SCHOOL VIOLENCE

School Violence: Tragic Headline Stories

In recent years, tragic headline stories about school shootings have become all too common. On April 29, 1999, two teenagers opened fire on classmates at Columbine High School in Littleton, Colorado, killing 15 people, including themselves. This was the eighth time in less than two years Americans have encountered a horrifying tableau: guns, bullets, and bodies of students and teachers—another school, another community, another shooting. Prior to this shooting, the following stories made headline news:

- May 21, 1998: A freshman boy opened fire with a semiautomatic rifle in a Springfield, Oregon high school cafeteria, killing two students and wounding 22 others. The teenager's parents were later found shot to death in their home.

- May 19, 1998: A high school senior shot and killed another student in the school parking lot at Lincoln County High School in Fayetteville, Tennessee three days before they were to graduate. They had had an argument about a girl.

- April 24, 1998: In Edinboro, Pennsylvania. A 14-year-old shot a teacher and wounded two students at an eighth grade dance. He said he wanted the dance to be "memorable."

- March 24, 1998: Two boys opened fire with rifles on classmates and teachers when they came out during a false fire alarm at the Westside Middle School in Jonesboro, Arkansas. Four girls and a teacher were killed and eleven people were wounded.

- December 1, 1997: A youth opened fire on a student prayer circle in a hallway at Heath High School in West Paducah, Kentucky. Three students were killed and five others were wounded.

- October 1, 1997: In Pearl, Michigan, a 16-year-old killed his mother, then went to school and shot nine students. Two of them died, including the boy's ex-girlfriend.

- February 9, 1997: A 16-year-old student opened fire in a common area at the Bethel Alaska High School, killing the principal and a classmate. Two other students were wounded.

■ February 2, 1996: A 14-year-old student turned an assault rifle on his algebra class, killing two classmates and a teacher in the central Washington city of Moses Lake.

Americans are recognizing that this type of violence is happening across the country, but people do not want to believe that it can happen in their community. Educators, however, have long recognized that incidents of school violence are not more frequent, they are more severe. People cannot pretend that none of this is ever going to happen in their community because it already is. School violence is societal violence that has penetrated the walls of our schools. These tragic headlines have captured the attention of all, but beyond the headlines, everyday in every school our children face smaller acts of violence.

Adolescents aged 12 to 19 have the highest victimization rate for violent crimes and theft. One-third of violent crimes committed against teens involve weapons and some sort of physical injury. Homicide rates are the second leading cause of death among all teenagers, but the leading cause of death for African-American males and females aged 15 to 24 (American School Health Association, 1989). More than one-fourth of male adolescents commit at least one violent offense before reaching adulthood. The median age of first gun ownership is 12-and-a-half. The peak age of arrests for serious violent crimes in America is 18 (Herchinger, 1994). About 40 percent of arrests for all serious crimes are accounted for by youths between 10 and 20 years of age. Yet, despite the prevalence of delinquent behavior, a small proportion of adolescents—about 6 percent—are responsible for two-thirds of all violent crimes committed by juveniles (U.S. Department of Justice, 1993). The Centers for Disease Control and Prevention found that one in 25 high school students carry a gun (Herchinger, 1994). One in five teachers can cite incidents of verbal or physical threats from students during the past 12 months (Crowley, 1993).

In his book, *Fateful Choices,* Fred Hechinger (1992) wrote about adolescent death and violence and reported the following information:

1. Researchers at the University of Maryland's School of Medicine surveyed 168 teenagers who visited an inner-city clinic and reported that 24 percent had witnessed a murder and 72 percent knew somebody who had been shot.

2. According to the National Center for Health Statistics, young black males face the most serious threat of harm to life and limb. They are seven times more likely than white youths to die as a result of homicide. The rates for Native-American and Hispanic-American youths were about three to four times that of white Americans; that for Asians was virtually the same as white Americans.

3. Forty-one percent of juveniles held for violent crimes had used a weapon, most frequently a gun.

4. Each month, 300,000 high school students are physically attacked, many in, or on the way to, school.

5. The National Adolescent Health Survey found that 41 percent of boys and 24 percent of girls report that they could obtain a handgun if they wanted one.

In addition:

- The U.S. Bureau of Justice, 1992 statistics, reported that of the crimes committed in the United States, 7.9 percent of all rapes reported occurred on school property, 3.9 percent of all robberies reported occurred on school property, and 14.1 percent of all assaults occurred on school property (School Net, 1996).

- The Department of Education, Justice, and Health and Human Services in 1994, reported that every school day more than 150,000 students stay home because they are "sick of violence and afraid they might be stabbed, shot, or beaten (School Net, 1996)."

- Younger students (aged 6–10) are much more likely to be victims of violence than are senior high school students (U.S. Department of Education, 1993c).

- Students whose families moved frequently and students from racial and ethnic groups that are minorities within the school are more likely to be physically assaulted (U.S. Department of Justice, 1991).

- Thirty-eight percent of teachers and 57 percent of students rank strict teachers as more at risk of victimization than any other members of the teaching staff (The American Teacher, 1993).

- Most acts of violence occur where adult supervision is minimal or where there are large crowds of people moving to and fro. Students, especially those who have been victims, learn quickly which areas to avoid (The American Teacher, 1993).

- The National School Violence and Safety Study in 1995 reported that 71 percent of 7–10 year olds fear they might get shot or stabbed at school or home; 22 percent of 11–12 year olds said they knew someone their age who was in a gang (School Net, 1996).

Such statistics are shocking. More shocking is that only approximations of the number of incidents of school violence are available because neither federal nor state agencies require schools by law to (1) track incidents of school violence, (2) maintain records of statistics, or (3) supervise the tracking and maintenance of school violence statistics (School Net, 1996). Reporting is not even required by the Departments of Education.

Students as Victims of Violence

Victims and perpetrators of school violence represent all racial, ethnic, and economic groups. Although males are more likely to be involved in acts of violence in schools, females are engaging more frequently in such acts.

Most disturbing is that in many acts of violence the perpetrators do not have a serious reason for lashing out. Toby (1994) reported it could be something as simple as a look or stare or an accidental bump into someone that triggers a violent reaction. Acts of violence often erupt from idle gossip, boyfriend-girlfriend jealousies, extortion, feeling slighted or disrespected, or an attempt to impress friends. It could result from the perpetrator's dislike for a person or the perception that someone is weak or is a nerd (gets good grades). In other words, a logical reason for the incident is not necessary.

Baker (1994) stated that "another school factor that impedes the progress of many children is *negative school climate*. This term refers to the sum total of qualities that make up the school environment. A school that is physically unsafe, that suffers vandalism and violence against teachers and students, and that features constant disruptions, interrupting class time, is a difficult place in which to learn."

When fear stalks the halls of a school or the streets to and from school, education is also a victim. As a result of this epidemic, many schools have incorporated anti-violence programs. Schools have adopted programs that have included strict rules and regulations, safety classes, conflict resolution workshops, stronger counseling referral systems, primary intervention programs, and peer education and mentoring programs.

It is imperative that schools establish safety zones that are free of violence, weapons, and drugs. The goal for any school is to assure that children and youths are able to go to and from school without fear of bodily harm. Educators, administrators, community leaders, police authorities, the courts, parents, youth organizations, the media, and politicians must find avenues of true cooperation to stem the tide of adolescent violence. In addition, violations, such as possession of firearms, knives, and other weapons, and the sale or use of drugs, must be instantly and severely penalized through legal action.

Characteristics of At-Risk Youth

The National School Safety Center (1998) has created a checklist of 20 characteristics that could indicate a youth's potential for harming himself or herself or others. These characteristics are taken from youngsters who have caused school-associated violent deaths in the United States from July 1992 to the present:

1. Has a history of tantrums and uncontrollable outbursts.
2. Characteristically resorts to name calling, cursing, or abusive language.
3. Habitually makes violent threats when angry.
4. Has previously brought a weapon to school.
5. Has a background of serious disciplinary problems at school and in the community.
6. Has a background of drug, alcohol, or other substance abuse or dependency.
7. Is on the fringe of his or her peer group with few or no close friends.
8. Is preoccupied with weapons, explosives, or other incendiary devices.
9. Has previously been truant, suspended, or expelled from school.
10. Displays cruelty to animals.
11. Has little or no supervision and support from parents or a caring adult.
12. Has witnessed or been a victim of abuse or neglect in the home.
13. Has been bullied and/or bullies or intimidates peers or younger children.

14. Tends to blame others for difficulties and problems he or she causes himself or herself.

15. Consistently prefers TV shows, movies, or music expressing violent themes and acts.

16. Prefers reading materials dealing with violent themes, rituals, and abuse.

17. Reflects anger, frustration, and the dark side of life in school essays or writing projects.

18. Is involved with a gang or an antisocial group on the fringe of peer acceptance.

19. Is often depressed and/or has significant mood swings.

20. Has threatened or attempted suicide.

If you have students who have many of these characteristics, they may be at risk for violent behavior. You cannot handle this situation alone. Contact the school counselor and principal to establish a strategy of intervention.

Developing School Safety Programs

Educators should adopt violence prevention programs that are tailored to their school's unique needs, resources, and safety goals. On school campuses where there is crisis and emergency, schools should place priority on developing crisis management plans that include detailed procedures for preventing and responding to violent situations, communication links between students and faculty, as well as specific programs for counseling and enforcing the school conduct code. Violence prevention programs should be developed through partnerships with the teachers, administrators, parents, school personnel, the students, and representatives from the community.

In some schools it may be necessary to incorporate unannounced locker searches, metal detectors, surveying trouble areas with closed-circuit television, and security guards. In less severe situations, schools might implement safety programs that include conflict resolution programs, peer mediation curricula that teaches young people to handle anger and disagreements nonviolently, and/or multicultural and bias identification programs that target racial and ethnic prejudices that are often at the core of violence.

Some schools are developing long-term prevention programs by modifying their curriculum to emphasize students taking responsibility for their actions and caring for one another, as well as instruction that focuses on building students' moral reasoning and decision-making skills. Many schools have adopted conflict resolution and anger-management classes beginning in kindergarten. Many school districts are investing in training teachers, counselors, and parents to recognize early warning signs. Schools also need to create an atmosphere where students are comfortable coming forward with information about dangerous situations.

Other long-term strategies include peer tutoring programs and community service programs that will, hopefully, translate to a more caring society. Mentoring programs have also been designed to help alienated youth.

Gangs

The American School Health Association (1989) reported a significant gang presence in public schools. Fifteen percent of students aged 12 to 19 reported the presence of street gangs in their school. The Attorney General's Report on the Impact of Criminal Street Gangs on Crime and Violence in California by the year 2000 (1993) reported that criminal street gangs have become one of the most serious crime problems in California. Gang violence—particularly assaults, drive-by shootings, homicides, and brutal home invasion robberies—accounts for one of the largest, single, personal threats to public safety in California and throughout the United States.

A street gang is a group of people who unite for a common purpose and engage in violent, unlawful, criminal, and antisocial behavior. They are usually territorial, often but not always of the same gender, and operate by creating an atmosphere of fear and intimidation in a community. Gangs are usually made up of males in age from 12 to 22 years old. Members represent all racial and ethnic groups. Females play an important role because they often carry weapons and transport or hold drugs for male gang members. It is believed that females are less likely to be searched by police. Young members are also used to carry, hide, or sell drugs and weapons because of the less severe legal punishment if they are caught. Schools, unfortunately, have become breeding grounds for gangs and this can have a tremendous negative impact on the learning environment.

Identifying Gang Members in Your School How can you identify which of your students might belong to a gang? The answer to that question is pretty easy because most gang members are proud of their gang and freely display their membership. You can identify gang members by becoming aware of the signs and symbols that gang members use to communicate their affiliation to one another. Many openly display tattoos and adopt a style of dress and color which identifies their gang. Gang members often use hand signs to identify the gang to which they belong and often use nicknames when they are among other gang members. Graffiti is often used to advertise the gang and is used as a means of communicating, marking territories, identifying sources of illegal drugs, and claiming responsibility for violent acts. It is also used to intimidate and to provide individual gang members with a means of showing gang association and allegiance. Flashing gang signs to opposing gang members often results in verbal and/or physical conflict.

Gang Clothes Dress is an important component of gang identity. Gang fashion, like regular fashion, changes over time and gang dress is constantly evolving. However, students at your school know the gang dress and keeping in touch with non-gang members will help you identify any emerging gang trends. Hispanic gangs, for example, painstakingly iron khaki pants to have a clear distinct crease in the pant leg. Pants are often baggy because weapons can be easily concealed. White cotton T-shirts that are heavily starched are worn under plaid flannel shirts that are buttoned only at the top. Headgear may include bandannas or black hairnets. The color of the bandannas and scarves signify gang membership. Black gang members often wear the same khaki pants, but wear them so low that their boxer shorts are exposed. Flannel shirts are also worn, but unbuttoned. Baseball caps are worn backwards, a fashion statement that was spawned because the brim gets in the way when firing a gun. Expensive leather athletic shoes are also worn.

Gang Signs, Tattoos, and Graffiti Gang members often use hand signals to identify and communicate with other gang members or as taunts to other gangs. For example, the thumb and index finger of the left hand form a "C" to represent "crip." The "C" is flashed to fellow gang members. The traditional okay sign with the index finger and thumb forming the letter "o" with the other three fingers pointing up means "cousin." Tattoos are often worn and used to identify and communicate with other gang members. Tattoos are often found on the hand or across the chest or stomach. Graffiti is used by gang members to communicate with one another and with other gangs. Gang writing is very angular and follows a set pattern. Gang members often use gang graffiti on book covers and folders, but it is most often seen on public buildings. Crossed-out graffiti is a signal that rival gang members have been in the territory and is considered a direct challenge. It means, "I can come and go as I please" or "I can come onto your turf whenever I want." Such challenges often result in gang fights.

Disciplining Gang Members Affiliation with a gang, gang activities, or claiming gang membership should be considered extreme misconduct within the school environment because gang membership is a form of intimidation to the student body and is disruptive to the educational process. Disciplining gang members is an administrative process and not a classroom teacher's responsibility. It is the teacher's responsibility to report any gang membership or activity to the administration. Consequently, corrective action from short-term suspension to long-term suspension must be considered by the administration. Schools must establish fair, firm policies that reflect a "no-nonsense policy." Gang behavior is often criminal behavior and must be disciplined differently from normal school disruptions. Gang activity must be dealt with individually and swiftly and not allowed on any school campus. If criminal behavior occurs, law enforcement must be contacted to deal with the situation.

Reasons Why Children Join Gangs The Department of Justice estimates there may be as many as 175,000 to 200,000 gang members in California (Attorney General's Report, 1993). The *Gangs 2000: A Call to Action Report* (The Attorney General, 1993) determined that seven major factors are involved in why youth, especially high-risk youth, join gangs. A close investigation of the factors reveals that all seven are related to the basic needs discussed earlier.

1. Gangs provide them with a sense of friendship, camaraderie, and family; things that they are not receiving at home or school. This factor is related to the need to be accepted and to belong.

STANDARD GANG SYMBOLS
& DEFINITIONS. Timmy

-R- RIFAMO, RIFA, RIFAN
Meaning: "We're the best, I'm the best they're
the best."

CONTROLZA
Meaning: "The gang controls the area."

c/s - CON SAFOS -
Meaning: "Same to you" or "There's nothing you
can do about it."

"C": crip

GANG
SIGNS. Timmy

"Victory"

"Power"

"Blood"

Number one

2. They experience a kind of success in gangs; whereas, they experience failure at school and in the home. This factor is related to the need to feel significant and capable.

3. There is nothing else to do; they have no hope and see no alternative but to join a gang. This factor is related to feeling capable and significant.

4. They feel their survival may depend on joining a neighborhood gang. They fear for their safety and believe that being in a gang gives them protection. This factor is related to feeling safe.

5. They have not developed the skills to express feelings of anger and rage constructively. This factor is related to feeling capable.

6. It is a way to gain respect and money. Gangs can provide lucrative economic opportunities, status, and prestige, especially for youths who do not believe they have employment opportunities, or who have no job skills. This factor is related to feeling capable and significant.

7. Some youths grow up in families in which parents and relatives are active gang members, and joining a gang is part of family tradition. In Hispanic neighborhoods, for instance, gangs have been an integral part of the barrio for generations. This factor is related to acceptance, significance, and belonging.

To counter these seven factors, we must develop strategies to fulfill the basic needs in a healthier way. This can be accomplished by providing a reason and means for young people to get out of gangs and to empower individuals, families, schools, and communities so that they can take action to solve problems associated with gangs.

REPORTING CHILD AND SEXUAL ABUSE

Child abuse includes any act of commission or omission related to the physical, mental, and sexual well-being of a minor (less than 18 years of age). This would include any physical assault, corporal punishment, emotional deprivation, emotional assault, sexual exploitation, or inadequate supervision (Project TEACH, 1993).

It is hypothesized that one in four girls and one in eight boys will be sexually abused before the age of eighteen. Incest is a profound form of sexual abuse where members in one's own family are involved sexually with children. Seventy-five percent of prostitutes report having been victims of childhood sexual abuse, and as many as 75 percent of children on the street report having been victims of sexual abuse (Reagan & Brookins-Fisher, 1997).

Since 1986, the California Penal Code Section 11166 has required not only teachers, but also any adults who work with minors, to report any suspicion of child abuse. Other states have similar laws. Child abuse is no longer a family matter, and teachers must truly act in *loco parentis*. The intent of the law is to provide for the immediate protection of the minor child while under the direct supervision of the classroom teacher (Project TEACH, 1993). You are required to report any possible abuse, both in writing and by phone within 36 hours of making the observation (either real or suspected). Failure to report can lead to jail sentencing, loss of teaching credentials, and possible charges of obstruction of justice.

Teachers must also be aware of the ever-present possibility of accusations against them. It is important that teachers protect themselves from this possibility by taking preventive measures. Following are some suggestions:

- Learn to identify signs of abuse.
- Always make a written notation of any injury you see on a student. Regular documentation will protect you against parents who might falsely claim that an injury occurred at school.
- Touch students appropriately. A safe zone of touch is from the shoulder to the hand. A pat on the shoulder, a handshake, and a "high five" are just some of the ways that a teacher can show caring and acceptance. Always ask

Teachers are required to report any possible abuse, both in writing and by phone within thirty-six hours of making the observation (either real or suspected).

the students respectfully if it is okay to shake their hands or pat them on the shoulder or arm. A student may not want to be touched.

- Try to avoid being alone with a student, especially in closed or isolated places.

- Avoid mixed messages by being clear with your students about the nature of your relationship with them.

PHYSICAL SAFETY/
ACCIDENT PREVENTION

Threats to one's physical safety include fear of injury due to feelings of being unprepared, undertrained, unprotected, overwhelmed, or overmatched. The student may also fear participating in an unprotected classroom environment where there are safety hazards and unsafe equipment.

Physical safety problems are usually associated with physical education classes, shop classes, and athletics. However, common principles can be applied to all classes. Elkow reported the primary considerations of any classroom program are to:

1. prevent accidents

2. eliminate hazards

3. develop individual and group safety consciousness

4. develop wholesome attitudes, habits, and practices pertaining to safety

5. develop attitudes of personal responsibility for safety

It is important to remember that all the latest equipment; controls, and procedures will not keep students safe until these are properly used. Most accidents involve human error, so safety is primarily a people problem. In order to achieve these five considerations, Elkow reported that "a teacher must have a thorough understanding of the class, equipment, and facilities; the leadership provided; fitness requirements of the participants; nature of the skills necessary for success; and the demands placed on personnel involved in the activity by themselves and their community." Fewer accidents occur when the students believe that the teacher is committed to their safety. And, until the student is comfortable within the environment, he or she will never be fully aware of his or her full potential.

Is it Possible to Be Too Overprotective?

Because there are so many hazards and so many different degrees of risk in different classes, such as physical education and shop, you must seek a practical changing balance between protection and classroom participation. If students are overprotected, their personal responsibility and adjustment may be retarded. On the other hand, if students are underprotected, in the absence of proper safety practices they may be seriously injured or even killed. This is a fine line, and you must always teach on the side of safety before moving to the next level.

EMOTIONAL SAFETY

Human interrelationships are integral to any classroom situation. The student's emotional development can be positively or negatively affected by this experience. If you use harsh words, threats, sarcasm, and undesirable discipline and place too much stress on performance and competition, many students become uneasy and nervous.

Emotional safety also means that students can trust you to be there for them and that you are willing to respect their points of view. They know that you won't always agree with them, but you are on their side and you are willing to work with them rather than against them. They can count on you because they know that they are valued and you will not hold their actions against them personally. An important part of emotional safety is feeling respected.

The emotional setting is just as important as the physical one, and the teacher is responsible for establishing a safe emotional atmosphere within the classroom arena. The overall atmosphere should be one of acceptance, one in which you know the students well and are sensitive to their individual needs. Students should feel free to express their feelings honestly without fear of ridicule or rebuke. They should also feel free to fail occasionally without punishment. You can promote well-being by being kind but fair, promoting teacher-student relationships, setting reasonable goals for each student, encouraging positive behavior, challenging students within their capabilities, and tolerating occasional frustration.

You may find the following categories useful in determining whether or not you provoke emotional fear in students.

1. *Warning and threatening tells the student that you have little respect for his or her needs or concerns.* "You're going to stay here all night until you get it right" and "If you don't get your act together you're out of here" are examples of making the student feel fearful and submissive.

2. *Being criticized makes students feel stupid, unworthy, and inadequate.* Demeaning words will chip away at the student's self-confidence and self-image. Critical remarks usually provoke defensiveness and anger on the part of the student. Teachers who use criticism usually find that their students have little respect for them.

3. *Name-calling and ridiculing have effects similar to those of criticism.* Teachers who send these messages in an attempt to influence students are usually disappointed.

4. *Sarcasm usually tells the student that you are not interested in him or her and do not really care or have any positive feelings toward him or her.* Sarcasm usually hurts and is viewed as a put-down.

The Effects of Emotional Assaults

When students are emotionally assaulted, they feel both hurt and anger. If the students cannot express those feelings, they will suppress them, and resentment will build. It is unhealthy to be consumed inwardly by resentment. Students usually pay a price when they "swallow" feelings, and the relationship between you and them will be impaired.

In addition, you must be aware of the dynamics that are taking place between students. With regard to safety issues, you must also be aware of the class bully. Almost every parent has listened to a child's complaints about the class bully whose antisocial behavior often includes extortion and threats to personal safety. A bully usually picks on smaller, relatively defenseless, classmates. The class bully should not be regarded as a form of acting-out. To regard violent behavior in young people as a phase of normal development is wishful thinking.

Interventions to eliminate bullying require the active involvement of teachers and parents, setting firm limits against unacceptable behavior, and protecting potential victims.

The Progression from Unexpressed Anger to Resentment to Hostility

If emotional assaults continue and the student repeatedly represses the anger and resentment, internal pain builds up, causing an intense rage or hostility. The student becomes a time bomb, easily able to explode at even the most minor irritations or annoyances. The hostile student will eventually withdraw from the entire situation by quitting or express rage in the form of insulting behavior or words at classmates or others in inappropriate situations. What the classmates do not know is that the hostile student is responding not to the present situation, but to the accumulation of unresolved pain and anger.

The Toll on the Body Marks (1978) reported that "strong fear and anxiety cause unpleasant feelings of terror; paleness of the skin; sweating; hair standing on end; dilation of the pupils; rapid pounding of the heart; rise in blood pressure; tension in the muscles and increased blood flow through them; trembling; a readiness to be startled; dryness and tightness of the throat and mouth; constriction of the chest and rapid breathing; a sinking feeling in the stomach; nausea; desperation; contraction of the bladder and rectum leading to urges to pass urine and feces; irritability and a tendency to lash out; a strong desire to cry, run, or hide; difficulty in breathing; tingling in the hands and feet; feelings of being unreal or far away; paralyzing weakness of the limbs; and a sensation of faintness and falling."

Students can live under fear for only so long. The body and mind can endure only so much. Eventually, over time, students who feel personally victimized by continued physical or emotional assaults are likely to develop anxiety, depression, and helplessness and will live in fear, not knowing when the abuse will happen next. They will lose faith in the teacher and develop a persistent preoccupation with the problem. Some think that there is no escape except to quit. Others become preoccupied with revenge.

When students view the environment as hostile, they are likely to dislike the class, the teacher, and their classmates. Fear promotes anxiety, stress, and depression. It reduces the ability to perform and creates an atmosphere of distrust. These are all typical symptoms of an unhealthy classroom.

SUMMARY OF MAJOR POINTS
IN CHAPTER 6

1. In order to improve academic achievement, schools and other institutions must devote more attention to the health and safety of students.

2. *Healthy People 2000: National Health Promotion and Disease Prevention Objectives* was designed to significantly improve the nation's health in the twenty-first century.

3. The number one killer of children 14 years and under is injuries.

4. The leading causes of death of young people 15–24 are, in rank order: injuries, homicide, suicide, cancer, heart disease, congenital anomalies, HIV, pneumonia / influenza, stroke, and chronic lung disease.

5. Teachers may teach health in three ways: direct instruction, integrated instruction, and incidental classroom health education.

6. Native-Americans and Alaska Natives, as a whole, still lag behind the United States general population in terms of general health.

7. Twenty-two percent of Hispanic Americans live below the poverty level.

8. African-Americans have high infant mortality rates, lower life expectancies, higher mortality rates at earlier ages, and higher rates of homicide, stroke, cirrhosis, diabetes, and AIDS.

Time-out: Recognizing Symptoms of Stress

It is important that teachers be aware of the physical and emotional reactions to fear, anxiety, and/or distress. Your physician can make the best determination of your medical condition, of course, but these guidelines can provide a rough measure of your stress level. You can get a measure of how well you manage stress by checking how much you are bothered by the following symptoms.

Check the Symptoms or Signals You Have:

1. Feeling hot ____
2. Feeling dizzy or light-headed ____
3. Feeling unsteady ____
4. Having trembling hands ____
5. Having a flushed face ____
6. Pounding of the heart ____
7. Dryness of mouth and throat ____
8. Insomnia ____
9. High pitched , nervous laugh ____
10. Diarrhea, indigestion, queasiness in the stomach, and sometimes vomiting ____
11. Migraine headaches ____
12. Pain in the neck and lower back ____
13. Loss of appetite ____
14. Increased smoking ____
15. Increased use of prescribed drugs ____
16. Alcohol and other drug abuse ____
17. Nightmares ____
18. Hypermobility, an increased tendency to move about without any reason ____
19. Accident proneness ____
20. Bruxism (grinding of the teeth) ____

21. General irritability, hyperexcitation, or depression ____
22. Impulsive behavior, emotional instability ____
23. Overpowering urge to cry or run or hide ____
24. Inability to concentrate, flight of thoughts, disorientation ____
25. Feelings of unreality, weakness, dizziness ____
26. Fearing the worst happening ____
27. Being terrified ____
28. Feeling nervous ____
29. Feeling a loss of control ____
30. Being unable to relax ____

Items 1 through 5 measure somatic symptoms; items 26 through 30 measure subjective anxiety. These 10 items were adapted by the Beck Anxiety Inventory (Beck, Epstein, Brown, & Steer, 1988) as cited by Kleinke (1991). This inventory was developed as an index of anxiety independent of feelings of depression. There is no score to this inventory. It is a tool to help you recognize any symptoms of fear or anxiety that you or someone else may be having. Questions 1 through 20 are danger signals that focus on the physical symptoms common to tension stress. Items 21 through 30 are medical and emotional signals common to tension stress. Once the symptoms have been identified, it is important for individuals to deal with the problem. If you do not have the problem-solving skills or communicative tools to deal with the problem, seek help from a counselor or psychologist.

---

9. Acculturation has both positive and negative effects on health.

10. The California Health Framework states an effective nutrition services program is basic to successful learning in schools.

11. Teachers play an important role in identifying and referring children who may not be getting adequate nutrition or displaying unusual eating behaviors.

12. Extreme violence has infiltrated many schools and has compromised the safety of our children.

13. Victims and perpetrators of school violence represent all racial, ethnic, and economic groups.

Note: Review Appendix E before facilitating this activity.

Everything You Wanted to Know about Destroying a Student's Self-Concept But Were Afraid to Ask

Time: 20–25 minutes (discussion not included)
Objective: To help participants understand that sending negative messages has destructive consequences to both the sender and the receiver.
Materials: None

Procedure:

1. Divide the class into groups of six or seven participants.
2. Ask for a volunteer from each group who is willing to play the role of a student.
3. Take the volunteers from each group to an area outside of the classroom and explain to them that this exercise will involve receiving critical remarks from the other members of their group. Also explain that the purpose of the exercise is to help students understand the feelings that occur when negative messages are sent. Allow any of the volunteers to change their minds about participating if they feel they are too sensitive to critical remarks. Make substitutions if necessary.

   Tell the students that they are going to make two separate statements and that they should practice the following lines while you go back into the classroom to prepare the other group members.

   The two statements that the students need to practice are:
   a. "Teacher, I am really working hard and trying to get better."
   b. "Teacher, I'm really glad I'm part of this class."
4. Tell each group that they are going to get in a straight line, side-by-side, and that their responsibility for this exercise is to make critical remarks to the "student" when they come back to their individual groups.
5. Tell each group member that he or she will be approached by a student who will make a statement. After listening to the statement each group member will reply with a critical response such as a criticism, rejection, discouraging remark, insult, or lecture.
6. Ask the participants to role-play the situation and not to smile. Tell them to use body and facial gestures to emphasize their remarks. For example, they may point their fingers,

raise their voice, frown, put their hands on their hips, or whatever is appropriate to enhance the remark. However, they may not touch the "student."

7. Tell them that the student will move from one person to the next until he or she reaches the end of the line. This process will be repeated twice. The first time, the student will say, "I am really working hard and trying to get better." The second time, the student will say, "Teacher, I'm really glad I'm part of this class."
8. Reassure the group that the "students" are aware of what is going to happen and that they have consented to participate.
9. Return to the "students" and tell that they are to return to their respective groups and start at the front of the line, face the first person and say, "Teacher, I am really working hard and trying to get better."
10. They are to listen to the remark and then move on to the next person and repeat the same statement. After going through the entire line, return to the front of the line.
11. Repeat the same process, except say, "Teacher, I'm really glad I'm part of this class."
12. Bring the students back into the room and to their groups and on your signal, tell all students to start.
13. When all groups are finished, reassemble everyone together and have the group members welcome the "students" back to reassure them that they are really cared for and that they are sorry for any discomfort they may have caused them.

Suggested Discussion Questions:

1. How did the "students" feel about what had just happened to them?
2. How did the group participants feel about what had just happened to them?
3. Did any of the "students" feel any physiological changes taking place during this experience? If so, what?
4. What about the activity surprised the participants?
5. Can anyone relate this activity to any real life situations?
6. In what ways does this experience apply to the participants' experience as a student or teacher?
7. How will the participant be different after this experience?

**Teacher's Corner: Gang Assessment Tool for
School Personnel** (Curtis High School Gang Handbook)

Complete and discuss your school's assessment of the gang problem on your campus. Give yourself the points in the parenthesis if any of the following exist:

Do you have graffiti on or near your campus? (5)

Do you have crossed-out graffiti on or near your campus? (10)

Do your students wear colors, jewelry, clothing, flash hand signals, or display other behaviors that may be gang related? (10)

Are drugs available on or near your school? (5)

Has there been a significant increase in the number of physical confrontations/stare downs during the past 12 months on or near your campus? (5)

Is there an increasing presence of weapons in your community? (10)

Are beepers, pagers, or cellular phones used by your students? (10)

Have you had a drive-by shooting at or around your school? (15)

Have you had a "show-by" (display of weapons) at or around your school? (10)

Is your truancy rate increasing? (5)

Is there a history of gangs in your community? (5)

Is there an increasing presence of "informal social groups" with unusual names like: The Posse, Rip of A Rule, Kappa Phi Nasty, 13th Street Crew, or Females Chillin? (15)

A score of 50 or more indicates a need to develop a Gang Prevention and Intervention Plan in your school. Such programs are being introduced around the country and most school administrators are responsible for the development of programs in their schools.

---

14. Schools have become a breeding ground for gangs and this can have a tremendous negative impact on the learning environment.

15. Gang members can be identified by their clothes, signals, graffiti, and tattoos.

16. Gang activity must be dealt with individually and swiftly and not allowed on any school campus.

17. Educators must adopt violence prevention programs that are tailored to their school's unique needs, resources, and safety goals.

18. Emotional safety is when students feel safe from intimidation, emotionally painful put-downs, threats, and criticism from the teacher and their classmates.

19. How long students stay in school is directly related to how safe and orderly they perceive the classroom environment to be.

20. If emotional assaults continue to accumulate and the student repeatedly re-presses the anger and resentment, internal pain builds up, causing an intense rage or hostility. The student can become a time bomb ready to explode.

21. Strong fear and/or anxiety can cause a heavy physiological toll on the body.

Teacher's Corner: Students and Violence

Concern: Do nondominant culture students suffer more violence in the school setting than dominant culture students do?

Directions for Interview

This is a sensitive survey and schools may require administrative permission for conducting this type of survey with students. Some school districts may require parental consent forms. If the survey is approved, inform the student that the survey is strictly confidential and that it is for the purpose of accumulating information for your college teacher preparation class.

Yes	No	Question
__	__	Has anyone ever threatened to hurt you during school?
__	__	Have you ever been robbed at school?
__	__	Have you ever been attacked while at school or on a school bus during the past year?
__	__	Has anyone ever threatened to hurt you outside of school?
__	__	Have you ever been robbed outside of school?
__	__	Have you ever been attacked outside of school?
__	__	Do you know any students who carry a knife to school?
__	__	Have you ever seen a student with a handgun at school?
__	__	Has any classmate ever offered to sell or give you illegal drugs?
__	__	Do you know of any students who use illegal drugs during school?
__	__	Have you ever been in a physical fight with another student?
__	__	Has anyone ever called you a derogatory name that had sexual or racial overtones?
__	__	Has anyone ever made fun of you because of your ethnic/racial background?
__	__	Has anyone ever made fun of you because of your physical characteristics, language background, or gender?

Analysis

As a result of your observations and interview, what important lessons can you apply to your present or future teaching strategies?

PART III

Communication in the Healthy Classroom

This part consists of two chapters and focuses on helping teachers develop positive interpersonal relations through healthy communication. Success will depend not only on how well you communicate your thoughts and feelings, but also on how well you listen. Communication skills are just as basic as driving a car. A person needs to know how to start and stop it. In between starting and stopping, one needs to know when to accelerate, when to put on the brakes, and how to keep the vehicle on course. Chapter 8 pulls together all the concepts of the book in a process called the "Classroom Meeting." This meeting is designed to help teachers and students make plans and decisions, to provide encouragement, and solve problems. Classroom meetings improve communication, cooperation, and responsibility and, most important, reflect how fortunate the students are to have each other.

7

■

Communication Skills

He who listens, understands.

AFRICAN PROVERB

The process of communication makes it possible for you to carry out your teaching responsibilities. Your plans must be communicated to the students in order for them to be carried out. Leadership on your part requires communicating with the students so that the group goals can be achieved. The communication process is one of the most important processes in the healthy classroom because it is the process of interacting with others and the foundation upon which teaching functions depend.

A large share of your time is devoted to the activity of communication. The importance of your communication is best described from the research of Mintzberg (1975) that described the leader's job time in terms of three types of roles. Communication plays a vital part in each:

1. Teachers have *interpersonal roles* in which they interact with their classroom students.

2. Teachers have *informational roles* in which they seek information from others about anything that may affect their job and responsibilities. They also disseminate interesting or important information in return.

3. Teachers have *decisional roles* in which they implement new projects, handle disturbances, and allocate responsibilities to their students.

In the communication process, communication may be one-way or two-way. In one-way communication, the sender communicates without expecting or getting feedback from the receiver. If communication must be fast and accuracy is easy to achieve (school announcements), one-way communication is both more economical and more efficient. If orderliness is considered vital—as in a large school function in the auditorium—one-way communication might also be more appropriate. Two-way communication exists when the receiver provides feedback to the sender. When accuracy of communication is important, as in instructions for carrying out complex lessons and concepts, the two-way method is recommended. Without feedback from the receiver, the sender has little basis for judging the accuracy of the communication or the degree of understanding and comprehension experienced by the receiver.

LISTENING REFLECTS ACCEPTANCE
AND SIGNIFICANCE

Healthy and effective communication is one of the most important skills in teaching. Success will depend not only on how well you listen, but also how well you communicate your thoughts and feelings to the students, parents of the students, other teachers, administrators, and all other individuals who are actively concerned with the school.

Communication skills are just as basic as driving a car. You need to know how to start and stop. In between starting and stopping, one needs to know

Healthy and effective communication is one of the most important skills in teaching. Success depends on how well a teacher listens and communicates his or her thoughts and feelings.

when to accelerate, when to put on the brakes, and how to keep the vehicle on course.

Of all the things that can make any student feel accepted, significant, and worthwhile, none is more vital than being listened too. Yet learning how to listen is a skill that is usually overlooked. Teachers who are good listeners become very popular with all students. More important, they even learn something. Listening is a very powerful sign of respect. Listening is, perhaps, the most important vehicle for meeting any student's need for emotional acceptance, significance, and security. Being listened to makes a student feel worthwhile. For students, being listened to means being understood and feeling that his or her thoughts and feelings really do count.

If a teacher chooses to preach, advise, patronize, and evaluate his or her students rather than listen to and understand them, he or she mistakenly believes that what he or she has to say to the student is more important than what the students have to say. When a student expresses how he or she feels, some teachers may even tell them to deny those feelings and then proceed to tell them how they should feel. For example, a student expresses frustration because he feels that the other students don't like him, but the teacher says, "You shouldn't feel that way, I know that it isn't true." Or a student expresses disappointment because she lost the all-school spelling contest, and the teacher says, "You shouldn't feel disappointed. You did the best you could and that's what counts." It is a mistake for a teacher to believe that he or she can tell his or her students what and how they should feel and think. Unfortunately, the teacher who believes that he or she is communicating with his or her students by telling them how they should feel, in reality, is talking too much and hoping to hear his or her own words coming from the students' mouths.

Psychologists and counselors work with the principle that merely talking about one's inner emotions in relation to life's frustrations can be healing therapy. Letting clients talk is an important part of the foundation for most treatment. Careful study of good salespeople shows the importance of good listening. The best salespeople are those people who have empathy and listen the most. They know that if you want to get somebody to do something or to buy something, you cannot "talk them into it."

Empathy Not Sympathy

Empathy is a process that involves being sensitive to another individual's changing feelings and connecting emotionally to that other person. Empathy involves a process of "living for a time in the other person's life," entering his or her private perceptual world, and seeing events through his or her eyes. Empathy involves avoiding judgments about what the other person is feeling and instead trying to understand those feelings fully from the person's perspective.

You will witness countless cues to a student's emotional experience. These cues are found in what the student says and how he or she says it, as well as his or her actions and expressions. Empathy involves correctly perceiving what the student is expressing through nonverbal cues and responding in a manner that conveys understanding.

Empathy involves letting the student know that he or she is understood. It is more than just saying, "I understand how you feel." Rather, empathy requires the accurate perception of the student's emotional experience and then the communication back to the student precisely what is understood.

Empathy is not sympathy. Sympathy is the concern that you may feel or show for a student. Empathy is an attempt to feel with the student, to understand the feelings from the student's point of view. Empathy is focusing on the student's problem, not yours.

Can You Develop Empathy?

Developing empathy is a slow process that requires effort and discipline on three important dimensions. According to Mayer and Greenberg (1964), the cognitive component of empathy requires the teacher to observe the student's behavior carefully (body language and actions) and interpret the meaning of what is being observed. Empathy depends on knowing or being aware of what the physical and emotional effects of certain events are. For example, it is important for you to know about the emotional realities of being liked or not liked. These include the effects on a student's thoughts, emotions, and behaviors when he or she is faced with rejection or acceptance.

The affective component of empathy involves being sensitive to the student's feelings and listening to what the student is saying about those feelings in words, gestures, and actions. The affective component of empathy involves that you relate what you perceive to be the student's emotions to your own emotional experience. The communicative component of empathy focuses on communicating through words or gestures to the student that he or she is understood, that you know the facts about what the student is experiencing, and perceive accurately what the student is feeling.

When students feel understood, they are also more likely to follow any recommendations that you make. When given the opportunity to express their emotional needs and concerns, students feel they can trust you to function in their best interest. In addition, students will be more willing to share their concerns in the future.

Students Need to Be Understood

It is quite apparent that most people like to talk, express themselves, and be heard. When allowed to do that with an attentive listener, they respond positively and favorably. They become more receptive to the things that the listener suggests.

Students need to be understood. This is especially true when they are upset. They need the acceptance of others. Your acceptance does not mean that you must agree with the student's feelings and opinions. It simply requires that you listen and understand and allow the student to own his or her own feelings.

For example, a student comes to you and says that she hates school and is going to quit. You do not want her to quit, and she probably doesn't really want to quit, but something is obviously upsetting her. It would be difficult to convince her about the benefits of remaining in school because she would probably feel you do not understand her anger. Though you may already know the solution to the problem, jumping in too soon will usually result in rejection of the solution. When individuals are upset, they are not ready to hear instant solutions. They need to be heard and understood, and they need to have their feelings validated.

Acknowledge the student's feelings first. You might say, "Sounds like something is really upsetting you." Acknowledging the student's feelings gives her a chance to talk and sort out her feelings. If this process continues, she will gradually calm down and will be ready to look for ways to solve her problems. When you understand a student's thoughts and feelings, you establish a foundation for problem solving.

If a student expresses sadness, anger, or disappointment and wants to be left alone, you must acknowledge those feelings and wishes. If you believe that it is important to follow up on those feelings, you should allow those feelings to dissipate and discuss the issue at a less emotional time. Acknowledging a student's thoughts and feelings is not the same as approving of them, nor does it imply that the student is going to have his or her own way. It is simply a way of saying to the student that he or she is understood and that you can empathize with those thoughts and feelings.

Students need to be understood, especially when they are upset. A teacher can help by listening and allowing the student to own their own feelings

Listening for Feelings

Recognizing feelings is often difficult. Without a vocabulary for feelings, it is hard to explore and understand the needs of others. Following is a list of some words that describe internal feeling states:

angry	anxious	apathetic	bitter
bored	broken-hearted	calm	cautious
cheerful	comfortable	confident	confused
contented	daring	delighted	distressed
distraught	displeased	eager	ecstatic
elated	enchanted	excited	frustrated
foolish	glad	happy	hesitant
hopeful	hurt	humiliated	incensed
irritated	joyful	jubilant	nervous
proud	relieved	resentful	sad
selfish	silly	sorry	uneasy
uncomfortable	unhappy	weary	

The following attitudes are necessary for reflective listening:

1. You must be willing to hear what the student has to say and be willing to take the time to listen.

2. You must be willing to help the student.

3. You must be willing to accept the student's feelings.

4. You must see the student as a person who is capable and competent enough to understand his or her own problems.

Practice the Art of Listening

Most people are not taught to listen; however, listening skills are not difficult to learn—they are just difficult to use. The foundation of attentive listening skills is that you must want to listen. You must have a strong desire to hear what the other person has to say. Once you learn to use listening skills and use them with the students, you will transform relationships, help solve problems, and raise self-esteem.

1. *Stop.* Do not fidget, turn your back, or conduct some other business and try to listen at the same time. Show your students that you are interested in them. Be interested and look interested. Be sure your facial and eye expressions as well as your posture (body language) and tone of voice all communicate appropriate feelings and meanings. When a student shares something with you let your face express your interest. Make visual contact, face the speaker, and lean slightly forward.

2. *Look.* Be aware of the tone of voice, the pauses, movement, posture, speed, and inflection of voice, tears, facial expressions, hand gestures, and all the other things that relay important information to you. Sometimes the actions reflect a totally different meaning than the actual words. Be aware of nonverbal cues or behaviors. Try to hear the feelings and meanings behind the words.

3. *Listen.* Most of the time, when someone is talking, the listener is only partly listening because the listener is usually thinking about what he or she is going to say and waiting for the opportune time to cut in on the other person so that he or she can speak. Conversations that occur at this level are minimally effective. Try to focus on your students' words and feelings instead of thinking about what you are going to be saying next. Do not make impulsive judgments about your students and their feelings. Try to put yourself in their shoes and try to understand what is happening. Also, let the students own those feelings.

4. *Use caution.* Let them finish; do not interrupt the train of thought and feelings. Even though you may have a different opinion, keep it to yourself until your student requests it. If the students know they are really being listened to, they are more likely to choose their words carefully because they are more accountable for what comes out of their mouths. While you are a listener, let the speaker do the talking. It is occasionally okay to briefly interject an "uh-huh" or nod of the head. Any subtle gesture that reflects that you are listening is okay. The main point is that you do not interrupt the flow of words and feelings.

The Skill of Reflective Listening

Reflective listening is a way to show students that their message has not only been heard, but been understood as well. This skill becomes a way in which you can become the mirror by which the students can hear and "see" their feelings more clearly. While there is no one correct way to carry out this skill, a few guidelines follow:

1. *Reflect the content of the communication by paraphrasing what is being said instead of evaluating it.* Simply repeat exactly what is said. If a student says, "Nobody in the class likes me!" you would say, "You think no one in the class likes you?" Keep your voice calm, and be patient when you say this.

2. *Show that you empathize by reflecting the student's feelings.* When you reflect feeling, you listen with your eyes and hear the tone of voice that captures the nature and intensity of the emotion behind the words. In fact, the student may be saying a great deal more with his or her body language and tone of voice than the words alone convey.

3. *Ask open-ended questions to encourage the students to continue to share their feelings.* Asking them to elaborate on their thoughts and feelings shows that you are interested in what they have to say. Open-ended questions neither add to nor subtract from the student's message. It shows that you understand what your student is trying to tell you. When you are listening reflectively, it is better to ask the right questions than to provide the answers. Open-ended responses encourage dialogue. The opposite of an open-ended question is a closed question. Closed questions or responses are usually directive and require only a one-word response from the listener. Closed responses do not seek understanding. Closed responses discourage dialogue.

Following are some examples of open-ended and closed response questions:

1. Open-ended: "What options do you think are best?"
   Closed response: "Why don't you get a tutor?"

2. Open-ended: "What does Jim do that irritates you?"
   Closed response: "Why don't you try to get along with Jim?"

The important aspects of communicating with students are both understanding and building trust and confidence. When you listen, you make it clear to the students that you care about their concerns, needs, fears, doubts, and hopes. Listening is accepting the student's thoughts and feelings and being okay with the fact that this other point of view might be different from yours.

You should not think that you have to lecture and teach a lesson to the students at every turn, especially when emotions are intense. You should listen completely to all of the students' thoughts and feelings and be cautious about advising too quickly. Sometimes, when no advice is requested, you should try not to give any at all.

Cultural Differences Can Impair Communication

Difficulties in communication are not usually a result of words or language differences but are the result of cultural differences. In culture A, for example, communication may be direct and to the point. In culture B, the same topics may be approached with caution and reserve and the message is to be inferred as opposed to being direct. Members of culture A will have difficulty understanding what members of culture B are trying to say, while members of culture B will perceive members of culture A as being overbearing and rude.

In school it is important for you to understand cultural differences in communication habits. For example, students representing some ethnic groups are reluctant to challenge your opinions or even ask for clarification of unclear statements.

Intercultural Differences and Similarities
in Nonverbal Communication

We have all had the experience of talking to someone whose nonverbal messages or behaviors clearly contradict the words. Which message are we to believe? Irujo (1988) presented the following circumstances which elicit different emotional cultural responses:

1. A Japanese smile may represent embarrassment, sorrow, or anger.

2. Not looking another person in the eye is recognition of that person's authority for African-Americans, while whites interpret this as shiftiness and unreliability. When African-Americans roll their eyes, it is a sign of hostility, impudence, and disapproval.

3. Arabs, Latin-Americans, and Southern Europeans focus their gaze on their partners during conversation, while East Asians, Indian-Pakistani's and Northern Europeans show a peripheral gaze or no gaze at all. Arabs have difficulty carrying on a conversation if they cannot look each other in the eye, as when they are walking side-by-side down the street, or if one is wearing dark glasses.

4. Differences in gaze behavior may cause some misunderstandings. Latinos interpret a direct gaze as having sexual connotations, and a steady stare with raised eyebrows as anger. Greeks, who are used to being stared at in public, feel ignored when they go to countries such as England where staring is not considered polite.

5. The same gesture (making a circle with thumb and forefinger) means "okay" to a North American but can mean money to the Japanese, signify extreme hostility to an Arab, or be obscene to an Italian.

6. Africans, Arabs, and Hispanic-Americans touch a great deal in interpersonal relationships, whereas in Britain, Japan, and the United States there is very little touching. There was more physical contact among Americans compared to Japanese, and Americans had more "contact with the opposite sex." For many Japanese, touching causes embarrassment and discomfort.

Cultural differences can impair communication.

Schilling and Brannon (1986) have recommended the following suggestions to enhance communication between members of different cultures:

- Develop an understanding of your own cultural values and biases. Most of us tend to be somewhat ethnocentric, assuming that the ways of our own culture are best and judging other cultures by how closely they approximate our own.

- Develop an understanding of the cultural values, beliefs, and customs of other ethnic groups with which you interact.

- Be respectful of, interested in, and nonjudgmental about cultures other than your own. When two cultures are different it is not necessary to judge which one is better or right—we can simply accept them as being different. We can learn to enjoy and appreciate the richness that ethnic diversity brings to our classrooms and our communities.

- Speak in a way that promotes understanding and shows respect for someone from a different ethnic group. Be especially careful to avoid statements such as "She's really very (smart/tall/beautiful/etc.) for a (fill in the ethnic group)." Even though the intention may be good, such statements are certain to offend the subject and to reveal the speaker's biases.

- Avoid using slang or idioms that could be misunderstood by someone from a different ethnic group. Most of the everyday phrases that are instantly understood within one ethnic group might have no meaning or a totally different meaning to someone from a different group.

- Remember that the same gestures can carry different meanings in different cultures. Avoid body language that might be offensive or misunderstood. Observe closely the use of gestures by people in different cultures, it could save a

---

Time-out: Communication Skills Test

Directions: Respond to each of the following items by circling the number that corresponds to the description that most accurately reflects your behavior. *Treat the results as a guide only. There is a margin of uncertainty in all questionnaires of this kind.*

Rating Scale	*Never* 1	*Seldom* 2	*Usually* 3	*Always* 4

1. I like to listen to others.   1 2 3 4
2. I state one thought at a time.   1 2 3 4
3. I pretend that I'm paying attention.   1 2 3 4
4. I use sarcasm.   1 2 3 4
5. I repeat key points.   1 2 3 4
6. I respect others' right to express themselves.   1 2 3 4
7. I am easily distracted by other noises.   1 2 3 4
8. I listen to all of the other person's message.   1 2 3 4
9. I finish thoughts for the speaker.   1 2 3 4
10. I listen by nodding my head or verbally agreeing with what others are saying.   1 2 3 4
11. I keep the pitch of my voice level in tense situations.   1 2 3 4
12. I shake hands firmly.   1 2 3 4
13. I look directly at people when talking to them.   1 2 3 4
14. I walk slowly and hunch my shoulders.   1 2 3 4
15. I use my hands to augment my words.   1 2 3 4

Scoring: Simply add items 1, 2, 5, 6, 8, 10, 11, 12, 13, and 15. Then for items 3, 4, 7, 9, and 14, reverse the order of the numbering system. For example, if you circled 4 for the third item, you would score it as 1. Add these five reverse-scored items to the total for the first ten items summed to get your total communication score.

Total Score	Your Communication Style
51 and up	Clear Connection
40–50	Mixed Messages
39 and below	Tongue-tied

---

major embarrassment. For example, the hand gesture that means "perfect" in the United States refers to sexual intercourse in the Philippines.

Guidelines for Communicating with Students with Disabilities

Communication between the teacher and the student with a disability is a critical aspect of a healthy relationship. You must become aware of your responsibility to communicate with a person with a disability. Following are some suggestions to help you improve your communications with persons with disabilities:

- Speak directly with the person with the disability rather than with his or her companion.

- Be prepared to shake hands with the person. In some instances you may need to grasp the person's forearm or use your left hand as you meet or greet him or her.

- Do not raise your voice when speaking to a person who is visually impaired.

- Stoop or squat to communicate with a person in a wheelchair and position yourself in front and at eye level. If a chair is available, it is preferable to sit in the chair so that you are at an equal level.

- Greet the person as you would greet persons without a disability.

- Talk as you would talk with persons who do not have a disability. Do not patronize.

- Identify yourself and other persons in a group to the person who is visually impaired.

- Appropriately touch or tap a person who is hearing impaired so he or she is aware of your presence.

- Be patient and listen carefully when interacting with a person who has a speech impairment; use questions that require brief responses.

- If a person is able to lip read, stand where the person can see your lips clearly and speak slowly and enunciate carefully.

- Be careful about using such expressions as "see you later" or "let's do this one step at a time." In most cases, the person with a disability will recognize these as common expressions and will not take it personally. However, try to limit such expressions.

The Major Barrier to Healthy Communication

As far back as 1952, Rogers and Roethlisberger reported that the major barrier to the communication process is the tendency to judge, evaluate, and approve or disapprove of the statements that our students make to us. For example, suppose Jose comments that he "doesn't like having to take his math final on the last day of school." What will you respond? Almost invariably, your reply will be either to approve or disapprove of the attitude expressed. You respond either "I don't either" or "It doesn't really matter." In other words, you evaluate the statement from your own point of view or reference. In addition, evaluations are usually elevated when feelings and emotions are more deeply involved. Stronger feelings in the initial statement usually separate any mutual elements in the communication, resulting in two feelings and two evaluations that miss each other completely. The teacher could have replied, "You dislike taking the math test last?" or "What bothers you about taking the math test on the final day of school?"

Healthy communication, of course, occurs when we stop evaluating and empathetically listen with understanding. It means seeing the student's point of view and sensing how it feels to him or her.

When students have a problem and need to discuss something that is troubling them, you need to be a good listener. However, when you have a problem, you need to effectively communicate what you need.

The careful use of language is especially crucial in correcting a student's problematic behavior. Students who are given corrections without reasons tend to be less reasonable. Students who are not given clear statements of what is expected of them feel frustrated about doing anything right. It is difficult for a student to develop positive feelings when his or her behavior inspires only anger and annoyance in the teacher.

When Does the Teacher Get to Speak?

Reflective listening is a process that is used when something is troubling the student. The student "owns the problem." However, not every conversation involves a problem and reflective listening is not always required. The following diagram represents the typical situations that arise in any human relationship:

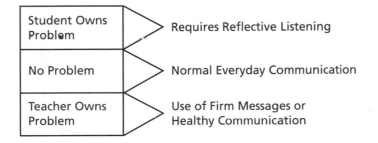

If no one has a problem, you and the student carry on with your everyday normal conversation. Listening is important, of course, but when no problem exists, reflective listening is not always necessary. You can talk as much as he or she wants, as long as the students are willing to listen. If you "own the problem" you should use healthy communication. Healthy communication is discussed in the next section of this chapter.

Wants into Words: Healthy Communication

The most important skill in asking students for what you want is formulating a request that is respectful and constructive. Preparing such a statement involves getting the facts and then putting them into a clear statement of your wants. This is usually all that is needed in everyday teaching. For example, simply stating that you want the class to do some math problems or to be quiet is all that is needed. In most cases, a clearly defined request suffices. You do not need to explain these requests.

However, sometimes it is not enough just to say what is wanted. On occasion, students need to know more background of your request. They need to know your understanding or perception. It may also be helpful for them to know how the situation has affected you emotionally. When you offer your

... encourages closeness and mutual respect.

thoughts (how the situation is perceived), feelings, and want statement, this is healthy communication.

Healthy communication encourages closeness and mutual respect. Students will be more likely to respond to your wants when they are aware of your feelings and perspective.

For example, you know that Cheryl is lying to you about why she hasn't been doing her daily English assignments. You are upset by the fact that Cheryl is not turning in her work but, more importantly, you are hurt that Cheryl is lying to you. It is rather abrupt to say to Cheryl, "I know you are lying to me, I can't trust you." It is better to deliver healthy communication like this, "I feel very hurt and disappointed about the fact that I am being lied to. What I want is for it to stop and find a way to develop a relationship that is based on honesty and trust."

When you leave your experience of a situation or your feelings out of a request, students may feel pressured to do something, but they won't know why. They are more likely to resist or argue and place barriers between themselves and you. It is better to give the students a window through which they can see and experience where you are coming from.

Anger Affects Healthy Communication

Teachers have moments of rage. No matter how much you care for students, it is inevitable that at some point you will get mad at them. Unfortunately, few teachers know how to communicate anger effectively. Most teachers will sometimes make the mistake of saying terrible things that are later regretted.

In moments of frustration, anger, or stress, teachers have said things that they knew they should not have. Unfortunately, many have engaged in personal attacks on students. Not knowing what else to do, they have said things that have insulted and hurt others. In their anger, they have blamed, ridiculed, and called their students unkind names. As a result, they usually got the opposite of what they wanted. Instead of encouraging cooperation, they invited anger, resistance, and rebellion.

Negative remarks are attacks on the student's self-esteem and promote defensiveness and counter-attacks. If the motivation behind such verbal attacks is to inflict emotional pain, character assassination is the ultimate weapon. However, if the goal is to create mutual understanding between the two parties, it is self-defeating.

Anger undermines healthy communication. Communication should be delayed until you feel that you are under control. Take a deep breath and say, "I am really upset and angry now. I need to move away from this situation. I will talk with you when I feel calm." Or ask for assistance from another adult or responsible student who is calm.

Angry confrontations are hurtful and punitive. Healthy communication guides, protects, and helps students to grow. An angry teacher may find it helpful to think about and answer the following questions:

1. Why do I feel this way?

2. What did I feel before I became angry? Was it embarrassment? Fear? Frustration?

3. Are there other problems bothering me that are making me less tolerant?

4. What is the student feeling at this moment?

5. Am I expecting too much from my students?

6. Am I being reasonable?

Teachers who lack assertiveness need to add healthy communication to their daily speech. Long-suffering martyrs who suppress their own feelings, wants, and needs to keep everyone happy are taken advantage of and eventually will erupt in anger and resentment. The more they give, the more people want. As they learn to take an assertive stance, they will discover less anger, greater feelings of appreciation, and a better feeling about themselves.

The more skilled you become in using healthy communication, the more successful you will become in confronting and resolving problems with your students. Students will respond with greater trust and confidence because they know they are being treated in a fair and respectful manner.

When a Student's Words or Actions Affect the Teacher's Emotional Well-Being

You need to develop positive ways to communicate your thoughts and feelings, especially when you are frustrated and upset. The language that you choose and the way you use it can ultimately affect student's performance. You need to model self-control, responsibility, and consideration to others.

Healthy communication is an effective way of dealing with undesirable behavior. It focuses on your feelings about a student's behavior, not about the student. The students are okay; their behavior is not. You can still accept and respect them, but you do not have to like what they did. Healthy communication expresses your feelings, thoughts, and wants. The first three steps of healthy communication are based on the I-Message model developed by Gordon (1970). The first three steps of healthy communication are:

1. *Describe Your Feelings* Your feelings help the listener to have empathy or your experience in a situation. The best way to express your feelings is for you to take responsibility for your emotions. You say:

I feel frustrated.

It makes me angry.

I'm confused.

I feel disappointed.

I was saddened.

I get discouraged.

I feel anxious.

This is in contrast to unhealthy or destructive communication, which is accusing and places all responsibility for your feelings on the listener. Unhealthy communications are You-Messages that put down, blame, or criticize. These destructive messages provoke anger, embarrassment, and feelings of worthlessness. Students may take such statements as "You're lazy" or "You're worthless" as an affirmation of their lack of personal value. Other examples of unhealthy communication are:

You hurt me.

You made me angry.

You're so inconsiderate.

You disappointed me.

At times you may have to use the pronoun "you" when you are referring directly to a specific student. However, you can still use it without placing blame. "When you come late to class" does not place blame; it merely states a fact. Whenever possible, talk about the situation rather than focusing on the individual.

2. *Describe Your Thoughts about the Action or Event That Concerns You* Your thoughts are your perceptions or understanding of a particular situation. You explain or describe what your understanding is of what is happening. You say:

When people do the exact opposite of what I requested.

When people lie to me.

When individuals spread rumors about me.

When people use that type of language with me.

3. Describe the Tangible Reason Why the Behavior Affects You Your explanation helps the listener to understand how his or her behavior is affecting you. You say:

Because it will adversely affect class unity.

Because I am afraid someone will get hurt.

Because I dislike leaving the locker room messy.

Because I don't like people questioning my abilities.

Because I don't like to be lied to.

The three part message is expressed as follows:

I feel _____

about/when _____

because _____

Other words or phrases may be substituted for any of the words used in the model. In addition, a person using healthy communication may state the three parts of the process in any order that he or she chooses.

Upon receiving the three parts of the message, the student is allowed to internally interpret the message and have the freedom to choose how he or she is going to respond to it. This is, of course, when the situation does not involve any immediate danger to anyone. This three-part message may not work with students unless a reciprocal environment of dignity and respect has been established. A fourth step may have to be added to the message until that environment has been established. The fourth part of the message follows.

4. Describe What You Want Done The most important skill is asking for what you want. Preparing a healthy request involves getting the facts and your thoughts and processing them into a clear statement of your wants or needs. Stay away from abstractions such as "show me some cooperation, " "show respect," or "be honest." Do not ask for a change in attitude or level of interest. Instead, specify the exact behavior: "I want you to tell me the real reason why you missed class yesterday" or "I want everyone to be here Monday morning at exactly 8:00." In some instances, it may be appropriate to omit the "therefore" portion of the statement and allow the listener to determine what he or she should do.

Putting It All Together: The Completed Message

The following is a model for healthy communication:

I feel _____

about/when _____

because _____

Therefore/so _____

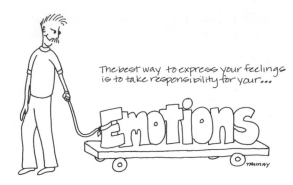

Further Thoughts about Healthy Communication

1. *Nonverbal communication is an important part of your message.* Remember that healthy communication is friendly, respectful, and honest; therefore, use appropriate body language. Maintain eye contact, sit or stand erect, do not cross your arms and legs, and make sure you are close enough to your listener. Speak clearly. If your tone of voice and body are out of sync with what you are trying to say, the student will be more influenced by the nonverbal behavior than your words. You should practice healthy communication in front of a mirror to correct problems in body language. You should also listen to your own words on tape to evaluate your voice and inflection.

2. *Don't overuse healthy communication.* Healthy communication should be used sparingly. If it is overused, students will be turned off, and it will consequently lose its overall effectiveness. Alternative approaches such as delaying the conversation to a time when there is no conflict or making simple requests for gaining cooperation are effective.

   "Is there anything that you can do to help me out?"

   "It would really be helpful if you _____."

   By making a request, you are giving the student the right to say no. If a "no" response is given, you must respect that decision. Doing so demonstrates respect and may very well encourage a willingness to cooperate in the future.

Using Encouragement Instead of Praise

It is equally important that you communicate good feelings. Be generous with good feelings, students need to know they are making important contributions. Encouragement is better than praise.

Time-out: The Teacher/Coach and the Overbearing Parents

Winston High School has just won a very close and important midseason conference game. They are well on their way to making the playoffs for the fourth straight year. The fans and the media have been supportive, and attendance and publicity have been exceptional. The season couldn't be going much better for Coach Thompson—except for Cheryl's aggressive and overly involved parents. Their recent "know-it-all" suggestions on what the team should be doing have been wearing away at Coach Thompson's nerves.

Parental interest and involvement are always appreciated, but over time, Cheryl's parents have crossed the line between what is acceptable and what has become obnoxious interference. The coach doesn't want to hurt their feelings, nor does she want to further embarrass an already embarrassed Cheryl; however, Coach Thompson has endured the situation long enough and is ready to tell Cheryl's parents where they can go. She also realizes that she could have prevented this situation if she had put a stop to their behavior earlier.

Coach Thompson, relaxing in her office after the game and quietly savoring the important victory is dreading the moment when Cheryl's parents "accidentally" run into her to tell her how great Cheryl played, what the team did wrong, and what the team needs to work on for the next important game.

Cheryl's Dad enthusiastically shouts, "Hi, Coach! Great game! We are going to make it to the playoffs." The supportive language continues in this direction until the manipulative conversation turns to the dreaded words that Coach Thompson has already anticipated: "You know, Coach, I noticed that Yolanda was making a lot of defensive mistakes. You might consider taking her out of the starting line-up or moving her to a different position. And . . ."

Coach Thompson is thinking to herself, "Oh no, here it comes again," as the words from Cheryl's Mom and Dad fade into space and are no longer heard. Coach Thompson's eyes are looking beyond them now, but she is not seeing anything in particular.

Multiple Choice

What would you do if you were Coach Thompson?

A. Tell Cheryl's Dad to "shut up" and keep his know-it-all, meddling opinions to himself and to stop coming to you with his comments.
B. Endure the situation and ignore his comments.
C. Use healthy communication to help Cheryl's Dad understand how you feel about the situation.

Response C is the correct answer. Healthy communication is a positive way to express your thoughts and feelings. It is respectful because it focuses on the behavior, not on the individual. Cheryl's parents are okay, but their behavior is not.

After recognizing her anger and calming down, Coach Thompson might reply something like this, "I truly appreciate all of the parent and fan support our team is receiving. I am, however, beginning to feel very frustrated with the unsolicited suggestions that I am constantly receiving. These comments suggest that I am not doing a good job. I would appreciate it if the suggestions would stop."

Response A is not appropriate because you are attacking Cheryl's Dad directly. This will result in hard feelings and put a huge barrier between you and Cheryl's parents. It might also damage your relationship with Cheryl.

Response B is not appropriate because enduring the behavior is not really fair to you. You should not have to endure any unsolicited behavior. Also, your negative feelings will only increase over time.

The Praise Craze

A controversy over the appropriate use of praise has arisen. Many educators and parenting experts have split on the merits of praise. Many believe that praise is overused, overrated, and used inappropriately. Some believe that Americans, in the name of self-esteem, have gone "praise crazy." Everyone agrees that self-esteem must arise from within, from a genuine sense of accomplishment and self-worth, but the approach has been an explosion of awards, gold stars, and certificates for such routine accomplishments as just showing up or "just being me." Many kids have become praise "junkies," expecting praise for every little thing they do.

The Ulterior Motives of Most Praise

Lillian Katz, president-elect of the National Association for the Education of Young Children and professor of education at the University of Illinois, in a *Newsweek* article (Surler, 1992) was quoted as saying, "Schools have established award structures—the happy helper of the week, the reader of the week. Teachers think that if they don't do this stuff, the kids won't work, but that's ridiculous. We don't need all this flattery. No other country does this."

Therein lies the fault of most praise. Teachers, parents, and other adults use praise to reinforce or change youngsters in some specific way. They have ulterior motives for their praise. Praise reinforces the "proper" behaviors that the adult wants the child to continue—such as good grades, neat appearance, good manners, and acting nice. Somewhere, hidden under most adult praise is the underlying purpose of making the adult feel good—getting the behavior he or she wants, having the kids dress the way he or she wants, having a quiet classroom. It does not take long for anyone to see through such praise and recognize the adult's intentions. Teachers who give out praise not only to make the student feel good, but to change the student so that the teacher can feel good, will soon be perceived by students as manipulative and dishonest.

Insulting Through Praise

Some teachers will give backhanded compliments by mixing their praise with an insult. They give students praise for what they did well, but at the same time remind them of earlier failures. Some examples are:

You certainly did better today than you did yesterday.

You scored really well on the test. I was really surprised since you loafed in class all week.

Congratulations, you got here on time. I didn't think you would make it considering you waited until the last minute to leave.

Do not use praise to punish or insult. Obviously, it does not make the student feel very good.

use encouragement instead of praise
to give positive feedback.

Praise That Does Not Match the Student's Perception

Another problem arises when the teacher's praise does not match a student's own perception of success. When praise does not match the student's self-evaluation of performance or behavior, the student loses respect for the teacher's integrity and honesty. More important, when praise does not match a student's self-evaluation, it denies the student's feelings. It tells the student that the teacher does not really understand him or her. Praise in this instance becomes a barrier to further communication.

Overpraising

A student often knows that he or she is not the best mathematician in the school, but overpraising the student because he or she got the highest test score today puts pressure on the student to be great everyday. When the student does not do well, will that make the student feel like he or she is lousy or inadequate?

Many teachers have come to realize that overpraising can become detrimental because as soon as they draw attention to what the student did well, he or she will do the opposite. This phenomenon is due to overpraising. The tension of being overpraised is too much of a burden to carry. Allow the student to be himself or herself and not the best mathematician.

An Alternative to Praise

This does not mean that teachers should never say anything nice to their students. Students do need encouragement and feedback; however, using the language of typical praise is not as effective as was once thought.

The healthy communication model is an excellent method for encouragement. These encouraging messages consist of the first three parts of healthy communication: (1) your reactions to or feelings about the behavior or performance, (2) a description of the behavior or performance, and (3) why it makes you feel that way. The following statements are examples of sharing good feelings through the healthy communication model:

Thank you for being so respectful during this talk, it really helped me focus on what I needed to say.

I appreciated how hard you worked in class today, I know it was a tough assignment.

The model for encouragement is summarized as follows:

1. I feel (share your feelings and emotions) _____
2. About (clarify the behavior) _____
3. Because (benefits to the teacher) _____

Sharing reactions such as these with students makes the teacher more understandable rather than someone who unpredictably goes from hot to cold without reason. This form of praise enables students to learn something about the teacher and themselves. For instance, "Thank you for being so respectful during my discussion with Keisha's mother and father, it really helped me focus on what I needed to say." You are glad that your students are able to diligently work while you talk with parents—you need quiet while you discuss important matters.

SUMMARY OF MAJOR POINTS
IN CHAPTER 7

1. Listening is a skill that is overlooked because many teachers would rather talk than listen.

2. Cultural differences are not usually a result of words or language differences but are reflected by cultural differences that impair communication.

3. Listening is, perhaps, the most important vehicle for meeting a student's need for emotional significance and security.

4. Empathy is a process of living for a time in the other person's life, entering his or her private perceptual world, and seeing events through his or her eyes.

5. Empathy is not sympathy.

6. Students need to be not only heard, but also understood.

7. The first step in the reflective listening process is the desire to want to listen reflectively.

8. Reflective listening requires the teacher to:

    a. stop all other activity,

    b. look for body language and emotions to help understand the meaning behind the words,

    c. listen to words and search for the meaning rather than thinking about what you are going to say, and

    d. use caution. Do not interrupt the flow of words and feelings.

Class Discussion	CHAPTER 7

Note: Review Appendix E before facilitating this activity.

Active Listening

Time: 15–20 minutes (discussion not included)
Objective: Group members will demonstrate the behavior characteristics of an active listener.
Materials: A copy of "Active Listening Skills" for each participant.

Procedure:

1. The facilitator distributes "Active Listening Skills."

2. The facilitator explains each of the qualities of an active listener, demonstrating appropriate eye contact, body language, and other aspects. Modeling is an essential component of learning appropriate listening skills.

3. Group members form triads. Members are asked to choose the role of listener, speaker, and observer. There will be three timed sessions. The facilitator asks the speaker to choose a personal issue and talk for three to four minutes. During this time, the listener practices the qualities of an active listener as previously presented. The observer watches the listener and checks listening behaviors noted on the "Active Listening Skills" sheet. At the end of the timed session, there is a two-minute sharing. Positions are traded until each member has had an opportunity to try each role.

4. If members have a difficult time choosing a talk topic, the following are suggested:
   a. A unique experience
   b. A special teacher, friend, classmate, or relative
   c. A memorable vacation
   d. An embarrassing moment

5. Bring the groups back together.

Suggested Discussion Questions:

1. What pleased you about the experience?
2. What did you learn about yourself?
3. How did you feel during this experience?
4. In what ways can this experience apply to the teaching profession?
5. How are you going to be different from this experience?

Active Listening Skills

1. Make eye contact and use "listening" language

   Make eye contact with the speaker to show you are attentive

   Lean slightly toward speaker, but not too close

   Tilt head slightly forward to acknowledge understanding

   Be aware of hand position. Crossing the arms in front of the chest may reflect that you are closed off to the listener. Crossing the hands in front of your lap is a more open posture.

   Give speaker complete attention

   Remain silent when person speaks

   Listen attentively

2. Encourage the speaker by acknowledging his or her words

   "Uh huh."

   "Yes, I see what you mean"

   "Okay"

   "That sounds right"

3. Reflect feelings or paraphrase

   "What I heard you say was . . ."

   "It sounds as if you're feeling . . ."

   "You sound . . ."

4. Be empathetic and nonjudgmental

   Value the speaker and what he or she says

   Accept the speaker's feelings

   Forego judgments

Class Discussion	CHAPTER 7

Note: Review Appendix E before facilitating this activity.

Sending Nonverbal Messages
Time: 10 minutes (discussion not included)
Objective: To help participants understand that body language is an important part of the message. Sometimes it speaks louder than the words.
Materials: None

Procedure:

1. Participants choose one partner and decide who will be the speaker and who will be the listener.
2. Partners face each other about 4–6 feet apart.
3. The speaker is to convey his or her message by using only facial or body movements. Emphasize that the speaker may not touch the listener. The listener may not move from the spot in which he or she is standing.
4. Tell the speaker to display the following feelings to the listener as you describe them. Allow about 10 seconds for each message.

   frustrated—I am frustrated with you

   anger—I am angry at you

   bashful—I am very shy

   admiration—I admire you

   scared—I was really scared

   joy—I am happy for you

   support—I am rooting for you

empathy—I understand your feeling

sad—I am really sad

optimistic—I am optimistic about our chances

puzzled—I don't understand

5. Reverse the procedure and have the speaker be the listener and the listener becomes the speaker. Again, allow about 10 seconds for each message.

   disappointment—I am disappointed in you

   guilt—I am guilty over what I did

   hurt—You hurt me

   disapprove—I really disapprove of what you did

   like—I like you

   envious—I am really envious of you

   helpfulness—I want to help you

   boredom—I am bored with you

   shame—I am ashamed of you

   discomfort—I am too cold

   loaded—I had to much to drink

Suggested Discussion Questions:

1. What did you learn about yourself?
2. How did you feel during this experience?
3. What physical reactions did your body show?
4. What did this experience remind you of?
5. What did you think your partner was thinking or feeling?

---

9. Reflective listening also requires that the listener:

   a. reflect the content of the communication,

   b. reflect feelings, and

   c. ask open-ended questions.

10. Some of the major barriers to the communication process are the tendency to judge, evaluate, or approve or disapprove of the statements that the student is making.

11. Communication between the teacher and the student with a disability is a critical aspect of a healthy relationship. You must become aware of your responsibility to communicate with a person with a disability.

Teacher's Corner: Observing Teachers' Recognition of Students in the Academic Process

Concern: Do teachers give students the opportunity to perform in class by asking them questions or allowing them to perform some meaningful task? Secondly, do teachers listen to their responses?

Directions for Observation

Observe a teacher for about one hour. The observer uses the following observation sheet.

A. Recognition: The observer makes a slash mark by the R box (Recognition) by the student's name each time the teacher recognizes a student in an academic lesson by:

1. requesting a student to answer a question
2. asking the student to contribute to the lesson in some other way (e.g., setting up an experiment, preparing the media equipment, writing on the board, etc.)

Note: A response is not recorded when the teacher:

a. asks a non-academic question, such as "Do you have a pencil?" "Are you ready for PE?" or "Did you bring the permission slip?"
b. receives an entire class response to a question or responds back to the entire class.

B. Listening: One recognition is also recorded in the L box (listen) when the teacher:

1. verbally or nonverbally accepts, not accepts, or redirects the response to the teacher's question.
2. accepts the answer of a student who responds even though the student was not called upon.

Note: If the teacher has one continuous interaction, only one response is recorded in the R and L box.

Summary

The observation data is tallied to determine which students are recognized and listened to and which are not. Discuss the results of the observations.

---

12. Healthy communication is when the teacher puts his or her wants or needs into words.

13. Healthy communication encourages closeness and mutual respect.

14. In moments of frustration, anger, or stress, teachers have said things that they later regretted.

15. Healthy communication includes the following three steps:

    a. The teacher describes his or her feelings.

    b. The teacher describes his or her thoughts about the action or event that concerns him or her.

    c. The teacher describes what he or she wants.

16. Nonverbal communication (body language) is an important part of a message.

17. Do not overuse healthy communication. A teacher should use it only when something really bothers him or her.

18. Many people believe that praise is overused and used inappropriately.

19. Use the healthy communication model to encourage instead of praising.

Observation Sheet

NAME OF OBSERVER _____   DATE _____

NAME OF TEACHER _____   TIME _____

OBSERVATION: RECOGNITION   (R)   CLASS _____
                            LISTENING   (L)

ETHNIC CODE: AF = AFRICAN AMERICAN
                      AS = ASIAN AMERICAN
                      HA = HISPANIC AMERICAN
                      NA = NATIVE AMERICAN
                      EA = EUROPEAN AMERICAN
                      DS = DISABLED STUDENT
                      PC = POVERTY STUDENT

NAME	ETHNIC	GENDER	RECOGNITION CODE							
			R		R		R		R	
				L		L		L		L

8

■

Communication:

Resolution and the Class Meeting

We cannot expect children to learn
democracy unless they live democracy.

WILLIAM H. KILPATRICK

HEALTHY RESOLUTION

Autocratic teachers do not have to be concerned about conflict or solving problems because they make all the decisions. They take the position that they are right and if the student does not like it, tough. However, most teachers do not operate completely in that manner, so, like it or not, a teacher must be a negotiator when conflict occurs. Negotiation is a basic means of getting what the teacher wants from others. It is a process in which a teacher and student(s) reach an agreement when both sides have some interests that are shared and others that are in conflict.

The process of negotiation has become an important tool in the lives of most people who work with others. Students want to participate in decisions that affect them; most are unwilling to accept decisions that are dictated to them. Over time, directive teachers will lose control.

Negotiating a conflict, of course, is not easy. If a teacher does not have the tools or strategies for effective negotiation, both students and teacher will usually end up frustrated, tired, and/or alienated. Typically, teachers approach negotiation from one of two positions: (1) afraid of personal conflict, the teacher makes amicable compromises that leave him or her feeling exploited and angry, or (2) the teacher must win because the teacher feels that if he or she does not, control and authority are lost. Some teachers may also find themselves fluctuating somewhere between these two positions because they do not have a clear perspective of what is right. Both positions are wrong.

Before specific steps for resolving conflict are discussed, it is important to discuss certain principles that set the foundation for fair negotiations. Negotiating conflict in a fair and dignified manner requires the following prerequisites: (1) caring and respect, and (2) the seven operating assumptions defined by Gerstein and Reagan (1986).

Caring and Respect as
the Foundations of Negotiations

Understanding basic human needs and how they become frustrated or satisfied is the first step in understanding how conflicts between individuals can be resolved. Most everyday conflicts have either a psychological or a social basis rather than a physical or material foundation. Conflict usually results from unfulfilled psychosocial needs, such as the desire to feel accepted, significant, and capable. Most conflicts you have with students and others can be resolved through improving human relations and satisfying each other's basic needs.

Most conflicts cannot be completely resolved or prevented if respect and empathetic caring do not exist between the individuals who are in conflict. Only when people respect each other and care about each other's basic needs can conflict be turned into mutual respect and cooperation with lasting agreement and order. Consequently, caring and respect are the most important ingredients in conflict resolution in all aspects of one's life.

Operating Assumptions for Approaching Conflict

Gerstein and Reagan (1986), in their book *Win-Win: Approaches to Conflict Resolution,* listed the following seven operating assumptions for approaching conflict:

- All needs are legitimate and important and must be attended to.
- There are enough resources to meet all needs.
- Within every individual lies untapped power and capacity and people in conflict know better what they need than outside experts can.
- Process is as important as content because it provides direction and focus.
- Improving situations is different from solving problems.
- Everyone is right from his or her own perspective.
- Solutions and resolutions are temporary states of balance and are not absolute or timeless.

Each of the seven operating assumptions is discussed in the following paragraphs:

1. *All needs are legitimate and important and must be attended to.* When all needs are considered to be of equal importance, the task shifts to a search for options to meet all needs instead of seeing the task as having to prove which need should be addressed. For example, a teacher may feel that the student is ready to advance to more difficult skills while the student argues against it because he or she is focused on the fear of failure. At this point it is exceedingly difficult for either side to hear the needs of the other.

2. *There are enough resources to meet all needs.* There is no limitation on the human potential to create new ideas and resources. The concept of human synergy tells us that all of us collectively know more than any one of us.

3. *Within every individual lies untapped power and capacity and people in conflict know better what they need than outside experts can.* Teachers cannot impose their own solutions based on their own idea of what they believe is the student's problem. Imposing solutions without recognizing the need will create unwilling students.

4. *Process is as important as content because it provides direction and focus.* Process is the flow of feelings, thoughts, and events. When one becomes too fixed on particular details of content, one misses important valuable clues and information about what is going on and what people are doing. Often the intended listener is so caught up in specific pieces of content, either rehearsing an attack or thinking of evidence to support a position, that the process that is going on is totally missed.

5. *Improving situations is different from solving problems.* Improving situations focuses on the underlying causes rather than just eliminating the problem or symptom. For example, physical exercise may relieve tension that arises from the stresses in people's lives, but it does not focus on what causes the stress or the problem.

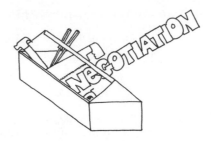

The process of negotiation has become an important tool in the lives of most people who work with others. A teacher must have the tools for effective negotiation when negotiating conflict.

6. *Everyone is right from his or her own perspective.* Therefore, if it is possible to move inside the situation to see it from the other person's perspective, a teacher can come up with a resolution that is more favorable to both parties. In conflict situations people spend an inordinate amount of time defending or supporting their own positions and points of view. This can be exhausting and wasteful. Continual arguing only teaches people more ways to argue and leads to lose-lose outcomes.

7. *Solutions and resolutions are temporary states of balance and are not absolute or timeless.* Solutions and resolutions depend on the flux of circumstances and human changeability. That is why contracts are renegotiable and not irrevocable. When circumstances change, we also expect an adult to recognize those changes and alter his or her actions so that a dynamic balance can be reached.

The Four Steps to Problem Solving
for Teachers and Students

It is important to remember that problem solving and negotiations are not debates or trials. They are processes of building relationships. They require that you focus on the problem and separate the people from the issue. The basic approach to problem solving is to deal with people as human beings who deserve the respect and dignity that you expect from them. You should negotiate the problem or conflict only on its own merits. The following four steps are useful in resolving conflict:

1. Self-Perception You must believe that "I can solve the problem." The first step in successful problem solving is for you to develop the belief that you are a problem-solver and can negotiate a fair and honest settlement. A problem-solver accepts the fact that problem situations are a normal part of life and that it is important to face such challenges calmly and rationally, not impulsively.

Some teachers despise personal conflict and make concessions to try to reach quick and amicable resolutions that leave them feeling exploited and angry. A true problem-solver knows that he or she can rely on his or her problem-solving skills to decide on a reasonable and fair course of action.

In addition, some teachers have attitudes that reflect the opposite extreme. They feel that "Someone has to suffer," "This can't make a difference," "You really can't trust anyone," or "I can't let you win, so I'm going to argue." These are examples of negative beliefs that obstruct progress in conflict resolution. "It is possible to make a difference," "It is possible for everyone to win," and "It is possible to learn to trust ourselves and others" are examples of positive beliefs that can lead to fair resolutions.

2. What's Wrong Identify the problem or situation to be improved. The first thing to do when faced with a challenge or conflict is to understand exactly what is happening by defining the problem. The process of identifying the true problem is extremely important because your emotions often distort objective thinking.

Unfortunately, many teachers try to argue or defend their position rather than focusing on the underlying concerns of all parties. Consequently, fair resolution is unlikely, and less satisfactory decisions are usually made.

To avoid taking positions, a simple process is to have each party write in one sentence, on a separate sheet of paper, what he or she thinks the problem is. This simple procedure will often solve the problem without any further steps. Viewing the problem from the other person's perspective often creates an immediate understanding of the situation. Seeing the problem from the other person's point of view puts the problem into a mutual perspective. Then, together, describe the situation on one single sheet of paper.

3. What Could Be Done? Brainstorm to generate options to improve the situation. The procedures for brainstorming are as follows:

a.   List all options that could be taken to improve the situation. All ideas are valid and welcomed. They are not judged, criticized, or commented on. Write down each option on a blackboard or large sheet of paper so that all concerned can see. This process gives the parties involved a tangible sense of collective achievement, encourages greater participation and creativity, reduces the tendency to repeat, and helps to stimulate other ideas.

b.   Whenever appropriate, consolidate ideas by joining or combining one with another. After viewing them, mark the most promising ideas that may be worth developing further.

c.   Select a plan of action. Become selective by evaluating each of the ideas. Through a process of discussion without criticism, choose the best of the listed options. Be willing to invent ways to make some of the more

FOUR STEPS TO PROBLEM SOLVING

1. Self-perception.
2. What's wrong.
3. What could be done.
4. Get commitments from each party and follow through on accountability.

promising ideas better or more realistic. If more than one option is going to be used, make a rank-order list of what you will do first.

4. Get Commitments from Each Party and Follow Through on Accountability This final step is to carry out the appropriate option(s) to improve the situation. The selected option is then evaluated after a predetermined period of time to determine whether it is working. If it is not working, the brainstorming process is started over.

Regardless of the conflict, the process of problem solving is consistent, and the basic steps do not change. Problem solving can be used whether there is one or several issues and whether there are two or more individuals. This simple process is a great equalizer because it eliminates two major factors that may be perceived as advantages: experience of individuals and dominating personalities. Most important, conflict resolution through problem solving becomes easier with practice.

When Students Do Not Want to Participate
in the Spirit of Fair Negotiation

If the student attacks you or your proposals instead of the problem, Fisher and Ury (1983) suggest three basic approaches to resolve this problem. Focus on what you should not do and what you can do. Do not push back. If the students attack your ideas, do not defend them. If they attack you, do not counter-attack. If they assert their position, do not reject them. Break the vicious cycle by refusing to react. Instead of pushing back, sidestep the attack and deflect it against the problem by using these three maneuvers:

1. Do not attack the student's position, look behind it by seeking out the principles that it reflects, and think about ways to improve it. Instead of making statements, ask questions. Statements usually generate resistance, whereas questions generate answers. Questions allow students to get their point across and help you to understand them. If you ask respectful and honest questions, wait in silence to allow the student to respond. If the answer is insufficient, just wait. People who have doubts about what they have just said are uncomfortable with silence. When you ask questions, pause. Some of the most effective negotiating is accomplished when you are not talking.

2. Do not defend your ideas but invite evaluation and advice. Instead of asking the students to accept or reject your idea, ask them what is wrong with it. Say, for example, "What concerns of yours do my suggestions fail to take into account?" Rework your ideas in light of what you learn from them, and turn criticism from an obstacle into a working solution to the problem.

3. Remember that an attack on you is really an attack on the problem. Listen to and show the students that you understand what they are saying. When they are finished, redirect their attack on you and focus on the problem. Use healthy communication to help the student or students rechannel or refocus their verbal energies toward solutions to the conflict.

What If the Teacher Makes a Mistake?

Nobody is perfect. We all make mistakes. Sometimes we do or say things that we truly regret. We tend to criticize ourselves and make negative judgments about our behaviors. However, instead of viewing mistakes as negative elements in our lives, if we see them as opportunities to learn, we can grow and change in more positive ways.

Nelsen and Lott (1988) recommend that by using the "Four R's of Recovery (Recognition, Responsibility, Reconciliation, and Resolution)," you can make your relationship with your students better than it was before you made a mistake.

1. *Recognition.* Nobody is perfect and we all make mistakes. Admit that you made a mistake and that what you did or said was inappropriate. It is important to be comfortable with saying, "I made a mistake."

2. *Responsibility.* Responsibility means describing what you did. Your description should be void of any guilt as well as any accusing remarks that may have provoked your outburst. Take responsibility for your part in the conflict that was created by your mistake. Be specific in telling your student the nature of your mistake: "I am sorry for swearing at you. My language was entirely inappropriate, and there really is no excuse for what I said."

3. *Reconciliation.* Apologize. Say, for example, "I apologize for making fun of you in front of your classmates. I treated you disrespectfully, and I'm sorry for any hurt that I may have created." One of the wonderful aspects of young students that you may have already discovered is their readiness to forgive when we are willing to apologize.

Time-out: What Should I Do?

Situation: A number of students in a high school class are disgruntled by the teacher's favoritism. He is coddling and catering to only the high GPA students. In the teacher's eyes, these star students can do no wrong. He pays little attention to the less-skilled students. On many occasions he has even forgotten student names and, on occasion, has called students by the wrong name. Even on parent night he has a tendency to talk only with the parents of his star students and ignores the parents of the less-skilled students.

Multiple Choice

The students are frustrated and do not know how to handle the situation. Should they:

A. Get another teacher, administrator, or an outsider to confront the teacher about his problem?

B. Put the problem on the agenda for the next class meeting?

C. Confront the teacher about their concerns?

D. Do nothing and ignore the whole issue, hoping it will go away or the students will learn to live with the situation?

There are two possible answers for this situation.

Response B is the easiest way to deal with both situations. The class meeting is the logical place for these kinds of problems to be addressed.

Response C is also a possibility. Of course, it depends on the individual's ability to use healthy communication techniques. If these techniques have been learned and modeled by the teacher and students, this procedure is probably the quickest and most efficient way of dealing with these kinds of situations. However, if the individuals do not know how to communicate in a

healthy, face-to-face manner, confrontations will, in all likelihood, lead to further conflict.

Response A is appropriate only when both parties have reached an impasse and a third-party mediator is needed to facilitate a solution. The accused individuals in the previous situations are not even aware that there is a problem. Calling in a third party would, in all probability, create an immediate barrier based on the following logic: "Why didn't they come and see me first and talk about it instead of going behind my back and bringing in someone else to confront me?"

Response D will only bring on more frustration. If the individual does not know that a problem exists, he or she will probably continue the behavior. The class meeting was designed to help teachers and students make plans and decisions, provide encouragement, and solve problems. It provides an opportunity for all to be heard on issues arising within the classroom. The topics that can be discussed in a class meeting cover a wide range of issues such as beliefs, values, wishes, complaints, plans, questions, and suggestions. A healthy class thrives on making decisions together. Class meetings improve communications, cooperation, and responsibility and, most importantly, reflect how fortunate the students are to have each other.

You will be impressed by the results that occur when your students meet to decide what needs to be done and how to do it. You will discover that students are likely to be more responsible and cooperative in following through when they have input into the decision-making process. Successful class meetings help students learn to share responsibility and solve problems together.

---

4. *Resolution.* When appropriate, take action to fix any damage that might have occurred from your actions. Also, if necessary, design a strategy that you and the students are satisfied with in case the problem occurs again.

Of course, students, make mistakes too. You can teach them the Four R's of Recovery. The best way to teach this skill is to model it with your own behavior when working with your students.

WHAT IS A CLASS MEETING?

The class meeting is a regularly scheduled meeting that is designed to provide an opportunity for the teacher and the students to learn the democratic procedure of cooperation, mutual respect, emotional honesty, and responsibility. These class meetings:

- promote class harmony through the establishment of rules
- help to solve problems in a cooperative manner
- help students to make decisions through a democratic process
- encourage students by recognizing the good things happening within the class and pointing out strengths of individual students
- allow everyone to be listened to—not just heard, but understood
- allow individual students to express concerns, feelings, and complaints
- enable students to practice honest dialogue
- provide leadership opportunities by providing each student the chance to chair a class meeting
- allow each student to be taken seriously—not just understood but accepted and respected
- allow each student to feel genuinely appreciated for his or her own personal worth, contributions, and significance

What a Class Meeting Is Not

A class meeting is not a meeting in which the teacher can lecture and moralize to the students. Nor is it an opportunity for the teacher to exercise excessive control. Students will see through this behavior and will not cooperate. You are simply an equal member within the group. You have equal input and one equal vote. The same principles apply to students as well. A class meeting is not an opportunity for one or two students to dominate the situation. Every student has an equal opportunity for input.

The Class Meeting Foundation: Mutual Respect and Emotional Honesty

Two of the most exciting aspects of the class meeting are working with the established ground rules of mutual respect and emotional honesty. Dr. Jane Nelsen (1996), in her book *Positive Discipline,* states that mutual respect incorporates attitudes of (1) faith in the abilities of yourself and others, (2) interest in the point of view of others as well as your own, and (3) a willingness to take responsibility and ownership for your own contribution to the problem. Thus, mutual respect means that you must allow for differences, staying away from judgments of right or wrong and blaming stances, and respect your own feelings as well as the feelings of others.

Lynn Lott, in an article about family meetings (Lott & Nelsen, 1988), viewed emotional honesty as a learned skill. She defined emotions as feelings that happen inside of us. She used such words as angry, happy, irritated, joyful, and hopeless. Feelings are not judgments about others and are different from thoughts. Feelings are neither good nor bad and they are not actions or behaviors. The feeling of anger is very different from a display of anger. We cannot always tell how a person is feeling from just observing his or her behavior. For example, people can smile even though they are angry. To really know how someone is feeling, we must ask how or what they are feeling.

Communicating the honesty part of your feelings can be very frightening. When we communicate feelings we are vulnerable, and sometimes the people around us do not listen sensitively, but take things personally and react defensively. Listeners may try to explain our emotions away or correct them. But without emotional honesty there is little growth in the acceptance of oneself and others.

Emotional honesty works in both directions. We are emotionally honest when we communicate our feelings; on the other side, we are emotionally honest when we hear another's feelings without judging, criticizing, defending, assuming, explaining, or fixing. A major concern is that emotional honesty will hurt someone else's feelings. In an environment of mutual respect and cooperation the exact opposite is true. Emotional honesty opens communication and invites closeness and respect.

The Class Meeting Structure

Class meetings should be held at least once a week at a regularly scheduled time. This assures all students of a specific time at which they can discuss the issues that are important to them. These class meetings become an important ritual and tradition when they are regular and predictable.

Establish an appropriate amount of time for the class meeting. Thirty minutes to a maximum of one hour is the recommended time. Any issue that has not been concluded by the end of the meeting can be the first item on the agenda for the next class meeting. Stick to time limits.

A specific agenda is discussed at each class meeting. The agenda can be as simple as a sheet of paper on a clipboard. The agenda is kept in a designated but easily accessible place and students add items to it during the week as issues arise that involve anyone on the clipboard. The items are discussed in the order in which they were written on the agenda.

Each student should have the opportunity to chair the class meeting. A rotation schedule should be determined. The teacher can chair the first few meetings to model the procedures. The chairperson starts and closes the class meeting at the times agreed on. He or she makes sure that all points of view are heard and tries to keep the discussion focused on the issue.

Have a secretary keep minutes for each class meeting so that a record of issues, plans, and decisions is kept. Some classes may find it helpful to post the minutes of each meeting so students can check on the agreements that were made. The role of the secretary should also be rotated.

How To Have Effective Class Meetings

The following steps provide helpful guidelines that teachers can use for a successful class meeting:

1. Meet in a circle for the class meeting. Meeting in this fashion reduces some of the physical barriers that prevent dialogue.

2. Begin with compliments, appreciations, or acknowledgments. This step is important because it sets the tone for pleasant communication.

   Because criticism and complaints are common in most classes, starting the meeting with statements of "appreciation" helps to focus on the strengths and positives of individuals. Individuals who want to give a classmate or the teacher a compliment will raise their hand, and the chairperson should go around the circle in a specific order and call on everyone who has a hand raised. The chairperson must not call on individuals randomly or arbitrarily choose when to stop. Instead of raising hands, an object such as an eraser may be used. The person who has the object in his or her hands may either speak or pass it on. In the beginning, individuals will have difficulty verbalizing compliments and you may have to model this behavior by giving several compliments. For example, "I would like to compliment (a person's name) for (something specific that person did)" or "I appreciated it when (name of person) (something specific that person did)" or "I want to thank (a person's name) for (some specific action)."

   During the first few meetings, everyone should give at least one appreciation. After this, appreciation can be optional. It is also a good idea to teach students to say thank you after receiving a compliment or acknowledgment.

3. Read and, if necessary, discuss the minutes from the previous meeting.

4. Discuss old business (items left over from previous agenda).

5. Read the first item on the agenda. Ask the individual who wrote the item whether it is still an issue. If the problem no longer exists, simply move on to the next item. If the problem still exists, ask the person to briefly explain the item on the agenda.

6. If another person is involved, ask the "accused" if he or she has a suggestion for a solution. If the "accused" does, ask the group to vote on the suggestion. If the majority vote agrees with the suggestion, go on to the next item.

7. If the "accused" has no suggestion or the suggestion is voted down, go around the circle twice for comments and suggestions. Start with the person who wrote the agenda item and end just before this person after going around the circle twice. All students should be given the opportunity to make suggestions.

Especially in the early stages of class meetings, it is important that the teacher withhold his or her suggestions until the students have finished giving theirs. Jumping in too quickly may be interpreted incorrectly and some meeting students may think that the teacher is trying to force his or her ideas on them.

8. The secretary writes down every suggestion exactly as it is stated.

9. After the list of suggestions has been completed, evaluate each suggestion in the order in which they were given. If this brainstorming process is done with mutual respect, it will encourage the willingness to participate in generating solutions. If a member's suggestion is rejected as soon as it is said, the person will probably stop giving ideas. When evaluation is postponed until all suggestions have been given, a member's idea may be seen as one of many that are not accepted by the class.

10. Read all suggestions before asking for a vote. Instruct individuals to vote for only one suggestion. Read the suggestions again, one at a time, and have the secretary record the number of people voting for each suggestion. Some issues may require a secret vote if some individuals are reluctant to vote publicly or there is a potential for individuals to be influenced by the way other students vote.

11. If a consensus is not reached, table the item until next week with the words, "It looks as if we're not ready yet to agree on a solution. Let's think of some other ideas this week and talk about them at our next meeting." If it is an issue that needs immediate attention and a consensus cannot be reached, the teacher may have to make a temporary decision until the issue can be discussed again at the next meeting. Obviously, a teacher needs to be cautious with this procedure. You should never make such a decision in anger or revenge.

By using consensus students develop group solidarity and teach cooperation. When decisions are made by majority rule, factions may develop, and competition may divide the group. Consensus can demonstrate that, no matter how difficult the problem, if a class persists, they can come up with a solution that will be acceptable to all. If consensus cannot be reached, the making of a decision is put off until a solution that is mutually satisfactory is reached.

12. When the final consensus is in, ask the person for whom the solution was suggested when he or she would like to do it, and give two possibilities to choose from, such as today or tomorrow, or before or after class. The reason for allowing choice is to give the individual some sense of power and commitment.

13. A final summary settles the decisions and commitments that were made during the class meeting: "Today, we decided _____. Is that the way everyone understands it?"

14. Post the meeting notes in an appropriate place that is accessible to all students.

COMING TO A CONSENSUS

develops group solidarity *teaches cooperation*
TAMMAY

By using consensus students develop group solidarity and teach cooperation.

Ground Rules for a Class Meeting

1. Everyone is given the opportunity to speak.
2. One person talks at a time.
3. No interruptions.
4. Say what you feel, but without attacking or putting down another person.
5. You do not have to speak.
6. Everyone has to listen.
7. No one puts anyone else down.

Getting Started

Betty Lou Bettner and Amy Lew, in their book *Raising Kids Who Can* (1992), have a chapter called "Getting Started." Some of their "family meeting" ideas have been modified for a class meeting and incorporated in the following section. One way to get started is to have the teacher introduce the idea of the class meeting by saying, "I read this article about a process that teams can use for organizing themselves, making plans, and working out problems. I would like to try this plan with our class, maybe for a month, and see whether it can work for us."

Some teachers, excited about the idea of class meetings, expect that their students will also share their excitement and see the value in it. However, some students may be suspicious of the teacher's motives and may be resistant to the idea.

Start Slowly

One way to circumvent the possible resistance of students is to start off slowly. Instead of introducing the class meeting all at once, you can introduce the idea of problem solving and decision making by simply asking everyone to get together for a specific purpose, such as planning a social activity. The main point is that the topics should be of interest to the students. When fun is involved, most students are intrigued and are usually willing to take a chance. Other issues such as class rules could also be introduced. As these issues are being discussed, teachers can slowly introduce some of the ground rules of a class meeting.

To introduce the idea of future expanded class meetings, teachers can ask the students for their input and feedback about how the planning session went. Some useful questions might be: "Do you think this decision-making process worked well? What would you change? What made it fun? Was there anything that you didn't like? What other topics do you think we could discuss at future class meetings?"

The Class Vision

Classes may need several planning sessions before they develop the trust and skills that are necessary to add further agenda items. However, as the class members begin to recognize the advantages of establishing a regularly scheduled class meeting, they will be ready to develop it more fully. You can then introduce the idea of establishing a "class vision." You can introduce the idea of the class vision by asking the students to write down their answers to the following questions:

1. "What would our class be like if it was the way you wanted it to be?"

2. "Can you think of what this new and improved class might be like?"

3. "If you were a teacher, how would you like your class to be?"

It is important that everyone have the opportunity to come up with his or her own ideas before sharing with the others. It is important to make sure that everyone knows that nobody's ideas will be put down or judged. You will be surprised to hear what is of real value to the students.

Be sure to remind the students to focus on what they would like, not what they don't like. This process will eliminate put-downs and defensiveness.

(don't like)	"I hate the way John is always yelling at people."
(would like)	"I would like people to speak respectfully to others."
(don't like)	"I can't stand it when Susie loafs during physical education."
(would like)	"I would like everyone to give 100 percent when we play games in physical education."

After everyone has finished writing, it is time for sharing. Each person takes a turn reading his or her ideas. After the person shares his or her ideas, the other students may respond in the form of "what I agree/disagree with," "what surprises me," "what I don't understand," and so on.

Bettner and Lew recommend that all the ideas then be separated into two categories: (1) qualities, how we would like the class to be, and (2) actions, what the class needs to do to be that way. Examples of qualities are closeness, respect, and cooperation. Examples of actions are listening to someone's concern, being on time to practice, and maintaining good study habits.

Because the class vision serves as a guideline or ideal to be striven for, it should be a statement of qualities. A class vision might sound like this:

The two categories of the class vision are (1) qualities, how we would like the class to be, and (2) actions, what the class needs to do to be that way.

1. "We will respect each other, and we will do what we mutually agreed to do."

2. "Our class is a place where everyone can feel safe and respected. Everyone will help each other and make others feel important."

Once the class vision is established, the next step is to put the action statements into practice. Each student is to think about what he or she could do to reach the class vision. Each student can make an unpressured choice and pick one thing to work on during the coming week.

At the next meeting, each student will review his or her action and evaluate how it worked. New actions may now be chosen and/or old ones worked on for another week. The statement of the class vision should also be reviewed. Any changes to the class vision should be mutually agreed on. Once established, the class vision should be put in a prominent place, such as on the bulletin board or blackboard. In the future, when disagreements or conflicts occur, the students can refer to the class vision to determine whether their solutions and/or actions conform to the class vision ideals.

Common Questions about Class Meetings

Question: What are some examples of issues that are typically brought up in a class meeting?

Answer: The agenda is almost limitless but common issues brought up by students include:

Fighting	Disrespectful behavior	Swearing	Cheating
Blaming	Hitting	Lunchroom behavior	Bullying
Bus behavior	Bathroom issues	Playground behavior	Put-downs
Stealing	Taking turns	Teasing	

Question: Are there some issues that should not be discussed at a class meeting?

Answer: You will probably have items that the students do not think should be discussed at a class meeting. Although final responsibility for making certain decisions may lie with you, the opinions and concerns of others may provide additional possibilities or valuable insights and may even influence the final choice.

Question: What are the most common administrative mistakes in class meeting?

Answer: Starting late; meeting for too long; allowing one or more people to dominate the meeting; overemphasizing or focusing on the negative, such as complaints and criticism; and not putting agreements into action.

Question: What are the most common reasons why class meetings fail?

Answer: Nelsen et al. (1996) listed the following reasons why class meetings fail:

- Not sitting in a circle.

- Not holding meetings regularly (three to five times a week for elementary school and once a week or once every two weeks in middle and high school).

- Not trusting the process and consequently not allowing time for students to learn skills for effective meetings.

- Not understanding that even so-called tattletale problems provide opportunities to practice the class-meeting process or not understanding that solving similar problems over and over provides opportunities for practice.

- Not having faith in students' abilities, talking down to them (patronizing).

- Not going around the circle and allowing every student a chance to speak or pass.

Question: What happens when the class meeting merely becomes a gripe session?

Answer: If griping becomes chronic, establish a rule that complaints will be heard only if the complainer is willing to seek a solution. This can be done by asking whether he or she wants to solve it or only complain about it. Be sensitive to the complainer's feelings, and keep the focus on solutions. Say, "Do you have any suggestions that may solve this problem?"

Question: What happens if no one writes anything on the agenda?

Answer: Still hold the class meeting and go through the other aspects of the agenda, such as the minutes and giving compliments. When the agenda has been completed, end the meeting. This lets students know that no matter how angry we got at each other during the week, we can always find a few good things to say.

Question: Don't individuals need immediate solutions to their problems? I don't think some of my students can wait until the next class meeting.

Answer: The purpose of waiting is to provide a cooling-off period in which the individual has time to get control of his or her temper and calm down. Discussion of the problem will then be much more rational, helpful, and, most importantly, respectful. Incidentally, just the simple act of writing the problem on the agenda usually provides some immediate gratification for the individual.

Question: How receptive will students be to this concept?

Answer: Young students do not usually trust that adults are ready to listen to them or take them seriously and are usually skeptical of the idea of a class meeting. At first, things will often get worse before they get better because some individuals will use this newly acquired power to be hurtful and revengeful. For many individuals this is the only model they know. Do not forget the long-range goals of the class meeting, and do not quit. In the long run, you will be rewarded for your efforts.

Question: What if a consequence that has been decided on is not working?

Answer: The decision stays in effect until someone puts it back on the agenda. The item will then be discussed at the next class meeting.

Question: What if someone feels that a consequence is unfair?

Answer: He or she can put it on the agenda and it can be discussed at the next meeting. Logical consequences should be used whenever possible. Sometimes punishment is used instead of logical consequences. When punishment is used, it is very easy to get into a revenge cycle.

Question: What if an individual does not follow through on the agreement?

Answer: The time when agreements are made is the best time to discuss and settle on what will happen if they are broken. Try to build in logical consequences whenever possible, not punishment.

Question: What if someone puts something on the agenda that is inappropriate?

Answer: Do not censor agenda items. If a teacher censors agenda items, students will lose faith in the process. What may seem inappropriate to you may not be to the student. The important thing to remember is that the process is even more important than the solution. In addition, it is important to find the positive intent behind every behavior. This enables individuals to feel validated and respected.

Question: Can the teacher put something on the agenda?

Answer: Of course. You are equal to every student within the group.

Question: Can students put the teacher on the agenda?

Answer: Yes. This is a perfect opportunity for you to model appropriate behavior. You should feel comfortable discussing your own mistakes and view them as opportunities for learning. Remember a teacher who values open and direct communications is giving his or her students permission to disagree. The consequences (not punishments) should be equivalent to what other students might receive.

SUMMARY OF MAJOR POINTS
IN CHAPTER 8

1. Negotiating a conflict is not easy.

2. A teacher should not be afraid of personal conflict.

3. Do not use power in negotiating

4. Caring and respect are the foundations of negotiation.

5. The operating assumptions for approaching conflict are that:

   - all needs are legitimate

   - there are enough resources to meet all needs

- within every individual lies untapped power and capacity
- process is as important as content
- improving situations is different from solving problems
- everyone is right from his or her own perspective
- solutions and resolutions are temporary states of balance

6. The four basic steps to problem solving are:

- believe that "I can solve the problem"
- identify the problem
- brainstorm solutions
- get commitments from each party

7. The Four R's of Recovery are:

- recognition
- responsibility
- reconciliation
- resolution

8. Class meetings provide opportunities for open and honest communication. They establish a structure through which teachers and students can treat each other with mutual respect. They provide a process and a reflection of how we want to relate to each other. It is the working out that is important, and in class meetings, working things out takes place in an atmosphere of mutual respect and emotional honesty in which we may think and feel openly and listen openly to what others think and feel. Class meetings provide an opportunity for problem solving, cooperative planning, and shared encouragement.

9. The class meeting has a specific structure.

10. Effective class meetings follow specific guidelines within the designated structure.

11. Class meetings have specific ground rules.

12. Setting a specific class vision is a good way to start the class meeting process.

Class Discussion	CHAPTER 8

Note: Review Appendix E before facilitating this activity.

The Circle of Encouragement
Time: 10–15 minutes (discussion not included)
Objective: To help participants understand that in order to be an effective encourager, one must be comfortable with encouraging oneself.
Materials: A copy of the "Encouragement Profile" for each participant.

Procedure:

1. Distribute "Encouragement Profile" to each participant. (allow 5 minutes for completion)
2. Break class into groups of 4–5 participants.
3. Explain to the participants that in order to be an effective encourager we must feel comfortable encouraging ourselves. Ask participants to take turns reading their "Encouragement Profile" to their group. (3–5 minutes)
4. Explain to the group that they will now have the opportunity to practice encouraging each other and to experience what it feels like to be encouraged. Each person will be given the opportunity to be "it." Every other person in the group takes a turn sharing something he or she likes about the person ("it"). Each person is to begin by saying:
   "One thing I like about you is . . ."
5. Also explain the following rules:
   a. Speak directly to the person.
   b. Be specific (do not give general descriptions such as nice or neat)
   c. Be sincere (do not joke) If you do not know the person very well it is okay to be super-ficial (e.g., I like your warm smile or the bright colorful clothes that you always wear)
   d. Say "thank you" when you are encouraged. (5–10 minutes)
6. Gather all participants together.

Suggested Discussion Questions:

1. What did you learn about yourself?
2. Why do you think it is difficult for some people to accept praise or encouragement?
3. What pleased you about the experience?
4. How did you feel when others were encouraging you?
5. How did you feel when you read your "Encouragement Profile."
6. How did you feel when you encouraged others?

Encouragement Profile

I do very well at _____

One of my greatest strengths is _____ _____

What I like best about myself is _____

Something nice that I did for someone else was _____

One of my greatest accomplishments was/is _____

I really enjoy _____

I'm turned on by _____

One of my most meaningful possessions is _____

My primary life goal is _____

I am most proud of _____

Class Discussion	CHAPTER 8

Note: Review Appendix E before facilitating this activity.

Encouraging Personal Growth
Time: 20 minutes
Objective: To help participants understand how encouragement affects a students' feelings about him or herself.
Materials: A copy of "Encouraging Personal Growth" for each participant.

Procedure:

1. Distribute "Encouraging Personal Growth" to each participant. (5–10 minutes to complete)

2. Ask participants to share their responses.

Suggested Discussion Questions:

1. What is meant by "encouragement?"
2. What is the difference between praise and encouragement? When can praise be encouraging or discouraging?
3. Which do you believe is more effective—encouragement or praise? Why?
4. Why is it important to recognize effort and improvement as well as accomplishment?

Encouraging Personal Growth

The following situations require encouragement. What might each of the individuals believe about themselves? How would you respond? What would you do or say when:

1. Maria complains that the math is too difficult.

   _____

2. Alicia teaches Margaret a new gymnastics skill in physical education.

   _____

3. Jesus spent a lot of time writing a report that he thought was his best effort but received a "D" grade.

   _____

4. Carlos is worried that he will not do well on the next test.

   _____

5. Although Avery is ranked as the number one seed, he loses in the first round and is eliminated from the high school conference tennis championship.

   _____

6. Josh is discouraged because he was not elected as next year's class president.

   _____

Class Discussion	CHAPTER 8

Note: Review Appendix E before facilitating this activity.

Assessing Anger

Time: 5–10 minutes (discussion not included)
Objective: To help participants assess how they deal with anger.
Materials: Copy of "Assessing Anger" for each of the participants.

Procedure:

1. Distribute "Assessing Anger" to each participant.
2. Instruct participants to complete Anger Assessment as honestly as possible and to carefully read the evaluation that follows the assessment. (3–5 minutes)

Suggested Discussion Questions:

1. What did you learn about yourself?
2. What about the activity surprised you?
3. How do you feel when others express their anger at you?
4. What physical reactions does your body show when you get angry?
5. What physical reactions does your body show when someone expresses their anger at you?
6. Do you think that expressing anger at someone is good or bad?
7. Are there ways of dissipating your anger before confronting someone?
8. What will you try to change about yourself?

Teacher's Corner: Supporting Teacher Leadership

Assessing Anger*

Assess how much you agree or disagree with the following statements. Each of the statements below are related to assessing your anger. The assessment is divided into the following four parts:

- Anger arousal (intensity, duration, and frequency of your anger)
- Things you get angry about
- Your tendency towards hostility
- The ease with which you express your anger.

Do you agree or disagree with the following statements:

Anger Arousal (Intensity, Duration, and Frequency of Your Anger)

1. I tend to get angry more frequently than most people.
2. It is easy to make me angry.
3. I am surprised at how often I feel angry.

Things You Get Angry About

4. I get angry when something blocks my plans.
5. I get angry when I am delayed.
6. I get angry when people are unfair.

Your Tendency toward Hostility

7. People can bother me just by being around.
8. When I get angry, I stay angry for hours
9. I get angry when I have to work with incompetent people.

The Ease With Which You Express Your Anger

10. When I am angry with someone, I let that person know.
11. It is not difficult for me to let people know I'm angry.
12. I feel guilty about expressing my anger.

The more you strongly agree with the preceding statements the greater your anger quotient.
These statements come from the Multidimensional Anger Inventory (Siegel, 1986).

Teacher's Corner: Rate Your Class Strengths

Listed below are strengths that are commonly found in a healthy classroom. Interview a teacher and observe his or her class and consider the degree to which you think that each statement is true. Treat the results as a guide only. There is always a margin of uncertainty in all assessments of this kind.

1. Never   2. Rarely   3. Sometimes   4. Often   5. Always

1. _____ Students spend time together and do things with each other outside of class activities.
2. _____ Students have input into many class decisions.
3. _____ Students have good communication (talking, listening, and sharing of feelings with each other).
4. _____ All students are treated fairly.
5. _____ Students practice skills and learn in a physically safe environment (equipment, facilities, rules, etc.)
6. _____ Students are kept informed about what is going on in the class.
7. _____ The class actively seeks out challenges and solutions in a positive manner.
8. _____ Students easily manage the pressure of competition.
9. _____ Class rules and policies are fair.
10. _____ Students and teachers express words of appreciation to each other.
11. _____ Individual and class efforts are recognized and rewarded.
12. _____ There is a close relationship between teacher and students.
13. _____ Individual differences in lifestyle, language, and culture are appreciated.
14. _____ A spirit of happiness and excitement exists in the relationship between teacher and students.
15. _____ There is a spirit of enthusiasm, excitement and camaraderie among members of the class.

Scoring

66–75 Congratulations! You have a healthy class. High scores should be celebrated but should not lead to complacency. Continue to nurture your class, and it will continue to grow in strength.

50–65 You are in the average range and your class has a combination of both positive and negative traits. Your class still has room for improvement.

Below 50 Your score indicates below-average class strengths. Low scores on individual items identify areas that classes can profitably spend time on. You are undermining your most valuable assets. Take an honest look at your approach to leading your young students.

■

PART IV

Discipline in the Healthy Classroom

This part consists of two chapters and focuses on helping you to develop healthy discipline techniques that will help empower students to become self-reliant, self-disciplined, and responsible in their behavior. Part IV addresses discipline styles, why students misbehave, communicating appropriate behavior, and managing the classroom environment to reduce potential problems. Knowing the primary goal of most behaviors is the foundation for understanding most problems and knowing what kind of strategies to use in helping your students grow. Healthy discipline empowers students and is based on treating them with dignity and respect rather than punishment and humiliation.

9

■

Discipline:

Discipline Styles and the Goals of Behavior

The hardest faults to excuse in children are those they have observed in you.

UNKNOWN

STYLES OF DISCIPLINE

The purpose of discipline is to help students develop an inner guidance system so that they can ultimately function responsibly by themselves. In the short term, you start building self-discipline through the little things that occur on a daily basis so that in the long term the students can develop the inner strength to deal with the larger issues.

In the school environment, discipline is training a student in mind and character to enable him or her to become self-controlled and a constructive member of the class. How one goes about achieving and maintaining discipline has been one of the questions of the ages; however, discipline is immeasurably easier when the student feels genuinely liked and accepted. This makes it easier to accept your guidance without hostility. Without a relationship of mutual respect and dignity between you and your students, students react to discipline with anger, resistance, and resentment. In addition, it is important for you to control your emotions when you discipline. Uncontrolled anger is an especially detrimental barrier to good discipline.

Teachers try to teach students to behave responsibly both in and out of the classroom. Factors that influence how you go about disciplining students may include the way you yourself were disciplined as a student, what you believe the needs of the students to be, what you observe other teachers doing, and your own moral beliefs. Once you commit to teaching discipline to your students, you must discipline yourself to change any old destructive patterns and model new ones.

Good discipline is time-consuming because teaching students about discipline and responsibility requires planning and patience. Unfortunately, in the name of expediency, some teachers find that it is easier to control students than to teach them about discipline. However, in the long term the investment in teaching about discipline will give students a focused direction and a foundation on which a system of values can be built.

Most teachers discipline according to one of the three basic models described in the following sections. Each model is based on a different set of beliefs about how students learn about discipline. Each model also teaches a different set of lessons about cooperation, responsibility, and the rules teachers use for acceptable behavior. The remainder of this chapter focuses on the interpretation and application of the principles of autocratic, permissive, and healthy styles of discipline.

Autocratic Discipline

Autocratic leaders usually apply discipline that is based on punishment. Anyone can punish—it takes no sensitivity, no judgment, no understanding, and no talent. To depend on punishment to control people is to make the critical error in assuming that discipline equals punishment. Discipline is training that develops self-control, character, or orderliness and efficiency. Punishment is a method of maintaining discipline by imposing a penalty or retribution rather than correcting for a perceived or actual wrongdoing.

Let's examine a typical behavior problem in the classroom: a teacher reaches the scene of a heated argument, two angry students are pushing and yelling at each other. The argument is about to become a fistfight.

Teacher (*almost screaming*): "Hey, cut it out! What's going on? Can't you two get along?"

Student 1: "He's got a big mouth and I'm going to shut it!"

Student 2: "Yeah? Just try it, wimp!"

Teacher (*clearly angered*): "Both of you settle down. Who started this?"

Student 1: "He did with his big mouth."

Student 2: "He's been looking for a fight all day."

Teacher (*clearly frustrated*): "I've had enough of your fighting and lying. Both of you go to the principal's office."

Student 1 (*sarcastically*): "Just great! Thanks, teacher."

Student 2: "Come on, teacher, this isn't fair."

Teacher: "Don't talk back to me. You two just earned a period of detention."

Students (*turning their backs and walking away and quietly mumbling*): "Stupid teacher."

Teacher (*needing to get the last punitive words in*): "Get moving now, and don't let me catch you loafing."

Teachers who punish find themselves in the role of both policeman and judge. Their job is to investigate the crime, determine guilt, and impose penalties. Penalties are usually severe and unrelated to the misdeed. Students are viewed in terms of good or bad and right or wrong.

Punishment usually involves a threat that obligates the student to either obey or resist rather than to think constructively and respond. One may argue that punishment works. Very few people would disagree. Punishment does usually stop misbehavior. Punishment can work in an immediate situation, but the cooperation that punishment achieves may come at a high price that includes hurt feelings, impaired relationships, and angry power struggles. Students who must operate in this type of environment are more likely to rebel than are students who do not live in constant fear of their teacher.

Punishment degrades, dehumanizes, and humiliates students. Consequently, it hurts feelings, evokes anger, and incites resistance or withdrawal. When it comes to being humiliated, students respond much as adults do—they get mad. They rebel, seek revenge, and sometimes, withdraw in fearful submission. The long-range effects of punishment can be devastating, resulting in a student feeling one or all of the following:

1. *Indignation/Resentment.* Students feel anger or scorn resulting from the perception that they have been treated unfairly or out of meanness. Punishment creates distrust.

2. *Retaliation.* Students think about inflicting back some of the hurt and pain that has been inflicted on them. They want to get even for the meanness or injustice that has been imposed on them.

3. *Withdrawal.* Students think that they are deserving of punishment and will try to please through submissive compliance. Anxious docility along with a lack of confidence and spontaneity become part of the baggage that punishment creates.

Aside from the negative feelings and behaviors that might arise from punishment, teachers must ask themselves whether or not students will learn any new skills for resolving conflicts on their own. Will they learn anything about cooperation or responsibility? Will they learn how to solve problems? Punishment does not teach any of these. Teachers who use punishment make all the decisions, have all the power and control, and do the problem solving. Punishment takes responsibility and learning opportunities away from students because it leaves them out of the process.

A tragic consequence of punishment is when the student imitates the aggressor. The students begin to identify with the punishing teacher, coming to believe that being punitive is right. Then, of course, as students later become parents or teachers, they will treat their students as they themselves were treated. Teachers who use punishment were themselves usually mistreated. The use of punishment or the threat of it consequently becomes part of a vicious cycle.

Permissive Discipline

Permissive discipline is at the opposite end of the continuum. It is a democratic process without limits, rules, or order. Permissive discipline gives the students control over the final decision. Such freedom without rules, limits, or order creates anarchy, and students will not learn to respect rules or authority or how to handle freedom responsibly.

Permissiveness gives the teacher and students an equal voice in determining rules and privileges. When a student misbehaves, a permissive teacher appeals to the student's intellect and sense of responsibility by explaining the difference between right and wrong. The student, with that information, then decides what to do. Most students will manipulate the teacher into rescuing and protecting them from the consequences and results of their own behavior.

Let's return to the example of the student conflict and see how the permissive teacher handles this problem.

Teacher: "Hey, Cut it out! Someone is going to get hurt." *(The fight stops momentarily, then shoving and pushing erupt again)*

Teacher: "Did you two hear what I said? Cut it out!"

Student 1: "Teacher, tell him to keep his mouth shut! He's driving me crazy."

Student 2: "What's his problem?"

Teacher: "Why don't you two guys try to get along?"

Student 1: "He's getting on my nerves. He's constantly telling everybody what to do."

Student 2: "I am not."

Teacher: "Come on, you two. Why don't you try to get along? This fighting doesn't help anybody."

Student 1: "Yeah, we'll get along when pigs fly."

Student 2: "Jerk."

Teacher (*exasperated*)**:** "You two do what you want, but don't do it here."

The reason that the students did not cooperate was that they did not have to. Cooperation was optional, not required. Neither student was accountable for his behavior, and the teacher relied on reason or persuasion to get the message across. The teacher did not support the message with any effective action or consequences.

Students who are trained with permissiveness will become accustomed to getting their own way and will become experts at ignoring, avoiding, arguing, and defying. Permissive teachers are constantly shifting from strategy to strategy (e.g., repeating, pleading, reasoning) to get their students to cooperate. The teacher usually ends up frustrated and humiliated, giving up any hope of success, and the students end up getting their own way.

Can you imagine what a soccer game would be like if it was played in a permissive manner? Imagine the chaos that would result if every time there was an infraction the referee gave the players second and third chances without imposing penalties? Let's join such a game in progress:

A player on the yellow team is ready to kick a shot at the goal, but a player on the green team sticks a foot out to trip her. As play stops, the referee approaches the green player and says, "Was that an accident or was it intentional?" The green player apologizes, but indicates that it was an accident and that she did not mean to trip the yellow player.

"Well, okay," the referee says. "Be careful. I may call a foul on you the next time. Try not to let it happen again."

The next incident occurs when a ball hits the hands of the same green player. The referee blows the whistle, causing play to stop. The referee confronts the player.

"You know it is against the rules for you to touch the ball with your hands. First you tripped the other player, and now you touch the ball with your hands. I can't keep letting you get away with stuff like that. If it keeps up, I'm going to call a penalty."

Soon another infraction occurs and another confrontation: "Didn't you hear what I said the last time? Why would you do it again?" the referee pleads in exasperation.

The player looks down and sheepishly says, "I don't know."

The referee looks the player in the eye and says, "You have had your final warning. The next infraction and I'm calling it." Pointing at the player, the referee says, "Do you understand?"

As the game goes on, the referee continues to reprimand, lecture, threaten, complain, and everything else except to call a penalty. The game eventually is in shambles, and players are in a free-for-all.

Permissive teachers are a lot like the permissive referee. They give warnings and reminders and try to reason when their students break the rules. Without consequences to hold them accountable, the students have little cause to take the class rules or responsibilities seriously. Permissiveness does not usually stop behavior, nor does it teach anything about rules, cooperation, responsibility, or respect for authority.

Healthy Discipline

Autocratic discipline is discipline with firmness but requires no respect. Permissive discipline is discipline with respect but requires no firmness. Healthy discipline is discipline that requires a balance between firmness and respect. It is a process that decides on rules for the mutual benefit of teacher and students. It is a process that teaches about rules, cooperation, responsibility, and respect for authority.

Through healthy discipline, the teacher does not direct, but guides the students' misbehavior through a problem-solving process. The teacher provides clearly defined limits, acceptable choices, and clearly stated consequences that hold the students accountable for their behavior or actions.

Students can be cruel to other students. Occasionally they hit, kick, and call each other names. Sometimes students are cruel for lack of knowledge or sometimes they strike out at others because of their own inner pain. When these things happen in the classroom, you must not respond with more cruelty. To punish the student with more cruelty only teaches the student to lash out with more hostility. To yell at the student does not improve communication, it only makes it louder. To lecture, blame, threaten, or moralize turns the communication process off.

It is essential to stop the cruelty and remove the student from the situation immediately. Talk calmly with the student and say in a quiet clear voice, "Please take a time-out for a couple of minutes and when you are ready we need to talk about what just happened." We cannot ignore the damage that the student has done, but neither student nor teacher will benefit from more punishment.

A student who hurts another student is usually telling us that he or she is hurting. By allowing the student to gain his or her composure, you can now take some time to find out why the student is hurting. Once the student is able to express the hurt and have someone acknowledge it, he or she can now face his or her actions with greater understanding. You can now work out a plan for helping the student feel better again. When students are treated in a respectful manner, their behavior improves. In addition, you are modeling respectful

Healthy discipline requires a balance between firmness and respect.

behavior and self-control without trying to control the student. Children do better when they feel better.

Let's return to our familiar conflict and see how a healthy teacher handles the problem.

Teacher (*in a clear, matter-of-fact voice*): "Guys, stop the shoving and yelling. I'm sure there's a way we can solve your problem. Do you two need to take a little time to cool-off first before we talk?"

Student 1: "I'm ready to talk now."

Student 2: "Me too."

Teacher: "What would be another way to handle this problem without all of the shoving and pushing?"

Student 1: "I don't know. I just want him to shut up. I'm tired of him trying to boss everyone around and being a know-it-all."

Student 2: "Hey, I was just to trying make sure we finished. I wasn't trying to be bossy."

Teacher: "Well, you guys can either stop fighting and shake hands or go to the principal's office. Which would you like to do?"

Student 1: "I'll shake. I'm sorry I got so hot."

Student 2: "I'll shake. I'll try to control myself. I didn't realize I was coming off that way."

Teacher: "Good choice, guys. Shake hands, and let's get back to work."

With healthy discipline the teacher is able to stop the misbehavior and teach the intended lesson. There was no power struggle or conflict. The first step was to give a clear, direct, and matter-of-fact message about the behavior to be stopped. Second, the teacher sent a message of cooperation by using a "we" message expressing confidence in the students' abilities to solve the problem. Third, the teacher recognized that problems could not be cooperatively solved in a climate of anger. The teacher asked whether the students need a cooling-off period before talking. This choice forced the students to be responsible for controlling their own angry feelings.

Next, the teacher checked with the students to see whether they had the skills and information needed to resolve the conflict on their own. They didn't. The teacher then suggested solutions in the form of limited choices. By choosing the solution themselves, the students were responsible for their own problem solving. The conflict ended in an atmosphere of mutual respect and dignity.

In summary, the healthy discipline process includes:

1. communicating about expected behavior (firm limits) (see Chapter 10)
2. communicating confidence in the students' abilities to solve the problem (see Chapter 10)
3. offering a choice of a cooling-off period
4. providing an opportunity for the students to solve the problem
5. if necessary, giving limited choices with a logical or natural consequence

The following box contains a summary of the three discipline styles.

Autocratic Discipline (Punishing Method)	**Permissive Discipline (No-Limit Method)**	**Healthy Discipline**
Order without freedom	Freedom without order	Freedom with order
No choices	Unlimited choices	Limited choices
Compliance through force	Compliance through persuasion	Compliance through cooperation and accountability

Discipline and Cultural Bias

According to the annual Gallup Poll of Public Attitudes toward Education (Carter, 1987) lack of discipline was the number one problem in the public schools. Teachers from the United States and Canada listed classroom management or the control of students as their greatest concern. Each individual teacher sets different behavior standards as well as disciplinary actions. For example, a teacher may ask the student to leave the room, call a parent, send the student to the principal's office, add more homework, or make a student stay after school.

However, teachers' decision about how and who to discipline is not always based solely on the misbehavior.

Disciplinary policies often discriminate against particular students. Wehlage and Rutter (1986) determined that an important variable to dropping out of school is when students perceive disciplinary policies as being unfair and ineffective. Consistently, racial or ethnic minority students, especially African-Americans, will receiver harsher reprimands than Western European American students when measured by school suspension records. Dearman and Plisko (1981) reported that African-Americans were twice as likely to be disciplined than Western European Americans, and Arnez (1978) reported in a study of 21 school districts that 72 percent of all students disciplined were African-Americans. Nieto (1996) concluded that students who experience the least success in school are those students who bear the brunt of rigid school policies. Furthermore, poor students and minority students are more likely to be punished and suspended. This inequity is frequently related to poor communication in determining codes of behavior.

Meier and Stewart (1991) reported that (1) Hispanic students are more likely to receive corporal punishment than Anglo students, (2) Puerto Rican students are 43 percent overrepresented among students expelled from school, (3) as the African-American suspension rate increases, the relative level of suspension among Hispanics decreases, (4) African-American students are suspended for offenses that are often permitted of Anglo students, and (5) dress codes are more rigidly enforced against Hispanic students than Anglo students.

Discipline based on cultural biases is one of the most devastating forms of discrimination in the education system. It reinforces existing stereotypes and creates a situation where one group receives preferential treatment over another. In addition, these punishment trends can discourage these students from attending school or encourage them to rebel against school policies, procedures, and adults in authority.

Discipline and Gender

Alford (1979) reported that teachers, in particular male teachers, sent male high school students more frequently to the administration for disciplinary action than female students. Huffine (1979) reported that male students were reprimanded more frequently for verbal disruptions than female students; however, both male and female students were disciplined for aggressive behavior. These discipline patterns have some negative consequences for both males and females. For example, the male is viewed as aggressive and the female passive, or females may be perceived (by both genders) as receiving preferential treatment from teachers.

Discipline and the Exceptional Child

It is important that all of your students have the same privileges and the same limitations as much as possible. If expectations are clearly known by all students, they can easily separate what you consider right from wrong. When what is wrong for one child is right for another, all your students will remain confused. Treating all of your students equally is also important in terms of developing the exceptional child's self-image. Do not accept any behavior from a child with a disability that you would not accept from your other students unless that behavior is involuntary; such as, excessive movement, involuntary noises, or taking longer on certain tasks. In developing realistic expectations of a student with a disability, it may be necessary to make some adaptations in the environment, or to do some special training. For example, putting certain classroom materials away in a storage box may require making adjustments to the storage box by lowering its sides. The student with a disability is then expected to put away his or her materials. By making adaptations in the classroom, the teacher can then expect certain behaviors from his or her students with a disability. These behaviors should be realistic and comparable to the types of behavior the teacher expects from the other children.

As a member of your class, a student with a disability shares equally in the discipline process. He or she, like all other students, will look to you as an example of fairness. To make necessary exceptions for your disabled student would show understanding of his or her limitations. To make unnecessary exceptions for him or her would be to deny whatever moral and social growth he or she is capable of achieving.

Classroom Control Through Motivation

Waysons (1985) studied 500 well-disciplined schools to investigate the overlapping criteria that prevented violence and disruption in schools. He found that well-disciplined schools focused on positive attitudes and prevention rather than punishment. Instead of focusing on symptoms, they looked for solutions to the problems. They displayed faith in their students and their teachers. Most important, they emphasized that their schools were places to do valuable, successful, and productive work.

Gilliland (1988) states that "classroom control is about 95 percent motivation and interest and only 5 percent discipline. Motivation depends upon our learning the students' needs, and their interests. If we meet their needs, students will work willingly. If we provide for their interests, they will be enthusiastic. When students are discipline problems, it is well to look at our means of motivation."

Twelve Helpful Hints to Reduce Discipline Problems

1. Dump the old notion that to make students do better, a teacher must first make them feel bad. Do not say things to hurt feelings or create guilt with the idea that these statements will shame the students into better behavior. Nobody likes to feel humiliated.

2. Give students meaningful class and individual responsibilities. Students feel a sense of belonging when they believe that they are making real contributions to the class.

3. Make decisions together. When students have input into important decisions, they take greater ownership of the decision. This will increase cooperative behavior.

4. Punishment works only in the short term. In the long term it creates negative feelings of anger and resentment.

5. If you are angry, cool off before you confront the student. Go some place private and say all the negative things you feel like saying—but say them alone. When you have vented your anger and are ready to talk, approach the student in a respectful manner.

6. Use natural and logical consequences whenever possible. Allow the student to learn from the consequences of his or her choices. Natural and logical consequences are discussed in Chapter 10.

7. Teach and model mutual respect. A teacher can be kind and still be firm. When in conflict, maintain respect. Focus on correcting the behavior without attacking the student's personality. The student needs to know that he or she is still respected even though the behavior is not.

8. Encouraging students will make them feel accepted and capable and, consequently, more motivated to participate responsibly.

9. Make sure the environment is both physically and emotionally safe for the student. Fearful students are more likely to get hurt and become less cooperative.

10. Teach students what you want by being specific. For example, the phrase "a clean room" may mean different things to the teacher and to the students. If a process or procedure is important, demonstrate it.

11. When one or more of the basic needs in life are not being met, students may adopt certain misbehaviors to try to get those needs fulfilled.

12. Hold regular class meetings to solve problems through cooperation and respect. See Chapter 8 for a detailed discussion of the "Class Meeting."

Common Classroom Discipline Problems

Although each teacher and situation is a little different, the following five situations usually lead to potential discipline problems in the classroom. These situations are not listed in any particular order:

1. *Arguing.* Students often challenge the teacher's and other student's beliefs and attitudes.

2. *Insults and vulgar language or gestures.* Students often swear to create excitement or to gain peer acceptance.

3. *Forgetting.* Some students will "conveniently" forget as an excuse for not fulfilling a responsibility. Sometimes students will forget to get their teacher's or peer's attention.

4. *Arguing, put-downs, and fighting among classmates.*

5. *Students not being responsible.* For example, missing assignments, being tardy, or not staying on task.

Each of these problems is unique, and each requires a different strategy that depends on the situation. Strategies for solving these problems are discussed throughout this entire book. Examples are reflective listening, setting firm limits, applying natural and logical consequences, conflict resolution strategies, and the use of healthy communication.

UNDERSTANDING THE
GOALS OF BEHAVIOR

Whatever a student does, no matter how peculiar or strange it may seem, he or she does it for a reason. And what the student does usually shows something about himself or herself. It is, of course, very difficult to determine what the behavior means. Sometimes people do things that are so destructive or peculiar that a psychologist needs to be consulted. Psychologists know, however, that people do things because they expect to make matters a little better. They expect to be a little happier because of their behavior.

You may not always understand the goal of a student's behavior. When you begin to judge the behavior from your own perspective rather than the student's, it becomes very confusing. Many behaviors will ultimately lead to conflict. You must realize that if you are ever to understand what a student does, you must understand what the student needs.

When you and the student are in conflict, it is important to have the student involved in the resolution, but it is equally important to break a chronic cycle of dysfunctional behavior. You must take steps to ensure that the student's emotional needs are being met.

Dreikurs (1964) theorized that the true primary purpose of most behavior is (1) to find a sense of belonging, (2) to feel that one has significance by having control over one's own life, (3) to feel that one has been fairly treated, or (4) the need to avoid stressful and frightening situations.

Students want desperately to belong. They achieve that sense of belonging through participation and their sense of usefulness to the group. Healthy children who feel good about themselves will generally find positive ways to contribute and be recognized. They enjoy cooperating and participating. They enjoy the people they are with. A young student, however, who is discouraged and, for whatever reason, feels left out or insignificant will turn his or her attention from participation in the group to a desperate attempt to find his or her place within the group. The discouraged student may adjust to the situation with either pleasing or disturbing behavior; one way or another, he or she will find a place.

When one or more basic needs are not being met, the healthy student will generally choose positive approaches to fulfill them. The unhealthy and discouraged student will often adopt certain negative behaviors in his or her attempt to fulfill needs. Dreikurs (1964) hypothesized that discouraged children, as well as adults, may use inappropriate behaviors or "mistaken goals" to help achieve fulfillment of their needs. He proposed four mistaken goals of behavior that he hypothesized to be the root of chronic patterns of dysfunctional behavior. Dreikurs called them mistaken goals because they lead to misbehavior due to mistaken beliefs about how to find belonging and significance. The remainder of this section focuses on the interpretation and practical application of Dreikurs "Mistaken Goals Model."

When Dreikurs refers to the mistaken goals of behavior he is referring to the actions of the discouraged, unhealthy child. Popkin (1998) prefers to drop the term "mistaken" because these goals of behavior are universal to all people. Healthy students have the same goals, but go about fulfilling them in positive ways. The goals are not mistaken, but the key difference is how students go about attaining those goals. If students are going about fulfilling these goals in unhealthy ways, these negative behaviors act as "red flags" indicating that some need is not being met.

THE FOUR MISTAKEN GOALS
OF BEHAVIOR

Attention-Seeking

Discouraged students suffer from low self-esteem and have the mistaken assumption that they belong and are significant only when they are the center of attention. Being the center of attention gives them a sense of power and control over others. Consequently, discouraged students will develop great skill at attention getting. Discouraged students develop a variety of ways to keep you and others busy with them. Obviously, students need your attention; however, when you find yourself chronically busy with the student at times when situations do not justify it and you feel annoyed or distressed, it is usually a sign of undue attention. You must realize that as pleasant or as disturbing as the student may be, his or her goal is to win attention rather than to participate. The following list gives examples of attention-seeking behavior.

The Class Clown This is the student who is constantly clowning around, acting out, or being overly silly to get attention from both the teacher and his or her classmates. He or she needs to be the center of attention or uses this behavior when he or she feels embarrassed or pushed into a corner. It is used as a way of "saving face."

The Obnoxious Student This student usually does not feel good about himself or herself and consequently does things that receive negative attention from the teacher or classmates.

The Lazy Student This student is similar to the obnoxious student in that he or she receives negative attention while the teacher nags and other students do work for him or her.

The Helpless Student This student pretends that he or she cannot do anything without help. He or she only feels loved when he or she is being fussed over and cared for.

The Artificial Charmer This student plays the role of the adorable and charming student by spouting insincere compliments to everyone. This niceness vanishes as soon as the attention is diverted toward someone else. He or she becomes a cold competitor in seconds.

Power

The battle for power is the second mistaken goal of behavior and most frequently occurs after the teacher has tried for some time to restrain the discouraged student's demands for attention. Discouraged students feel a sense of belonging and significance if they are in charge and do what they want to do. Power becomes a mechanism by which the student can defeat the teacher or others. It is an attitude that implies that one belongs only if one is winning or, if one cannot win, one prevents others from winning the power struggle. Discouraged students feel an enormous satisfaction when they refuse to comply with your demands. This situation is like the small child who calmly smirks in the face of the parents' screams and tears. The child knows that he or she has won because the parents were driven to complete exasperation and frustration. The following list gives examples of types of students who use control or power behaviors.

The Rebellious Student This student controls the teacher by being so out of control that the teacher feels helpless. He or she controls some of his or her classmates by bullying them with size and strength.

The Stubborn Student When this student fails to get his or her way, he or she gains control by refusing to participate or causing a scene.

Revenge

The third mistaken goal of behavior is usually a consequence of the power struggle. The student in his or her discouragement may retaliate. Revenge becomes a means of feeling significant and important. It implies that if one cannot belong, at least one can hurt back. Discouraged students are now convinced that they do not belong, are not liked, and do not have any significance. They become mistakenly convinced that they will count only if they can hurt others, as they believe others have hurt them. The following list give examples of disruptive or revengeful behaviors.

The Destructive Student This student feels a sense of hopelessness and believes that everyone has rejected him or her, so it does not really matter what he or she does. No one will like him or her regardless of how he or she behaves. He or she loses control over his or her impulses and acts out against others and the environment with destructiveness and aggressiveness.

The Defiant Student This student strikes out against those who he or she believes have hurt him or her. He or she strikes back with fits of anger, temper tantrums, and defiance.

The Contemptuous Student This student has so much mistrust of others that he or she seems to despise everyone. A student who feels that others have continually treated him or her unfairly will find it difficult to have a trusting relationship.

Self-Imposed Inadequacy

Completely discouraged students use the fourth mistaken goal of behavior. The discouraged student demonstrates his or her self-imposed inadequacy by simply giving up. He or she believes that there is no way of succeeding by useful or destructive means and avoids the hurt of even trying to achieve what he or she mistakenly believe is not possible. These discouraged students believe that they lack the ability and stamina to perform competently; they have a low opinion of their abilities. When they do not think they can be the best, they give up. The discouraged students do not believe that it is possible for them to belong, to be liked, and to have any significance. They give up and hope that people will leave them alone. You generally feel despair and may also want to give up on the student. You may actually come to agree that the student is incompetent and inadequate. The following list gives examples of self-imposed inadequacy behaviors.

The Socially Inept Student This student is the severely withdrawn individual who has turned all of his or her negative feelings inside. He or she does not make eye contact, refuses to talk most of the time, and stays apart from others whenever possible. Fear, anger, and frustration are repressed and never expressed. He or she is a loner who is sometimes seen as a "good child" because he or she never causes trouble.

The Depressed Student This student exhibits feelings of ineptness, hopelessness, and despair. He or she has no energy and has given up. He or she no longer wants to be involved.

Why Mistaken Goals of Behaviors Do Not Work

Unfortunately, the mistaken goals of behavior provide only temporary relief to the student and, in the long run, worsen and compound the problem. There is a snowball effect because the student's inappropriate behavior increases the negativity and hostility in the teacher and the environment; these in turn enhance the student's emotional neediness and the likelihood that the student will behave more and more inappropriately in the future.

Most people's natural reaction is to respond in a way that is precisely opposite to the actual response that the student needs. For example, one is usually tempted to ignore the student who is acting out for attention, but that usually causes the student to increase the behavior. One usually wants to "show who's boss" in a power struggle, but this usually makes the student feel more of a need to demonstrate his or her power. One usually wants to punish the revengeful student, but that only makes the student want to seek greater

FOUR MISTAKEN GOALS
OF BEHAVIOR

revenge. Finally, you may want to give up on the inadequate student, and that only allows the student to sink deeper in his or her isolation.

To bring about real change, you must relieve the problems that cause the chronic misbehavior and find appropriate methods to meet the student's emotional needs. When you become aware that a student's chronic misbehavior is a consequence of one of the four mistaken goals, you have a basis for action. Once you identify the need behind a behavior, you can understand the hidden purpose of the behavior. What seemed illogical now begins to seem logical and make sense. You are now in a position to act.

Students are usually not aware of their mistaken goal of behavior, except when the goal is revenge. Even when their goal is revenge, students do not know that they have decided that the only way to deal with feeling hurt is to hurt back. They are acting on an unconscious level. Nothing is gained by you telling the student what he or she suspects is the mistaken goal. This disclosure should be left to someone who is more professionally trained to deal with such matters; however, once you are aware of the mistaken goal of behavior, you can develop a plan of action.

It is also important to recognize that not all behaviors are based on these four goals. Some antagonistic or senseless behavior of students and adults may be explained in terms of the four mistaken goals, but other forms of behavior may be linked to such things as financial gain and risk-taking behavior, which do not necessarily fall within the scope of these goals.

Identifying the Mistaken Goal of Behavior

The only way for you to determine the mistaken goal of behavior is to identify your own feelings and the student's reactions to your attempts to correct the misbehavior. Nelsen (1996) discussed two clues that can help you identify the mistaken goal:

1. Identifying the feelings of the teacher as he or she responds to the misbehavior. The following chart categorizes the teacher's feelings followed by the student's mistaken goal:

Teacher's Feelings	Student's Mistaken Goal
Irritation or annoyance	Attention-Seeking
Threatened	Power
Hurt	Revenge
Inadequate	Assumed Inadequacy

2. The student's response when you tell him or her to stop the misbehavior. The following chart identifies the mistaken goal and student's response:

Mistaken Goal	Student's Behavioral Response
Attention-Seeking	Behavior stops momentarily but usually resumes
Power	Continues behavior and verbally defies or passively resists the teacher's request to stop
Revenge	Retaliation by doing something destructive or saying or doing something hurtful.
Assumed Inadequacy	Passive, hoping the teacher will soon give up and leave him alone. She or he simply quits.

PRESCRIPTIONS FOR EACH
MISTAKEN GOAL

When you realize that a student is demanding undue attention, you can simply ignore the behavior. What is the point of demanding attention if you do not respond? When you are in a power struggle, you can withdraw from the contest. What is the point of being the victor of a noncontest? When a student seeks to hurt, you can become aware of the student's deep discouragement, avoid feeling hurt, avoid punishing, and develop a plan of action. Finally, you can help the "helpless" student by structuring experiences that will lead to success and help the student to discover old and new abilities.

Obviously, there is no one simple way to solve such complex problems. You need to think out the solutions that best fit the situation. It is always reasonable and prudent to consult others. The important thing to remember is that these problems, like all other situations, should be approached with continued

Teacher's Corner: Identifying the Student's Mistaken Goals

Quiz 1: Fill in the student's mistaken goal on the basis of the teacher's feelings:

Student's Goal	Teacher's Feelings
1. Power	Angry
2. _____	Hurt
3. _____	Despair
4. _____	Irritated
5. _____	Provoked
6. _____	Worried
7. _____	Threatened
8. _____	Disbelieving
9. _____	Hopeless
10. _____	Disappointed

3. _____	Rude
4. _____	Quitting all the time
5. _____	Disobedient
6. _____	Truant
7. _____	Outlandish dress
8. _____	Minor mischief
9. _____	Defiant
10. _____	Arguing

Answers to Quiz 1

1. Power 2. Revenge
3. Inadequacy 4. Attention
5. Power 6. Attention or Inadequacy
7. Power 8. Revenge
9. Inadequacy 10. Revenge

Quiz 2: Fill in what you believe is the student's goal on the basis of his or her behavior. Remember the real clue is how you feel in response to those behaviors. You may not completely agree with the answers because each situation is different and some of these behaviors may elicit a different response in you.

Student's Goal	Student's Behavior
1. Attention	Forgetting
2. _____	Clowning around

Answers to Quiz 2

1. Attention 2. Attention
3. Revenge 4. Inadequacy
5. Power 6. Inadequacy
7. Attention 8. Attention
9. Power 10. Power

attitudes of encouragement, understanding, dignity, and mutual respect. Some general guidelines for effective responses to each mistaken goal follow. These are only suggestions based on the principles of this book.

Responses to Attention-Seeking Behavior

- Ignore the misbehavior. Do not acknowledge the misbehavior and, whenever possible, walk away from it. Be aware that ignoring the behavior may cause the student to increase his or her attention-seeking behavior; however, if you are consistent, over time the behavior will be extinguished. Give positive attention during cooperative, enjoyable, and agreeable times. This will help the student to reevaluate his or her methods.

- Schedule some special time with each student on a regular basis. Take a little extra time to help validate the student's feelings and needs. Be interested, and learn to listen. This strategy should be a part of the solution for all mistaken goals.

- Redirect the misbehavior into some positive contributing behavior that reinforces participation. Give all students some genuine responsibility that is essential to the functioning of the class.

Responses to Power Behavior

- Remove yourself from the power struggle to give yourself and the student some time to calm down or cool off. This gives you an opportunity to seek a respectful and friendly solution that will help you to decide what you will do, not what you will try to make the student do.

- Act in one of the following ways: (1) remain calm and act thoughtfully, but firmly, (2) follow up with a one-to-one problem-solving session. Remember to practice encouragement, understanding, and mutual respect. Learn to listen and be open-minded. Do not go in with a hidden agenda or the student will see through it, and the power struggle will be exaggerated.

- Do whatever has to be done to keep a student from harming others and the physical environment.

- Provide limited choices whenever possible. Allowing the student a choice is essentially saying, "You may make your own choices—within reasonable limits—but you must also live with the consequences of your choices."

- Avoid head-to-head confrontations. Aggressive behavior further establishes a model for this type of undesirable behavior.

Responses to Revenge Behavior

- Withdraw from the revenge cycle by avoiding retaliation or punishment. Withdrawal does not mean withdrawal from the student. Acceptance, respect, and friendliness still remain. Withdrawal from the revenge cycle helps to maintain a positive relationship. If teachers continue in the conflict, they feel more inclined to punish or retaliate. Punishment will only enhance the revenge cycle.

- After withdrawing from the conflict, remain respectful and friendly during the cooling off period.

- Do whatever has to be done to keep a student from harming others and the physical environment.

- Follow up with a one-to-one problem-solving session. Maintain the same rules that were discussed previously in the "power" behavior guidelines.

- Build cooperative relationships with defiant students to become the students' ally and friend while refusing to participate in inappropriate interactions with them.

- Avoid overreacting to expressions of defiance such as vulgar language.

- When necessary, remove or restrain any student in extreme circumstances with firmness and resolve, not anger or punitiveness.

- Earn the student's trust through consistent fairness, honesty, true acceptance, and good modeling.

- Model trust by placing the student in situations in which the teacher knows that the student is likely to succeed and, if he or she should fail, it can be easily overlooked.

Responses to Assumed Inadequacy Behavior

- Arrange nonthreatening experiences that result in success by creating small, achievable steps.

- Do not make assumptions about the student's abilities and knowledge. Take adequate time for training.

- Use encouragement.

- Special guidance from outside sources may be required.

- Reduce stress in the student's training by introducing nonthreatening activities and easing the student into more active involvement with things and people around him or her.

GOALS BEYOND DREIKURS BASIC FOUR

Eugene Kelly and Thomas Sweeney (as cited in *The Parent's Guide: Systematic Training for Effective Parenting (STEP),* Dinkmeyer & McKay, 1983) extended the list of goals to include excitement, peer acceptance, and superiority. These goals, of course, can be used in positive ways, but they can also be negative and destructive. They were not discussed with the four mistaken goals because they are usually more of an issue between parent and child than between student and teacher. It is especially important that you know the basic four goals discussed in the chapter. Following is a brief discussion of the other three:

- *Excitement.* Some young people use negative behavior to pursue this goal. For example, speeding in a car, taking drugs out of curiosity, and promiscuous sex are not acceptable to most adults.

- *Peer acceptance.* Having a peer group is usually fine until the individual joins an "unacceptable" group. For example, joining a gang that is identified with crime would not be acceptable to most parents or teachers.

- *Superiority.* Most adults will approve of kids who seek to be superior in achievement in school or sports; however, some young people seek superiority in destructive ways. For example, putting down others and consuming more alcohol than anyone else are destructive.

SUMMARY OF MAJOR POINTS
IN CHAPTER 9

1. Discipline is training students in mind and character to enable them to become self-controlled and constructive members of society.

2. Good discipline is time-consuming because teaching students about discipline and responsibility requires planning and practice.

3. The three basic models of discipline discussed in this chapter are:

   ■ Autocratic discipline, which is based on punishment

   ■ Permissive discipline, which allows freedom without rules, limits, or order

   ■ Healthy discipline, which requires a balance between fairness and respect

4. Anger can get in the way of healthy discipline.

5. Teachers must control their anger before they discipline.

6. Punishment usually involves a threat that obligates the student to either obey or resist rather than to think constructively and respond.

7. Punishment degrades, dehumanizes, and humiliates students. Consequently, it hurts feelings, evokes anger, and incites resistance and withdrawal.

8. The lack of discipline is the number one problem in public schools.

9. Consistently, racial and ethnic minority students, especially African-Americans, will receive harsher reprimands than Western European American students.

10. Dreikurs theorized that the true primary goals of most behaviors are to:

    ■ find a sense of belonging

    ■ feel that one has significance by having control over one's life

    ■ feel that one has been treated fairly

    ■ avoid stressful and frightening situations

11. The four mistaken goals of behavior are:

    ■ attention-seeking

    ■ power

    ■ revenge

    ■ self-imposed inadequacy

12. Mistaken goals do not work.

13. Teachers can identify the mistaken goals by identifying their own feelings as they respond to the misbehavior and recognizing how the students are responding when the teacher tells them to stop the misbehavior.

14. There are specific strategies that a teacher can use to help solve the problems associated with mistaken goals.

Class Discussion	CHAPTER 9

Note: Review Appendix E before facilitating this activity.

The Giant Teacher*
Time: 15 minutes (discussion not included)
Objective: To help participants understand the effects of a controlling and/or hostile teacher.
Materials: One chair for each pair of participants.

Procedure:
1. Participants will pair up and decide who will be "**S**" and who will be "**T**."
2. Instruct **T** to stand on a chair facing forward with the back of the chair behind **T**. It can now be revealed that **T** stands for teacher.
3. Instruct **S** to stand very close to and facing the teacher. It can now be revealed that **S** stands for student. Tell **S** to now look up at "Teacher."
4. The facilitator now reads the following script to the participants:
   "You are looking at the Giant Teacher. This Teacher knows everything. This Teacher is smarter than you, can think faster than you, knows more than you do, and can do almost everything better than you. The Giant Teacher knows all the answers and solves all problems and does everything right. You can't do anything right! Almost everything you do is wrong and imperfect and needs to be corrected by the Giant Teacher."

Scolding Exercise:
5. Instruct the Giant Teacher to stand straight and tall on the chair, extend one arm and point his or her index finger with a tapping motion.
   Tell the Giant Teacher something like this:
   "In 10 seconds you are going to lower that finger and wave it in front of the student's face and give him or her insults and criticisms such as: 'You are really incompe-

tent, You're the worst student in this class, Can't you ever do anything right, Why do I have to tell you everything.' Be stern and no smiling. Ready—lower that finger and give it to the student." (allow about 20 seconds)

Head-Patting Exercise:
6. Next, instruct the Giant Teacher to bend over and very gently pat the student's head and give patronizing and sugary comments like: "You're so nice and sweet, You always do such a great job, I wish everyone behaved like you, You are just super." (allow about 20 seconds) Remind the Teacher not to rub or stroke too hard.
7. Have the students switch roles and repeat the exercise (steps 1 through 6).

Suggested Discussion Questions:
1. How did you feel during this exercise?
2. How often is this situation a reality in teaching?
3. How does humiliation or patronizing behavior affect relationships?
4. How many of you, when you were standing on the chairs, felt that you were in complete control? (Leader should point out that most teachers are feeling out of control when they are acting controlling.)
5. How many of you have noticed that when you hear others humiliating a youngster it sounds so terrible; but when you are doing it, it is because that person darn well deserves it?
6. Process more by asking participants what they learned about the long-range effects of humiliation.
7. What are some sources of inferiority feelings?

SOURCE: Adapted from an activity (The Competent Giant) by John Taylor from his book, *Person to Person: Awareness for Counselors, Group Leaders, and Parent Educators,* R&E Publishers.

Class Discussion	CHAPTER 9

Note: Review Appendix E before facilitating this activity.

Punishment Exercise

Time: 10–15 minutes (discussion not included)
Objective: To help participants understand the feelings that are generated in the one who is being punished.
Materials: None

Procedures:

1. Class members are to pair up.
2. One partner will play the teacher and the other the student.
3. The teacher is going to play the role of the punisher and verbally admonish the student with strong words (scolding, insults, threats, criticisms, name-calling, etc.) and exaggerated body language (finger pointing, hands on hips, glaring at student, etc.). However, touching of the student is not allowed.
4. Read the first role-playing situation. Give the teacher a few seconds to think how he or she is going to play out the scene.
   Role-Playing Situation #1
   Your student was caught taking a pencil from another student's desk.
   Teacher: Do your scolding and be sure to insult him good and don't forget to "get in his face."
5. Allow about 15–30 seconds for the scolding.
   Role-Playing Situation #2
   This time you will be punishing your student for "bullying" a smaller student.

6. Repeat the process for the second role-playing situation.
7. Ask the participants to reverse roles and repeat the same process or the 3rd or 4th role-playing situation.
   Role-Playing Situation #3
   New teachers, you are now going to punish your student for starting a physical and verbal fight with one of his or her classmates.
   Role Playing Situation #4
   You are now going to punish your student because you notice he or she doesn't seem to be putting in a strong effort in memorizing the lines for the new school play.
8. Assemble all the groups together again.

Suggested Discussion Questions:

1. How did you feel during this experiment?
2. Why do you think people punish?
3. How did you feel when others treat you in this manner?
4. What physical reactions did your body show?
5. What did you think your partner was thinking or feeling?
6. In what ways does this experience apply to you as a teacher or student?
7. Did this experience remind you of anything?
8. What will you start or stop after this experience?
9. Reviewing each situation again, how would a democratic or empowering teacher handle them?

Class Discussion	CHAPTER 9

Note: Review Appendix E before facilitating this activity.

The Push Activity

Time: 2–5 minutes (discussion not included)
Objective: To show participants that when we try to control people by being controlling and hostile, they are more likely to rebel and push back.
Materials: None

Procedures:

1. Ask the participants to pair up. Each designates who will be A or B.
2. Ask the A's to leave the room for one moment.
3. Explain to the B's that upon returning, the A's will return to their seats. When all the A's are seated they will be asked to stand. The

(Continued)

B's will then stand in front of the A's and both A's and B's will raise their hands with their palms facing outward.

4. Tell the A's that when it is announced to "begin the experiment" they will push gently against the B's hands, gradually increasing the pressure.

5. The B's will notice that the A's will resist. Upon resistance, the B's should increase their push.

6. Instruct B's that when they recognize that the two are in a deadlock, B's should gently stop pushing.

7. Instruct B's they should then step backward and **without saying anything,** invite the A's to sit down.

8. After the activity, gather all participants together.

Suggested Discussion Questions:

1. What were you feeling during the activity?
2. What physical reactions did your body show?
3. What were you thinking as the activity progressed?
4. What did you think your partner was thinking or feeling during the activity?
5. What happened when you stopped pushing?
6. How is this activity similar between a power struggle between a teacher and student?
7. What did the experience remind you of?
8. What other techniques can you use to influence people other then force?
9. How are you going to be different after this experience?

Teacher's Corner: Observing Teacher's Responses to Student Misbehavior

Concern: Do teachers unconsciously discipline, disapprove of, reprimand, scold, or reproach minority students differently than majority students? Are some students reprimanded for minor misbehavior while others are not?

Directions for Observation
Observe a teacher for about one hour. Whenever you observe a student misbehaving, check one of the two boxes:
Minor Misbehavior (MM) or Serious Misbehavior (SM)
Note: One box is marked for each interaction. One continuous interaction is marked only once. If the teacher moves away and returns a second reprimand is recorded.

Interview
Ask the teacher some of the following questions:

1. What are the rules in your class?
   _____
   _____

2. How are they maintained and enforced?
   _____
   _____

3. Which of the rules are most commonly violated?
   _____
   _____

Summary
The observation data is tallied to determine if the teacher has different responses for different students. Discuss the results of the observations and interview.

Observation Sheet

NAME OF OBSERVER _____   DATE _____

NAME OF TEACHER _____   TIME _____

OBSERVATION: MINOR MISBEHAVIOR   (MM)   CLASS _____
              SERIOUS MISBEHAVIOR (SM)

ETHNIC CODE: AF = AFRICAN AMERICAN
               AS = ASIAN AMERICAN
               HA = HISPANIC AMERICAN
               NA = NATIVE AMERICAN
               EA = EUROPEAN AMERICAN
               DS = DISABLED STUDENT
               PC = POVERTY STUDENT

NAME	ETHNIC	GENDER	RECOGNITION CODE							
			AD		AD		AD		AD	
				UD		UD		UD		UD

10
∎

Discipline:

Rules, Consequences, and Controlling the Physical Environment

> The school should never lay down a rule without giving an adequate
> explanation as to why this rule is good for the pupil.
>
> JAMES GIESEL

SENDING FIRM MESSAGES AND
ESTABLISHING RULES AND PROCEDURES

When you send messages that communicate class rules and expectations or demands, you are setting the boundaries for acceptable behavior. These boundaries provide the limits within which the students can freely participate without being reprimanded. How you send your messages determines the parameters of behavior and answers the question of what is acceptable and what is not acceptable.

Students clarify your message through their behavior. Testing is the best way to determine whether you really mean what you say and whether those demands and expectations are going to be enforced or the limits can be stretched. Some students will simply go ahead and do whatever you said you did not want them to do and then wait to see what happens. Your actions after the violation will determine what the student will do next.

Firm Messages

Firm messages are when "no" really means "no." You are using firm messages when both your words and their actions say "stop." Your students receive a clear message that says that compliance with the rule or request is both expected and required. In addition, the students are given all the information they need to make more acceptable choices in the future. Firm messages send clear communications about rules and expectations. Your words must also be consistent with your actions.

Let students know that you want them to learn and grow and that you may have to correct them at times. This, of course, does not mean that you do not like them or that you are rejecting them; it means that there is a better way to do something. You should like the students, but should not have an urgent need to be liked in return every minute of the day.

When giving guidance to students, you must give a clear message about rules and expectations. Following are some suggestions for communicating a clear, concise, verbal message:

Focus Your Message on the Behavior, Not on the Student Be sure to correct the behavior while it is happening or as soon as you become aware of it. Do not focus on the student's attitude or make a judgment about his or her worth. Tell the student (in nonjudgmental language) that what he or she did was not acceptable. If you want a student to stop interrupting you while you are talking, your message should be, "Joe, stop interrupting, please," or "Joe, you need to wait until

I'm finished speaking." It should not be, "Can't you see I'm busy!" or "Do you have to be such a pain in the neck?" or "Are you always so inconsiderate?"

Be Direct and Specific Speak directly to the students and use language that tells them precisely what you want them to do. Such statements as, "I want you to be here at 3:00 this afternoon," or "It's time for you to turn in your tests, right now," or "You need to leave the classroom right now," are direct and specific. Speak in terms that are clear rather than abstract. "I want you to quit your fooling around during class," is vague. "When we have a class discussion, I want you to sit quietly in the front row and in front of me," is clear and concise.

If necessary, be prepared to tell the students when and how you want things to be done. If it is the class's responsibility to keep the room clean, but they are leaving the classroom a mess, your message should be, "Each of you needs to be responsible for keeping this room clean. That means putting all chairs on the desks, putting away all books and personal materials in your lockers, and picking up any trash before you leave the classroom to go home. If your message was, "You have to do a better job of keeping the classroom clean," who decides what "a better job" means? Without a direct and precise message, a student's performance will probably fall short of your expectations. If you want your students to do something, you must tell them in no uncertain terms. The more uncertain your terms, the more uncertain the outcome.

Be Concise and Use Your Normal Voice The fewer words the better. Do not use 100 words when 10 will do. Do not lecture; you are sure to lose your students' attention. When expressing your carefully chosen words, keep your tone of voice calm and under control. State your matter-of-fact message in a normal voice.

Firm messages do not need to be stated emotionally. There is no need to yell or raise your voice to convince your students that you really mean what you say. Your actions or the consequences will communicate your message more forcefully than your words can.

Nonverbal Communication Is an Important Part of Your Message Firm messages should be respectful. Therefore, appropriate body language is important. Maintain eye contact, do not cross your arms and/or legs, sit or stand erect, and make sure you are close to your listener(s). If your voice, words, and body language are out of synchronization, the student will be influenced more by the nonverbal behavior than by your words.

State Your Consequences When Appropriate, and Follow Through with Actions When Necessary If you are expecting a power struggle or to be tested, you may need to specify the consequences of noncompliance at the same time that you make your request. This is not a threat, nor should it be punishment. It is far better to solve a problem than to apply consequences; however, when you apply a consequence, you are bridging any credibility gap that may have existed between what has been said and what action was to be taken.

For example, if you ask a student to stop swearing when he or she gets upset, but you expect him to continue swearing, your message should be, "Do not swear in my presence or in the classroom. If you do, I'll have to ask you to bring your parents in after school to discuss how we can resolve his problem."

Now your student has all the information he or she needs to cooperate. If he or she swears again, follow through with your action and call the parents in for a conference. Making your action consistent with what you say will establish your credibility and your students will begin to take your words seriously and do what you request. Your words are only the first part of your message, and that may be all you will need. But your words will be ineffective if you fail to support your message with action.

Following are examples of effective firm messages:

Stop fighting right now!

All students must be out of the classroom by 3:30 p.m.

You can play by the rules of the game or leave this field and find another game to play elsewhere. What would you like to do?

It's 10:30—time for study hall. You must leave now.

It is time for you to work on your social studies project.

It is time for you to come in to physical education. You need to say good-bye to your friends and come inside the gym now.

Remove any rings, bracelets, earrings, or necklaces before getting on any piece of gymnastics apparatus.

Following are examples of effective actions after firm messages have been communicated:

- Removing a student from the room for swearing.
- Not allowing a late student into the classroom if he or she was warned about coming late.
- Not replacing a piece of equipment that was damaged because of carelessness.

Soft Messages

Soft messages are rules that are only expressed in words but not put into consistent practice. Soft messages are when "no" means "yes," "sometimes," or "maybe." The verbal message of "no" says to stop, but the action message says that it is okay to continue.

Following are examples of soft messages:

Please try to get here on time, okay?

Do some homework after school.

That is enough from you.

Come on, shape up.

I don't like your attitude.

Don't be stupid.

It is time to do our math drills, okay?

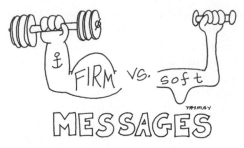

Firm messages are clearly stated when compliance with the rule or request is both expected and required.
Soft messages are only expressed in words but not put into consistent practice.

Come on, let's have a little cooperation.

Would you just try to cooperate once in a while?

Come on, stop acting like a jerk.

Can't you see that I'm busy?

Keep the noise down.

How about picking up those balls before you leave?

I want you to be good when we travel on a field trip.

Let's clear the classroom, okay?

Following are examples of ineffective action:

- Ignoring misbehavior in the hope that it will go away.
- Not enforcing the predetermined consequences of rule violations.
- Trying to persuade an academic teacher to consider giving a student a passing grade
- Making exceptions for the star students.
- Overlooking unacceptable behavior when you are in a good mood.
- Allowing students to walk away from assigned responsibilities.

CLASS RULES AND PROCEDURES

Just as in athletics, students need to know the rules, but they also have to know the reasons for them, and they have to be applied consistently. Students function and cooperate best within a structured environment. Students know what is expected of them because the classroom environment has been planned with their needs in mind. Rules are implemented to maintain harmonious interactions within the school, as well as the appropriate use of equipment and property. Rules provide a structure and a pattern to daily routines.

It is your responsibility, sometimes with the help of the class members, to establish rules to guide the behavior of all class members. You may have issues about which you feel very strongly, and you alone establish the rules for those issues. There is nothing wrong with this procedure as long as the established rules have the "five characteristics of a good rule" which are discussed in the next section. However, at times, you may be very receptive to having student input about the rules. In this case you and your students can work together to make good rules.

Setting limits on behavior means making good rules and teaching the value of the rules. Making rules and consistently enforcing those rules provide the foundation for building the inner discipline that is necessary in and out of school. Without rules, there is disorder. Without rules, there is nothing to refer to when a choice about behavior arises. However, making rules requires planning and patience. Good rule making is a skill that must be learned and practiced.

What Makes a Good Rule?

There are five characteristics that make a good rule:

1. *The rule must be reasonable.* A rule is reasonable when it takes into consideration the student's age and ability to perform according to the rule. If it is reasonable, it must be understood. Safety rules are the most reasonable because the reason for the rule can be explained in terms of the consequences. Other rules are not as easy to explain.

2. *The rule must be clearly communicated.* The rule must not be confusing or ambiguous. It should not imply what needs to be done, it must state it clearly. "All students must attend classes," is not a clearly communicated rule. A clearer version of this rule would be, "All students must attend all classes every school day unless they have a written excuse from their parents or school counselor."

3. *The rule must be enforceable.* The rule must be one that the teacher can enforce with a consequence. An example of an unenforceable rule is "Don't ever swear." The enforceable rule is, "Do not swear in my presence." Ideally, we do not want kids swearing, but it would be almost impossible for the teacher to enforce such a rule when the student swears at home or with his or her friends.

4. *The rule must be consistent.* The rule must be one that has general application and few circumstances in which it may or may not apply. "Do not fight unless you are attacked and must defend yourself or you are going to the defense of one of your classmates" is not a good rule because there are too many circumstances or conditions.

5. *The rule must be flexible.* The rule must have room for flexibility due to changes of circumstances. There are times when other priorities take precedence over a rule. For example, if your class is on an overnight trip and

The five characteristics that make a good rule.

the curfew for being in the hotel is 9:30 p.m. and the students are attending a movie that ends at 9:25 p.m., some degree of flexibility would be prudent.

Making rules is not easy. For practice in making rules with these five characteristics, make rules for the following classroom situations:

1. Cleaning up after class
2. Fighting
3. Not attending class
4. Not completing academic class assignments
5. Swearing
6. Using alcohol, tobacco, or other drugs on school grounds
7. Tardiness from class to class

Administering Consequences: Making Students Accountable for Their Behavior

Early planning can prevent many behavioral problems; however, every class will have a few students who will choose to become disruptive. They will violate rules and procedures. When rules are broken, it is the teacher's responsibility to consistently and firmly apply the pre-established consequences for violating the rule. If you are not consistent in your enforcement and your application of consequences, the rules will soon become ineffective.

When Students Keep Challenging Certain Rules

If students are engaging you in long explanations, debates, or arguments, they are probably testing your limits and finding out whether the rules can be renegotiated (Do you really mean what you say?). Remain firm with your limits and arguments will diminish over time. Do not get into any arguments when the consequences are being applied; this is the time when students will try to test you. If a student needs any clarification of rules, this can be done at a later time when things are calmer.

Student Input

How much input you allow students to have in establishing rules depends on their age and readiness. Obviously, a 6-year-old does not have the same capacity as a 17-year-old to make good rules. If students have input and their opinions are received, respected, and implemented whenever possible, the students are usually more willing to abide by them.

If a rule is broken, the consequences must be consistently applied. If the student believes that the consequence is unfair, it can be renegotiated at a later time, after the consequence has been allowed to run its course.

Rules Should Be Flexible and Negotiable

Rules should be flexible in the sense that they can be negotiated and revised as the students outgrow them or as changing circumstances require; however, you cannot be flexible at the moment when the rules or firm limits are being violated. They can be open to discussion at more appropriate times.

Using Procedures to Prevent Problems

Many of the problems that are associated with student misbehavior can be prevented through early planning and effective class management. Effective teachers use the preventive approach.

Rules, as was previously stated, are statements that specify what students can or cannot do. *Procedures* are the ways of doing things. Procedures provide order and sequencing to make activities flow more efficiently. Establishing class procedures beforehand can prevent a lot of potential problems and disruptions. Effective teachers must take the time to teach their students about procedures. You should not assume that the students know how to behave; however, when you explain procedures, you must walk a thin line between providing helpful explanations and sounding patronizing or overly moralistic.

It is, of course, important for you and your students to establish rules of behavior that concern attendance, tardiness, drug use, and general behavior both in and out of the classroom. However, many teachers overlook some of the most important activities that require rules to govern behavior and procedures that make everyday practices flow efficiently. These include student movement, downtime, and talking.

1. *Student movement.* Many large functions are an efficient way for large groups of students to learn important skills. Effective teachers devise ways to make needed movements flow smoothly. They use efficient cues, such as whistles and hand signals, and they establish rules that ensure (1) safety and the prevention of potential injuries, and (2) fairness; for example, taking turns, limiting the number of people in an activity, and movement from place to place.

   Setting safety rules is essential in school. These rules, in particular, must be firm and enforced. Students may not always agree with the teachers, but safety rules are usually the most reasonable because the reason for the rule can be explained in terms of consequences. Rules that encourage responsible behavior and inner discipline are not as easy to explain.

2. *Student downtime.* This refers to the time in between activities. A simple rule to be applied during downtime is that students must respect the rights of others to finish their activity without any disruptions.

3. *Student talking.* Students who talk while you or others are talking are annoying and disruptive. Effective teachers have a clear set of rules governing student talking. Most teachers have a no-talking rule when they or others are lecturing or explaining. Such procedures as listening to others, raising hands, taking turns, and talking one at a time are also used.

Procedures and routines help students learn to manage their classrooms by themselves, without teacher supervision. Routines encourage students to become self-disciplined by following a set schedule. Early in the term students will learn to organize their daily routines as you make your expectations clear. Students of any age can self-start with routines and not wait for the teacher's directions.

Procedures and routines have value, but do not let them become overbearing to the students. For example, having students form lines to get them from one place to another often creates more problems than solutions. Problems such as shoving, hitting, butting in line, and control commonly occur when teachers demand strict adherence to lines. If students, however, are treated respectfully, line problems can present positive opportunities for training in life skills. For example, as long as students can quickly get from one place to another in a quiet and safe fashion, it is not really necessary for the class to travel in a line. If there is a problem, you can use this opportunity to problem solve the situation with the entire class. When students have the opportunity to identify the problem and offer solutions, this is often enough to stop the problem.

Daily schedules or the general daily routine—how you sequence your classes and activities—is important for both you and your students. Routine offers security and comfort in knowing what is expected and when. Every teacher is different and each has his or her expectations of behavior for entering, participating in, and leaving the class. It is, therefore, important that you inform your students of your specific expectations. Not knowing the norms of appropriate behavior causes insecurity and misunderstandings. Let the students know what is expected of them before the bell rings (are they allowed to mill around or should they be seated?), where to place their homework (in a basket or on the right side of the desk?), and how to clean the classroom before leaving (putting away equipment and materials, arrangement of seats, etc.). Creating a classroom routine helps to create an environment that is predictable and comprehensible and reduces confusion and loss of instructional time. By helping students establish a routine, you enable students to carry out many of these routines without your direct supervision, freeing you to concentrate on the important classroom instruction.

The job of the daily schedule is usually determined by school administration, such as recesses, lunch, study periods, and planning periods. Like it or not, you and your students have to organize your day around these set activities. Sometimes class scheduling can be complicated at the junior and senior high level and it may require that you take some students through it several times before assuming they know the routine.

What you do have control over is how you plan your individual classes. Young children, in particular, will have difficulty staying on task for long periods of time and you should provide some type of routine physical movement at least every hour to counteract boredom. A simple stretching session or allowing students to get a drink of water are good strategies. An important routine that you need to attend to revolves around student interactions. When student talk is allowed and how it is to occur is very important.

Canter (1992) provided the following examples of some routine procedures:

- When students enter the classroom
- When students leave the classroom
- When a student needs to sharpen a pencil
- When students turn in homework
- When the teacher gives a signal to begin an activity
- When students transition from one activity to another
- When the fire drill bell rings
- When the class goes to a school assembly
- When guests come to the classroom
- When students are in the library
- When students put certain materials away (music, sports, art equipment)

Canter also reinforces the idea that the ultimate goal of procedure and routine is not to control behavior, but to help your students succeed at their various activities.

Minor Misbehaviors: Keeping Students On Task

If you are paying attention to what is going on in the classroom, you can usually "nip minor misbehaviors in the bud" by applying some simple intervention strategies. It is difficult for many students to consistently stay on task throughout the school day. As a result, some students simply forget or become bored and get distracted from their task. Minor misbehaviors are common and teachers usually expect them to happen throughout the day, therefore, having prepared strategies for minor misbehaviors are important. Minor misbehaviors occur when students get distracted from or distract others in the classroom from the activity or task. They include such things as frequent whispering, talking unusually loud, passing notes, moving unnecessarily around the room, day dreaming, putting on make-up, constantly tapping or twirling a pencil, or disturbing others.

Using respectful nonverbal or nondirective verbal prompts or cues are simple intervention tools with the purpose of getting the student(s) back on task in a respectful and unobtrusive manner. Nonverbal cues include eye contact, facial expressions, hand gestures or signals, appropriate touch, and moving close to the student(s). When students are in an activity that requires quiet, for example, a teacher's "look," a thumbs down hand gesture, a light touch on the student's shoulder, a slight disapproving facial gesture, or moving close to the misbehaving student is usually enough to stop minor misbehaviors. Nonverbal interventions let the student(s) know that you are aware of the misbehavior and that you would like it to stop. Nonverbal cues are always presented in a calm and respectful manner with the purpose of not distracting other students or making an issue of the misbehavior and most importantly, encouraging the misbehaving students to assume the responsibility for changing their misbehavior and getting back on task.

The principles of nondirective verbal interventions for minor misbehaviors are similar to nonverbal interventions in that you are still attempting to get the student(s) back on task in a respectful and unobtrusive manner. Verbal strategies include simply stating the student's name, calling on the student to answer a question, or incorporating the student's name in the lesson. Simply saying the student's name might be enough to get the student back on task. By simply stating the student's name, he or she knows that you recognize the misbehavior, but more importantly, you have left the responsibility up to him or her to figure out what to do. Given that responsibility, many students will stop. Calling on a student to answer a simple question or to do a task allows you to capture the student's attention without focusing on the misbehavior. After the question or task is completed, you can reply with a simple "thank you." This strategy shows the student that you were aware of the misbehavior but treated him in a respectful way and did not try to embarrass him. Most students will return to their task. Incorporating a student's name in the lesson is another simple way of distracting the student away from the misbehavior and back into the lesson. For example:

> Jennifer is slouching down in her seat with her book opened, propped up on her desk. However, she is putting on make-up while the health lesson continues. The teacher continues to talk about alcohol while moving closer to Jennifer and says, "Let's say Jennifer was my 16-year-old daughter and she came home both late and intoxicated from a party. What do you think I should do with her?" Jennifer puts her make-up away and pays attention.

If nondirective verbal messages are ineffective, it may require that you use firm messages or healthy communication (I-messages) as discussed in earlier chapters. Firm messages give clear messages about rules and expectations. Firm messages are when "no" really means "no." You give your students a clear message that says compliance with a rule or request is both expected and required. In addition, the students are given all the information they need to make more acceptable choices in the future. If you are expecting a power struggle or to be tested, you may need to specify the consequences of noncompliance at the same time you make the request.

Healthy communication is an effective way of dealing with undesirable behavior. It focuses on the teacher's feelings about a student's behavior, not about the student. The students are okay; their behavior is not. Remember, the model for the four steps of healthy communication is:

I feel _____

about/when _____

because _____

therefore/so _____ .

Cueing with Hand Signals

Many experienced teachers also use signals as a warning mechanism to alert students about an upcoming activity or task change that they need to get ready for. Just as a referee drops his raised hand to start play in a football game, you may use a hand signal to signify quiet or clap them together to get the attention of the class. For example, a common method of getting the class's attention is for you to rhythmically clap four beats and the students respond with a two-clap echo. This signals that all activities stop and all attention is turned to the teacher. Flicking the light switch three times or quietly ringing a bell will also have the same effect. When students are grouped and being dismissed, holding up two fingers means that students may leave two at a time. It is also effective to warn students that the activity will end in five minutes.

Managing the Physical Environment

The physical environment of the classroom has a direct impact on the health, safety, comfort, and motivation of both students and teacher. The heating, ventilation, illumination, glare, noise, size, and color are aspects of the room that have a direct and indirect effect on the comfort of the students. Students and teachers will find it difficult to learn in a classroom that is either too hot or too cold, poorly lighted, or acoustically too noisy. These factors fall under the category of school and classroom maintenance. It is the specific charge of the administration and custodial staff and, therefore, not discussed in this book. This section focuses on what you can do as a teacher to maximize your classroom for learning.

Teachers do have the responsibility of organizing and managing their classroom space so that they maximize the learning environment. Making the classroom a hospitable place for learning is controllable. How important is the physical environment in which a student learns? If people have the motivation to learn, they will probably do so in almost any physical environment; however, does the physical classroom environment enhance learning? Research by Doyle (1986) suggests that careful design of the physical space within a classroom influences the attitudes and conduct of the students and ultimately influences student behavior and learning. Proshansky and Wolfe, as far back as 1974, determined that the classroom setting has both direct and indirect effects on student learning. Something as simple as students sitting in a straight row may reduce their ability to hear one another, making it difficult to carry on a discussion. Students may also correctly or incorrectly perceive the straight row seating arrangement as a way the teacher purposely arranged the seats to inhibit discussion. The way space is managed has important behavioral and cognitive effects.

In addition to the hard physical make-up (linoleum, concrete, Formica surfaces, hard wooden chairs, desks) of the classroom, Sommer (1974) suggested students tend to feel more comfortable and secure in environments that contain items that are "soft" and responsive to touch. Soft items include such things as plants, small animals, area rugs, soft and warm colors, and bean bags. In addition, softness can be increased when classroom space is less crowded, allowing for "personal space," cubicles for private work, and ample space for aisles. Studies (Maslow & Mintz, 1956; Horowitz & Otto, 1973; and Sommer & Olson, 1980) have also demonstrated that aesthetically pleasing environments can influence behavior. Plants, mobiles, banners, bulletin board displays, pictures, posters, maps, globes, paintings, statues, books, magazines, student projects, sculptures, calendars, and puzzles are just a few of the many aesthetic objects that can enhance pleasure, beauty, and the personal growth of your students.

The physical environment, both hard and soft, must also support the social functions that take place within any classroom. The teacher must communicate and interact with students and students must communicate and interact with each other. As you plan the arrangement of students' desks, you must think carefully about the lesson plan activity and how often and how much you want the students to interact with each other. There are an infinite number of ways in which you can arrange clusters of desks to promote social discussion, sharing, and cooperative learning activities.

In a physical sense, there is no such thing as the perfect classroom setup because the needs and requirements of the learning activities and the students are continuously changing. Therefore, every teacher should be flexible enough to move furniture and change student learning groups as often as necessary. Trying to fit every learning activity into the same physical classroom setup will lead to disruption, discipline problems, and decreased motivation. In addition, at the high school level, many classrooms maintain a sterile environment because of the constant shifting of classes. Although students are shifting from classroom to classroom, most teachers maintain the same classroom throughout the day. When this is the situation, the teacher has the opportunity to "soften" his or her classroom. If you have more than one classroom environment, work together with the other teachers who share the same classrooms.

The Action Zone

In their classic study of the traditional classroom seating arrangement of rows and columns, Adams and Biddle (1970) reported that in most lessons and at all grades, a central group of actively participating students emerged and they became the central focus of the teacher's attention. The teacher talked to them the most and asked them the most questions. The students reciprocated with active dialogue in discussions. The other students did not actively participate; they remained silent, did other things, or talked with classmates. Some of these later behaviors may ultimately lead to discipline situations.

Adams and Biddle reported that the students who participated the most were located in what they called "the action zone." The action zone consisted of the front three middle students and the three down the middle aisle. These students received 64 percent of the questions. Also contributing to this effect was that most teachers maintained the front and center position during class. Do only the motivated students sit in the action zone? No. Schwebel and Cherlin (1972) concluded that it is the action zone that influences students. Teachers must find ways to expand the action zone. Teachers can do this by changing their location, moving away from the front and center position, and by being flexible in changing the seating and learning groups depending on the learning activity.

```
        T
  ○  ⊗  ⊗  ⊗  ○
  ○  ⊗  ⊗  ⊗  ○
  ○  ○  ⊗  ○  ○
  ○  ○  ○  ○  ○
  ○  ○  ○  ○  ○
```

The Action Zone
⊗ represents students in the action zone
T represents the teacher

```
             →       T
  ○  ○  ⊗  ⊗  ⊗
  ○  ○  ⊗  ⊗  ⊗
  ○  ○  ⊗  ⊗  ⊗
  ○  ○  ○  ○  ○
  ○  ○  ○  ○  ○
```

Changing positions changes the action zone
⊗ represents students in the action zone
T represents the teacher

```
      T  →    T    →  T
      ⊗  ⊗  ⊗  ⊗  ⊗
  ↑   ⊗  ⊗  ⊗  ⊗  ⊗   ↓
  T   ⊗  ⊗  ⊗  ⊗  ⊗   T
      ⊗  ⊗  ⊗  ⊗  ⊗   ↓
      ⊗  ⊗  ⊗  ⊗  ⊗
  T   ←    T    ←   T
```

A circular pattern around the room includes all students in the action zone
⊗ represents students in the action zone
T represents the teacher

Today, many teachers have moved toward alternative classroom arrangements because no single room arrangement will be appropriate for every lesson taught. Teachers must arrange the furniture in the room, have a variety of activity areas available to facilitate different learning situations, and use alternative facilities on a temporary arrangement. For example, some of the following may be incorporated into a teaching area:

- *Activity areas.* Activity areas contain appropriate materials and equipment where activities (such as science experiments) can be performed.

- *Resource center.* A resource center involves the teacher and librarian planning units which integrate resources with classroom assignments and teaching students the processes needed to find, analyze, and present information. Some of the resources within these centers include: books, magazines, films, audio and video tapes, computer software and databases, manipulative objects, commercial games, maps, artifacts, media production equipment, etc.

- *Conference areas.* Conference areas are used for discussion, reading, investigation, writing, or tutorials.

- *Learning center.* In a learning center, students have access to additional activities related to a unit of work.

In a large classroom, all four areas may remain set-up at all times. In more limited situations, resource and learning centers should remain available and activity and conference areas set-up as appropriate.

Whatever tasks will occur in your classroom, Weinstein (1996) recommends that you keep the following guidelines in mind:

- *Frequently used classroom materials (e.g., calculators, scissors, textbooks) should be accessible to students.* Decide which materials will be kept in locked or closed cabinets and which will be kept on open shelves.

- *Shelves and storage areas (e.g., in-out boxes) should be well-organized and labeled so that it is clear where materials and equipment belong.*

- *The seating arrangement should allow students to have a clear view of instructional presentations.*

- *The location of the teacher's desk depends on where you will be spending your time.* Do you move around the room a lot? Will a central location disrupt student conferences? Will you stay at your desk too long and not move around the room if you create a central location?

- *Decide where to store your own personal teaching aids and supplies.* Maintain a desk drawer or storage cabinet for your own personal use. If you move from classroom to classroom, a moveable cart or carrying case is practical.

Horowitz and Otto (1973) reported that students in alternative classrooms that had moveable panels and flexible comfortable seats had better attendance, group cohesion and participation, and more visits with the instructor when compared to the traditional classroom setup. Simply changing the arrangement of the room, however, does not guarantee positive results and behavior. An initial change in classroom arrangement must be viewed as temporary and one that will continuously evolve. For example, a teacher must study each learning area for possible overcrowding, gender utilization of certain areas, undesirable behaviors in some areas, space utilization, and other potential problems.

Gathering information is the key to control. Only through the systematic gathering of information and facts are you able to analyze your situation. This analysis enables you to help predict behavior. Once you are in a position to predict behavior you are in a position to control behavior. Your ability to control events, rather than being controlled by them, helps determine your success at managing classroom behavior.

There is only one way to gather, store, and retrieve information and that is through a written record. You should get in the habit of writing down your observations of specific events. Such documentation should answer the following questions:

- What happened?
- When did it happen?
- Where did it happen?
- Who was involved?
- How did you respond to the event?

The more information that you gather at the time of the event is important because when it is fresh in your mind the better off you will be. On a practical level, this is not always possible. If it is not possible to record information at the time of the event, make every attempt to write down the information before the end of the day because trying to recollect what happened yesterday or last week is more difficult.

Arranging Student Space

Because of the changing nature of how teachers teach, the traditional row and column seating design has limitations. For example, rows and columns are not conducive to class discussion or small-group activities. Circles are much more useful for classroom discussion and independent seatwork. Circles are, however, not the best arrangement for presentations and demonstrations because some students would inevitably face the teacher's back. Many teachers favor "seating clusters" of four or six students that are conducive to small group discussion, cooperative learning, and other small group tasks. It is, however, the students who will ultimately determine the success of any seating arrangement. It is critical that you manage student location and student grouping. Listed below are two suggestions to help reduce potential disruptions in cluster arrangements:

1. Mix low-achieving students with high-achieving students when making seating arrangements. Good and Brophy (1987) reported that low-achieving students participate in class activities more frequently when they are next to high-achieving students. Make sure that whichever classroom arrangement

you choose, the low-achieving student receives your attention and special attention when needed.

2. Mix peer-dependent and distractible students with well-motivated, socially skilled, and task-oriented students. Although it is not the responsibility of the well-motivated student to teach and control other students, Spaulding (1992) suggested that well-motivated students may be better off in the long run when they are involved in teaching and helping others. This situation, however, must be closely scrutinized because it is important that the well-motivated students not be penalized in their learning process.

Other Factors That Contribute to the Emotional Environment of the Classroom

An underlying assumption of this book is that a drab, barren, uninspiring learning environment helps create situations where behavior problems are more likely to occur. The environment, therefore, should be inspiring. The teacher does not have to be an interior decorator to make his or her classroom a pleasant place for students to be. Nor does it require a lot of money. Many teachers have involved their students in decorating the room. Most teachers are aware of the artistic ideas and talents that their students possess. Getting them involved also gives students ownership, responsibility, and pride for their classroom. Listed below are two other ideas for improving classroom ambience:

1. The room should be clean and free of clutter and trash.
2. Bright cheerful colors should be used throughout the room to contrast with the predominant room color. Some ways in which this might be accomplished are:
   a. Using bulletin boards that are colorful, cheerful, informative, and motivating.
   b. Displaying projects, posters, essays, or artwork developed by the students.

As mentioned in the beginning of this section, the teacher does not have complete control over the physical maintenance of the classroom environment (heating, ventilation, illumination, glare, noise, size, and color). He or she can, however, make accommodations for his or her students within that environment. Making adjustments to the physical environment of the classroom will help reduce behavior and learning problems. So what can a teacher do when the physical environment affects the students? With regard to the students, the teacher can:

■ Permit students to arrange or change seats whenever this will provide better conditions for seeing.

■ Arrange seats so that no student will face a window or work in his or her own shadow.

- Insist that the minimum type-size of textbooks be 10-point type or higher. Young children should have books with larger type.

- Make sure all duplicated materials are of good quality.

- Write on chalkboards or dry-erase boards in large clear letters, in the line of the student's vision.

- Insist that the classroom temperature be between 68 and 73 degrees F.

- Insist on proper ventilation and lighting.

- Maintain meticulous enforcement of rules with regard to hallway and classroom conduct, which will aid in reducing noise.

- Make sure students have the needed supplies, equipment, and resources for teaching and learning.

- Establish rules that include clear expectations and guidelines for student behavior.

In summary, the physical condition and environment of the classroom and the school, whether new or old, will influence the desire of the students and teachers to be there.

NATURAL AND LOGICAL CONSEQUENCES

Humanistic psychology seeks to understand people in terms of how they see themselves and what goes on inside of people in terms of how their needs and their unique ways of perceiving themselves influence them to behave the way they do. In other words, it centers on humans who are influenced and guided by the personal meanings they attach to their experiences. In contrast, behavioral theorists believe that external or environmental stimuli are reinforcers that either increase or maintain a behavior. The use of rewards and punishment are common in behavioral psychology. External rewards, such as praise, prizes, and other external stimuli, are used to motivate behavior change. Punishment is used to decrease a behavior.

Dreikurs (1964) did not advocate the use of rewards or punishment as motivators for behavior. Dreikurs instead recommended the use of natural or logical consequences to motivate behavior change. Students sometimes need to experience a concrete consequence of their actions in order to understand their behavior. The use of consequences also allows the student the freedom of choice on how to respond to a situation. The remainder of this chapter provides practical applications of natural and logical consequences in the classroom.

In life, one's actions are often followed by natural or logical consequences. If a person is late getting to the busstop, he will miss the bus (natural consequence). If a runner goes out too quickly in the mile run, she will fade in the end (natural consequence). If the employee does not attend work regularly, he may be fired (logical consequence). If a student does not turn in an assignment,

Time-out: Are You A Respectful and Trustworthy Teacher?

Instructions: Read each statement carefully. Circle the letter that corresponds to your response. *Treat the results as a guide only. There is a margin of uncertainty in all questionnaires of this kind.*

   If you are currently not teaching, you may respond according to how you think you would respond to the situations, or you can choose a former or present teacher and try to respond as you think he or she would respond.

1. A student has begun to show unsettled behavior just before a major examination, complaining of sickness, aches, and pains that you suspect are caused by stress rather than anything else. Do you:
   A. Speak to the student firmly and say that he or she must take the examination, like it or not?
   B. Allow the student to postpone the examination and send him or her to the nurse's office?
   C. Continue as if the student will take the examination but resolve to keep an eye on the situation?
2. How do you respond if one of your students openly swears at you?
   A. A stern reprimand at the instant the act is performed, followed by punishment.
   B. No punishment, but a quietly spoken reprimand.
   C. A reprimand followed by a determined attempt to reward the student for positive behaviors.
3. If a student does something that is outside of school (examples: stealing, vandalism, drinking, sexual behavior) and that you very much disapprove of, do you:
   A. Try to have the student disciplined?
   B. Tell the student how you feel and keep your distance?
   C. Tell yourself that the behavior is not a school issue and behave toward the student as you always did?
4. You are trying to concentrate on getting some important matters finished, but the noise of the students fooling around outside your office distracts and irritates you. How would you feel?
   A. That kids are kids and be happy that they are having a good time.
   B. Furious with them.
   C. Annoyed, but acknowledge to yourself that kids do make noise.
5. Do you discuss a student's behavior critically with other students?
   A. Often
   B. Rarely or never
   C. Sometimes
6. A student comes to you and confides that he is really unhappy with his life. Would you:
   A. Listen with empathy?
   B. Tell him what to do?
   C. Do things to try to cheer him up?
7. If a student openly questioned your authority, would you:
   A. Feel uneasy?
   B. Think that it is okay to do so?
   C. Feel very angry?
8. Do you believe:
   A. That some class rules are necessary, but the fewer the better?
   B. That students must have specific rules because they need to be controlled?
   C. That class rules are unnecessary?
9. Which statement do you most agree with?
   A. Don't judge a student's actions because we can never fully understand his true motives.
   B. Students are responsible for their actions and have to take the consequences.
   C. People's actions must be judged.

(Continued)

Time-out: Are You A Respectful and Trustworthy Teacher? *(Continued)*

10. State whether you strongly agree (SA), tend to agree (TA), tend to disagree (TD), or strongly disagree (SD) with each of the following:

A. SA TA TD SD   Students should be seen and not heard.

B. SA TA TD SD   The majority of misbehaviors and problems can be traced to a lackof firm discipline.

C. SA TA TD SD   It is better to reward good behavior than to punish bad behavior.

D. SA TA TD SD   A teacher should never raise his or her voice in anger to a student.

E. SA TA TD SD   The best way to eliminate bad behavior is with severe punishment.

F. SA TA TD SD   Students will always take advantage of a teacher who is not strict.

G. SA TA TD SD   When misbehavior begins to appear, stop it immediately before it becomes a pattern.

H. SA TA TD SD   "Spare the rod and spoil the child."

Scoring: Find your score by adding up the sum of your responses

1. A. 4   B. 2   C. 0
2. A. 4   B. 2   C. 0
3. A. 4   B. 2   C. 0
4. A. 0   B. 4   C. 2
5. A. 4   B. 0   C. 2
6. A. 0   B. 4   C. 2
7. A. 2   B. 0   C. 4
8. A. 2   B. 4   C. 0
9. A. 0   B. 4   C. 2

10.	SA	TA	TD	SD
a.	4	3	2	0
b.	4	3	2	0
c.	0	2	3	4
d.	0	2	3	4
e.	4	3	2	0
f.	4	3	2	0
g.	4	3	2	0
h.	4	3	2	0

Score	Analysis
Over 48	You are a very intolerant person. You are probably authoritarian, defensive, and opinionated. If you scored in this category, you may want to ask yourself why you are unable to accept faults in others.
32–47	You are not as tolerant as most other people are. You are probably bothered by little things and waste a lot of emotional energy. Try to focus on the significant problems rather than trivia. Try to have more genuine relationships with other people and experience more of life. If you do, your score will come down.
16–31	You are usually respectful and trustworthy and people will see these values in you. You are accepting of the views of others.
Below 16	You are a very respectful and trustworthy person. You are able to put yourself in another person's shoes and have empathy for their problems and difficulties. You are accepting even when you are offended.

she receives a zero (natural consequence). If a student makes a racial remark, he is suspended from school (logical consequence). If a player commits five personal fouls in a basketball game, she is out of the game (logical consequence). If a student brings a gun to school, he is expelled (logical consequence). No one is trying to hurt or annoy anyone. These consequences are merely the way things work. Through them, however, people learn to behave in certain ways if they want to avoid undesired results and achieve their goals.

You should not rescue students from the logical and natural consequences of their actions and choices as long as the consequences are reasonable and safe. A physical education teacher, for example, would never risk a non-swimmer being hurt as a natural consequence of jumping into the swimming pool or you would not fail a student as a logical consequence of missing a test due to sickness.

Natural Consequences

Natural consequences follow naturally after an event. If you play golf in the rain, you get wet. If you wear shoes that are too tight, you get blisters. If you do not drink water while running the marathon, you get dehydrated. If you do not water the plants, they will die. If you forget your bus money, you walk to school. The connections are direct and clear. Natural consequences place the responsibility for the behavior directly on the student performing that behavior. A natural consequence is a natural lesson for the student and does not require any intervention on the part of the teacher. Natural consequences are easy to use. Following are some situations in which you can use natural consequences.

When Students Keep Forgetting If students are in the habit of forgetting, the teacher must allow the consequence of forgetting to occur. You cannot keep reminding students or rescuing them from their forgetting by doing things for them that they should be doing for themselves.

During a recent lunch hour, Jose has forgotten his money to purchase his lunch. His teacher muttered, "Jose, this is the second time this week you have forgotten your lunch money. Wait just one minute and I will get you some money for your lunch."

The teacher would have used natural consequences if he had said, "Jose, I'm sure you feel terrible about forgetting your money. Can you think of anything you can do to solve your problem?"

Jose might suggest that he would try borrowing some money from somebody or he would see if someone might share his or her lunch. If neither of the suggestions is workable, the natural consequence of Jose's forgetting would be that he is not able to eat lunch.

By helping Jose find ways to solve his own problem (rather than solving it for him), the teacher guides Jose to focus on his problem of forgetfulness. Jose will realize that his discomfort results from the natural consequence of his forgetfulness. If Jose is not allowed to eat because of his forgetfulness, he will probably never forget his lunch money again.

The decision not to let Jose eat is a difficult one because you do not want Jose to be hungry for the rest of the day. If this were a first-time offense, the teacher might decide to help problem solve the situation with Jose and find a way to help Jose; however, if it is habitual for Jose to forget, the teacher must let the consequences occur.

When Students Fail to Live Up to Their Responsibilities Let the student experience the results of his or her actions.

Maria was late in turning in her term project. The class was reminded numerous times of the due date during the semester. The teacher reminded the class that any late papers would be severely penalized. Upon receiving her lowered grade, Maria was upset and at first blamed the teacher for being unfair; however, this incident caused Maria to reevaluate her behavior. She never turned in a late paper again.

When Students Lose or Damage Equipment or Clothes Due to Carelessness, Misuse, or Lack of Responsibility Do not repair or replace the damaged or lost item until enough time has passed for the student to experience its loss.

Within three days of receiving her new high school volleyball uniform, Courtney forgot her sweatshirt and left it on a chair in the school cafeteria, and it disappeared. She begged for another one and blamed the other students for their dishonesty in taking the sweatshirt. The coach recognized how important it is for young students to proudly wear team clothing in public. Sympathetic to Courtney's pleading, the coach gave her another sweatshirt. One month later, Courtney lost it.

The teacher had learned her lesson, but Courtney had not. After the first incident the teacher could have offered another plan: "I'm going to give you an old team sweatshirt. When you show me you can be responsible for it, we will be ready to talk about how you might get a new one."

Logical Consequences

Logical consequences require the teacher's intervention. They are the result of structured situations in which young students learn to be responsible within a social order. If a student does poorly on a school project, the student's grade is lowered. If a student is tardy, the student must go to the attendance office and check in. If a basketball player commits a fifth personal foul, the player is out of the game. If a student hits another student, the student is disciplined according to the school rules.

The connection between the situation or the behavioral act and the consequence must be logically related. It is important that the student see the connection between cause and effect. Fighting results in the removal of the student from the classroom and disciplinary action by the assistant principal.

When students know what is expected and do not comply with the rules, they learn from the consequences of their behavior. A logical consequence is not punishment. For example, if a student knows that he is not going to be able

Natural consequences follow naturally after an event and do not require intervention by the teacher.

to go to a school dance if he does not turn in his homework, that is not a logical consequence. Nelsen (1996) suggests that consequences must be *related* to the behavior, *respectful*, and *reasonable* to both the teacher and student. In addition, logical consequences should be agreed on in advance by both the teacher and students; therefore, it must be *revealed*. If misbehavior occurs that was not previously discussed, student(s) and teacher should problem solve the situation. Logical consequences can then be determined for future reference.

What If a Behavior Does Not Have an Obvious Consequence? Unfortunately, some teachers think of logical consequences as a way to punish students for what they have done instead of focusing on solutions for the future. What happens if a logical consequence for a particular behavior is not obvious? The answer is that a logical consequence is not appropriate if it is not obviously related to the behavior.

There is not a logical consequence for every problem or behavior. If there is no logical consequence, look for a solution. This situation gives you a tremendous opportunity to work together with students in finding a solution through problem solving. Getting students to help in deciding on the consequences is a wonderful learning opportunity for all.

Following are situations in which you can use logical consequences:

Purposeful Destruction of Equipment Make the student repair, replace, or pay for the item.

In a fit of anger, Ahmed threw and damaged his book against the wall. After Ahmed calmed down, the teacher calmly asked him how he might vent his anger more constructively. After getting a reasonable response, the teacher added, "How do you want to pay for a new book?" Ahmed never threw a book again.

When Students Make a Mess Make the students clean up the mess.

The exuberant students left the classroom in a mess after a class party. The teacher announced, "Nobody leaves until the mess in the room is cleaned up." Chris replied, "We promise we will do it after the assembly." "There won't be any assembly until it's done," the teacher responded. Everyone wanted to go to assembly. The classroom was quickly picked up within five minutes.

Misuse of Classroom Equipment Temporarily take the item away from the student.

While doing lab experiments, Tim started playing with the Bunsen burner in the chemistry lab by burning paper with it. The teacher said, "Tim, that's not what the Bunsen burner is used for. You can use it tomorrow provided you use it right."

When Students Misuse or Abuse Any of Their Class Privileges Temporarily withdraw or modify the privilege.

Keesha borrowed a volleyball to practice her setting skills at home. She forgot to bring it to class the next day. On its return the following day, the physical education teacher said, "You may not bring the volleyball home for the rest of the week. You can try again next week."

Help Students Learn from Their Mistakes

Teachers often interrupt the natural process of learning from consequences by rescuing students from adversity. When you rescue, the students miss out on important lessons. The undesirable behavior is, therefore, more likely to be repeated. For example, the logical consequence for a student-athlete failing a class is athletic ineligibility; however, if the coach rescues the athlete by asking the teacher to make special allowances, it teaches the student that rules can be bent and that his or her athletic ability has precedence over scholastic responsibilities.

You must make a strong commitment to help students learn about life from their own behaviors and from the social system. This must be done in an atmosphere of dignity, respect, and firmness. The choice not to rescue is a difficult one. The choice must be appropriate to the age and maturity level of the student and the situation. Obviously, if a student is being abused and does not have the resources to deal with it, a teacher must choose to rescue. When the situation endangers a student's emotional or physical safety, the teacher has the moral obligation to intervene. However, when a student' safety is not at issue, you must be careful not to step in too quickly. If you step in too quickly, the student will not have the opportunity to develop the tools that are necessary for positive growth.

Rather than rescuing, it is more appropriate to help the student learn from the experience. By reflecting on the experience, students can learn to make decisions on how to handle future situations. Explore the situation with thoughtful questions such as, "What is your understanding of what happened? Why do you think that happened? How do you think you might handle the situation differently the next time?" By exploring the experiences, you will help young students to develop good judgment skills.

Mistakes give us an opportunity
to learn and grow so we can change
in positive ways.

Time-Out as a Logical Consequence

Time-out is the removal of the student from the situation. It stops the misbehavior by removing the student from the problem environment. Generally,
time-outs are applied for aggressive, hurtful, disrespectful, or defiant behavior.
This method utilizes a time-out room or area that is devoid of interesting objects so that during this period the student talks to no one and has nothing to
play with or to occupy his or her attention.

A time-out should not be used as punishment. It is not a prison sentence to
force the student into compliance. Punitive time-outs are not constructive and
cause aggression on the part of the student. A punitive time-out sounds like this:
"Sit in the corner and keep your mouth shut until I'm ready to deal with you."
The student is to remain in the corner for a lengthy period of time until he or
she "learns his or her lesson." The value of any lesson is now lost.

Time-outs should simply be removal of the student from the environment in
which the misbehavior is occurring. They are brief and used to help the student
calm down and learn the rules. Once calm, the student and teacher can communicate in a friendlier atmosphere to resolve the problem and learn from the
situation.

Following are guidelines for using time-outs:

1. *Select the appropriate time-out area in advance.* Make sure it does not contain
   any stimuli that will hold the attention.
2. *Keep the time-outs brief.* Use a timer if necessary. Time-outs should not exceed 15 minutes. Older students can usually be given the option of returning
   when they feel they are ready to discuss the issue.

Time-outs are logical consequences that remove the student from the problem environment to help the student calm down and learn the rules.

3. *Time-outs should be applied immediately after a rule has been violated.* For example, fighting is not okay, and the students should be given a time-out directly. If the student refuses to go to the time-out area, limited choices or consequences are applied to the situation.

4. *Once the time-out is over, it is over.* If the student is no longer misbehaving, do not use the incident as ammunition in future conflicts or as grounds for punishment in later incidents.

5. *Apply time-outs every time they are required.* Do not hesitate to use time-outs when they are needed. Over time, the students will learn the appropriate behaviors.

The Difference between Punishment and Consequences

The following chart lists the differences between punishment and natural and logical consequences.

Punishment	*Natural and Logical Consequences*
Makes teachers responsible for their behavior. They become policeman and judge.	Makes students responsible for their own behavior
Decisions are made by the teacher. Students must obey or resist.	Students must decide which actions they want to take. Students must think constructively and respond.
Penalties are usually severe and unrelated.	Teacher's behavior results in a natural order of events rather than results that are based on the teacher's mood.

Problems, like all other situations, should be approached with continued attitudes of encouragement, understanding, dignity, and mutual respect.

Students are degraded, humiliated.	Students feel powerful and secure in the outcome of events.
Creates anger and hurt feelings and invites resistance or withdrawal.	Creates less guilt and hostility in the teacher because he or she is not directly involved in the decision.

Teaching Beyond Consequences

It is important to use logical consequences as a way of focusing on solutions rather than punishment. Nelsen, Lott, and Glenn (1992) have given the following seven suggestions for going beyond consequences and/or making sure consequences are not disguised punishment:

1. *If a consequence is not obvious, it is not appropriate.* If a physical education student kicks the ball over the fence in anger, it would be logical (also related, respectful, and reasonable) to have that student retrieve it. It would not be logical to have the student run ten laps around the track.

2. *Focus on solutions.* Rather than looking for consequences, look for solutions.

3. *Involve students in solutions.* The students can be your greatest resource. Tap into their wisdom and talent for solving problems when you are looking for a solution.

4. *Logical consequences might be appropriate when opportunity = responsibility = consequence.* For every opportunity (such as new equipment) there is a responsibility (such as taking care of equipment). When students choose not to take

Avoid piggybacking or following
a consequence with punishing
statements or acts.

care of equipment, the consequence is to lose the opportunity of having new
equipment; however, consequences are effective only if they are enforced
respectfully and students have another chance when they are ready for the
responsibility.

5. *Focus on the future.* Look for solutions that will help students to learn instead
of focusing on the past.

6. *Avoid piggybacking.* Teachers must avoid following a consequence with punishing statements or acts. For example, the teacher piggybacks a consequence
with such statements as, "Maybe you'll think twice the next time!" or "Just
sit there and think about what you've done!" Do not make the students
"pay" for their actions. Help the students learn from their experience with
dignity and respect.

7. *Plan ahead.* Enlist the aid of your students in deciding on consequences in
advance. For example, the teacher might say, "What would be a logical consequence for swearing in class?" Class meetings (discussed in Chapter 8) and
problem-solving sessions are excellent opportunities to ask students for their
help.

SUMMARY OF MAJOR POINTS
IN CHAPTER 10

1. How teachers send their message determines the boundaries or parameters of
behavior and answers the question of what is acceptable and what is not.

2. Firm messages are when "no" really means "no."

3. Clear and concise verbal messages requires that the teacher:

- focus the message on the behavior and not the student

- be direct and specific

- be concise and use a normal tone of voice

4. Understand that nonverbal communication is an important part of the message.

5. State the consequences when appropriate and follow through with actions when necessary.

6. Soft messages are rules that are only expressed in words but not put into consistent practice.

7. Soft messages are when "no" really means "yes," "sometimes," or "maybe."

8. The five characteristics of a good rule are that they must be:

   - reasonable
   - clearly communicated
   - enforceable
   - consistent
   - flexible

9. Many of the problems associated with student misbehavior can be prevented through early planning and effective class management.

10. Rules are statements that specify the things that students can and cannot do.

11. Procedures are the ways of doing things by providing order and sequence to make things flow more efficiently.

12. Many experienced teachers use signals as a warning mechanism to alert students about an upcoming activity or task change that they need to get ready for.

13. Experienced teachers use respectful verbal and nonverbal cues as simple intervention tools with the purpose of getting the student(s) back on task in a respectful and unobtrusive manner.

14. The physical environment of the classroom has a direct impact on the health, safety, comfort, and motivation of both students and teacher.

15. Appropriately managing the physical environment in which the students learn can significantly reduce classroom misbehaviors.

16. Dreikurs advocates the use of natural and logical consequences to motivate students to change.

17. Natural consequences follow naturally after an event.

18. Logical consequences require the teacher's intervention and are the result of structural situations in which young students learn to be responsible within a social structure.

19. Logical consequences must be:

   - related to the behavior
   - respectful
   - reasonable to both the teacher and student
   - revealed or agreed on in advance.

Class Discussion	CHAPTER 10

Note: Review Appendix E before facilitating this activity.

Sending Firm Messages
Time: 15–20 minutes (discussion not included)
Objective: To practice sending firm messages
Materials: "Firm Message Checklist" for each participant and six role-playing cards for each triad of students.

Procedure:

1. The facilitator distributes "Firm Message Checklist."
2. The facilitator explains each of the qualities of sending a firm message, demonstrating appropriate eye contact, body language, and other aspects. Modeling is an essential component of learning appropriate listening skills.
3. Group members form triads. Members are asked to choose the role of listener, speaker, and observer.
4. The facilitator gives each triad the six role-playing cards. Each member randomly selects two cards.
5. The speaker reads aloud his or her role-playing card and then delivers a firm message to

the listener while the observer and listener evaluate the "firm message."

6. The listener and observer share their thoughts about the firm message with the speaker.
7. The process is repeated as each member in the group rotates their role so that a new role-playing card is read and another firm message sent. Continue the process until all six role-playing cards are processed.

Suggested Discussion Questions:

1. What did you learn about yourself?
2. Is it difficult for you to send firm messages? Why?
3. How did you feel during this experience?
4. Why is it important to focus on the behavior instead of the person?
5. What happens when the messages are "soft?"
6. In what ways can this experience apply to the teaching profession?
7. How are you going to be different from this experience?

Checklist for Sending Firm Messages

1. Use Appropriate Body Language
   - maintain eye contact
   - uncross your arms and/or legs
   - sit or stand erect
   - make sure you are close, but not to close
2. Use a Clear but Normal Tone of Voice
   - the fewer the words the better
   - keep calm and keep your voice under control
   - be "matter of fact"
3. Focus Your Message on the Behavior and not the Student
   - "Joe, please stop interrupting."
   - "Mary, you cannot be late again."
4. Be Direct and Specific
   - "I want everyone here at 2:00."

Role-Playing Situations

1. An angry Joe has just shoved Travis to the floor because he thought Travis stole something from his locker. You are the teacher and must give Joe a firm message.
2. Maria is talking to a classmate and disturbing your concentration while you are trying to explain a new lesson to the class. You are the teacher and must give Maria a firm message.
3. Mark has been sleeping and not completing assigned lessons. You are the teacher and must send Mark a firm message.
4. Mitsuko copied off of a classmate's laboratory report. You are the teacher and must send Mitsuko a firm message.
5. Miguel calls a classmate a "jerk." You are the teacher and must send Miguel a firm message.
6. Laura throws a basketball in anger and kicks the ball off the court after losing the game. You are the physical education teacher and must send Laura a firm message.

Class Discussion   CHAPTER 10

Note: Review Appendix E before facilitating this activity.

Alternatives to Punishment
Time: 20–30 minutes (discussion not included)
Objective: To help the participants understand that there are more effective methods to discipline than punishment.

Materials:

Chart of "Alternatives to Punishment"

Role-playing cards of the following:

- A student has been fooling around and disturbing others during class.
- A student deliberately tries to hurt another student during recess.
- Your students have been leaving the classroom in a terrible mess after school.
- A student says something derogatory to you.
- A student keeps disturbing you while you are trying to talk with others.

Have participants within the group list some of their past or present discipline experiences and add them to the above list.

Procedure:

1. Display the "Alternatives to Punishment" chart.
2. Ask participants to get into groups of three.
3. Give each group a role-playing card. Ask them to choose an alternative to punishment from the chart and set up a demonstration of how they would handle the problem situation with one of these skills.
4. Allow time for each group to demonstrate their role play.

Suggested Discussion Questions:

After each demonstration ask the following questions:

1. What did you learn from this activity?
2. What did you learn about yourself from this activity?
3. How do you feel when others treat you fairly or unfairly?
4. What will you try to change after this activity?

Alternatives to Punishment

Decide what you will do, not what you will make your student do.

Set a limit and follow through.

Say how you feel.

Take care of your own needs.

Trust him/her to be who he/she is.

Natural consequences

Logical consequences

I can't make you and I would like your help.

Work on an agreement with your student and follow through.

Teacher's Corner: Observing Teachers' Disciplinary Behavior of students

Concern: Do teachers unconsciously discipline, disapprove of, reprimand, scold, or reproach specific students more severely than other students?

Directions for Observation
Observe a teacher for about one hour.
A. Appropriate Discipline. The observer makes a slash mark by the AD box (appropriate discipline) by the student's name each time the teacher uses a calm and unemotional voice and respectfully attempts to stop unacceptable student behavior. Relaxed nonverbal responses that stop inappropriate behavior are also recorded in the AR box.
B. Unacceptable Discipline. The observer makes a slash mark by the UD box (unacceptable discipline) by the student's name each time the teacher verbally or nonverbally responds with disrespectful words and anger. Touching such as pushing or grabbing a student in anger is also marked in the UR box.
Note: One reprimand is marked for each interaction. One continuous interaction is marked only once. If the teacher moves away and returns a second reprimand is recorded.

Summary
The observation data is tallied to determine which students are recognized and listened to and which are not. Discuss the results of the observations.

---

20. Time-outs should simply be the removal of the student from the environment in which the misbehavior is occurring.

21. A time-out should not be used as punishment.

22. Punishment and natural and logical consequences are not the same.

23. Rather than always looking for logical consequences, a teacher should look for solutions. In this way, teacher and student can be working together for the common good.

Observation Sheet

NAME OF OBSERVER _____   DATE _____

NAME OF TEACHER _____   TIME _____

OBSERVATION: APPROPRIATE DISCIPLINE   (AD)   CLASS _____
                UNACCEPTABLE DISCIPLINE   (UD)

ETHNIC CODE: AF = AFRICAN AMERICAN
                AS = ASIAN AMERICAN
                HA = HISPANIC AMERICAN
                NA = NATIVE AMERICAN
                EA = EUROPEAN AMERICAN
                DS = DISABLED STUDENT
                PC = POVERTY STUDENT

NAME	ETHNIC	GENDER	RECOGNITION CODE							
			AD		AD		AD		AD	
				UD		UD		UD		UD

Appendix A

■

Humanistic Psychology

Humanistic psychology focuses on human interests and values such as warmth, fair play, meaning, becoming, and emotional health. It characterizes that each person:

1. is inherently and intrinsically good and, therefore, deserving of dignity and respect

2. is aware of his or her own feelings and is ultimately in control of his or her own destiny

3. is expressed through his or her interpersonal relationships

4. has an "intent" or purpose that is the basis on which he or she builds his or her identity and distinguishes himself or herself from other species (Gensemer, 1980).

Abraham Maslow (1987), whom many consider the "father" of humanistic psychology, developed a theory that people achieve emotional well-being by meeting a triangular hierarchy of needs. These needs are discussed in the following paragraphs.

Physiological Needs These needs are at the base of the triangle, and as these needs are met we move upward in the triangle to safety and security needs. Physiological needs are taken as the starting point for motivation theory and refer to such functions as homeostasis, hunger, and thirst. Physiological needs are the most powerful of all the needs and, if unsatisfied, all others will be of secondary importance.

Safety Needs Examples of safety needs include security; stability; dependency; protection; freedom from fear, anxiety, and chaos; and need for structure, law, and order. Safety needs can encompass such situations as endangerment to one's life; job tenure and protection; insurance plans; religion; emergencies, such as catastrophes, crime, injury; verbal abuse and hostility; and disorganization. Maslow suggests that the human organism is a safety-seeking mechanism.

Belongingness and Love Needs Examples of these needs include giving and receiving of affection, being accepted by others, and being a part of a group. People hunger for relations with people—for a place in the group or family—and will strive with great intensity to achieve this goal.

Esteem Needs Esteem needs refers to the belief that all people in our society (with a few pathological exceptions) have a need or desire for a stable, firmly based, usually high evaluation of themselves; for self-respect or self-esteem; and for the esteem of others. These are, first, the desire for strength, achievement, adequacy, mastery and competence, confidence in the face of the world, and independence and freedom. Second, we all have a desire to feel important, appreciated, and to be recognized. Satisfaction of the self-esteem needs leads to feelings of self-confidence, worth, strength, capability, and adequacy; of being useful and necessary in the world. Unfulfillment of these needs produces feelings of inferiority, weakness, helplessness, and ultimately discouragement. Basic needs are discussed in Chapters 4 to 7.

Self-Actualization Need This need is at the peak of the hierarchy and refers to the desire for self-fulfillment, for becoming what one has the potential to become. For example, musicians must make music, artists must paint, and poets must write if they are to be ultimately at peace with themselves. Each individual has a desire to achieve what he or she believes is his or her potential; consequently, the course that one takes will vary greatly from person to person.

Many educators have applied humanistic-social psychology to parenting skills and education by defining and applying aspects of the basic needs concept to raising children and educating children in a classroom setting. Even though different humanists have applied their own individual interpretation of the basic needs theory, they are all very similar in concept.

Dreikurs (1964) also supported the theory that all behavior is purposeful and is always directed toward specific goals. To understand behavior, one must see behavior in terms of its purpose. Dreikurs placed a great emphasis on the significance of "belonging." Dreikurs supported the concept that all people have the desire to belong to someone or something and cannot be self-actualized unless he or she belongs. He believed that the need to be part of the group and to find one's significance through belonging explains many kinds of behavior. In his book, *Children: The Challenge,* Dreikurs believes that when a child believes he or she does not belong, he or she feels discouraged. Out of that discouragement the child will choose a "mistaken goal of misbehavior" to fulfill that sense of belonging. The Four Mistaken Goals of Behavior—undue attention, power, revenge, and assumed inadequacy—are discussed in Chapter 9. Dreikurs also focused a great deal of attention on ways adults "discourage" children and provided ways of encouraging children in his book, *Encouraging Children to Learn* (Dinkmeyer & Dreikurs, 1963). Encouragement strategies are also provided in Chapter 9.

Although society is continually changing and today's mix of students may think somewhat differently from the students of the past, humanistic psychologists believe that past and present students share the same basic needs. Today's students, regardless of gender, disability, color, or ethnic background, still have the same basic physical and emotional needs that require fulfillment. Understanding and meeting these needs is the positive connection between teacher and student and the focus of this book.

Glasser (1995) proposed a needs theory he calls the "control theory." Although Glasser is a cognitive psychologist, his theories are very similar to humanistic psychology. His theory holds that behavior is never caused by response to outside stimuli, but instead by what we want most of the time: probably one of five basic needs of survival that Glasser feels is genetically programmed within each individual. The needs that Glasser has identified are survival, love and belonging, power, freedom, and fun.

Survival needs are the physiological needs such as eating, sleeping, keeping warm, and feeling physically safe and secure.

Love and belonging is the need to feel connected with other people such as family, friends, classmates, or other significant people. When students say that a teacher cares about them, that teacher is meeting the students' need for love.

Power is related to feeling significant, important, or respected. Each person needs to feel that they have some significant power within a relationship and that what they have to say is not just heard but acted upon. When students say a teacher talks and listens to us, that teacher is meeting the need for power. When a person believes he or she has little or no power in a relationship, he or she will usually distance themselves from that relationship.

Freedom refers to the belief that most people will struggle to be free to live as they think best. This struggle for freedom often takes the form of attempting to get out from under the control of others. When students say that a teacher gives them the chance to do what they want to do, that teacher is meeting the need for freedom.

Fun refers to the idea that when we learn anything that is need-satisfying it makes us feel good, and when we feel good, we believe it is because we are having fun. When students are asked what good teachers do, the usual answer is that they make learning fun.

Glasser also believes that all living creatures "control" their behavior to maximize need satisfaction. If students are not motivated to do schoolwork, it is because they understand schoolwork as unconnected to their basic needs. Glasser proposes that the real challenge for the classroom teacher is to negotiate content and method with students so that what is learned can be seen as directly contributing to their basic needs.

EXISTENTIALISM

Existentialism is defined in Webster's New World College Dictionary (1996) as "a doctrine that focuses on the concrete; individual existence takes precedence over abstract, conceptual essence and holds that human beings are totally free and responsible for their acts and that this responsibility is the source of their feelings of dread and anguish." Individuals, consequently, are responsible for making themselves what they are. Not only can we think and feel, we can correct our thinking and have feelings about our feelings. Existentialism is a process of coming into being, or becoming, rather than a state of being.

In existential thought man is responsible for his becoming in the sense that by choosing among different alternatives for behavior he becomes authentically himself—that self which he really is—and it is this exercise of freedom that distinguishes man from all creatures (Graham, 1985). An individual has the right to experience freedom and he or she is free to choose not only what to do on a specific occasion, but what to value and how to live. Tillich (1952), however, observes that from this perspective man is essentially finite—inasmuch as he is free within the limits imposed by "being in the world" to make himself what he wants to be.

Maslow (1987) suggests that the concept of freedom is also a precondition to the basic needs. Freedom to speak, freedom to do what one wishes so long as no harm is done to others, freedom to express oneself, freedom to investigate and seek information, freedom to defend oneself, justice, fairness, honesty, and orderliness in the group are examples of such preconditions for basic need satisfactions. Without these freedoms the basic satisfaction of needs are quite impossible. Rogers (1951) has said that such a state of "feeling free" can be a reality only when the complete educational environment allows students to express their feelings, impulses, and precepts without fear of punishment for doing so. Psychological freedom, then, is the result of an environment intentionally arranged to permit full expression of values. It allows for the openness, spontaneity, and creativity that are released with a feeling of the inner spirit (Gensemer, 1980). Secrecy, censorship, dishonesty, and blocking of communication threaten all the basic needs.

PERCEPTUAL PSYCHOLOGY

Perceptual psychologists believe that the reality of an event lies in the perception of that event. Fundamental to this point of view is the belief that our behavior is influenced by the personal meanings we attach to our perceptions of those experiences (Hamachek, 1978). How we feel about the event determines our perceptions of the event and, consequently, we may be powerless to change the event, but can change how we feel about the event.

Hamachek (1978) summarized some of the most important features of Roger's "self-theory." They include: (1) the self strives for consistency, (2) a person behaves in ways which are consistent with the self, (3) experiences that are not consistent with the self are perceived as threats and are either distorted or denied, (4) the self may change as a result of maturation and learning. Although Roger's self-theory represents a synthesis of phenomenology (perceptual psychology), social interaction theory, and interpersonal theory, it represents the concepts of perceptual psychology that are utilized throughout this book. Rogers (1951) provided some of the following basic propositions derived from the mentioned concepts:

1. Every individual exists in a continually changing world of experience of which he or she is the center. In this sense, each person is the best source of information for himself or herself.

2. Each individual reacts to his or her perceptual field as it is perceived and experienced. Consequently, knowledge of a person's experiences is not sufficient for predicting behavior; one must know how the person perceives the experiences and what it means to him or her.

3. Each individual has a basic tendency to strive, actualize, maintain, and enhance the experiencing organism.

4. As a result of interaction with the environment, and particularly as a result of interactions with others, one's perception of oneself is formed—an organized, fluid, but consistent conceptual pattern of perceptions of characteristics and relationships of the "I" or the "me."

5. Perception is selective, and the primary criterion for selection is whether the experience is consistent with how one sees oneself at the moment.

6. Most ways of behaving that are adopted by the individual are those that are consistent with his or her concept of self.

7. When a person perceives and accepts into one integrated system all of his or her sensory and visceral experiences, then he or she is in a position to be more accepting and understanding of others as separate and different individuals. For example, a person who feels threatened by his or her own hostile or sexual feelings may tend to criticize or move away from others whom he or she perceives as behaving in sexual or hostile ways. On the other hand, if he or she can accept his or her own sexual or hostile feelings he or she is likely to be more tolerant of his or her expression of others.

Appendix B

■

Activities to Enhance Acceptance

A teacher must establish an appropriate classroom atmosphere that encourages acceptance. A number of requisite skills to help students accept other students can be developed through warm-up activities. Warm-ups are used in the first portion of a class when people are new to each other or just arriving. Some of the requisite skills developed through activity-oriented warm-ups are:

1. Familiarity with, and trust of other students in the class.
2. Listening skills.
3. Knowledge of and experience with the decision-making process.
4. Cooperation and participation of one's own feelings and the feelings of others.
5. Open communication among disagreeing factions and empathy with people who have opposing viewpoints.
6. An appreciation and understanding of both one's own feelings and the feelings of others.
7. An appreciation of individual differences and unique potentials.

Warm-ups are nonthreatening and are conducted in an informal but structured manner. They are designed to help students verbally interact in an open and trusting atmosphere. Warm-ups help to build trust and acceptance among classmates. The following pages offer only a few of an infinite number of warm-up activities. The activities are listed in random order and no activity is more important than another. Choose the activities that are most appropriate to your situation. The activities are universal in that they can be used at any level; however, appropriate language and situations must be adjusted to the grade level of the class.

Classroom Acceptance	**Warm-up**

Name Tags
Time: 10–20 minutes
Objective: Warm-up or ice-breaker to help students become acquainted. It also helps students increase their awareness of their uniqueness as an individual with different ideas, likes, values, and opinions.
Materials: Large index cards or colored paper
Tape, paper clips, or pins to hold the tags on participant's shirts or blouses
A variety of colored large felt tip pens

Procedure:

1. Distribute cards and pins to participants.
2. Ask each person to write their first name in the middle of the card, using a large felt tip pen. However, tell them to leave some space around the outside of the card for some additional information.
3. Tell students to:

A. Write the name of the person they most admire above their name.
B. Below their name, write the animal that best represents them.
C. Along the right border in a vertical column write what they feel is their most important virtue.
D. Along the left border in a vertical column write their greatest accomplishment.
4. When the students have completed their cards, they are to move freely around the room and become acquainted with each other.

Suggested Discussion Questions:

1. What made this exercise pleasant or unpleasant?
2. What did you learn about other people in the group?
3. What, if anything, surprised you about this activity?

Classroom Acceptance	**Warm-up**

Who or What Am I?

(The Guessing Game)
Time: 10 to 15 minutes
Objective: To help participants relax, get acquainted, and get actively involved with each other.
Materials: Index cards and tape or computer mailing labels
Thick felt tip pen

Procedure:

1. Assemble several index cards or computer mailing labels so that there will be one for each participant.
2. On each card write the name of a famous person, a college mascot, an academic subject, the name of a professional sports team, or some other specific category relevant to the lives of your students.

(Continued)

3. Tape one label on the back of each participant without letting him or her see what it says. Make a few extras for students who may want to participate more than once.
4. Instruct the participants to try and guess what is written on the label by asking only yes-no questions of the other participants. Each participant can only ask another participant three yes-no questions. After three questions have been asked, he or she must move to another participant. At the same time he or she is asking fellow group members about his or her own label, the participant must answer their yes-no questions so they can figure out what their labels say.
5. Continue until everyone has succeeded. If time is a factor, the leader can announce that the other group members can give the participants clues.
6. When the participant guesses correctly, he or she is to remove the label from his or her back and put in on his or her right shoulder area.

Suggested Discussion Questions:

1. What made this exercise pleasant or unpleasant?
2. What did you learn about the people in the group?

The Scouting Report
Time: 15 minutes
Objective: To get acquainted and begin to disclose personal information.
Materials: Printed sheet of "The Scouting Report" for each participant.
Procedures: Members are given a copy of the "The Scouting Report." Each student is to match other students who fit the descriptions on the worksheet. A student may only use a name once; however, more than one person may sign the same item. After completing the "Report," members may share things that they learned.

Suggested Discussion Questions:

1. What elements make this exercise pleasant or unpleasant?
2. What did you learn about people in the group?
3. After looking over your list, do you have any questions that you would like to ask people within the group?
4. How do you feel about being a member of this group?

The Scouting Report

Find Someone Who:

1. Is on a school athletic team _____
2. Participates in a school club _____
3. Speaks more than one language _____
4. Has been to a rock concert _____
5. Plays a musical instrument _____
6. Has more than two sisters or brothers _____
7. Has been on television _____
8. Traveled to another country _____
9. Likes school _____
10. Was born in the same month as you _____
11. Is a left hander _____
12. Carries a good luck charm _____

Classroom Acceptance	Warm-up

Getting Acquainted

Time: 10–15 minutes

Objective: To allow participants an opportunity to learn some things about each other and provide an environment where people practice good listening skills.

Materials: None

Procedure:

1. Have the participants pair off with someone that they do not know very well. Instruct them to find a place where they will not interfere with other pairs.
2. Give them at least 6 minutes to talk about themselves.
3. Bring the group back together in one large circle with each student sitting next to his or her partner.
4. Ask each participant to introduce and speak about his or her new friend. Remind the group that no one else should talk while the speaker has the floor.
5. After everyone has made introductions, the facilitator can moderate a question and answer period.

Suggested Discussion Questions:

1. What did you like about this activity?
2. What did you learn about others that surprised or pleased you?
3. How did you feel during this activity?

Classroom Acceptance	Warm-up

Likes and Dislikes

Time: 20–25 minutes

Objective: To help participants share some of their values and experiences.

Materials: A copy of the "Likes and Dislikes" list for each participant.

Procedure:

1. Divide the class into groups of four to six participants and distribute "Likes and Dislikes" list.
2. Tell each group that they are to come to a consensus for each of the categories found on the "Likes and Dislikes" list. It is important that "honesty" be stressed in this activity. (10–15 minutes)
3. After the list is completed, each group must choose three items to share with the entire class. (5–10 minutes)

Note: This activity can also be competitive by placing point values on the items where consensus is reached. A suggested format is 1 point for each of the likes and dislikes and 3 points for each of the common experiences. The group with the highest point total wins. Remind the group that honesty is imperative in this activity.

Suggested Discussion Questions:

1. What were some items that you had difficulty coming to consensus with?
2. What did you like about this activity?
3. What did you learn about others?

Likes and Dislikes List

Part A: Likes and Dislikes
The object of this activity is for each group to reach a consensus.

	Like	Dislike
1. Sport	_____	_____
2. TV show	_____	_____
3. School subject	_____	_____
4. A movie star	_____	_____
5. A politician	_____	_____
6. Food	_____	_____
7. Drink	_____	_____
8. Exercise	_____	_____
9. Animal	_____	_____
10. Summer vacation	_____	_____

Part B: Common Experiences
Participants are to search for experiences they have had in common.

1. A time when they felt uneasy at school.
   _____

2. A time when they got away with something they should not have.
   _____

3. Something they have done with their friends about which they are very proud.
   _____

4. A pleasant childhood memory.
   _____

5. Something that they did for someone that really made a difference in that person's life.
   _____

Classroom Acceptance   Warm-up

Introduction Skits
Time: 20–30 minutes
Objective: To help participants build trust by working together in a fun activity.
Materials: None

Procedure:

1. Divide the class into groups of five or six.
2. Allow each group 15 minutes to put together a three-minute skit that will serve to introduce the members of that group.
3. Allow the students to be as creative as possible. If groups are stuck, suggest some ideas:

   A drug raid where a policeman asks the suspects things about their lives.

   A psychiatrist asks patients questions as they visit his or her office.

   Television show formats: Quiz Shows, Dating Game, Late night talk show, interviews, etc.

4. At the end of the skits, all participants gather together.

Suggested Discussion Questions:

1. What pleased you about the activity?
2. What did you learn about others in the group?
3. What did you learn from this activity?

Classroom Acceptance   Warm-up

The Auction

Time: 15–20 minutes

Objective: To help participants examine their priorities and make choices on the basis of those priorities.

Materials: "Auction List" for each group of 3–4 students.
Play money (monopoly money or any teacher-made bogus currency).

Procedure:

1. The class is divided into groups of 3–4 participants.
2. Each group gets a copy of the "Auction List" and a predetermined amount of money (e.g., $500.00).
3. Explain to the groups that each item will be auctioned off in order of appearance on the "Auction List" to the highest bidder.
4. Once a team runs out of money, its members can no longer bid.
5. Only groups can make purchases, individual students within the groups cannot make independent decisions.
6. The money cannot be divided among the members of the group.
7. Gather the groups back together.

Suggested Discussion Questions:

1. Was your group happy with what it received?
2. Why was your selection important to you?
3. If you did not receive what you wanted, how did that make you feel?
4. Were any members within the group unhappy with the group's decision?
5. What did you learn from this activity?

Note: This activity works well when the facilitator gets into the spirit of the activity and has fun auctioning off the items. He or she should keep trying to raise the price without dwelling too long on any one item. The instructor can also choose an outgoing student to be the auctioneer.

Auction List

1. The perfect mate for the rest of your life.
2. A feature article in the newspaper about you.
3. A chance to spend the day with your classmates at Disney World.
4. A chance to be the special guest of your teacher at a teacher's banquet where he or she is being honored.
5. A guarantee to attend any college of your choice.
6. Participation as an athlete in the Olympics
7. Perfect health for your entire life.
8. The promise to have a perfect friendship for life.
9. The chance to solve the social problem of racism.
10. To have others accept you for who you are and not what they want you to be.
11. A report card of straight A's.
12. A future job in which you are liked and respected by your friends, colleagues, and community.

Classroom Acceptance   Warm-up

Tell Me Questions
Time: 10 minutes
Objective: To help participants get to know each other on a more personal basis.
Materials: A copy of "Tell Me" questions for each participant. The "Tell Me" questions should relate to the feelings of the participants, therefore, there are no right or wrong answers.

Procedure:

1. Divide the class into groups of four.
2. Distribute the "Tell Me" questions to each group.
3. Tell the participants that they are to designate a person to be the starting point for the activity.

4. That person directs the first statement to each individual within the group.
5. After each person has completed the first statement, the next person to the right directs the next statement to each of the individuals within the group.
6. This process continues until all statements are read and answered.
7. Gather all participants into one group.

Suggested Discussion Questions:

1. What did you like about the activity?
2. What did you learn about others?
3. How did you feel during this activity?
4. Did you learn anything about yourself through this activity?

"Tell Me" Questions

1. Tell me something about your best vacation.
2. Tell me something that frightens you.
3. Tell me something that really makes you happy.
4. Tell me something that really irritates you.
5. Tell me something about a favorite childhood memory.

6. Tell me something about someone in your family.
7. Tell me something that makes you laugh.
8. Tell me something that _____ _____.

Classroom Acceptance   Warm-up

My Worry List
Time: 30 minutes
Objective: To have students share some of the pressures and worries they face, as well as to help them get to know themselves a little better.
Materials: Paper, pens/pencils, chalkboard, chalk, and eraser

Procedures:

1. Have students list at least five of the pressures or stressors they personally face (grades, parents, friends, money, etc.)

2. After a designated time, ask members to volunteer some items on their list. Write their responses on the board.

Suggested Discussion Questions:

1. Do students in the class have some common pressures?
2. How do you cope with some of the pressures you have?
3. What are some other healthy ways of coping with minor pressures?
4. What can some people do when the pressures become too great?

Appendix C

■

High Risk Health Behaviors

The California Task Force to Promote Self-Esteem and Personal and Social Responsibility (1990) is convinced that self-esteem is central to most of the personal and social problems that plague human life in today's world. The task force was mandated by California legislature to investigate the relationship between self-esteem and various social concerns and through their three year research reported that self-esteem plays a central role in the social of our society. It is imperative that teachers be aware of the severity of these problems and their impact on some of our youth.

SEXUAL INTERCOURSE

By age 18, 57 percent of teens have had sexual intercourse while half of American teens at this age have had no sexuality or HIV education. In addition, the American School Health Association (1989) reported that only 26 percent of twelfth-grade teens who are sexually active use condoms. The task force reported studies that have correlated low self-esteem with infrequent use of contraceptives by females while high self-esteem females are more apt to rely on contraception to avoid pregnancy.

The task force reported that teens engage in sexual activity in an attempt to bolster low self-esteem. A boy may hope to enhance his self-worth by proving his sexual prowess and virility. Some girls become sexually involved because they couldn't say no, because they wanted to satisfy a boyfriend, or because they felt it was expected of them—all reasons consistent with feelings of low self-esteem.

TEEN PREGNANCY

Each year in the United States, 20 percent (one million) teenage girls become pregnant and have 25 percent of all abortions each year. Forty percent will choose abortion and 470,000 will complete their pregnancy. In 1990, some 10,000 teenage unintended births occurred with girls 14 years of age and under. Of all the teens between the ages of 15 and 19, Hispanic girls make up more than one-third of them; yet, only 9 percent of all adolescent females are Hispanic.

Teenage girls who become pregnant are more likely to drop out of school and end up on welfare than those who do not become pregnant. Children of teenage mothers tend to be sicker and smaller then those born to older mothers, and they wind up pregnant or in prison in disproportionate numbers. The good news is that between 1990 and 1996, there was a dramatic decline (11.9 percent) in the birth rates for all female teenagers. More importantly, this decline cut across geographic, racial, and ethnic lines. The pregnancy rate for African-American teens dropped 21 percent during this time period and the teen pregnancy rate among Hispanics, though still highest in the nation, dropped 4.8 percent between 1995 and 1996 (Wingert, 1998). In addition, abortions among teens are also falling.

The task force reported data indicated that many teenage fathers have histories of delinquency, substance abuse, failing to graduate from high school, financial difficulty, and exposure to family violence. This background makes it difficult for the teenage father to create a stable self-esteeming environment for his offspring. The task force also reported that a female adolescent might expect motherhood to improve her status because as a mother she is someone with important tasks to perform; someone loved and needed.

SEXUALLY TRANSMITTED DISEASES

More Americans are infected with STDs now than at any other time in history. The most common sexually transmitted diseases include chlamydia, genital herpes, genital warts, gonorrhea, syphilis, and HIV/AIDS. It is estimated that each year 3 million teenagers are infected with an STD. The National Adolescent School Health Study reported that 30 percent of teens do not know that most people get STDs by having sexual intercourse, and 25 percent do not know that using condoms is effective in avoiding some STDs.

No one is immune to STDs. Everyone who is sexually active can get or transmit an STD. Race, religion, sexual preference, and socioeconomic status are not protective barriers to any of the sexually transmitted infections. "Nice" people get syphilis; heterosexuals get AIDS. STDs are equal opportunity diseases. However, the Division of Sexually Transmitted Disease Prevention of the Centers for Disease Control (1995) reported that surveillance data show high rates of STDs for some minority racial/ethnic groups when compared with rates for white Americans.

There are no known biologic reasons to explain why racial or ethnic factors alone should alter risk for STDs. Rather, race and ethnicity in the United States are risk markers that correlate with other more fundamental determinants of health status, such as poverty, access to quality health care, health care seeking behavior, illicit drug use, and living in communities with a high rate of STDs. Acknowledging the disparity of STD rates by race and ethnicity is one of the first steps in empowering affected communities to organize and focus on this problem. Some of the most prevalent sexually transmitted diseases are discussed in the following paragraphs.

HIV/AIDS Throughout the first half of the 1990s, there was a great increase in the number of cases of HIV/AIDS in African-Americans and a substantial increase among Hispanic Americans. In 1994, an accumulation of 441,528 U.S. cases had been reported. Hispanics accounted for 18.7 percent of the cases and African-Americans for 39 percent, or three of every eight cases (Centers for Disease Control, 1995).

There is no evidence to suggest that African-Americans or Hispanic Americans are more biologically susceptible to AIDS than white Americans; however, some ethnic groups have a greater proportion of people exhibiting certain risk behaviors. White males account for 77 percent of AIDS cases in homosexual men (Mays, 1989). In 1989, among black males, 35.4 percent reported exposure to the disease through homosexual risk behaviors and 39.4 percent through intravenous drug use (National Center for Health Statistics, 1990).

Women represent the fastest growing group of HIV-infected people in the United States and abroad. African-American women and Latinas are the fastest growing group at risk of HIV infection; 52 percent of female AIDS patients are listed as black, non-Hispanic; 20.5 percent are Hispanic; and 26.5 percent are white, non-Hispanic (Centers for Disease Control, 1990), although black and Latina women make up only 19 percent of all U.S. women. AIDS is now the leading cause of death among women aged 15 to 44, and half of these women are African-American.

The increasing numbers of cases of AIDS among African-American women is of concern because of the impact on pediatric cases of AIDS. Currently, 58 percent of all pediatric AIDS cases are African-American children (Centers for Disease Control, 1992).

Gonorrhea Gonorrhea has had a devastating impact on African-Americans and Hispanic Americans who represent, respectively, 12.4 percent and 9.5 percent of the U.S. population. In 1994, the Division of Sexually Transmitted Diseases (U.S. Department of Health and Human Services, 1995) reported that African-Americans accounted for about 81 percent of all reported cases of gonorrhea. The overall gonorrhea rates in 1994 were 1,219.3 cases per 100,000 for African-Americans and 84.5 cases per 100,000 for Hispanics, compared with 30.1 for non-Hispanic whites.

Age-specific rates are very high for African-American adolescents and young adults. African-American 15- to 19-year-old women had a gonorrhea rate of

4,911.9 cases per 100,000. African–American males in this age group had a gonorrhea rate of 4,007.5. These rates are, on average, more than 28-fold higher than those in white American adolescents aged 15- to 19-years-old. Among 20- to 24-year-olds in 1994, the gonorrhea rate among blacks was 38 times greater than that of whites (4,479.3 versus 116.3, respectively).

Gonorrhea rates are rising in various Native American populations. Native American women, in particular, have a prevalence rate much higher than any other group of women in the United States. In 1992, the gonorrhea rate for Native American women was nearly 1,200 per 100,000 population, compared to less than 200 per 100,000 in all other female populations (Centers for Disease Control, 1993).

Syphilis An Atlanta (AP) article titled "Syphilis Rate at an All Time U.S. Low" (1998) summarized a Centers for Disease Control and Prevention study which reported that the syphilis rate in the United States has plummeted 84 percent in this decade to its lowest level on record. For every 100,000 people, 3.2 contracted syphilis in 1997—the lowest rate since health officials started tracking the disease in 1941. This disease, however, still has a racial component. Twenty-two out of every 100,000 blacks contracted syphilis, compared with 0.5 of every 100,000 whites and 1.6 per 100,000 Hispanics.

Chlamydia Nonspecific bacterial infections and chlamydia are the most common of all sexually transmitted diseases. They may affect as many as 45 percent of sexually active U.S. teens and college students (3 to 4 million a year) (Reagen & Brookins-Fisher, 1997). The Centers for Disease Control (1993) estimated that over 10 percent of sexually active young females and over 5 percent of sexually active young males have genital chlamydia.

Genital Warts Med. Help International (no date) reported that an American College Health Association study found that 1 in 10 college women is infected with genital warts (HPV, the human papilloma virus), one of the fastest growing sexually transmitted diseases. This sexually transmitted virus is responsible for the vast majority of the nearly 16,000 new cases of cervical cancer diagnosed in the United States. Several of the HPVs many different strains cause genital warts or lesions that have been linked to both dysplasia and cancer. Having sex before age 18 or having more than three sexual partners in a lifetime increases a woman's likelihood of contracting HPV and cervical cancer.

SUICIDE

Suicidal behavior is a serious health problem for adolescents, second to accidents as the leading cause of death among young people. Suicide among teens between 15 to 24 years old is the second leading cause of death. In 1992, one in every twelve high school students reported having tried suicide. Every 6 hours, a youth aged 10 to 19 commits suicide with a gun. Across ethnic groups, adolescent suicide has increased over the years.

Native Americans, one of the most impoverished ethnic groups, often live without adequate nutrition, shelter, and sanitation. They suffer from a high rate of mental illness, which stems from feelings of hopelessness, desperation, and family dissolution, all of which are related to poverty, harsh living, social injustices, and discrimination. As a result, Native Americans suffer from depression, anxiety, violence, substance abuse, and family conflicts. Native Americans have the highest rate of completed suicide of any ethnic group in the United States, even though the rate is decreasing (McIntosh, 1990). Alcohol abuse is a critical risk factor associated with suicidal behavior; 80 percent of Native Americans who attempt suicide also have alcohol abuse problems (Young, 1998). Age is also a risk factor. High rates of suicide are found primarily among young American Indians from 15 to 34 years, the age group that makes up the largest proportion of the population.

Suicide is the third leading cause of death among African-American youth aged 15 to 24 after homicides and accidents (Gibbs, 1988). African-American males between the ages of 15 and 19 have a suicide rate of 8.2 per 100,000. The suicide rate for African-American males is lower than white American males at all ages. This also applies to African-American females in comparison to white American females.

The U.S. Department of Health and Human Services (1991) reported that, until boys and girls are 9-years-old, their suicide rates are identical. From 10 to 14, the boys' rate is twice as high as the girls'; from 15 to 19, four times as high; and from 20 to 24, six times as high. Women are twice as likely to attempt suicide, but men have a higher completion rate (National Institute of Mental Health Report, 1992). Men are more likely to use more violent means, like a gunshot to the head. Women are more likely to take an overdose and then can be saved. Those who complete suicide also have a higher rate of substance abuse.

SUBSTANCE ABUSE: ILLEGAL DRUGS

The epidemic of drug abuse has plagued our nation and, in particular, our youth for too long. Drugs have destroyed individuals, families, and communities. The use of psychoactive drugs occurs in all 50 states.

The reason for people abusing drugs is, of course, multifaceted; however, low self-esteem in most drug education textbooks is consistently listed as one of the variables that contribute to drug abuse. The task force reported one major study that concluded that low levels of self-esteem are the cause, not the result, of deviant behavior.

The 1995 National Household Survey on Drug Abuse reported the following:

- An estimated 12.8 million Americans were current illicit drug users (used an illicit drug in the past month) and represent 6.1 percent of the population 12 years old and older.

- Marijuana still continues to be the most commonly used illicit drug, used by 77 percent of current illicit drug users. Approximately 57 percent of current illicit drug users used marijuana exclusively, 20 percent used marijuana and another illicit drug, and the remaining 23 percent used an illicit drug other than marijuana in the past month.

- An estimated 5.6 million Americans (2.6 percent of the population) were current users of illicit drugs other than marijuana and hashish.

- The current illicit drug use (within the past month) for African-Americans (7.9 percent) was somewhat higher than for white Americans (6.0 percent) and Hispanics (5.1 percent).

- Among youths, the rates of illicit drug use are about the same for the three groups. These numbers may be reflecting a change in the use of illicit drugs by different minority groups. Most current illicit drug users were white Americans.

- There were an estimated 9.6 million whites (75 percent of all users), 1.9 million African-Americans (15 percent), and 1.0 million Hispanics (8 percent) that were current users in 1995.

- An increase in illicit drug use (between 1992 and 1995) occurred among white American, African-American, and Hispanic American youths.

- The rate of current illicit drug use for youths in other race/ethnicity groups increased from 2.7 percent to 11.2 percent between 1994 and 1995. This result should be viewed with caution, however, as the National Household Drug Abuse Survey sample size is small for this group. This racial/ethnic group comprises mainly Asian-Americans, Pacific Islanders, and Native Americans.

The following section discusses some independent drug research on Native Americans and Asian and Pacific Americans, the members who make up the "other" category of the National Household Drug Abuse Survey. Unfortunately, the number of published studies describing prevalence rates are limited in scope and few in number. Caution must be taken in their interpretation.

Native Americans One of the few longitudinal studies on Native American drug use reported over a three year period that (1) 80 percent of the Native American youth reported using alcohol and 20 percent used alcohol every weekend, (2) 70 percent reported using marijuana, with 40 percent of those using it at least 10 times during the past month, and (3) 40 percent reported using other drugs at least three times in the past month (King et al., 1992).

Segal (1989) conducted a comprehensive survey of Alaska Natives and reported the youth showed higher drug and alcohol use than all other ethnic groups, including white Americans. Segal reported 71 percent of Alaska Natives and 66 percent of Native Americans tried marijuana, 40 percent reported using stimulants, 33 percent used inhalants, and 70 percent of the Alaska Natives and 53 percent of the Native Americans used chewing tobacco. Eighty-eight percent of Native Americans and 75 percent of Alaska Natives tried alcohol. Table C.1 reports the percentage of high school seniors who reported using selected drugs in the past year, 1985–1989.

**Table C.1 Percentage of High School Seniors Who Reported
Using Selected Drugs in the Past Year, 1985–1989
Data have been combined for 1985 to 1989**

Native Am.		White		African Am.		Hispanic Am.		Asian Am.	
M	F	M	F	M	F	M	F	M	F
Marijuana									
42	44	40.2	36	29.8	18.4	34.5	24	19.6	17.1
Cocaine									
14.2	15.5	11.9	9.3	6.1	2.6	15	7.6	5.8	5.7
Alcohol									
82	81.3	88.3	88.6	72.5	63.9	81	75	69.3	67.5
Inhalants									
5.2	0.9	3.4	2	1.4	1.4	2.1	1.5	1.3	0.8
LSD									
3.1	2.2	2.8	1.1	0.6	0.2	1.8	0.25	1.1	0.1
Cigarettes									
36.8	43.6	29.8	34	15.6	13.3	23	21	16.8	14.3

SOURCE: Adapted from U.S. Department of Education, National Center for Education Statistics, The Condition of Education, 1992, Washington, DC: 1992. Primary Source: U.S. Department of Health and Human Services; Alcohol, Drug Abuse, Mental Health Administration; National Institute of Drug Abuse, *Drug Use Among American High School Students and Other Young Adults,* 1991.

The average percentage of Native American high school seniors (both male and female) who have used drugs in the past 12 months (1985 to 1989) was higher than other racial/ethnic groups (U.S. Department of Health and Human Services, 1991).

Asian-Americans There is a relatively small number of research papers devoted to the Asian and Pacific Americans and drug use. Most of the information pertaining to alcohol, tobacco, and other drug use among Asian-Americans comes from isolated, non-random surveys. Unfortunately, the number of published articles describing prevalence rates among Asian and Pacific American ethnic groups are limited in scope and few in numbers. In general, the research reports that Asian and Pacific Americans use and abuse substances less frequently than do members of other racial and ethnic groups (McLaughlin, Raymond, Murakami, & Gilbert, 1987; Trimble, Padilla, & Bell, 1987, and Tucker, 1985). Flaskerud and Hu (1992) found lower rates of substance abuse among Asian-Americans than among white Americans, African-Americans, or Latino Americans. However, most samples are small and primarily drawn from West Coast cities like San Francisco and Los Angeles.

There are no prevalent data pertaining to the Asian-American populations at the national level. Most of the available survey data are on the use of alcohol and tobacco. The three major surveys—the National Institute on Drug Abuse (NIDA) National Household Survey, the NIDA National Adolescent School Health Survey, and the National High School Seniors Survey—do not report data on Asian-American groups. In addition, the majority of studies have been conducted primarily on Chinese and Japanese populations and do not include recent immigrant and refugee groups. These later groups are at high-risk status for illegal drug use and are also the fastest-growing populations among Asian Pacific groups.

SUBSTANCE ABUSE: TOBACCO

Smoking remains the single most preventable cause of death (U.S. Department of Health, Education, and Welfare, 1985), accounting for approximately 125,000 deaths per year or 30 percent of all deaths from cancer (American Cancer Society, 1989). The 1995 National Household Survey reported that an estimated 61 million Americans were current smokers in 1995. This represents a smoking rate of 29 percent for the population aged 12 and older. In addition, current smokers were more likely to be heavy drinkers and illicit drug users.

The 1995 National Household Survey summary was prepared by Joseph Gfroerer of the Substance Abuse and Mental Health Services Administration, Office of Applied Studies (SAMHS/OAS). The National Household Survey reported that:

- Among adults, men had somewhat higher rates of smoking than women, but rates of smoking were similar for males and females aged 12 to 17.

- Approximately 4.5 million youths aged 12 to 17 were current smokers in 1995. This rate is about 20 percent of all youths in this age category. The rate was 18.9 percent in 1994.

- Youths aged 12 to 17 who smoked were about eight times as likely to use illicit drugs and eleven times as likely to drink heavily as nonsmoking youths.

- The level of educational attainment was correlated with tobacco use. Thirty-seven percent of adults who had not completed high school smoked cigarettes, while only 17 percent of college graduates smoked.

African-Americans and Smoking Hildreth and Saunders (1992) reported that smoking-related diseases are more prevalent among African-Americans than whites and are prevalent among African-American women in particular (Klonoff et al., 1995). One in five college-aged African-American males are current smokers—more than twice the number of female African-Americans. For African-American men, lung cancer is the leading cause of cancer deaths. Over twice as many African-American males than females die from lung cancer. African-American women smoke more than nonminority women and this difference is partially responsible for mortality rates for lung cancer that are twice as high for African-American women (National Cancer Institute, 1989).

Hispanic Americans and Smoking The 1985 National Health Interview Survey (Centers for Disease Control, 1987a) reported that 31 percent of Hispanic men and 32 percent of non-Hispanic whites smoke cigarettes. The corresponding figures for women were 21 percent among Hispanics and 28 percent for non-Hispanic whites. Further studies by Marin and his colleagues (1995) also reported differences in the number of cigarettes smoked per day. Non-Hispanic whites reported smoking more cigarettes (mean = 21.5) per day than Hispanics (mean = 12.0).

Latina females are much less likely than African-Americans or Anglos to smoke (Marin, Perez-Stable, & Martin, 1989) and much less likely to use drugs (Smith-Peterson, 1983). Latinas drink much less than Anglo and African-American women. Indeed Latinas are the group most likely to be abstainers (Gilbert, 1987).

Asian and Pacific Islanders and Smoking Cigarette use among Asian immigrant or refugee groups is higher than in other ethnic groups in the United States. Among California immigrants, smoking rates among men are 72 percent to 92 percent for Latinos, 71 percent for Cambodians, and 65 percent for Vietnamese (U.S. Department of Health and Human Services, 1990), compared with 30 percent for the overall white American male population. Table C.2 reports cigarette use from the data taken from the 1991 National Household Survey on Drug Abuse by race and age.

The results of the survey reflect greater cigarette use by males when compared to females and white Americans smoke more than minority Americans.

Smokeless tobacco products include both chewing tobacco and snuff. Chewing tobacco can be loose-leaf, pressed into bricks or cakes (plugs), or twisted into rope-like strands. Snuff is made from powdered or fine-cut tobacco leaves. Smokeless tobacco contains carcinogens, nicotine, and abrasives to the teeth and gums. Smokeless tobacco can cause halitosis, stained teeth, gingivitis (inflammation of the gums), ulcerations of the gums, leukoplakia (a precancerous condition) and cancer of the mouth, tongue, and palate.

Recently, the National Institute on Drug Abuse estimated that as many as 22 million Americans have used smokeless tobacco. Most users are male, but unfortunately, in some Native American tribes, smokeless tobacco use rates among adolescent females approach 45 percent. Table C.3 reports the use of smokeless tobacco by race and age.

One out of every four males has used smokeless tobacco—eight times the number of females. More than one out of five college-age males uses smokeless tobacco (11 times the number of females). The 1995 National Household Survey found that an estimated 6.9 million Americans (3.3 percent of the population) were current users of smokeless tobacco in 1995. In addition, the rate of smokeless tobacco use continues to be significantly higher for men than for women in 1995 (6.2 percent vs. 0.6 percent). Over 90 percent of smokeless tobacco users were men.

In 1995, the National Household Survey reported that smokeless tobacco use was more prevalent among whites (3.9 percent) than among blacks (1.3 percent) or Hispanics (1.2 percent).

Table C.2 Cigarette Use By Race, Sex, and Age
(Estimates are shown for 1991)

	Total	Hispanic	White	Black
(Percent rate estimates)				
Ever Used				
Age				
12–17	37.9	31.9	41.7	25.6
18–25	71.2	58.0	76.5	57.0
26–34	76.4	69.2	78.4	74.0
35+	78.0	66.3	80.0	75.6
Sex				
Male	77.3	70.7	79.7	70.2
Female	72.7	60.6	75.8	65.4
Used in Past Year				
Age				
12–17	20.1	16.7	23.2	9.6
18–25	41.2	33.0	45.3	28.9
26–34	38.0	34.6	38.3	40.8
35+	30.0	31.1	29.2	35.7
Sex				
Male	34.7	35.8	34.3	36.3
Female	39.7	24.8	30.7	28.5
Used in Past Month				
Age				
12–17	10.8	8.7	12.7	4.3
18–25	32.2	24.7	35.7	22.0
26–34	32.9	28.6	33.2	36.8
35+	26.6	27.7	25.8	32.6
Sex				
Male	28.7	29.7	28.1	31.5
Female	25.5	19.7	26.5	24.8

SOURCE: Adapted from *National Household Survey on Drug Abuse: Population Estimates, 1991.*
U.S. Department of Health and Human Services; Alcohol, Drug Abuse, Mental Health Administration; pp. 91–93. National Institute of Drug Abuse, 1991 National Household Survey on Drug Abuse.

SUBSTANCE ABUSE: ALCOHOL

Alcohol, a depressant drug, is one of the most widely used and abused drugs in the United States and throughout the world. Abusive alcohol consumption is related to a variety of health problems such as destruction of brain cells, cirrhosis of the liver, cardiomyopathy, ulceration of the stomach lining, menstrual irregularities, and sexual impotency. However, the leading alcohol-related cause of

Table C.3 Smokeless Tobacco Use By Race and Age (Estimates are shown for 1991)

	Total	Hispanic	White	Black
(Percent rate estimates)				
Ever Used				
Age				
12–17	11.8	4.2	14.9	4.0
18–25	21.8	9.2	26.4	7.6
26–34	16.4	8.9	19.2	7.5
35+	11.7	4.7	12.4	12.8
Used in Past Year				
12–17	6.1	2.0	7.9	1.2
18–25	8.7	2.7	11.0	2.0
26–34	5.0	2.0	5.9	2.3
35+	3.4	0.6	3.7	2.9
Used in Past Month				
12–17	3.0	1.1	3.8	0.8
18–25	5.8	1.7	7.5	1.2
26–34	3.5	0.8	4.3	1.5
35+	2.8	0.4	3.0	2.8

SOURCE: Adapted from *National Household Survey on Drug Abuse: Population Estimates, 1991.* U.S. Department of Health and Human Services; Alcohol, Drug Abuse, Mental Health Administration; National Institute of Drug Abuse, 1991 National Household Survey on Drug Abuse.

death is injury due to drunk driving. Young drinkers are at highest risk of dying in an alcohol related driving accident, while drinkers over 60 years face a higher risk of premature death from cirrhosis of the liver, hepatitis, and other alcohol-linked illnesses.

Table C.4 reports the use of alcohol by race and age. The data was taken from the 1991 National Household Survey on Drug Abuse.

White Americans have the highest overall rate of alcohol use. Rates for Hispanics and African-Americans were slightly lower. The survey also reported that 58.1 percent of men were past month alcohol users, compared to 44.3 percent of women.

The following National Household Survey summary was prepared by Joseph Gfroerer of the Substance Abuse and Mental Health Services Administration, Office of Applied Studies (SAMHS/OAS). The 1995 National Household Survey on Drug Abuse reported that:

■ Approximately 111 million persons aged 12 and over were current alcohol users. About 32 million persons (15.8 percent) engaged in binge drinking, and about 11 million Americans (5.5 percent of the population) were heavy drinkers.

Table C.4 Alcohol Use By Race and Age
(Estimates are shown for 1991)

	Total	Hispanic	White	Black
(Percent rate estimates)				
	Ever Used			
Age				
12–17	46.4	45.9	48.2	40.3
18–25	90.2	82.2	93.2	82.5
26–34	92.4	85.7	94.4	88.6
35+	87.5	81.0	88.9	84.4
Sex				
Male	89.0	86.0	90.6	84.2
Female	80.7	68.9	83.3	74.7
	Used in Past Year			
Age				
12–17	40.3	40.2	41.9	35.2
18–25	82.2	72.3	86.8	72.8
26–34	80.9	74.4	83.7	72.7
35+	65.1	64.4	66.4	56.6
Sex				
Male	72.7	75.0	73.6	66.1
Female	63.9	54.9	66.8	54.5
	Used in Past Month			
Age				
12–17	20.3	22.5	20.4	20.1
18–25	63.6	52.8	67.2	56.0
26–25	61.7	57.2	63.8	57.1
35+	49.5	47.8	50.9	40.3
Sex				
Male	58.1	60.2	59.2	52.2
Female	44.3	34.9	46.6	36.5

SOURCE: Adapted from *National Household Survey on Drug Abuse: Population Estimates, 1991.*
U.S. Department of Health and Human Services; Alcohol, Drug Abuse, Mental Health Administration, pp. 85–87. National Institute of Drug Abuse, 1991 National Household Survey on Drug Abuse.

- About 10 million of those binge drinkers were under the age of 21. Of these, 4.4 million were binge drinkers, including 1.7 million heavy drinkers.
- The level of alcohol use continues to be strongly associated with illicit drug use in 1995. Of the 11.3 million heavy drinkers, 25 percent (2.8) million people were current illicit drug users. Among binge (but not heavy) drinkers, 18 percent (3.8 million) were illicit drug users.

- Education also plays an important role in patterns of alcohol use and abuse. The 1995 National Household Survey found that 68 percent of adults with college degrees were current drinkers compared with only 42 percent of those having less than a high school education. However, the rate of heavy alcohol use was 3.7 percent among adults who had completed college and 7.1 percent among adults who had not completed high school. Binge drinking use rates were similar across all levels of education.

- White Americans continue to have the highest rates of alcohol use at 56 percent. Rates for Hispanics were 54 percent and African-Americans were at 41 percent. The rate of binge use was lower among blacks (11.2 percent) than among whites (16.6 percent) and Hispanics (17.2 percent). Heavy use showed no statistically significant differences by race/ethnicity (5.7 percent for whites, 6.3 percent for Hispanics, and 4.6 percent for blacks).

- The survey also reported that 60 percent of men were past month alcohol users, compared to 45 percent of women, and that men were much more likely to be heavy binge drinkers (23.8 percent and 8.5 percent, respectively) and heavy drinkers (9.4 and 2.0 percent, respectively).

African-Americans and Alcohol Herd (1988) reported that African-American youth use alcohol less often than youth from other ethnic groups. However, Herd also reported that African-American adult males consume more alcohol than white males on a per capita basis. Schinke et al. (1988) reported of those that do drink that when compared to white Americans and Hispanics, African-Americans show higher polydrug use, such as alcohol and heroin, alcohol and PCP, and cocaine and heroin.

Barnes and Welte (1986) reported that African-American youth have a lower rate of alcohol use and overall drug use (Skager, 1986; Hartford, 1985) than white youth. The proportion of abstainers is higher among African-Americans than whites, mainly because of the high proportion of abstainers among African-American women. Lillie-Blanton, Mackenzie, and Anthony (1991) reported that white women with 12 years of education or more were heavier drinkers then black women with similar educational background.

The homicide rate is much higher for African-Americans compared to white Americans. In 1991, over 10,000 African-Americans were victims of homicide (U.S. Bureau of the Census, 1994). If 50 percent of the homicides are attributable to alcohol, more than 5,000 African-Americans lost their lives due to alcohol abuse.

Harper (1981) suggested that one of the major barriers to the treatment of alcoholism for African-American males is that heavy drinking is considered the norm and is positively associated with manhood and camaraderie. Harper (1979) also suggested that African-American men generally do not draw a clear distinction between alcohol use and abuse.

Asian-Americans and Alcohol Asian-Americans consume less alcohol and have fewer cases of alcoholism than white Americans, Hispanic-Americans, African-Americans, and Native-Americans. Comberg (1982) reported that this may be

Table C.5 Alcoholism Deaths and Mortality Rates for Native-Americans and Alaskan Natives, 1986–1988

Age adjusted rates are shown, per 100,000 population, for Native-Americans, Alaskan Natives, and U.S. all races.

Year	Native-Americans and Alaskan Natives		U.S. All Races		Ratio of Native-Americans and Alaska Natives to All U.S. Races
	Number	Rate	Number	Rate	
1988	389	33.9	16,882	6.3	5.4
1987	288	25.9	15,513	6.0	4.3
1986	272	24.6	15,525	6.4	3.8

SOURCE: Adapted from *Trends in Indian Health, 1991,* U.S. Department of Health and Human Services, Public Health Service, Indian Health Service, p. 49. Note: All deaths include deaths due to alcohol dependence syndrome, alcoholic psychosis, and chronic liver disease and cirrhosis, specified as alcoholic.

due to the genetic-racial differences in alcohol sensitivity and aversion and Asian-American attitudes and values toward the use of alcohol. Within Asian-American groups, only Native Hawaiians drink alcohol at levels similar to those of white Americans (Murakami, 1989). Outside of Hawaii, there is considerable variation in drinking patterns among different Asian groups, although it is generally believed that Japanese-Americans drink the most, followed by Korean-Americans, and Chinese-Americans (Chi, Lubben, & Kitano, 1989). When comparisons are made within various Asian and Pacific American cultures a relatively high proportion of heavy drinkers exists among Japanese-American and Filipino-American males. Foreign-born Korean-Americans and Japanese-Americans drink quite heavily in business entertainment and after work hours in drinking establishments such as bars and nightclubs. By contrast, Chinese-American men and women tend to have significantly lower prevalence of alcohol use and abuse.

Native-Americans and Alcohol Alcoholism and alcohol abuse remains the number one health problem facing Native-Americans, although patterns vary from tribe to tribe and region to region. The Report of the Secretary's Task Force on Minority Health (U.S. Department of Health and Human Services, 1985) found that five of the top ten leading killers of Native-American people were directly related to alcoholism and alcohol abuse. Table C.5 presents the alcoholism deaths and mortality rates for Native-Americans and Alaskan Natives from 1986 to 1988.

The rate of Native-American deaths due to alcohol is extremely high in comparison to all other races in the United States. The ratio of deaths between Native-Americans and all other U.S. races is 5.4, an increase over the two previous years. Table C.6 reports the alcoholism mortality rates for Native-Americans by age and sex.

Table C.6 Alcoholism Mortality Rates for Native-Americans and Alaskan Natives, by Age and Sex

Rate per 100,000 population for Native-Americans, Alaskan Natives, all races, 1955–1988.

Age Group	Native-Americans and Alaska Natives			U.S. All Races			U.S. Other Than White		
	Both Sexes	Male	Female	Both Sexes	M	F	Both Sexes	M	F
15–24 years	1.0	0.8	1.2	0.1	0.1	0.1	0.3	0.2	0.4
25–34 years	19.3	21.8	16.8	2.3	1.4	1.4	5.7	7.9	3.7
35–44 years	50.1	65.5	35.1	8.5	12.9	4.2	22.1	34.2	11.9
45–54 years	76.5	96.8	57.3	15.8	24.4	7.6	32.6	53.1	15.4
55–64 years	72.0	95.4	50.2	20.5	33.1	9.4	33.0	55.4	14.7
65–74 years	47.3	79.5	20.1	16.0	27.0	7.3	19.8	34.8	8.4
75–84 years	36.0	58.1	18.7	8.9	17.5	3.8	12.1	24.8	4.08
85 years +	10.6	13.3	8.9	3.2	7.3	1.6	5.1	10.8	2.3

SOURCE: *Trends in Indian Health*, 1991, U.S. Department of Health and Human Services, Public Health Service, Indian Health Service, p. 50.

The National Technical Information Service (1986) reported a high rate of deaths among Native-American youths due to causes related to substance abuse, particularly alcohol. Weibel (1984) reported that Native-American youth also have been found to begin abusing various substances at a younger age compared to white Americans.

Native-American deaths from alcohol occur at younger ages, usually violently, and related to risk-taking behaviors. In fact, of all Native-American deaths annually, over 35 percent are to persons under the age of 44, compared with 11 percent for all U.S. races. The two leading causes of death for Native-Americans between the ages of 15 and 44 are accidents and cirrhosis of the liver (U.S. Indian Health Services, 1993). Among Native-American people, alcohol has also been found to be a contributor to 90 percent of all homicides and 80 percent of suicides (Gunther, Jolly, & Wedel, 1985).

ETHNIC AND GENDER DIFFERENCES IN ALCOHOL CONSUMPTION

A few random facts about alcohol consumption by different minority groups follows:

- Hispanic-American males generally tend to drink heavily and to have a disproportionate number of alcohol-related problems, including alcohol dependence, compared to African-American and white American males.

- African-American women have higher rates of medical and other alcohol-related problems than white American women.

- Hispanic-American females are at considerably lower risk for developing alcohol-related problems than are white American females.

- Native-American women drink much less than Native-American men do.

- Three times as many African-American males as females use alcohol once a week or more.

- The death rate for African-American men is more than one and a half times that of white American men and almost two and a half times that of African-American women.

- The U.S. Department of Health and Human Services (1985) reported that Hispanic-American adolescents have a higher percentage of abstainers than the general student population.

- Menon, Burrett, and Simpson (1990) showed that problems in school performance, school conduct, peer associations, and attitudes of the school-based peer group were significantly related to adolescent Mexican-American inhalant use. Students with better grades were also less likely to use inhalants regularly.

- McRoy, Shorkey, and Garcia (1985) reported that higher alcohol and other drug use by Mexican-American youth is associated with lower grades, increased school dropout rates, and high unemployment in adulthood.

- Latina females drink much less than Anglo and black women. Indeed, Latinas are the group most likely to be abstainers. (Gilbert, 1987)

- Latinas are much less likely than blacks or Anglos to smoke (Marin, Perez-Stable, and Martin, 1989) and much less likely to use drugs (Smith-Peterson, 1983).

- Earlier theories of Native-American alcoholism that suggested a genetic predisposition and the inability to metabolize alcohol at a normal rate are no longer accepted. Alcohol genetic traits and alcohol metabolism are traits of individuals and not race or ethnic background.

- Five times more males than females are heavy drinkers.

- Nearly one-third of the estimated 15 million alcohol-dependent Americans are women.

- Alcohol is involved in nearly one-half of all male accidents, homicides, and suicides.

- Only 1 in every 10 drivers arrested for drunk driving is female.

- Three and one-half times more males than females die from "alcohol-induced causes," which does not include accidents and homicides.

- The time period between onset of drinking-related problems and entry into treatment appears to be shorter for women than for men.

- Adult females' role deprivation—loss of one's role as wife, mother, or worker—seems to increase a woman's risk for abusing alcohol.

- When compared to males, females have less body fluid and lower water content in which to dilute any alcohol consumed. Women, therefore, become more intoxicated than men do after drinking the same amount of alcohol.

- Women are more susceptible to alcohol's effect because, when compared to men, they have less of the enzyme alcohol dehydrogenase in their stomachs. This enzyme helps break down a portion of the alcohol before it enters the bloodstream.

DRUGS AND WOMEN OF
CHILDBEARING AGE

Joseph Gfroerer of the Substance Abuse and Mental Health Services Administration, Office of Applied Studies (SAMHS/OAS) prepared the National Household Survey summary. The National Household Survey on Drug Abuse (1995) reported the following facts about women of childbearing age:

- Overall, 7.3 (4.3 million) of women aged 15 to 44 in 1995 had used an illicit drug in the past month. The corresponding rate for men aged 15 to 44 was 11.6 percent.

- Of the 4.3 million women aged 15 to 44 who were current illicit drug users, more than 1.6 million had children living with them. About 400,000 had at least one child under 2 years of age.

- Among women aged 15 to 44 with no children who were not pregnant, 9.3 percent were illicit drug users. Only 2.3 percent of pregnant women were current drug users, which suggests that most women may reduce their drug use when they become pregnant. However, women who recently gave birth (have a child under 2-years-old, and not pregnant) have a rate use of 5.5 percent, suggesting that many women resume their drug use after giving birth. Similar patterns are seen for alcohol and cigarette use.

- Among pregnant women, rates of illicit drug use and cigarette use were highest among women in the first trimester and lowest among women in the third trimester.

- Among pregnant women, rates of substance use generally varied as they do among non-pregnant women. Rates were higher among women 15 to 25 than among those 26 to 44, and they were higher among unmarried women than among married women. One exception to this pattern was evident in smoking rates by age. Non-pregnant women aged 15 to 25 and aged 26 to 44 had about the same rates of smoking. However, among pregnant women, those aged 26 to 44 had a significantly lower past month smoking rate than those aged 15 to 25, suggesting that older women smokers are more likely to reduce their smoking during pregnancy than are younger women smokers.

Appendix D

■

Barriers to Health Care
for Minority Populations

FACTORS THAT INFLUENCE ACCESS
TO HEALTH CARE

Equal access to health care in the United States is a noble aspiration; however, implementation of such goals is not void of complications. It is not surprising that, because of the diversity and political issues within the United States, those particular problems have arisen in implementing this goal. Barriers to achieving this goal were identified some time ago, yet many still continue to exist today. Although teachers may not have a direct connection to these barriers, it is important that teachers be aware of them and be a resource for students and parents when these barriers are encountered.

Access to health care can be examined in a variety of ways. For the purpose of this chapter, the aspects of access to health care will be discussed by identifying those factors that influence access to health care. Because of the diversity of the various minority populations within the United States, it is very difficult to examine the complexity of the health access issues that each minority population faces. Because of the vast differences in such factors as language and culture, the limited data available, and immigration status, only a superficial view of the health access issues is possible.

Lack of access to medical care is frequently cited as the single greatest problem that ethnic/racial minority populations face in the health care system. This lack of access results from (1) socioeconomic factors, and (2) cultural and institutional barriers. Each of these factors is discussed in the following paragraphs.

Table D.1 Persons and Families Below Poverty Level

Selected Characteristics by Race, Age, and Family	1994	1995*
All persons	%	%
All Races	14.5	13.8
White American	11.7	11.2
African-American	30.6	29.3
Hispanic-American	30.7	30.3
Asian/Pacific Islander	14.6	14.6
Families		
All Races	11.6	10.8
White American	9.1	8.5
African-American	27.3	26.4
Hispanic-American	27.8	27.0
Asian/Pacific Islander	13.1	12.4
Families with female householder, no husband present		
All Races	34.6	32.4
White American	29.0	26.6
African-American	46.1	45.1
Hispanic-American	52.0	49.4

SOURCE: Adapted from U.S. Bureau of the Census: Poverty in the United States 1996
www.census.gov/main/www/subjects.html

Socioeconomic Factors

Poverty It is almost impossible to talk about health and wellness of minority groups without talking about their economic circumstances. Many poor minorities are undereducated, unemployed or have minimum wage jobs, and geographically concentrated in central cities and ghetto areas. Substantial evidence suggests that poverty, unemployment, and living in a single-parent home poses significant risks for the development of health problems, particularly in behavioral health areas (Reed et al., 1993). Therefore, poverty significantly affects health and wellness. Poverty, in particular, affects the ability to afford preventive and routine health care. Women and children represent 80 percent of the poor people in the United States. The majority of these poor are people of color. Table D.1 provides a picture of poverty for the years 1994 and 1995. The United States 1994 federal poverty level for one person was $7,500, $9,000 for a couple, and $14,500 for a family of four. The 1995 poverty threshold for a family of four was $15,569.

The 1994 U.S. Bureau of the Census: Poverty in the United States, did not include a separate category for Native-Americans; however, according to the 1990 census data, 35 percent of Native-Americans live below the federal poverty level, 14 percent live in deep poverty, compared with 9.8 percent of white persons, and 21 percent of Native-American and Alaska Native households are headed by women.

Minorities with the worst health status and poorest access to health care live in communities that have inadequate housing, poor nutrition, poor sanitation, and high rates of physical, emotional, and sexual abuse. People living in poverty experience poorer health that is reflected in a higher incidence of chronic diseases, a higher mortality rate, and poorer survival rates (National Center for Health Statistics, 1991).

Lack of Health Insurance "Health insurance is an indispensable key to health care in this country—it opens doors to access, quality, and at least some choice of care. Many Americans, especially members of minority groups, are still locked out of the care they need to live full, healthy lives," said Thomas Chapman, CEO, George Washington University Hospital (Commonwealth Fund Survey, 1994). This lack of insurance is also a primary reason for the failure of many ethnic minorities to seek preventive health care services.

Twenty-nine percent of ethnic/racial minority adults do not have insurance, compared to 12 percent of white American adults (Commonwealth Fund Survey, 1994). Acosta-Belen and Sjostrom (1988) reported that 39 percent of Hispanics, 7.2 million Hispanics under the age of 65 years, have no health insurance. Brown and colleagues (1991) reported that 20 percent of non-elderly Asian Pacifics and "others" in California were uninsured, and 21 percent nationally were uninsured. Although health insurance statistics on African-Americans is limited, the Children's Defense Fund (1989) stated that 10 to 12 million African-American children are without health coverage and even more are underinsured. They further stated that African-American children are 63 percent more likely than white children to be uninsured.

Minority adults are nearly twice as likely to have "very little" or "no choice" in where they obtain their health care according to the Commonwealth Fund Survey. Many minority groups lack access to a broad array of health services, especially primary care. Many studies have documented that minorities are less likely than any other group to be linked to a regular source of care. The Commonwealth Survey reported minority adults (66 percent) are less likely than white adults (80 percent) to have a regular doctor or other health professional, particularly Asian-American (60 percent) and Hispanic adults (59 percent). A regular source of care refers to an established and identifiable or medical source that an individual or a family uses on a routine basis. Having a regular source of care not only improves continuity and quality of care, but also helps facilitate entry into the health care system. Poor and uninsured minorities who turn to public medical facilities for routine care often confront a lack of bilingual and bicultural services, long waiting lines, and distant appointments. These barriers contribute to the advancement of their illnesses and their disproportionate use of costly emergency room services.

Finally, the Commonwealth Survey reported 46 percent of minority adults are very satisfied with the quality of their health care services, compared with 60 percent of white adults. Fifteen percent of adults in all minority groups—five times the number of whites (3 percent) believe their medical care would have been better if they were of a different race.

Education and Literacy Limited reading skills (in English or native languages) has a negative impact on access. The ability to read and comprehend health-related information and application or registration forms in medical facilities is crucial in aiding the patient through the health access process. Even the simple process of reading and comprehending the signs in health facilities can become complicated. Limited education and literacy serve to obstruct the path to health care access.

National standardized tests illustrate continuing gaps in educational attainment measurements between Native-Americans, Hispanic-Americans, and African-Americans, despite improvements by ethnic minorities over the last decade. Disparities occur largely in national achievement test scores in critical areas such as reading, mathematics, and science (U.S. Department of Education, 1992). For many ethnic minorities, schools have become alienating places for them and the absenteeism, truancy, and dropout rates for these groups is higher compared to white students (Roberts, 1992; Schorr & Schorr, 1988). Roberts (1992) also reported that there is consensus among scholars that, given the proper health care and educational conditions, school performance among black children is comparable with that of their white counterparts, particularly at the elementary level. High school graduation rates are a significant indicator of actual as well as potential socioeconomic status. In 1986, the non-high school graduation rate for certain groups of ethnic minorities was still significantly higher than that for whites (U.S. Department of Health and Human Services, 1990).

A truncated educational experience diminishes prospects for student's success in employment and leads, ultimately, to an increased risk of continued poverty. Deficits in critical cognitive skills restrict opportunities for competitive jobs, improved salary, and, ultimately, social and economic mobility (Turner et al., 1990).

CULTURAL AND INSTITUTIONAL BARRIERS

Lack of Cultural Understanding For many minority groups, Western health care practices conflict sharply with their own cultural health and healing practices. Cultural barriers are built into the very structure of the Western health care model, which emphasizes isolating and treating different ailments through specialized practitioners, rather than a holistic approach. This fragmented health care system is even more formidable for those who possess different conceptions of health care and healing and use different health care-seeking practices. In addition, there is usually a lack of bicultural and culturally competent staff to provide appropriate care. Most health care professionals are not educated and trained to be culturally sensitive.

Language Gap In conjunction with cultural awareness, practitioners face a language gap with some minority groups. The inability of the patient to speak English and the inability of the practitioner to speak the patient's language is one of the most formidable obstacles that immigrants and medical practitioners face. The U.S. Department of Health, Education, and Welfare (1980) stated, "The inability to speak English is a major obstacle for immigrants as most practitioners are not bilingual. As a result, even the simple exchange of information is very difficult without an interpreter. Often, interpreters are not available at crucial times in the delivery of health care. These events further isolate the immigrant, and lead to fragmentation of care."

The Commonwealth Fund Survey (1994) reported that language differences are a problem for 24 percent of minority Americans who do not speak English as their primary language. Twenty-six percent of Hispanic adults and 22 percent of Asian-American adults need an interpreter when seeking health care services. The survey quoted Grace Wang, the medical director of Chinatown Health Council, as saying, "Talking with your doctor and being understood is basic to getting good care. Many minority Americans do not speak English as a primary language. They are often frightened and confused about their health and problems, and cultural traditions and differences can add to their difficulties in communicating. Patience, empathy, as well as interpreters, can make a real difference in the effectiveness of the treatment that they receive."

CONCLUSION

The increasing racial and ethnic diversity within our nation has become one of the most significant challenges our teachers, medical practitioners, politicians, and employers of today and tomorrow face. It is also a challenge that many are ill-prepared to meet.

Every individual should have equal access to quality health care and services, but good personal health is not an entitlement. No individual, regardless of race or gender, can attain good health without a certain amount of personal responsibility and involvement regardless of the environment and society in which he or she lives. This is not to say that the "victim of poor health is totally responsible" because he or she is the one who chooses to smoke, drink, and eat too much; engage in unprotected sex, and violence; and not exercise. This view, of course, is too narrow. Taking control of one's own fate and assuming personal responsibility is one aspect of this effort (Braithwaite & Taylor, 1992). Very few people would argue that economic stratification, politics, and access to health care facilities does not play a major role in one's health. If every citizen is to enjoy an equal opportunity for health, both individual and collective action will be needed to overcome the many obstacles to good health care.

Even though acculturation does take place, structural assimilation or gaining access to U.S. institutions, including medical care systems for prevention, screening, and treatment, continues to be difficult. Sociometric factors, such as lacking health insurance, very low income, and lack of a regular health care provider, appear to be the strongest determinants of gaining entry into the health care system. In addition, the policies and practices in the medical care system have limited flexibility to meet the needs of populations who are poor or may have different illnesses, cultural practices, or language. Obviously, the needs of all Americans cannot be addressed through a generic approach. The unique characteristics and needs of special populations must be taken into account.

It also appears, that for many minority populations, there are more dimensions to "health" and "wellness" than what traditional Western society considers. Many minority groups practice culturally conditioned health-related behaviors that are different from those of the Western mainstream culture. Therefore, good health must be viewed as a product of cultural considerations such as behavior and customs, human ecological systems, education, exercise, proper diet, healthy self-esteem, social supports, healthy lifestyles, and acceptable health care services. Policies must support strategies that will increase cultural, linguistic, and geographic access to care while attempts are being made to remove financial obstacles that deprive tens of millions of people of excellent health care.

Finally, quality health care should be accessible to everyone and should not vary depending on the language, culture, race, and financial status of the patient. Providing equal access to ethnic/racial minority populations must be seen in the context of improving health care access for all Americans.

Appendix E

■

A Facilitator's Guide to Healthy Classroom Management:

Motivation, Communication, and Discipline

PURPOSE OF THIS GUIDE

This guide can be used in University teacher training programs where the professor encourages student participation or teachers can use these activities in elementary, middle school, or high school teacher workshops to explore the principles discussed in this book.

This guide provides a variety of "learn by doing" exercises to help pre- and in-service teachers to understand the principles discussed in each of the chapters. The activities are designed with a consistent format or structure to help participants know what to expect, how to "behave," and what is expected of them. Each activity follows the same format. Most importantly, most can be done with little or no advance preparation.

THE LEADER'S GUIDE

The purpose of the guide is to provide activities that will encourage the learning process. The activities, of course, do not replace the teacher. The activities set the environment that enables the teacher to set the foundation for the learning process. The activities are structured and organized. The teacher does not have to be an expert in the content area or a beginner—the essential qualification is only that he or she be an effective facilitator.

Activity Format

Title: Each activity has a title that is intended to capture the basic principle involved.
Time: The time statement provides an "estimate" of the minimum time needed to conduct the activity. It does not account for any spontaneous extension of the activity or the discussion period that follows.
Objective: The objective defines the intended teaching point, purpose, or principle.

Materials: The preparation statement provides the necessary pre-class preparations and the list of materials that are needed before the class begins.
Procedures: The procedure subheading gives step-by-step instructions for actually conducting the activity with the participants.
Suggested Discussion Questions: A list of discussion questions is given at the end of each activity.

The Facilitator's Guide contains the activities and the discussion questions related to the activities. The design of each activity is simple and sufficiently detailed that a beginning teacher can follow the step-by-step directions and lead a successful class.

THE FACILITATOR'S/TEACHER'S ROLE

The teacher for *Healthy Classroom Management* is really a facilitator. He or she provides a structure for the "learn by doing" or experiential activities by supplying materials, organizing time, giving directions and facilitating interactions.

The activities in this guide are designed to help students to understand their own values and ideas through their participation in the activities. In order for this to occur, the facilitator must:

1. Establish the appropriate classroom atmosphere. It should be one built on trust and a feeling of warmth and acceptance in the classroom. It is a place where differences of opinion are accepted, in fact, desired. Students and facilitator must be supportive of each other and sensitive to each other's needs. It must be an atmosphere where students feel comfortable with their privacy and their voluntary self-disclosure. It is a place where participants are not forced or pressured to explain their positions nor to defend their choice to "pass" on a discussion.

2. Not force or teach his or her values, ideas, or perceptions to the group. He or she can only provide possible alternatives, but be accepting of the participant's values, ideas, or perceptions.

3. Provide an emotionally safe environment where there are no put-downs, criticisms, or insults. No person's growth can be gained at the expense of someone else's. It is an atmosphere where all students and facilitators are treated with mutual dignity and respect.

GROUP LEADERSHIP SKILLS

The role of the teacher is not to present the information. The activities and discussions that follow each activity will accomplish that. The teacher's role is to facilitate the learning process so students learn to apply that information in their own lives and future teaching behaviors and philosophy. Following are some helpful hints:

1. *Become acquainted with the activity.* Although the activities are reasonably simple, the facilitator should allow a short time to acquaint himself or herself with the activity. This should be done at least one day before the activity is presented.

2. *Be prepared.* Prepare all materials a day before you plan on doing the activity. Be aware of the importance of thinking out beforehand how to divide participants into groups.

3. *Explain the activities.* Although each activity has detailed directions on how it should be run, the leader should read them over carefully, have a full understanding of the activity, and be prepared to answer any questions that might arise.

4. *Facilitate discussion.* The discussion phase of the activity is critical. In fact, discussion is so important that ideally it should far outweigh the time spent in the activities. It is here where the real meaning of the activity or experience becomes part of the participant's life and actions. In discussing what has just happened, the participant is forced to relive it, explain its impact, and in other ways digest and integrate the experience.

The discussion can take place between pairs or groups of more than two people. Following discussion between partners or small groups, the entire group can share their reactions to the activity so that the variety of feelings evoked can be better understood by all.

Several types of questions have been found useful in helping participants process learning. Although each activity has a list of discussion questions, facilitators are encouraged to ask their own based on the make up of the group. Some of the most effective discussion questions that can be used in the discussion phase follow:

What did I learn?

What did I learn about myself?

What did I learn about others?

How did I feel during this experience?

How do I feel when others treat me this way?

What physical reactions did my body show?

What did I think my partner was thinking or feeling?

In what ways does this experience apply to my experiences as a teacher or student?

How am I going to be different after this experience?

What will I start or stop doing after this experience?

Helpful Hints for Facilitating

1. When someone asks a question, open it up to the group. For example, "How do the rest of you feel about that?"

2. Facilitators must listen to all—even to those you do not agree with.

3. When students are working in small groups, the facilitator should not sit in the groups.

4. To remember what a participant has said, you can either repeat what the person said, or take notes to refer to it later.

5. Be sure to use open-ended questions rather than yes/no questions.

6. Nonverbal messages are very important.

7. Give the participants time to think and answer—be comfortable with silence.

8. Participate in sharing your feelings and concerns as an equal member of the class.

9. Hold back your own response to better understand the speaker's feelings. Question and/or restate the speaker's message, then check for accuracy.

10. When asking participants to share a situation, problem, or feeling, be ready to share an example from your own life to clarify what you are asking of them.

11. Invite participants to let themselves be learners instead of experts.

12. Let participants decide what fits for them. There is no absolute right or wrong way to teach.

13. Be aware of cultural differences.

Appendix F

■

The Student with a Disability*

INTRODUCTION

The Americans with Disabilities Act (ADA), signed into law by President Bush in 1990, has been characterized as an "emancipation proclamation" for people with disabilities. This law opened the door to employment for millions of Americans with disabilities. However, even though ADA and earlier legislative acts guarantee equal access to employment, people with disabilities must be qualified for jobs that are now available. Thus, schools play a vital role by providing educational opportunities for both able and disabled students to adequately compete in a chosen career.

One of the many important goals of the school is to assist students with disabilities by providing them physical access, appropriate support services, adaptive equipment, and reasonable adaptations, alterations, and accommodations in order to benefit from instruction. The role of the teacher in making educational programs accessible to students with disabilities is critical in helping schools reach this goal. This appendix has been designed to serve as a guide to help teachers understand how disabilities affect learning in an academic setting and suggests adjustments that can be made in the environment or teaching style.

---

* This appendix is a modification of *The College Student with a Disability: A Faculty Handbook,* a publication by Disabled Student Services (DDS), Cal Poly University, San Luis Obispo, CA 93407. This appendix is based on a similar publication by the President's Committee on Employment of the Handicapped of the same title, now out of print.

STUDENTS WHO ARE BLIND

The major challenge facing students who are blind in school centers around the overwhelming mass of printed material with which they are confronted—textbooks, class outlines, bibliographies, posters, tests, and so forth. The increasing use of films, videotapes, overhead projectors, CD-ROMs, computers, and closed-circuit television adds to the volume of visual material to which they must have access in some other way.

By the time students who are blind are mainstreamed into the classroom, they have probably developed various methods for dealing with the volume of visual materials. Most students who are blind use a combination of methods including Reader's Brailled books, audiotape recorded books, and lectures. If the student uses a reader, the teacher is responsible for accommodating the blind student and the reader. If a teacher knows he or she will be receiving a blind student into his or her classroom, a helpful practice is have the textbooks audiorecorded or brailled.

Students may use the raised line drawings of diagrams, charts, and illustrations; relief maps; three-dimensional models of physical organs, shapes, microscopic organisms; and so forth. Modem technology has made available other aids for blind people including talking calculators and speech-time compressors, paperless Braille machines, Braille computer terminals, and reading machines. Many of these devices, unfortunately, are rarely accessible for convenient student use.

Most students who are blind who use Braille prefer to take their own notes in class using a slate and stylus, a Perkins Brailler, or a laptop computer. Some students have a classmate make a copy of his or her notes using a copy machine. The blind student's reader later reads the notes onto tape for future use. Some blind students audiorecord lectures and later transcribe notes for them into Braille.

When there is a student who is blind in the classroom, the teacher should remember that "this and that" phrases are basically meaningless to that student; for example, "the sum of this plus that equals this" or "the lungs are located here and the diaphragm here." In the first example, the teacher may be writing on the chalkboard and can just as easily say, "The sum of 4 plus 7 equals 11." The student who is blind in this case is getting the same information as a sighted student. In the second example, the instructor may be pointing to a model or to the body itself. In this instance, the professor can "personalize" the locations of the lungs and diaphragm by asking class members to locate them by touching their own bodies. Examples of this type will not always be possible; however, if the teacher is sensitized not to use strictly visual examples, the student who is blind and probably the rest of the class will benefit.

Another area in which the student who is blind will need an adaptation is in testing. Most students will prefer to take examinations with a familiar reader. This is often beneficial to the student because it does not add anxiety to what is already an anxiety-producing situation. However, some teachers prefer to administer the tests themselves. Although this approach is certainly within the prerogative of the teacher, it can be an uncomfortable situation for the student. If a teacher is concerned about "test security" or prefers not to rely on the "honor system," a take-home test can be given to the blind student. However, it is better to avoid giving the student "different" tests because it creates segregation, makes it difficult to compare test results, and may create negative attitudes in the other students. Another method that may be used is to administer the test orally or by audiotape to the blind student who, in turn, either records answers orally on another tape recorder or types the answers.

Some students who are blind use dog guides. There is no need to worry that the dog will disturb the class. The opposite is usually the case. The other students are more intrigued by the guide dog and usually have to be oriented toward what is appropriate behavior. Dog guides are highly trained and disciplined. Most of the time the dog will lie quietly under or beside the table or desk. The greatest disruption a teacher can expect may be an occasional yawn or stretch. (Sometimes a rescue siren can cause a low moan.) It is good to remember that, as tempting as it may be to pet a guide dog, the dog, while in harness, is responsible for guiding its owner who cannot see. It should not be distracted from that duty.

Classes that are extremely "visual" by their very nature may be waived for the student who is blind; however, it should not be assumed automatically that this will be necessary. Conversations between the student who is blind and teacher can lead to new and even exciting instructional techniques that may benefit the entire class. For example, it is often thought that a blind student cannot take a course in art appreciation. However, the student who is blind should have the opportunity to become familiar with the world's great art (just as any other "educated" person). A classmate or reader who is particularly talented at verbally describing visual images can assist the blind student as a visual "interpreter" or "translator." There is no reason for the student who is blind not to know what the Mona Lisa (or other great work of art) looks like. It can be described, and there are poems written about the Mona Lisa that may be used as teaching aids to give more insight and understanding to the work. Miniature models of great works of sculpture can be made available for display and touching in the classroom. Many modern museums have tactile galleries.

One student was able to learn roper technique in an archery class when a rope was stretched perpendicular to the target. A "beeper" added to the target assisted with positioning. The point being made here is that certain disabilities (in this case blindness) do not automatically preclude participation in certain activities of classes. Students, teachers, and counselors must be careful not to lower expectations solely on the basis of disability.

If there are classes that involve field trips to out of class locations, discuss traveling needs with the blind student. In most instances all that will be required is for a member of the class to act as a sighted guide. In those localities where public transportation is adequate, many blind persons travel quite independently.

STUDENTS WHO ARE PARTIALLY SIGHTED

Between 70 to 80 percent of all persons who are legally blind in the United States have measurable vision. The student who is partially sighted meets the challenge of disability in much the same way as the student who is blind. This includes the use of readers, audiotaped texts, raised line drawings, and so forth. In addition, the partially sighted student may be able to use large print books, a closed-circuit TV magnifier, or other magnifying device. The student may also use a large print typewriter, or computers for papers. Some partially sighted students will be able to take notes in class by printing very large with a felt tip pen or marker. Others will tape record lectures for later use.

The student who is partially sighted is confronted with two basic difficulties that the student who is fully blind does not. First, the student who is partially sighted is sometimes viewed by the teachers and classmates as "faking it." Because most students who are partially sighted do not use white canes for travel and because most are able to get around much like everyone else, people have difficulty believing that the student needs to use adaptive methods when utilizing printed materials.

One student who is partially sighted commented that, having been observed playing Frisbee by one of the instructors, she was sure the instructor would no longer believe that she was partially sighted. As she explained, she had more peripheral than central vision and was able to see a red Frisbee. If any other color Frisbee were used, she could not see it well enough to play. Playing Frisbee and reading a printed page present quite different visual requirements. These differences are often difficult for the person who is fully sighted to understand.

Another difficulty that the student who is partially sighted experiences has a more subtle effect and can be troublesome. This is the psychological response that large print evokes in the sighted reader. Such handwritten communications tend to give the reader the idea that "a small child has written this." Needless to say, this may lead to the conclusion that a student with this kind of handwriting is immature or childish and that the written communication is less than sophisticated. Even when the student uses a large-print typewriter, this can still be a problem.

In addition, the assumption is sometimes made that the student is merely trying to make an assignment appear longer, as in the case of a term paper of a required length. When the number of words instead of pages required is stated, this is not a problem.

These potential difficulties can be alleviated if the student and the teacher discuss the student's needs early in the school year. Sitting in the front of the room, having large print on the chalkboard, or the use of enlarged print on an overhead projector *may* assist a partially sighted student; however, the capacity to read printed materials depends so greatly on conditions, such as the degree of contrast, brightness, and color, that it is preferable that the student and instructor discuss what methods, techniques, or devices may be used to maximum advantage. If the teacher discovers that a partially sighted student has not had an evaluation at a low vision clinic, it may be appropriate to refer the student for this service.

STUDENTS WHO ARE DEAF
OR HEARING IMPAIRED

Obviously, the major challenge facing the deaf student is communication. Speech reading (lip reading) is a partial solution. At best, a person who is deaf can read only 30 to 40 percent of the sounds of spoken English by watching the speaker's lips.

Another form of communication used by many, but not all persons who are deaf or hearing impaired, is American Sign Language (ASL). Research has shown that ASL is a complex language, with its own grammatical structure and syntax, as different from English as any foreign language. The intensity of repetition of the hand movements, as well as facial expression and body language, are also important elements of ASL. Finger spelling, which consists of finger and hand positions for each letter of the alphabet, is frequently incorporated as part of the language. Students who are deaf will also communicate in writing when speech reading, sign language, or finger spelling cannot be used effectively. Teachers should not hesitate to write notes when necessary to communicate with a deaf student.

Many students who are deaf can, and do, speak. Most deaf people have normal organs of speech and many learn to use them in speech classes. Some people who are deaf cannot automatically control the tone and volume of their speech so the speech may be initially difficult to understand. Understanding improves as one becomes familiar with the person's speech.

At least one Telecommunication Device for the Deaf (TDD) should be made available in every school. This device allows the deaf person to use a telephone by providing a keyboard for typing a visual message back and forth. At least one amplifying telephone receiver should also be made available for the hard of hearing student.

Students who are deaf, just like hearing students, vary to some degree in their communication skills. Factors such as personality, intelligence, degree of deafness, residual hearing, age of onset, and family environment all affect the kind of communication the student uses. As a result of these and other variables, a student who is deaf may use a number of the communication modes discussed above.

The main form of communication within the deaf community is sign language. In view of this, many persons who are deaf have not mastered the grammatical subtleties of their "second language"—English. This does not mean that teachers should overlook errors in written (or spoken) work; however, they should know that this difficulty with English is not related to intelligence, but is similar to that experienced by students whose native language is not English.

In the classroom, many students who are deaf will use an interpreter. The presence of an interpreter in the classroom enables the student who is deaf to understand what is being said. There are two types of interpreters—oral and manual. The oral interpreter "mouths" what is being said, while the manual interpreter uses sign language. The two methods are often used in combination. There is a time lag, which will vary in length depending on the situation, between the spoken word and the interpretation or translation. Thus, the student's contributions to the lecture or discussion may be slightly delayed.

Interpretation will be easiest when the teacher uses the lecture method and more difficult in discussion classes. Because class formats are so varied, it is recommended that the teacher, interpreter, and student arrange a conference early in the class to discuss any special arrangements that may be needed.

Students who are deaf usually have someone take notes for them because it is difficult to follow an interpreter or to speech read the teacher and take notes at the same time. It is best if a classmate can be found who takes good notes. This student can make a copy of the notes and give them to the student who is deaf.

Assumptions should not automatically be made about the deaf student's ability to participate in certain types of classes. For example, students who are deaf may be able to learn a great deal about music styles, techniques, and rhythms by observing a visual display of the music on an oscilloscope or similar apparatus or by feeling the vibrations of music. Some students who are deaf will have enough residual hearing so that amplifications with hearing aids will allow participation. It is always best to discuss with the student the requirements of a class and to determine if there are ways that the materials can be modified so that the student can participate in what may become an exciting learning experience for all concerned. The student who is hearing impaired may require nothing more than some form of amplification to participate in a class—a hearing aid, public address system, or a teacher/student transmitter/receiver unit (also known as the phonic ear).

In conclusion, the following hints compiled from practical experience and from publications of the National Technical Institute for the Deaf, the Registry of Interpreters for the Deaf, and Gallaudet College, will facilitate the participation of students who are deaf or hard of hearing in (and out of) the classroom:

Look at the person when you speak.

Do not smoke, chew gum, or otherwise block the area around your mouth with your hands or other objects.

Speak naturally and clearly. Do not exaggerate lip movements or volume.

Try to avoid standing in front of windows or other sources of light. The glare from behind you makes it difficult to read lips and other facial expressions.

Using facial expressions, gestures, and other "body language" is helpful in conveying your message.

If you are talking with the assistance of an interpreter, direct your conversation to the deaf individual. This is more courteous and allows the deaf person the option of viewing both you and the interpreter to more fully follow the flow of conversation.

When other people speak who may be out of the deaf or hard of hearing person's range of vision, repeat the question or comment and indicate who is speaking (by motioning) so the individual can follow the discussion.

The use of visual media may be helpful to deaf students since slides and videotaped materials supplement and reinforce what is being said. Alteration in lighting may interfere with the deaf student's capacity to read manual or oral communication. These materials may be difficult to interpret because of sound quality and speed of delivery. Therefore, interpreter "lag" may be greater. If a written script is available, provide the interpreter and student with a copy in advance.

In addition, videotapes produced in recent years may be captioned for hearing impaired viewers. Use a telecaption decoder when you plan to show a captioned videotape during class.

When particularly important information is being covered, be sure to convey it very clearly. Notices of assignments and announcements can be put in writing or on a chalkboard to ensure understanding.

Establish a system for getting messages to the deaf student when necessary. Class cancellations can be particularly costly if an interpreter is not informed, in advance, of such things.

STUDENTS WHO USE WHEELCHAIRS

Access is one of the major concerns of the student who uses a wheelchair. The student must learn routes to and from classes and across campus that do not present barriers. A barrier may be a stair, curb, a narrow walkway, a heavy door, an elevator door that has no delay mechanism or one that is too fast, a vehicle blocking a curb cut or ramp, a sign in the middle of what would otherwise be a wide enough walkway, and so forth.

Theater-type classrooms may present difficulties unless there is a large enough flat floor space in the front or rear of the room for a wheelchair to park (there must also be an entrance to and from that level). Classrooms with tables (provided there is an under-table clearance of at least 27-1/2") are more accessible to students in wheelchairs than rooms with standard classroom desks. It is better if the tables and chairs are movable rather than stationary.

It is difficult to make generalizations about the classroom needs of students who use wheelchairs because some students may be able to stand up for short periods of time while others will not be able to stand up at all. Some will have full use of their hands and arms while others will have minimal or no use of them. There are, however, some general considerations that will apply to most, if not all, students who use wheelchairs:

1. If breaks between classes are short (10 minutes or less), the student who uses a wheelchair may frequently be a few minutes late. Often, the student must take a circuitous (but accessible) route, wait for assistance in opening doors, and maneuver along crowded paths and corridors. If a student who uses a wheelchair is frequently late, it is, of course, appropriate to discuss the situation with the student and seek solutions.

2. If a class involves a field trip or field work, the teacher or the student will need to assess the site for type of terrain (hard pack, gravel, sand) and slope, and availability of handicap restrooms. The school must also provide accessible transportation for students who use wheelchairs.

3. Classes in physical education can almost always be modified so that the student in a wheelchair can participate. Classmates are usually more than willing to assist, if necessary. Most students who use wheelchairs do not get enough physical exercise in daily activity, so it is particularly important that they be encouraged, as well as provided the opportunity, to participate. Information on adaptive physical education programming is available from the American Alliance for Health, Physical Education, and Recreation for the Handicapped, Information and Research Utilization Center.

4. Classes taught in laboratory settings (science, wood and metal workshops, home economics, language labs, art studios) will usually require some modification of the workstation. Considerations include undercounter knee clearance, working countertop height, horizontal working reach, and aisle widths. Working directly with the student may be the best way to provide modifications to the workstation; however, if a station is modified in accordance with established accessibility standards, the station will be usable for most students in wheelchairs.

5. For those students who may not be able to participate in a laboratory class without assistance of an aide, the student would be allowed to benefit from the actual lab work to the fullest extent. The student can give all instructions to an aide—from what chemical to add to what type of test tube to use to where to dispose of used chemicals. The student will learn everything except the physical manipulation of the chemicals.

6. Students are not "bound or confined" to wheelchairs. A "wheelchair user" is a more appropriate term for someone who uses a wheelchair. They often transfer to automobiles and to furniture. Some who use wheelchairs can walk with the aid of canes, braces, crutches, or walkers. Using a wheelchair some of the time does not mean an individual is "faking" a disability. It may be a means to conserve energy or move about more quickly.

7. Most students who use wheelchairs will ask for assistance when they need it. Do not assume automatically that assistance is required. Offer assistance if you wish, but do not insist, and accept a "no, thank you" graciously.

8. When talking to a student in a wheelchair, if the conversation continues for more than a few minutes, sit down, kneel, or squat if convenient.

9. A wheelchair is part of the person's personal body space. Do not automatically hang or lean on the chair—this would be similar to hanging or leaning on the person. It is fine if you are friends, but inappropriate otherwise.

Wheelchairs come in a variety of styles and sizes, with many types of optional attachments available. Some of the standard accessories that college students may add to their wheelchairs are special seat cushions (to prevent pressure sores which result from long periods of sitting), tote bags that attach to the chair back or arms, and trays that fit over the arms of the chair to serve as a desk. Some wheelchairs are designed with desk arms that are lower in front so that the chair will fit under a desk or table. Most students use this type of chair. There are also wheelchairs that are modified for athletic competition.

STUDENTS WITH LEARNING DISABILITIES

Learning disability has come to be the general term for a variety of specific disabilities that are neurologically based. These include dyslexia, developmental aphasia, dysgraphia, expressive dysphasia, aural receptive dysphasia, and sequential memory disorder. A common misconception among those not familiar with learning disabilities is that the student with a learning disability is retarded—this is not true.

The teacher should keep in mind that the needs of a student with learning disabilities center around information processing. Students with learning disabilities have trouble taking information in through the senses and bringing that information accurately to the brain. The information often gets "scrambled." These students may have difficulty with discrimination (perceiving differences in two like sounds, symbols, or objects). Because the information does not reach the brain accurately, the brain often does not do a good job of storing the information. Thus, it is important that students with learning disabilities receive and transmit information in a form or modality that works best for them. Some ways of assisting the learning disabled student are suggested here for the teacher.

The student who has difficulty with written symbols can use readers or texts that are recorded verbatim (as does the blind student). In this case, the student should be encouraged to listen and read along. The student can be shown how to obtain textbook information in "economical" ways by using chapter summaries, pictures and captions, graphs, tables, bold type, italics, tables of contents, paragraph and unit headings, indices, and glossaries.

Some students with learning disabilities are unable to communicate effectively through printing or cursive writing (dysgraphia). This condition may manifest itself in written work that appears careless. Some of these students may be able to use the computer for written communication; many cannot. Another solution is for a student aide to take dictation from the student.

Other students with learning disabilities, for all practical purposes, will be "lecture deaf" (aural receptive dysphasia). Many of the adapted techniques that assist the deaf student will also assist these students—TV, movies, role playing, and role taking. Still other students will have difficulty with sequential memory tasks involving letters (spelling), numbers (mathematics), and following step-by-step instructions. For these students it will help to break up tasks into smaller parts, or provide time and a half proctoring for exams. In general, the student with learning disabilities will learn more effectively by using multisensory approaches in the teaching/learning process—visual, auditory, tactile, and kinesthetic.

Because the *expectation* is that a student will absorb information, communicate it, and be evaluated through the printed page, the student with learning disabilities will need assistance and support from teachers in finding innovative ways of receiving and transmitting information and in being evaluated. Because a learning disability is "hidden," the instructor may have understandable doubts about the validity of these alternative approaches; however, the fact remains that the student's capacity for learning is intact—it is only the means by which information is processed that is different.

STUDENTS WITH SPEECH IMPAIRMENTS

Speech impairments may be congenital or the result of illness or injury. They may be found alone or in combination with other disabilities. In any case, the student with a speech impairment (unless it has been recently acquired) will probably have received some speech therapy.

Impairments range from problems with articulation or voice strength to being totally non-vocal. They include stuttering (repetition, blocks, and/or prolongation occasionally accompanied by distorted movements and facial expressions), chronic hoarseness (dysphonia), difficulty in invoking an appropriate word or term (normal aphasia) and esophageal speech (resulting from a laryngectomy).

Many students with a speech impairment will be hesitant about participating in activities that require speaking. Even if the student has adjusted well to speech impairment, new situations may aggravate old anxieties. It is important that self-expression be encouraged, but pressure to speak is not apt to be helpful. It is important to allow time for the speech-impaired student to express himself or herself so that confidence can be gained. Speaking in front of a group can be an agonizing experience for anyone—the speech-impaired student is no exception. It is also important for the instructor to accept and respond to all appropriate attempts at communication. When speaking to a speech-impaired person, continue to talk naturally. Resist the temptation to complete words or phrases for a speech-impaired person.

For persons who cannot speak and who are otherwise physically disabled so that they cannot sign, write, or type, various communication aids are available. These aids may range from sophisticated electronic "speaking" machines activated by punching a keyboard with a head pointer or mouth wand to a spelling board that consists of a layout of the alphabet, a few common words or phrases, yes and no, to which the speech-impaired person points and an assistant may speak out loud. Some devices provide a "ticker tape" print-out or display the message on a calculator-like screen across which the characters move. With some less portable devices, the message is displayed on a TV screen.

Depending on the severity of impairment, various adapted methods may be required for the speech-impaired student. Many of the adapted methods for evaluation suggested for other disabilities will be appropriate for the speech-impaired student. Some speech-impaired students will require no adapted methods at all. Most will need patience, encouragement, and an opportunity to develop self-confidence in an unfamiliar group. The teacher can set the tone that encourages appropriate self-expression.

STUDENTS WITH OTHER DISABILITIES

There are other disabilities that largely affect student's behavior, mobility, or movement, such as cardiac conditions, arthritis, chronic back pain, active sickle cell anemia, diabetes, Tourette's syndrome, Attention Deficit Disorder, epilepsy, and others.

Students of short stature (little people) will have in-classroom access problems similar to those facing students in wheelchairs.

The student with epilepsy will have little problem in the classroom. In most cases a seizure will be controlled by medication. Students with epilepsy will have learned to manage seizure activity through adequate rest, proper diet, and regular medication. Most of them will be able to participate in sports and lead active, normal lives.

Students with diabetes may need to schedule classes and other activities in order to accommodate eating and taking medication. Heat and stress also may affect these students' physical well-being.

As a final note, some of the conditions described may require medication for control of symptoms. If a teacher has valid educational questions about the potential effect of various medications on a student's performance, the student or parent, if willing, can probably provide some information. The teacher should not hesitate to discuss such issues tactfully with the student.

In closing, the following guideline may be helpful: Many disabilities are obvious, and the question then is one of the degree of accommodation and assistance required. However, there are cases in which a teacher may have no way of knowing that a student has a disability. For example, an epileptic student on medication may not expect to need any adaptation and may not mention his or her condition to the teacher.

One good policy is for the teacher to send a note home to parents requesting any recommendations for accommodating any sort of disability for their children. Appointments can be arranged with the parent and child to discuss any necessary strategies. This approach preserves the student's privacy and also indicates the willingness of the teacher to provide assistance.

GLOSSARY

Amplifying Telephone Receivers. Telephone receivers with a volume control built into the hand grip allow the hearing impaired person to amplify the incoming conversation.

American Sign Language. Within the last three decades, American Sign Language (ASL) has been recognized as a natural and complex language with its own culture and literary tradition. It is visual/gestural in nature, having a complex grammar and syntax and is the language used by the majority of deaf adults in the United States. Sign language is not universal; deaf people from different countries use different sign languages. There are also various sign systems based on English which are used by some deaf students and interpreters; Pidgin Signed English (PSE) and Signing Exact English (SEE) are two of the most common of these systems.

Barriers. Some common standards that eliminate barriers are:

Walks: 4' minimum width

Doors: 32" minimum *clear* opening

Toilet Stall: minimum 3' wide, 5' deep, 2'8" outswing door

Telephone: dial, handset, and coin slot not over 48" from floor

Elevator: controls no higher than 48" from the floor

Braille Computer Terminals. This terminal can interact with existing on-site or remote information processing systems. When connected to computers or data banks, they can deliver brailled pages of information at a rate of at least 100 words per minute. Students can request information on a standard keyboard and obtain a brailled response in a manner of seconds.

Brailled Books. Most of the legally blind population does not read Braille. About 7-1/2 percent of this population use Braille as their primary reading mode. Braille is extremely bulky and requires a great deal of storage space.

Brailler. The Perkins Brailler is an all-purpose Braille writer. It is operated by six keys, one for each dot in the Braille cell. There are spacing, line advancing, and backspacing keys.

Captioned Films. Public Law 85-905 established the Captioned Films Program to provide for distribution of captioned films through appropriate agencies to bring to deaf persons an understanding and appreciation of those films that play a part in the general and cultural advancement of hearing persons. Theatrical, short subject, documentary, training, and educational films are available. Certain copyright restrictions apply to certain showings.

Closed-Circuit TV Magnifier (CCTV). This consists of a television camera which views the printed page or other materials and a television monitor which displays the image in enlarged form. Light and dark contrast can be adjusted. Most models allow reversing the image from black on white to white on black depending on individual preference. The extent of enlargement is also usually adjustable for individual needs. Students commonly refer to these by brand name (Visualtek, Apollo, etc.).

Curb Cut. Also called a curb ramp, it is a depression built into the curb of a sidewalk to permit passage by a wheelchair. The incline should not exceed a gradient of 1:12 and the flat surface width should be no less than 3′ wide.

Dog Guide. The dog guide ("seeing eye" and "guide dog" are brand names) undergoes extensive specialized training to assist blind persons. It must learn basic obedience, to lead rather than "heel," to avoid obstacles (including overhead objects), cross streets, ride various forms of public transportation, etc. Dog guides are legally permitted to accompany their owners into all places of public accommodation, including all federal and state buildings, hotels, motels, restaurants, grocery stores, airplanes, trains, and buses. To refuse entry to any of these places is a violation of the law, punishable by a fine or imprisonment. There are also dog "guides" that assist the physically disabled person and alert deaf or hearing impaired persons.

Electric Powered Wheelchair. Such chairs provide maximum independence for people who must do a great amount of moving around or who cannot use their arms. They are powered by rechargeable batteries. Because a wheelchair does not maintain a constant full battery charge as does an automobile, short battery life is expected. Students must pay close attention to battery maintenance.

Finger spelling. Finger and hand positions for each letter of the alphabet. It is most often used for titles, proper names, and convenience.

Head Pointer. A stick or rod which is attached to a person's head with a head band so that by moving the head an individual can perform tasks that would ordinarily be performed by hand or finger movement.

Hearing Aid. Consists of a receiver and amplifier of sound. *All* sounds in the environment are amplified with the same intensity. A hearing aid does not sort, process, or discriminate among sounds. Because someone is wearing a hearing aid, it does not mean that the person can hear normally. Aids do not correct hearing, but they improve hearing in some people. They may enable someone to hear a voice even though he or she may not be able to understand words.

Interpreter/Transliterator. A professional person who assists the deaf person in communicating with hearing people who cannot sign. The following certifications are awarded by the Registry of Interpreters for the Deaf (RID) National Certification Board:

Certificate of Interpretation: Ability to interpret between American Sign Language (ASL) and spoken English. This includes skills in both sign-to-voice and voice-to-sign.

Certificate of Transliteration: Ability to transliterate between English-like signing and spoken English, including both sign-to-voice and voice-to-sign. A directory, which lists members by states, certified members, chapter officers, and suggested reimbursement for professional services, is available for a nominal fee.

Large Print Books. A number of sources produce large print books for the individual with low vision. The American Foundation for the Blind, Inc. can provide a list of publishers of large print books.

No Carbon Required (NCR) Paper. A special paper developed by the National Institute for the Deaf for taking notes facilitates making a duplicate copy of class notes for sharing with a deaf or learning disabled classmate.

Phonic Ear. A wireless electronic amplification system consisting of an instructor microphone/transmitter, binaural student FM receiver, and a recharging unit. The system allows the hard-of-hearing student to have personal amplification in the classroom setting. Newer models are available that are compact and inconspicuous.

Reader. A volunteer or employee of the blind, learning disabled, or partially sighted student who reads printed material in person or onto audiotape. The reader sometimes performs other tasks, such as mobility assistance for the blind student.

Recorder Books. Recordings for the Blind (RFB), a national, non-profit voluntary organization which is supported primarily by contributions from the public, provides taped educational books, free on loan, to print-handicapped elementary, high school, college, and graduate students. Service is somewhat slow during the beginning of the academic year. Students must place their orders early.

Residual Hearing. The amount of hearing remaining after hearing loss. Few deaf people hear no sound at all.

Registry of Interpreters for the Deaf (RID). The RID, Inc. a national organization with over 50 chapters and membership of over 1,800, was organized for the purpose of providing translating/interpreting services to deaf people of America and its trust territories.

Telecaption 300 Decoder. The fast pace of many in-class videotapes makes it difficult for the interpreter to keep up with the speaker, and some of the content can be lost. Many video programs are now closed captioned for hearing impaired viewers. The Telecaption 300 Decoder picks up an electronic signal which allows the information to be printed across the bottom of the screen.

Telecommunication Device for the Deaf (TDD). TDDs are instruments such as the teletypewriter (TTY) that allow deaf persons to communicate over the telephone. Such a device must be located at each end of the telephone conversation. Some devices type the message on a paper roll while others display the message on an electronic calculator-like display panel with the letters moving from right to left across a screen. Some TDDs display the message on a television-like screen.

Appendix G

■

Multicultural Magazines and Journals

Some of the magazines listed below are general publications and should be reviewed by teachers before displaying them in the classroom. All materials in the following magazines need to be reviewed for age appropriateness.

GENERAL MULTICULTURAL MAGAZINE

TEACHING TOLERANCE
400 Washington Ave.
Montgomery, AL 36104
Order Department Fax (334) 264-7310

Teaching Tolerance is mailed twice a year at no charge to educators.

The goal of the journal is to provide high-quality educational materials to help teachers promote interracial and intercultural harmony in the classroom.

HISPANIC AMERICAN
MAGAZINES/JOURNALS

AMERICA'S MAGAZINE
Organization of American States
19th & Constitution Ave. NW, Ste. 300
Washington, DC 20006
Ph: (202) 458-6218

Bimonthly magazine in Spanish and English.
Focuses on Latin American art, culture, history, literature, and current events.

HISPANIC
Hispanic Publishing Corp.
111 Massachusetts Ave. NW, Ste. 200
Washington, DC 20001
Ph: (202) 682-3000

Monthly magazine.
Focuses on Hispanics in various fields such as education, politics, business, the arts, etc.

LA OFERTA REVIEW
2103 Alum Rock Ave.
San Jose, CA 95116
Ph: (408) 729-6397

Bi-weekly bilingual newspaper.

LATINA
www.latina.com

A magazine devoted to the lifestyles of Latinas.

MIA
165 W. 29th St.
New York, NY 10001
Ph: (212) 643-3484

A magazine about life in the Latino community

URBAN LATINO
www.urbanlatino.com

Bi-monthly magazine devoted to the lifestyles of urban Latinos.

AFRICAN-AMERICAN
MAGAZINES/JOURNALS

AMERICAN LEGACY
Ph: 1-800-454-4997

Celebrates African-American history and culture.

THE BLACK COLLEGIAN
Black Collegiate Services
1240 S. Broad St.
New Orleans, LA 70125
Ph: (504) 821-5694

Quarterly publication that is the national magazine of black college students.

EBONY
U.S. Johnson Publishing Co.
820 S. Michigan Ave.
Chicago, IL 60605
Ph: 1-800-272-6602

Articles related to African-American history, politics, entertainment, sports, etc.

EMERGE
Emerge Communications, Inc.
One Bet Plaza
1900 W Place NE
Washington DC 20018-1211

Monthly magazine focusing on contemporary African-American life.

ESSENCE
1500 Broadway, 6th Floor
New York, NY 10036-4071
Ph: (212) 642-0600

Magazine oriented toward African-American women. Includes fashion, health, fiction, etc.

JET
Johnson Publishing Co.
820 S. Michigan Ave.
Chicago, IL 60605
Ph: (312) 322-9200

African-American news magazine focusing on current events and stories.

NATIVE AMERICAN
MAGAZINES/JOURNALS

AMERICAN INDIAN ART MAGAZINE
7314 E. Osborn Dr.
Scottsdale, AZ 85251
Ph: (602) 994-5506

Quarterly magazine devoted to American Indian Art.

COWBOYS AND INDIANS
e-mail: mail@cowboysindians.com

A magazine that partially focuses on modern lifeways of Native Peoples of the West.

NATIVE PEOPLES
Media Concepts Group, Inc.
5333 North Seventh St.
Suite C-244
Phoenix, AZ 85014
Ph: (602) 252-2236

Monthly magazine that portrays the arts and lifeways of Native Peoples of the Americas.

SOUTHWEST ART
Ph: (713) 296-7900

A portion of the magazine is devoted to contemporary Native-American Art.

ASIAN-AMERICAN
MAGAZINES/JOURNALS

A MAGAZINE: INSIDE ASIA AMERICA
677 Fifth Ave.
New York, NY 10022
Ph: (212) 593-8089

Provides an insight into the lives of Asian-Americans.

ASIAN ART NEWS
Ph: (760) 747-8327

Articles on contemporary Asian Art.

ASIAN WEEK
809 Sacramento St.
San Francisco, CA 94108
Ph: (415) 397-7258

Focuses on the Asian-American community.

KYOTO JOURNAL
31 Bond St.
New York, NY. 10012
(212) 674-6788
Provides perspectives of Asia.

KOREAN CULTURE MAGAZINE
Korean Culture Service
5505 Wilshire Blvd.
Los Angeles, CA 90036
Ph: (213) 936-5712

Focuses on art, culture, and contemporary life in Korea.

MINARET
434 South Vermont Ave
Los Angeles, CA 90020
Ph: (213) 381-5762

Bi-monthly magazine that provides a source of information on Islam.

SEOUL
HEK Communications
1-12 Hoehyon-dong 3-ga
Chung-ku, Seoul, Korea

Monthly magazine where the land, people, culture, customs, and events of Korea are illustrated.

YOLK
Inform Asian Media, Inc.
PO Box 861555
Los Angeles, CA 90086-1555
Ph: (310) 817-7252

Monthly magazine that focuses on contemporary Asian-American life.

References

Chapter 1

American Association of Colleges for Teacher Education (AACTE). (1989). RATE 111. *Teaching teachers: Facts and figures*. Washington, DC.

American Council on Education. (1988). *One-third of a nation*. Washington, DC.

Brylinsky, J., & Hoadley, M. (1991). A comparative analysis of wellness attitudes of "suicidal" and "at risk" college students. *Wellness Perspectives: Research, Theory and Practice, 8* (2), 59–72. In W. Payne & D. Hahn, *Understanding your health* (p. 4). St. Louis, MO: Mosby.

Chole, S. (no date). Minority teacher development program. http://MCA.NET/alliance/mca.mtdp.shtml

Donatelle, R., & Davis, L. (1997). *Health: The basics*. Boston: Allyn and Bacon.

Gollnick, D., & Chinn, P. (1998). *Multicultural education in a pluralistic society*. Upper Saddle River, NJ: Merrill.

Graham, H. (1985.) *The human face of psychology*. Philadelphia: Open University Press.

Guthrie, J. (1997, August 31). Race for minority teachers. *San Francisco Examiner*, p. 1.

Heward, W. (1996). *Exceptional children* (5th ed.). Upper Saddle River, NJ: Prentice-Hall.

Hope-Franklin, J. (no date). Introduction. In *Minority teacher development program*. http://MCA.NET/alliance/mca.mtdp.shtml

Maslow, A. (1987). *Motivation and personality* (3rd ed.). New York: Harper & Row.

National Multicultural Institute. (1997). *Facts about diversity*. Washington, DC. http://www.ncmi.org/nmci/statspag.html

Oakes, J. (1990). *Multiplying inequities: The effects of race, social class and tracking on opportunities to learn mathematics and science*. Santa Monica, CA: Rand Corporation.

Paplauskas-Ramunas, A. (1969). Development of the whole man through physical education. Ottawa, Canada: University of Ottawa Press.

Payne, W., & Hahn, D. (1995). *Understanding*

your health. St. Louis, MO: Times Mirror/Mosby College Publishing, 1995.

Peterson, P., Wilkinson, L., & Hallinan, M. (Eds.). (1984). *The social context of instruction: Group organization and group processes.* San Diego: Academic Press.

Pierson, F. (1999). *Principles and techniques of patient care* (2nd ed.). Philadelphia: W.B. Saunders Company.

Reed, W., Darity, W., Sr., & Robertson, N. (1993). *Health and medical care of African Americans.* Westport, CT: Auburn House.

Shapiro, J., Sewell, T., & DuCette, J. (1995). *Reframing diversity in education.* Lancaster, PA: Technomic Publications.

Trimble, J. (1995). Ethnic minorities. In R. Coombs & D. Ziedonis (Eds.), *Handbook on drug abuse prevention.* Boston: Allyn and Bacon.

U.S. Bureau of Census. (1990). *October current population survey.* Washington, DC: U.S. Department of Education.

Wellness Project Committee. (no date). *Wellness project.* San Luis Obispo, CA: Cal Poly University.

Wolfensberger, W. (1983). Social role valorization: Proposed new form for the principle of normalization. Mental retardation. In D. Gollnick & P. Chinn, *Multicultural education in a pluralistic society.* Upper Saddle River, NJ: Merrill.

World Health Organization. (1947). Constitution of the world health organization. *Chronicle of the World Health Organization, 1,* 29–43.

Chapter 2

Bey, T., & Turner, G. (1996). *Making school a place of peace.* Thousand Oaks, CA: Sage.

Boyd-Franklin, N. (1989). *Black families in therapy.* New York: Guilford.

Epstein, J. (1995, May). School/family/community partnerships: Caring for the children we share. *Phi Delta Kappan,* 701–772.

Goode-Vick, C. (1985). *You can be a leader: A guide for developing leadership skills.* Champaign, IL: Sagamore Publishers.

Greene, A. (1992, April). Social context

differences in the relationship between self-esteem and self-concept during late adolescence. *Journal of Adolescent Research, 7*(2), 266–280.

Henderson, A. (1997). *A new generation of evidence: The family is critical to student achievement.* Comprehensive Assistance Center, Region XI, West Ed, San Francisco.

Hidalago, N., Siu, S., Bright, J., Swap, S., & Epstein, J. (1995). Research on families, schools, and communities: A multicultural perspective. In J. Banks & C. Banks (Eds.), *Handbook of research on multicultural education.* New York: Macmillan.

McLaughlin, C. K. (1993). *The do's and don'ts of parent involvement.* Spring Valley, CA: Innerchoice Publishing.

Steinberg, L. (1996). *Beyond the classroom: Why school reform has failed and what parents need to do.* New York: Simon and Schuster.

Stevenson, D., & Baker, D. (1987, October). The family-school relation and the child's school performance. *Child Development, 58*(5), 1348–1357.

Sweet, J., & Bumpass, L. (1987). *American families and households.* New York: Russell Sage.

Teachers Leading the Way. (1998). Teachers leading the way: Supporting teacher leadership.http://www.oeri2.ed.gov/pubs/TeachersLead/support.html

Useem, E. L. (1990, April). Social class and ability group placement in mathematics in the transition to seventh grade: The role of parent involvement. Paper presented at the annual meeting of the American Educational Research Association, Boston, MA. In T. Bey & G. Turner, *Making school a place of peace.* Thousand Oaks, CA: Sage.

Vandegrift, J., & Greene, A. (1992, September). Rethinking parent involvement. *Educational Leadership,* 57–60.

Vega, W. A. (1995). The study of Latino families: A point of departure. In R. E. Zambrana (Ed.), *Understanding Latino families: Scholarship, policy, and practice* (pp. 3–17). Thousand Oaks, CA: Sage.

Chapter 3

AAUW. (1991). *Stalled agenda: Gender equity and the training of educators*. Washington, DC: Educational Foundation and National Education Association.

AAUW. (1992). *How schools shortchange girls: A study of major findings on girls and education*. Washington, DC: Educational Foundation and National Education Association.

Allen, J. (1986, Jan.–Feb.). Gender equity in computer education. *AEDS Monitor, 24,* 10–23, 26.

Berkman, L., & Syme, S. (1979). Social networks, host resistance, and mortality: A nine-year follow-up study of Alameda County residents. *American Journal of Epidemiology, 109,* 186–204.

Bernard, B. (1991, September). Prevention should emphasize protective factors. *Western Center News, 4*(4), 1–4.

Bernard, B. (1992). *Turning the corner: From risk to resiliency*. Portland, OR: Northwest Regional Educational Laboratory.

Brandon, N. (1969). *The psychology of self-esteem*. New York: Nash.

Brophy, J. E., & Good, T. L. (1974). *Teacher-student relationships: Causes and consequences*. New York: Holt, Rinehart & Winston.

California Task Force to Promote Self-Esteem and Personal and Social Responsibility. (1990). *Toward a state of esteem*. Sacramento, CA: California State Department of Education.

Conklin, R. (1979). *How to get people to do things*. New York: Ballantine Books.

Cooper, H. M., & Good, T. (1983). *Pygmalion grows up: Studies in the expectation communication process*. New York: Longman.

DeBoer, G. (1984). Sense and competence in science as a factor in career decisions of men and women. Paper presented at the annual meeting of the national Association for Research in Science Teaching. New Orleans, LA, 1984.

Donatelle, R., & Davis, L. (1997). *Health: The basics*. Boston: Allyn and Bacon.

Dreikurs, R. (1964). *Children: The challenge*. New York: Penguin Books.

Eckstrom, J., Goertz, M., Pollock, J., & Rock, D. (1986). Who drops out of high school and why? Findings from a national study. In G. Natriello (Ed.), *School dropouts: Patterns and policies*. New York: Teachers College Press, Columbia University.

Gamoran, A., & Berends, M. (1987, Winter). The effects of stratification in secondary schools. Synthesis of survey and ethnographic research. *Review of Educational Research, 157*(4), 415–435.

Gartner, J., Larson, D., & Allen, G. (1991). Religious commitment and mental health: A review of the empirical literature. *Journal of Psychology and Theology, 19,* 6–25.

Gensemer, R. (1980). Humanism and behaviorism in physical education. Washington, DC: National Education Association.

Goal 2 High School Completion. (no date). Defining dropouts: A statistical portrait. http://inet.ed.gov/pubs/ . . . als/Goal_2/Dropouts.html

Graham, H. (1985). *The human face of psychology*. Philadelphia: Open University Press.

Hamachek, D. (1978). *Encounters with the self*. New York: Holt, Rinehart & Winston.

Harris, A., & Carlton, S. *Pattern of gender differences on mathematics items on the scholastic aptitude test*. Paper presented at the annual meeting of the American Educational Research Association, Boston, MA.

Henderson, N., & Milstein, M. (1996). *Resiliency in schools: Making it happen for students and teachers*. Thousand Oaks, CA: Corwin Press.

Kids Count. *Minnesota kids: A closer look 1998 data book*. University of Minnesota Children, Youth and Family Consortium. www.cyfc.umn.edu.

Kobasa, S. (1979). Stressful life events, personality, and health: An inquiry into hardiness. *Journal of Personality and Social Psychology, 37,* 1–11.

Marmot, M., & Syme, S. (1976). Acculturation and coronary heart disease in

Japanese Americans. *American Journal of Epidemiology, 104,* 225–247.

Maslow, A. (1987). *Motivation and Personality* (3rd ed.). New York: Harper & Row.

Masten, A. (1994). Resilience in individual development: Successful adaptation despite risk and adversity. In M. Wang & E. Gordon (Eds.), *Educational resilience in inner-city America: Challenges and prospects.* Hillsdale, NJ: Lawrence Erlbaum Associates.

McKay, E. G. (1988). *Changing Hispanic demographics.* Washington, DC: Policy analysis center. National Council of La Raza.

Meyers, H. W. (1995). *Dropout prevention and recovery: It's only our future.* Presentation based on paper by H. W. Meyers and M. Bove.

Napoll, V., Kilbride, J., & Tebbs, D. (1996). Adjustment and growth in a changing world. Minneapolis: West Publishing Co. In S. Alters & W. Schiff (1998). *Concepts for healthy living.* Pacific Grove, CA: Brooks/Cole Publishing Company.

Noddings, N. (1988). Schools face crisis in caring. *Educationweek,* Dec. 7.

Oakes, J. (1987, April). *Race, class, and school responses to "ability": Interactive influences on math and science outcomes.* Paper presented at the annual meeting of the American Educational Research Association, Washington, DC. In D. Gollnick & P. Chinn (1998), *Multicultural education in a pluralistic society.* Upper Saddle River, NJ: Merrill.

Olson, L. (1988). *Crossing the schoolhouse border: Immigrant students and the California public schools.* San Francisco: Tomorrow.

Ortiz, F. I. (1988). Hispanic–American children's experiences in classrooms: A comparison between Hispanic and non-Hispanic children. In L. Weis (Ed.), *Class, race and gender in American education.* Albany: State University of New York Press.

Peterson, P., Wilkinson, L., & Hallinan, M. (Eds.). (1984). *The social context of instruction: Group organization and group processes.* San Diego: Academic Press.

Pollard, D. (1989). A profile of underclass achievers. *Journal of Negro Education, 58,* 297–308.

Poole, W. (1993). *The heart of healing.* Atlanta, GA: Turner Publishing.

Rogers, C. (1961). *On becoming a person.* Boston: Houghton Mifflin Company.

Rosenthal, R., & Jacobsen, L. (1968). *Pygmalion in the classroom.* New York: Holt, Rinehart & Winston.

Rosser, P. (1989). *The SAT gender gap.* Washington, DC: Center for Women's Policy Studies.

Rumberger, R. W. (1983, Summer). Dropping out of high school: The influence of race, sex, and family background. *American Educational Research Journal, 20* (2), 199–220.

Rutter, M. (1984, March). Resilient children. *Psychology Today,* 57–65.

Schwartz, W. (1995). School Dropouts: New information about an old problem. Eric Clearinghouse in Urban Education, New York, NY. http://www.eric-web.tc.columbia.edu

Seller, M. (1989). The United States. In G. Kelley (Ed.), *International handbook of women's education.* New York: Greenwood.

Thomas, D. (1997). Dropout rates remain stable over last decade. http://www.ed.gov/PressReleases/12-1997/dropout.html

U.S. Commission on Civil Rights. (1973, March). *Teachers and students, report V,* Washington, DC: U.S. Government Printing Office.

Williams, R., Barefoot, J., & Califf, R. (1992, January 22/29). Prognostic importance of social and economic resources among medically treated patients with angiographically documented artery disease. *Journal of the American Medical Association, 267,* 520–524.

Youngs, B. (1991). *The 6 vital ingredients of self-esteem and how to develop them in your child.* New York: Rawson Associates.

Chapter 4

Banks, J., & Banks, C. (1993). *Multicultural education: Issues and perspectives.* Boston: Allyn and Bacon.

Banks, J., & Banks, C. (1995). *Handbook of research on multicultural education*. New York: Macmillan.

Bernard, B. (1991, August). *Fostering resiliency in kids*. Paper prepared for the Western Regional Center for Drug-Free Schools and Communities.

Brookover, W., & Erickson, E. (1969). *Society and schools and learning*. Boston: Allyn and Bacon.

Clarke, J. I. (1978). *Self-Esteem: A family affair*. New York: Winston Press.

Eckstrom, J., Goertz, M., Pollock, J., & Rock, D. (1986). Who drops out of high school and why? Findings from a national study. In G. Natriello (Ed.), *School dropouts: Patterns and policies*. New York: Teachers College Press, Columbia University.

Gordon, E., Miller, M., & Rollack, D. (1990). Coping with communicentric bias in knowledge production in the social sciences. *Educational Research, 19.*

Kurth-Schai, R. (1988, Winter). The role of youth in society: A reconceptualization. *Educational Forum, 52*(2), 22–26.

Lasker, B. (1970). *Race attitudes in children*. New York: New American Library.

Love, J. (1985). Knowledge transfer and utilization in education. In E. W. Gordon (Ed.), *Review of research in education, vol. 12*. Washington, DC: American Educational Research Association.

Sarason, S. (1990). *The predictable failure of educational reform*. San Francisco: Jossey-Bass.

Sleeter, C., & Grant, C. (1991). Race, class, gender and disability in current textbooks. In M. Apple & L. Christian-Smith (Eds.), *The politics of the textbook*. New York: Routledge & Chapman Hall.

U.S. Commission on Civil Rights. (1973). *Teachers and students, Report V*. Wasington, DC: U.S. Government Printing Office.

Van Ekeren, G. (1988). *The speaker's sourcebook: Quotes and stories*. Englewood Cliffs, NJ: Prentice-Hall.

Wehlage, G. (Ed.). (1989). *Reducing the risk: Schools as communities of support*. Philadelphia: Falmer Press.

Chapter 5

Banks, J., & Banks, C. (1993). *Multicultural education: Issues and perspectives*. Boston: Allyn and Bacon.

Bloom, B. (1956). *Taxonomy of educational objectives: The classification of educational goals: HANDBOOK 1: Cognitive domain*. Longman, Inc.

Bossert, S. (1981). Understandiang sex differences in children's classroom experiences. *The Elementary Journal, 81*(95).

Boykin, W. (1982). Task variability and the performance of black and white school children: Vervistic explorations. *Journal of Black Studies, 12,* 471–485.

Burger, H. G. (1972). Ethno-lematics: Evoking "shy" Spanish-American pupils by cross-cultural mediation. *Adolescence, 6*(25), 61–76.

Burgess, B. J. (1978). Native American learning styles. In L. Morris (Ed.), *Extracting learning styles for social/cultural diversity. A study of five American minorities*. Washington, DC: Office of Education.

Campbell, P. (1984, April). *Girls, boys and educational excellence*. Paper presented at the annual meeting of the American Education Research Association, New Orleans, LA.

Cortes, C. (1978). Chicano culture, experience and learning. In M. Sather & S. Scull (Eds.), *Extracting learning styles from social/cultural diversity: A study of five American minorities*. Norman, OK: Southwest Teacher Corps Network.

Dinkmeyer, D., & Dreikurs, R. (1963). *Encouraging children to learn: The encouragement process*. Englewood Cliffs, NJ: Prentice-Hall.

Dreikurs, R. (1964). *Children: The challenge*. New York: Penguin Books.

Fennema, E., & Peterson, P. (1986). Teacher-student interactions and sex-related differences in learning mathematics. *Teaching and Teacher Education, 2*(3), 19–42.

Franklin, M. (1992). Culturally sensitive instructional practices for African American learners with disabilities. *Exceptional Children, 59*(2), 115–122.

Garcia, R. (1982). *Teaching in a pluralistic society: Concepts, models, strategies.* New York: Harper & Row.

Gay, G. (1975, October). Cultural differences important in the education of black children. *Momentum, 30*–33.

Glenn, H., & Nelsen, J. (1989). *Raising self-reliant children in a self-indulgent world.* Rocklin, CA: Prima Publishing & Communications.

Grossman, H. (1984). *Educating Hispanic students: Cultural implications for instruction, classroom management, counseling, and assessment.* Springfield, IL: Charles C. Thomas.

Grossman, H. (1995). *Teaching in a diverse society.* Boston: Allyn and Bacon.

Hale, J. (1978). Cultural influences on learning styles of Afro-American children. In L. Morris (Ed.), *Extracting learning styles for social/cultural diversity. A study of five American minorities.* Washington, DC: Office of Education.

Hale, J. E. (1982). *Black children, their roots, culture and learning styles.* Provo, UT: Brigham Young University Press.

Howard, J., & Hammond, R. (1985, September 9). Rumors of inferiority: Barrier to black success in America. *The New Republic,* 17–21.

Kagan, S., Zahn, G., & Gealy, J. (1977). Competition and school achievement among Anglo-American and Mexican-American children. *Journal of Educational Psychology, 69*(4), 432–441.

Kolb, D. (1984). *Learning style inventory.* Boston: McBer.

Kolb, D. (1984). *Experiential learning: Experience as the source of learning and development.* New York: Prentice-Hall.

Morris, L. (Ed.). *Extracting learning styles for social/cultural diversity. A study of five American minorities.* Washington, DC: Office of Education.

Natriello, G., McDill, E., & Pallas, A. (1990). *Schooling disadvantaged children: Racing against catastrophe.* New York: Teachers College Press.

Oakes, J. (1988). Tracking in mathematics and science education: A structural contribution to unequal schooling. In L. Weis (Ed.), *Class, race, and gender in American education.* Albany, NY: State University of New York Press.

O'Neil, J. (1992, October). On tracking and individual differences: A conversation with Jeannie Oakes. *Educational Leadership, 50*(2), 18–21.

Pearlman, L., & Scott, K. (1981). *Raising the handicapped child.* Englewood Cliffs, NJ: Prentice-Hall.

Pepper, F. (1976). Teaching the American Indian child in mainstream settings. In R. Jones (Ed.), *Mainstreaming and the minority child.* Reston, VA: Council for Exceptional Children.

Ramirez, M., & Castaneda, A. (1974). *Bicultural democracy, bicognitive development and education.* New York: Academic Press.

Rogers, C. (1961). *On becoming a person.* Boston: Houghton Mifflin Company.

Rowe, M. (1986, Jan.–Feb.). Wait time: Slowing down may be a way of speeding up! *Journal of Teacher Education,* 43–50.

Rutter, M. (1984, March). Resilient children. *Psychology Today,* 57–65.

Sadker, D., & Sadker, M. (1985, January). Is the O.K. classroom O.K.? *Phi Delta Kappan, 66,* 358–361.

Scribner, S., & Cole, M. (1981). *The psychology of literacy.* Cambridge, MA: Harvard University Press.

Simpson, A.W., & Erickson, M. (1983, Summer). Teachers' verbal and non-verbal communication patterns as a function of teacher race, student gender and student race. *American Educational Research Journal, 20,* 183–198.

Torrey, J. W. (1983). Black children's knowledge of standard English. *American Educational Research Journal, 20,* 627–644.

Weinstein, R. (1991). Expectations and high school change: Teacher-researcher collaboration to prevent school failure. *American Journal of Community Psychology, 19*(3), 333–363.

Chapter 6

American School Health Association. (1989). *National adolescent student health survey.* California: Third Party Publishing.

American Teacher. (1993). *Violence in America's public schools. The Metropolitan Life Survey.* New York: Louis Harris and Associates.

Anspaugh, D., & Ezell, G. (1995). *Teaching today's health.* Boston: Allyn and Bacon.

Attorney General's Report on the Impact of Criminal Street Gangs on Crime and Violence in California by the Year 2000. (1993). *Gangs 2000: A call to action.* California Department of Justice, Division of Law Enforcement, Bureau of Investigation. http://electric.ss.uci . . . ica/Gangs2000/open.html

Baker, G. (1994). *Planning and organizing for multicultural instruction.* Menlo Park, CA: Addison Wesley.

California Department of Education. (1994). *Health framework for California public schools.* Sacramento, CA: Office of State Printing.

Crowley, M. (Ed.). (1993). *Schools, Congress sound alarm on student safety and security issues.* Child Protection Report.

Curtis High School Gang Handbook. (no date). *Gang information resource guide for parents and teachers.* http://www.upsd.wednet.e . . . /chs/ganghand.html#asses

Elkow, J. (no date). The injury problem in sports. *Sports Safety.* Division of Safety Education of the AAHPER/National Education Association, Washington, DC.

Goldman, B. (1991). *The truth about where you live.* New York: Times Books, Random House.

Hechinger, F. (1994). Saving youth from violence. *Carnegie Quarterly, 39*(1), 1.

Hechinger, F. and the Carnegie Council on Adolescent Development. (1992). *Fateful choices: Healthy youth for the 21st century.* New York: Carnegie Corporation of New York.

Kahn, H. S., & Williamson, D. F. (1991). Is race associated with weight change in U.S. adults after adjustment for income, education, and marital factors? *American Journal of Clinical Nutrition, 53,* 1566–1570.

Kleinke, C. (1991). *Coping with life challenges.* Pacific Grove, CA: Brooks Cole Publishing Company.

Kochanek, K. D. (1995, March 22). Advance report of final mortality statistics. *Monthly Vital Statistics Report, 43*(6) 2.

Marks, I. (1978). *Living with fear: Understanding and coping with anxiety.* New York: McGraw-Hill.

McBarnette, L. (1996). African American women. In M. Bayne-Smith (Ed.), *Race, gender, and health* (pp. 43–67). Thousand Oaks, CA: Sage.

McCord, C., & Freeman, H. (1990). Excess mortality in Harlem. *New England Journal of Medicine, 332,* 173–177.

Miller, D., Telljohann, S., & Symons, C. (1996). *Health education in the elementary and middle-school level.* Madison, WI: Brown & Benchmark.

National School Safety Center. (1998). Checklist of characteristics of youth who have caused school associated violent deaths. www.nsccl.org.

Olson, J., & Wilson, R. (1986). *Native Americans in the twentieth century.* Chicago: University of Illinois Press.

Porter/Novelli PR Agency. (1992, September). *Health care and a child's ability to learn: A survey of elementary school teachers,* Chicago.

Project TEACH. (1993). *Health education preservice resource manual.* Sacramento, CA: Healthy Kids, Healthy California Office, Department of Education.

Reagan, P., & Brookins-Fisher, J. (1997). *Community health in the 21st century.* Boston: Allyn and Bacon.

School Net. (1996). School violence is a national epidemic. http://www.schoolnet.org/spr96_epidemic.html

Toby, J. (1994). Violence in schools. In E. J. Hollingsworth, H. S. Lufler, Jr., & W. H. Clune, III (Eds.), *School discipline: Order and autonomy.* New York: Praeger.

U.S. Department of Education. (1993c). *The national education goals report: Building a nation of learners (vol. 1: The national report).* Washington, DC: U.S. Government Printing Office.

U.S. Department of Health and Human Services. (1990). *Healthy people 2000:*

National health and promotion and disease prevention objectives (Conference ed.). Washington, DC: U.S. Government Printing Office.

U.S. Department of Health and Human Services. (1990). *Report of the secretary's task force on black and minority health, vol. 1.* Executive summary (Publication No. 491–313/44706). Washington, DC: U.S. Government Printing Office.

U.S. Department of Health and Human Services. (1993). *Trends in Indian health.* U.S. Indian Health Service. Washington, DC.

U.S. Department of Justice. (1991, September). Office of Justice Programs, Bureau of Statistics. *School crime: A national crime victimization survey report.* Washington, DC: U.S. Government Printing Office.

U.S. Department of Justice. (1993). *Comprehensive strategy for serious, violent, and chronic juvenile offenders* (pp. 5–6). Washington, DC: Office of Juvenile Justice and Delinquency Prevention.

U.S. Office of Disease Prevention and Health Promotion. (1987). *ODPHP's prevention fact book: Life expectancy in the United States.* Washington, DC: U.S. Government Printing Office.

Williams, R., Barefoot, J., & Califf, R. (1992, January 22/29). Prognostic importance of social and economic resources among medically treated patients with angiographically documented artery disease. *Journal of the American Medical Association, 267,* 520–524.

Chapter 7

Gordon, T. (1970). *P.E.T.: Parent effectiveness training.* New York: Peter H. Wyden.

Irujo, S. (1988). An introduction to intercultural differences and similarities in nonverbal communication. In J. S. Wurzel, *Toward multiculturalism.* Yarmouth, ME: Intercultural Press.

Lott, L., & Nelsen, J. (1988). *Teaching parenting.* Fair Oaks, CA: Sunrise Press.

Mayer, D., & Greenberg, H. (1964, July–August). What makes a good salesman? *Harvard Business Review, 64411.*

Mintzberg, H. (1975, July–August). The manager's job: Folklore and fact. *Harvard Business Review, 53*(4), 49–61.

Rogers, C., & Roethlisberger, F. J. (1952, July–August). Barriers and gateways to communication. *Harvard Business Review, 52408.*

Schilling, B., & Brannon, E. (1986). *Cross-cultural counseling, a guide for nutrition and health counselors.* Alexandria, VA: U.S. Department of Health and Human Services, Nutrition and Technical Services Division.

Surler, C. (1992, February 17). Hey, I'm terrific. *Newsweek,* 46–52.

Chapter 8

Bettner, B., & Lew, A. (1992). *Raising kids who can.* New York: Harper Perennial Publications.

Fisher, R., & Ury, W. (1983). *Getting to yes: Negotiating agreement without giving in.* New York: Penguin Books.

Gerstein, A., & Reagan, J. (1986). *Win-Win: Approaches to conflict resolution.* Salt Lake City, UT: Gibbs M. Smith, Inc.

Glasser, W. (1969). *Schools without failure.* New York: Harper & Row.

Lott, L., & Nelsen, J. (1988). Teaching parenting. Fair Oaks, CA: Sunrise Press.

Nelsen, J. (1996). *Positive discipline.* New York: Ballantine Books.

Nelsen, J., Duffy, R., Escobar, L., Ortolano, K., & Owen-Sohocki, D. (1996). *Positive discipline: A teacher's A-Z guide.* Rocklin, CA: Prima Publishing.

Chapter 9

Alford, J. (1979, September). Male/female dynamics and student discipline. *NAASR Bulletin, 63*(428), 55.

Arnez, N. L. (1978). Implementation of desegregation as a discriminatory process. *Journal of Negro Education, 47.*

Carter, M. (1987). *A model for effective school discipline.* The Phi Delta Kappa Foundation.

Dearman, N. B., & V. W. Plisko. (1981). *The condition of education.* Washington, DC: U.S. Government Printing Office.

Dinkmeyer, D., & McKay, G. (1983). *The parent's guide: Systematic training for effec-*

tive parenting (STEP). Circle Pines, MN: American Guidance System.

Dreikurs, R. (1964). *Children: The challenge.* New York: Penguin Books.

Gilliland, H. (1988). *Teaching the Native American.* Dubuque, IA: Kendall/Hunt Publishing.

Huffine, S. (1979, Summer). Teacher responses to contextually specific sex type behaviors in kindergarten children. *Educational Research Quarterly, 4*(2), 29–35.

Meier, K., & Stewart, J. (1991). *The politics of Hispanic education: UN paso palante y dos patras.* Albany, NY: State University of New York Press.

Nelsen, J. (1996). *Positive discipline.* New York: Ballantine Books.

Nieto, S. (1996). *Affirming diversity* (2nd ed.). White Plains, NY: Longman Publishing.

Popkin, M. H. (1998). *Active parenting of teens: Leaders guide.* Atlanta, GA: Active Parenting Publishers.

Wayson, W. (1985, October). The politics of violence in school: Doublespeak and disruptions in public confidence. *Phi Delta Kappan, 99,* 127–132.

Wehlage, G., & Rutter, R. (1986). Dropping out: How much do schools contribute to the problem? In G. Natriello, *School droupouts: Patterns and policies.* New York: Teachers College Press, Columbia University.

Chapter 10

Adams, R., & Biddle, B. (1970). *Realities of teaching: Exploration with videotape.* New York: Holt, Rinehart & Winston.

Canter, L., & Canter, M. (1992). *Assertive discipline.* Santa Monica, CA: Canter and Associates.

Doyle, W. (1986). Classroom organization and management. In M. C. Wittrock (Ed.), *Handbook of research on teaching* (3rd ed.). New York: Macmillan.

Dreikurs, R. (1964). *Children: The challenge.* New York: Penguin Books.

Good, T., & Brophy, J. (1987). *Looking in classrooms* (4th ed). New York: Harper & Row.

Horowitz, P., & Otto, D. (1973). *The teaching effectiveness of an alternative teaching*

facility. Alberta, Canada: University of Alberta (ERIC Document Reproduction Service No. ED 083 242).

Maslow, A., & Mintz, N. (1956). The effects of esthetic surroundings. *Journal of Psychology, 41,* 247–254.

Nelsen, J. (1996). *Positive discipline.* New York: Ballantine Books.

Nelsen, J., Lott, L., & Glenn, H. (1992, Summer). Beyond consequences. *Capable People Quarterly.* Sunrise Books.

Proshansky, E., & Wolfe, M. (1974). The physical setting and open education. *School Review, 82,* 557–574.

Schwebel, A., & Cherlin, D. (1972). Physical and social distancing in teacher-pupil relationships. *Journal of Educational Psychology, 63,* 543–550.

Sommer, R. (1974). *Tight spaces: Hard architecture and how to humanize it.* Englewood Cliffs, NJ: Prentice-Hall

Sommer, R., & Olsen, H. (1980). The soft classroom. *Environment & Behavior, 12*(1), 3–16.

Spaulding, C. (1992). *Motivation in the classroom.* New York: McGraw-Hill.

Weinstein, C. (1996). *Secondary classroom management.* New York: McGraw-Hill.

Appendix A

Dinkmeyer, D., & Dreikurs, R. (1963). *Encouraging children to learn: The encouragement process.* Englewood Cliffs, NJ: Prentice-Hall.

Dreikurs, R. (1964). *Children: The Challenge.* New York: Penguin Books.

Gensemer, R. (1980). *Humanism and behaviorism in physical education.* Washington, DC: National Education Association.

Glasser, W. (1995). *Staying together.* New York: Harper-Collins.

Graham, H. (1985). *The human face of psychology.* Philadelphia: Open University Press.

Hamachek, D. (1978). *Encounters with the self.* New York: Holt, Rinehart & Winston.

Maslow, A. (1987). *Motivation and personality* (3rd ed.). New York: Harper & Row.

Rogers, C. (1951). Client-centered therapy. Boston: Houghton Mifflin Company. In D. Hamachek, *Encounters with the self.* New York: Holt, Rinehart & Winston.

Tillich, P. (1952). The courage to be. Nisbett and Co. Reprinted London: Collins, 1980. In H. Graham, *The human face of psychology.* Philadelphia: Open University Press.

Websters New World College Dictionary (3rd ed.) (1996). USA: Macmillan.

Appendix C

American Cancer Society. (1989). *Cancer facts and figures.* Atlanta, GA.

Barnes, G., & Welte, J. (1986). Alcohol consumption of black youth. *Journal of Studies on Alcohol, 47,* 53–61.

Centers for Disease Control. (1989). *Surgeon general's report on smoking.* Washington, DC: Central Office for Health Promotion and Education on Smoking and Health, U.S. Government Printing Office.

Centers for Disease Control. (1993, August 6). Recommendations for the prevention and management of chlamydia trachomatis infections. *Morbidity and Mortality Weekly Report, 42,* No. RR-12 1–39.

Centers for Disease Control. (1995). Sexually transmitted disease surveillance. In *The women's health data book* (2nd ed.) (p. 38). Washington, DC: Jacobs Institute of Women's Health.

Chi, I., Lubben, J. E., & Kitano, H. (1989). Differences in drinking behavior among three Asian-American groups. *Journal of Studies on Alcohol, 50,* 15–23.

Cigarette smoking among high school students. (1992, July 15). *USA Today,* p. 1d.

Comberg, S. (1982). Building on the strength of minority groups. *Practice Digest, 5,* 6–7.

Flaskerud, J., & Hu, L. (1992). Relationship of ethnicity to psychiatric diagnosis. *Journal of Nervous and Mental Disease, 180*(5), 296–303.

Gibbs, J. (1988). Conceptual, methodological and sociocultural issues in black youth surveyed: Implications for assessment and early intervention. *Suicide and Life Threatening Behavior, 19,* 17–29. In A. Stiffman & L. Davis (Eds.), *Ethnic issues in adolescent mental health.* Newbury Park, CA: Sage.

Gilbert, M. (1987). Alcohol consumption patterns in immigrant and later generations. *Hispanic Journal of Behavioral Sciences, 9*(3), 299–314.

Gunther, J. F., Jolly, E. J., & Wedel, K. (1985). Alcoholism and the Indian people: Problem and promise. In E. M. Greenman (Ed.), *Social work practice with clients who have alcohol problems* (pp. 229–241). Springfield, IL: Charles C Thomas.

Harper, F. (1979). *Alcoholism treatment and black Americans.* Rockville, MD: Department of Health, Education and Welfare, National Institute on Alcohol Abuse and Alcoholism.

Harper, F. (1981). Alcohol use and abuse. In L. E. Gary (Ed.), *Black men.* Beverly Hills, CA: Sage.

Hartford, T. C. (1985). Drinking patterns among black and non-black adolescents: Results of a national survey. In E. M. Greenman (Ed.), *Social work practice with clients who have alcohol problems* (pp. 229–241). Springfield, IL: Charles C. Thomas.

Herd, D. (1988). Drinking by black and white women: Results from a national survey. *Social Problems, 35,* 493–505.

Hildreth, C., & Saunders, E. (1992). Heart disease, stroke, and hypertension in blacks. In R. L. Braithwaite & S. E. Taylor (Eds.), *Health issues in the black community* (pp. 90–105). San Francisco: Jossey-Bass.

King, L., Beals, J., Manson, S., & Trimble, J. (1992). A structural evaluation model of factors related to substance abuse among American Indian adolescents. In J. Trimble, C. Block, & S. Niemcryk (Eds.), *Ethnic and multicultural drug abuse: Perspectives on current research.* Binghamton, NY: Haworth.

Klonoff, E.A., Landrine, H., & Scott, J. (1995). Double jeopardy: Ethnicity and gender in research. In H. Landrine (Ed.), *Bringing cultural diversity to feminist psychology: Theory, research, and practice* (pp. 335–380). Washington, DC: American Psychological Association.

Lillie-Blanton, M., Mackenzie, E., & Anthony, J. (1991). Black-white differences in alcohol use by women: Baltimore survey findings. *Public Health Reports, 106*(2), 124–133.

Marin, G., Perez-Stable, E., & Marin, B. (1989). Cigarette smoking among San Francisco Hispanics: The role of acculturation and gender. *American Journal of Public Health, 79*(2), 196–198.

Mays, V. M. (1989). AIDS prevention in black populations: Methods of a safer kind. In V. M. Mays, G. W. Albee, J. Jones, & S. F. Schneider (Eds.), *Primary prevention of AIDS: Psychological approaches* (pp. 264–278). Newbury Park, CA: Sage.

McIntosh, J. (1990). Suicide among Native Americans: Further tribal data and considerations. *Omega, 14*(3), 219–229. In A. Stiffman & L. Davis (Eds.), *Ethnic issues in adolescent mental health.* Newbury Park, CA: Sage.

McLaughlin, P., Raymond, J., Murakami, S., & Gilbert, D. (1987). Drug use among Asian Americans in Hawaii. *Journal of Psychoactive Drugs, 19*, 85–94.

McRoy, R. G., Shorkey, C. T., & Garcia, E. (1985). Alcohol use and abuse among Mexican-Americans. In E. M. Greenman (Ed.), *Social work practice with clients who have alcohol problems* (pp. 229–241). Springfield, IL: Charles C Thomas.

Med Help International. (no date). *Cervical Dysplasia.* http://medhlp.netusa.net/general/womens/displas.txt

Menon, R., Burrett, M., & Simpson, D. (1990). School, peer, and inhalant use among Mexican-American adolescents. *Hispanic Journal of Behavioral Sciences, 12*, 408–421.

Murakami, S. R. (1989). An epidemiological survey of alcohol, drug, and mental health problems in Hawaii. In D. Spiegler, D. Tate, S. Aitken, & C. Christian (Eds.), *Alcohol use among U.S. ethnic minorities* (NIAAA Research Monograph No. 18., pp. 343–353).

Rockville, MD: National Institute on Alcohol Abuse and Alcoholism.

National Cancer Institute. (1989). *Cancer in Hispanics.* Bethesda, MD: National Institutes of Health.

National Center for Health Statistics. (1990). *Health: United States, 1989.* (DHHS Publication No. 1232). Hyattsville, MD: Public Health Services.

National Clearinghouse for Alcohol and Drug Abuse (NCADI). (1995). *National household survey on drug abuse: Main findings 1995.* Rockville, MD: U.S. Department of Health and Human Services. http://www.health.org/pubs/95hhs/any.htm

National Institute on Drug Abuse. (1991). *National household survey on drug abuse: Main findings 1990.* DHHS Publication No. ADM (91-1788). Rockville, MD: U.S. Department of Health and Human Services.

National Institute on Drug Abuse. (1991). *National household survey on drug abuse: Highlights 1990.* DHHS Publication No. (ADM) 91-1789. Rockville, MD: U.S. Department of Health and Human Services.

National Institute on Drug Abuse. (1991). *Overview of the national household survey on drug abuse: NIDA capsules,* No. C-83-1(a). Rockville, MD: U.S. Department of Health and Human Services.

National Institute on Drug Abuse. (1991). *National household survey on drug abuse: Population estimates 1991.* DHHS Publication No. ADM (92-1887). Rockville, MD: Division of Epidemiology and Prevention Research, National Institute of Drug Abuse.

National Institute of Mental Health Report. (1992). *Suicidal facts.* Washington, DC: Author.

National Technical Information Service. (1986). *American Indian health.* Washington, DC: U.S. Department of Health, Education, and Welfare.

Reagen, P., & Brookins-Fisher, J. (1997). *Community health in the 21st century.* Boston: Allyn and Bacon.

Schinke, S., Botvin, G., Trimble, J., Orlandi, M., Gilchrist, L., & Locklear. C. (1988). Preventing substance abuse among American Indian adolescents: A bicultural competence skills approach. *Journal of Counseling Psychology, 35*(1), 87–90.

Segal, B. (1992). Drug-taking behavior among school aged youth: The Alaska experience and comparisons with lower-48 states. *Drugs and Society, 4*(1/2), 1–174. In R. Coombs & D. Ziedonis (Eds.), *Handbook on drug abuse prevention*. Boston: Allyn and Bacon.

Skager, R. (1986). *A statewide survey of drug and alcohol use among students*. Sacramento, CA: Office of the Attorney General.

Smith-Peterson, C. (1983). Substance abuse treatment and cultural diversity. In G. Bennett (Ed.), *Substance abuse: Pharmacological development and clinical perspectives*. New York: John Wiley and Sons.

Syphilis rate at an all time U.S. low. (1998, June). *San Luis Obispo County Telegram Tribune*, p. C-10.

Trimble, J., Padilla, A., & Bell, C. (Eds.). (1987). *Drug abuse among ethnic minorities*. DHHS Publication No. ADM (87-1474). Rockville, MD: National Institute of Drug Abuse.

Tucker, M. (1985). U.S. ethnic minorities and drug use: An assessment of the science and practices. *International Journal of the Addictions, 20*, 1021–1047.

U.S. Bureau of the Census. (1994). *Statistical abstracts of the United States: 1994* (114th ed.). Washington, DC: U.S. Government Printing Office.

U.S. Department of Health and Human Services. (1981). *Report on the secretary's task force on black and minority health*. Washington, DC: U.S. Government Printing Office.

U.S. Department of Health and Human Services. (1985). *Vital statistics of the U.S.: Vol. 11, Mortality*. National Center for Health Statistics. Washington, DC: U.S. Government Printing Office.

U.S. Department of Health and Human Services. (1991). *Drug use among high school students, college students, and other young adults*. Alcohol, Drug Use and Mental Health Administration, National Institute on Drug Abuse.

U.S. Department of Health and Human Services. (1991). *Vital statistics of the United States*. National Center for Health Statistics. Washington, DC: U.S. Government Printing Office.

U.S. Department of Health and Human Services. (1991). *Trends in Indian health*. U.S. Indian Health Service, p. 49. Washington, DC.

U.S. Department of Health and Human Services. (1993). *Trends in Indian health*. U.S. Indian Health Service. Washington, DC.

U.S. Department of Health and Human Services. (1995, September). *Sexually transmitted disease surveillance, 1994*. Public Health Service, Division of STD Prevention. Atlanta, GA: Centers for Disease Control and Prevention.

Weibel, O. (1984). Substance abuse among American Indian youth: A continuing crisis. *Journal of Drug Issues, 14*, 313–335.

Wingert, P. (1998, May 11). Boys will be boys. *Newsweek, CXXXI*(19), 55–60.

Young, T. (1998). Substance use and abuse among Native Americans. *Clinical Psychology Review, 8*(2), 125–138.

Appendix D

Acosta-Belen, E., & Sjostrom, B. (1988). *The Hispanic experience in the United States*. New York: Praeger.

Braithwaite, R., & Taylor, S. (Eds.). (1992). *Health issues in the black community*. San Francisco: Jossey-Bass.

Brown, E., Valdez, R., Morgenstern, H., Wang. C., & Mann, J. (1991). *Health insurance coverage of Californians in 1989*. Berkeley: University of California, California Policy Seminar.

Bureau of the Census. (1994). *Statistical abstracts of the United States: 1994*. Washington, DC: U.S. Government Printing Office.

Children's Defense Fund. (1989). *Lack of health insurance makes a difference*. Washington, DC: Author.

Commonwealth Fund Survey. (1994). *A comparative survey of minority health.* New York: The Commonwealth Fund. http://www.cmwf.org

National Center for Health Statistics. (1991). *Health, United States, 68.* DHHS Publication No. PHS 91-1232. Hyattsville, MD.

Reed, W., Darity, W., Sr., & Robertson, N. (1993). *Health and medical care of African Americans.* Westport, CT: Auburn House.

Roberts, V. A. (1994). Emeritus scientists, mathematics and engineers program: Evaluation report. In I. L. Livingston (Ed.), *Handbook of black American health* (pp. 331–343). Westport, CT: Greenwood Press.

Schorr, L., & Schorr, D. (1988). *Within our reach: Breaking the cycle of disadvantage.* New York: Anchor Press Doubleday.

Turner, R., Grindstaff, C., and Phillips, N. (1990). Social support and outcome in teenage pregnancy. *Journal of Health and Social Behavior, 31,* 43–57.

U.S. Department of Education. (1992). *Digest of education statistics, 1992* (NCES Publication No. NCES 92-097). Washington, DC: U.S. Government Printing Office.

U.S. Department of Health and Human Services. (1990). *Report of the secretary's task force on black and minority health, vol. 1.* Executive summary (Publicaion No. 491-313/44706). Washington, DC: U.S. Government Printing Office.

U.S. Department of Health, Education, and Welfare. (1980). *Special report to Congress on the primary health needs of immigrants.* Washington, DC: U.S. Government Printing Office.

Author Index

Subject Index